Study Guide and Reader to Accompany

EDUCATIONAL PSYCHOLOGY
Developing Learners

Fourth Edition

Jeanne Ellis Ormrod

University of Northern Colorado (Emerita)

University of New Hampshire

Merrill
Prentice Hall

Upper Saddle River, New Jersey
Columbus, Ohio

Vice President and Publisher: Jeffery W. Johnston
Executive Editor: Kevin M. Davis
Development Editor: Julie Peters
Editorial Assistant: Autumn Crisp
Production Editor: Mary Harlan
Design Coordinator: Diane C. Lorenzo
Cover Design: Ali Mohrman
Cover Image: Corbis Stock Market
Production Manager: Laura Messerly
Director of Marketing: Ann Castel Davis
Marketing Manager: Amy June
Marketing Coordinator: Tyra Cooper

Pearson Education Ltd.
Pearson Education Australia Pty. Limited
Pearson Education Singapore Pte. Ltd.
Pearson Education North Asia Ltd.
Pearson Education Canada, Ltd.
Pearson Educación de Mexico, S.A. de C.V.
Pearson Education—Japan
Pearson Education Malaysia Pte. Ltd.
Pearson Education, *Upper Saddle River, New Jersey*

10 9 8 7 6 5 4 3

Merrill
Prentice Hall

ISBN: 0-13-094197-2

PREFACE

As I wrote the fourth edition of *Educational Psychology: Developing Learners*, I had two primary goals in mind. First, I wanted to share many of the things that psychologists have discovered about school-age children and adolescents—how they change as they grow older, how they learn most effectively, what things motivate them, and so on—and to do it in a way that my readers would find informative, enjoyable, and at times perhaps even fascinating. Second, I wanted to give future teachers a toolbox of strategies and ideas for helping students with diverse backgrounds and abilities achieve academic, personal, and social success at school.

I hope that you learn a great deal from reading *Educational Psychology*. I have done several things in the book itself to help you learn and remember what you read more effectively. I've been selective about what I've included in the book, focusing on the concepts and principles that I think are most important for teachers to know and making sure that I explain those concepts and principles in a clear, understandable manner. I've included two classroom case studies in each chapter and incorporated numerous other examples of students and teachers in action throughout the text and in "Into the Classroom" boxes. I've created many "Experiencing Firsthand" exercises that illustrate important principles of thinking, learning, and behavior by showing you how *you* think, learn, and behave. I've presented numerous classroom artifacts (students' compositions, teachers' assignments, etc.) and interviews for you to analyze in "Interpreting Artifacts and Interactions" features. And I've used the margins of the book to encourage you to think further about ideas and connect them with concepts we've discussed in previous chapters.

This *Study Guide and Reader* provides additional ways of helping you learn and remember what you read in *Educational Psychology*. It begins with a summary of each chapter. It describes misconceptions that you might have before studying a particular topic—misconceptions that can interfere with your ability to understand and interpret chapter content accurately. It lists a number of "Focus Questions" that you should be able to answer once you've read each chapter. It provides many "Application Exercises" through which you can practice applying the concepts and principles you're studying to classroom situations. It answers some of the questions that appear in the margins of the textbook. It includes examples of the types of questions you may find on any tests that your instructor may give you. Finally, it includes several supplementary readings that your instructor may assign.

A Companion Website accompanies the textbook as well; this site can give you additional assistance as you read and study the textbook. In addition to presenting some of the same features you see here in the *Student Study Guide*, the site also provides a "Message Board" where you can communicate with your instructor and classmates, as well as a list of other Internet sites related to course content. You can find the Companion Website at www.prenhall.com/ormrod.

Enjoy the book!

J.E.O.

CONTENTS

USING THE CHAPTER STUDY GUIDES

Chapters 1 through 16 of this study guide include several features that should help you learn, remember, and apply the material presented in Chapters 1 through 16 of *Educational Psychology: Developing Learners*. Let me tell you a little bit about each one of these features.

Chapter Summary

At the beginning of each chapter in this *Study Guide and Reader*, I give a brief summary of the topics and ideas that its corresponding chapter in the textbook addresses. Such an overview can serve as an *advance organizer* that lays out the general structure and key ideas of each chapter. Numerous research studies have shown that students can more effectively remember the things that they read when they have a general idea ahead of time of what they will be reading about.

Common Student Beliefs and Misconceptions Related to Chapter Content

Research tells us that when students have erroneous beliefs about a topic they are studying, they often misinterpret new information so they learn and remember it incorrectly. Here in the *Study Guide and Reader*, I alert you to some of the beliefs and misconceptions I have observed in my own students over the years—prior "knowledge" that has occasionally wreaked havoc with their ability to learn successfully in my classroom. If you recognize any of these beliefs and misconceptions in yourself, I urge you to read the textbook with the mindset that you will encounter information that contradicts what you now believe.

Chapter Outline and Focus Questions

Each chapter includes a two-column table that lists headings for each section, along with "Focus Questions" that you should be able to answer once you've finished reading that section. Use these questions to test yourself on what you've learned from your reading. Use them again when you study for any exams that your instructor gives you. (The Companion Website for the book, which you can find at www.prenhall.com/ormrod, provides more general "Key Questions" that can guide your studying as well.)

Chapter Glossary

The chapter glossary presents definitions of all the key concepts that are introduced in boldface print in the chapter and then listed at the end of the chapter. (This glossary is also available on the book's Companion Website at www.prenhall.com/ormrod.)

Application Exercises

In the textbook itself, I've included numerous applications of the concepts and principles that I've described. Here in the study guide, I give *you* the opportunity to apply many of these same concepts and principles. Each application exercise includes a number of situations for you to analyze and interpret using the ideas that a particular chapter presents. As you do these exercises, I encourage you to proceed in the following manner:

1. First see if you can interpret each situation using only your *memory* of the ideas you have read in the textbook.

2. If you are unable to carry out Step 1 successfully, reread the relevant sections of the textbook and once again try to interpret the situation.

3. As a last resort, refer to the answers that follow each application exercise. Don't look at these answers until after you've made a concerted effort to apply the material on your own.

Keep in mind that the answers I provide are *my* interpretations of the situations, based on the concepts and principles presented in a particular chapter. If you disagree with, or perhaps don't understand, any of my analyses, you may want to consult your instructor for his or her opinion.

Answers to Selected Margin Notes

I've used the margins of the textbook to pose many questions that will, I hope, encourage you to think about and make sense of the things you are reading. Some of the questions might be answered very differently, yet equally correctly, by different students. But others have clear right and wrong answers. I address the latter set of questions here in the *Study Guide and Reader*.

Sample Test Questions

Ask your instructor if he or she will be using the test bank that accompanies *Educational Psychology* when constructing tests for your class. If so, you can find examples of the kinds of test questions your instructor will be using here in the *Study Guide and Reader*. Some questions have a number one (**1**) to their left; these items assess *lower-level skills* and ask you about the information actually presented in the textbook. Other questions have a number two (**2**) to their left; these items assess *higher-level skills* and ask you to apply, analyze, or synthesize concepts, principles, theories, and research findings. You may want to use both kinds of sample test questions to spot-check yourself on what you have learned. (Additional test questions appear on the Companion Website at www.prenhall.com/ormrod. The Companion Website provides hints about where in the textbook you can find information relevant to each question, and it gives immediate feedback about your answers to the questions.)

USING THE COMPACT DISK

Included with the fourth edition of *Educational Psychology: Developing Learners* is a compact disk (CD) called *Simulations in Educational Psychology and Research*. This CD contains five simulations that get you actively involved in the subject matter:

- The Pendulum Experiment (to be used with Chapter 2)
- Assessing Moral Reasoning (to be used with Chapter 3)
- Bartlett's Ghosts (to be used with Chapter 7)
- Intuitive Physics (to be used with either Chapter 7 or Chapter 8)
- Assessment in the Balance (to be used with either Chapter 8 or Chapter 16)

Each simulation will present one or more tasks and ask you to make certain responses (perhaps experimenting with a pendulum, recalling a story, or evaluating students' classroom work); it will also give you feedback about your responses. Following the task(s), you will learn more about the topic in question and consider implications for educational practice.

To use the CD, simply place it in the appropriate disk drive in your computer and double-click on the diamond-shaped *Sims* icon. The instructions and simulated "buttons" that appear on your computer screen will guide you from there.

USING THE COMPANION WEBSITE

The Companion Website for *Educational Psychology: Developing Learners* provides additional support for your learning. The site has the following features:

- Key questions, a glossary, links to relevant sites on the World Wide Web, and sample multiple-choice and essay questions for each chapter of the book

- A **Message Board** that allows you and your classmates to converse about chapter content

- A **Syllabus Manager** that your instructor may use to post and occasionally update your course schedule and assignments

- A **Student Artifact Library** that contains numerous examples of actual classroom artifacts, including students' writing samples, math and science assignments, and artwork, plus teachers' lessons and assessment instruments

You can find the Companion Website at **http://www.prenhall.com/ormrod**.

STUDY TIPS

As both a teacher and an educational researcher, I have discovered that many college students have little understanding of how they can study effectively. Following are a number of suggestions for reading and learning from textbooks. Many of them are from my 1989 book, *Using Your Head: An Owner's Manual*.

- **Determine your best learning times and use them wisely.** Are you a "morning person"? a "night owl"? Identify the times that you read and concentrate most effectively, and leave the dirty dishes, campus errands, and favorite television programs (use a VCR to record them!) for times when you're relatively brain dead.

- **Be realistic about how much you can learn in one sitting.** As you will discover when you read Chapter 6, you can think about and learn only a limited amount of information in a limited amount of time. Don't try to do too much too fast. And certainly don't leave everything until the last minute!

- **Minimize distractions.** Find a quiet place to study where you will have few things competing for your attention. Turn the radio and CD player off, or play soft background music that you will barely notice. And definitely turn off that television set!

- **Mark up the book.** Underline or highlight the main ideas of each section. Mark essential details that support the main ideas. Put brackets or stars beside examples that you find especially helpful.

- **Pay attention as you read.** Don't let your eyes wander mindlessly down the pages. Keep your mind actively attuned to the things you are reading.

- **Relate what you read to things you already know.** Think about how the ideas I present are consistent with personal experiences you've had or with things you've learned in other classes.

- **Elaborate on what you read, going beyond it and adding to it.** Draw inferences from the general statements I make. Generate your own examples of the concepts and principles I describe. Derive implications for your own teaching practice from the theories I present.

- **Use the tables to help you organize and summarize the material.** Use the "Compare/Contrast" tables to find similarities and differences among various positions and perspectives. Use the "Principles/Assumptions" tables to focus in on key ideas.

❑ **Use the pictures, photographs, and cartoons to help you remember the ideas they represent.** For most students, visual images provide one highly effective means of remembering information.

❑ **Use mnemonics to help you remember hard-to-learn information.** Use memory tricks that make difficult ideas more memorable. For examples of strategies you might use, see the section "Using Mnemonics in the Absence of Relevant Prior Knowledge" in Chapter 6 of your textbook.

❑ **Periodically check yourself to make sure you understand and remember what you've read.** Try to summarize each section as soon as you've read it. Ask yourself questions similar to the focus questions in each chapter of this study guide, or have a classmate ask you such questions. Try to explain a difficult concept to someone who doesn't yet understand it.

❑ **Answer the questions in the margins.** These questions encourage you to do some of the things I've just suggested, such as relating new ideas to your prior experiences, drawing inferences, and periodically checking yourself.

❑ **Know when to quit.** If you're tired or having a hard time concentrating, close your book for the time being. Pick it up again when you're more rested and less distracted.

❑ **Review.** Research is clear on this point: Periodic review of previously learned material definitely helps students remember it more effectively and accurately.

❑ **Reward yourself for your accomplishments.** Give yourself a break or a treat when you've finished a section or a chapter. Get a bite to eat. Call a friend on the telephone. Go to the mall, the movies, or the park.

As you read the textbook, you will learn even more about how you can learn most effectively. In fact, I urge you to skim Chapters 6, 7, and 8 (even before your instructor assigns them!) to get some ideas.

Chapter Study Guides

Chapter 1

EDUCATIONAL PSYCHOLOGY AND
TEACHER DECISION MAKING

Chapter Summary

This chapter gives you a taste of what educational psychology is all about. Early in the chapter you encounter the OOPS, a pretest that may alert you to certain misconceptions you have about learning, development, diversity, motivation, instruction, or assessment. Many people hold misconceptions about how students learn and develop and about how teachers can most effectively promote students' classroom success. The most accurate information about learning, development, and classroom practice comes from research findings. Different types of research studies—descriptive, correlational, and experimental—answer different questions about education, but all can help us in classroom decision making.

When research studies yield similar results time after time, educational psychologists derive principles and theories that describe and explain people's learning, development, and behavior. Our job as teachers is to translate these principles and theories into classroom practice. (For example, if research consistently tells us that "people learn more effectively when they relate new ideas to their existing knowledge," we know that we can facilitate our students' learning by helping them connect new material to what they have previously learned or experienced.) Yet to use psychological principles and theories most effectively, we must adapt them to our students' current knowledge and skills, and so we must continually assess students' progress toward instructional goals.

We don't yet have all the answers about how best to help children learn and develop, so we must continue to keep ourselves abreast of research results, theoretical developments, and educational innovations. Occasionally, we may also find it useful to conduct research ourselves to answer the questions we have about our own students, schools, and communities. As a beginning teacher, you may initially find the teaching profession a bit overwhelming, but with experience and continuing education, you can eventually become an expert.

Part 1 of the book examines the diverse characteristics that students bring to the classroom. Part 2 explores the nature of human learning and motivation. Part 3 draws on principles from Parts 1 and 2 to identify effective strategies for instruction, classroom management, and assessment.

You can use what you learn about learning and cognition not only to help your students be successful in the classroom but also to help *yourself* learn successfully. Among other things, you should relate new information to what you already know, elaborate on that information, and occasionally stop to test yourself on the content you've studied.

Common Student Beliefs and Misconceptions Related to Chapter Content

Below are several misconceptions that college students sometimes have when they first enroll in an educational psychology course. As you read Chapter 1, be on the lookout for evidence that contradicts these common misconceptions:

1. Sometimes students erroneously believe that the field of educational psychology deals primarily with counseling techniques or psychotherapy in the classroom.

2. Some students believe that good teaching decisions rest solely on "common sense" and that educational and psychological research findings have little relevance to classroom practice.

3. Students often infer cause-effect relationships from correlational data. In fact, only experimental studies allow us to draw conclusions about cause-effect relationships.

4. Some students think of tests and other forms of assessment only as mechanisms for measuring students' achievement *after* instruction. In fact, effective teachers assess their students' knowledge and skills throughout the instructional process.

5. Many students have misconceptions about effective study strategies. For example, some believe that they can learn course material through sheer exposure to it, even when they are not paying attention or otherwise thinking about it in any way.

CHAPTER OUTLINE	FOCUS QUESTIONS
OOPS—A PRETEST	• Do you have possible misconceptions about some of the topics discussed in the book?
DRAWING CONCLUSIONS FROM PSYCHOLOGICAL AND EDUCATIONAL RESEARCH Descriptive Studies Correlational Studies Experimental Studies An Example: Research on Visual-Spatial Thinking A Cautionary Note	• Can you describe the three types of research studies in your own words? What kinds of questions can each type of study answer? • Why is it important for teachers to be aware of cause-effect relationships whenever possible? • Why can we draw conclusions about cause-effect relationships only from experimental studies? What essential condition is absent in descriptive and correlational studies?
USING PRINCIPLES AND THEORIES IN CLASSROOM DECISION MAKING	• How are principles and theories different? • What role do principles and theories play in teacher decision making?

CHAPTER OUTLINE	FOCUS QUESTIONS
IMPORTANCE OF ONGOING ASSESSMENT IN CLASSROOM DECISION MAKING	• What forms can assessment take in the classroom? • What kinds of information does Justin's story "The Pet Who Came to Dinner" provide? How seriously should we take the conclusions we reach from students' classroom products and behaviors?
DEVELOPING AS A TEACHER	• In what way does the job of teaching become easier as time goes on? • How can you continue to grow as a teacher?
LOOKING AHEAD TO THE FOLLOWING CHAPTERS	• What topics will you learn more about as you read the book? • What do we mean by the term *students with special needs*? What implication does the practice of *inclusion* have for classroom teachers?
STUDYING EDUCATIONAL PSYCHOLOGY MORE EFFECTIVELY	• What three strategies does the book suggest you use as you read and study?

THE BIG PICTURE
    Importance of Research for Teachers
    Principles, Theories, and Assessment in Decision Making
    Developing as a Teacher
    Reading About and Studying Educational Psychology
	• Identify the main ideas in each section of the chapter.

Supplementary Readings

Your instructor may assign one or both of these supplementary readings:

• Appendix A, "Describing Relationships with Correlation Coefficients," in the textbook.

• Supplementary Reading #1, "Common Themes Throughout the Book," which appears in the final section of this *Study Guide and Reader*.

Chapter Glossary

Action research. Research conducted by teachers and other school personnel to address issues and problems in their own schools or classrooms.

Control group. A group of people in a research study who are given either no treatment or a presumably ineffective (placebo) treatment. The subsequent performance of this group is compared to the performance of one or more treatment groups.

Correlation. The extent to which two variables are related to each other, such that when one variable increases, the other either increases or decreases in a somewhat predictable way.

Correlational study. A research study that explores relationships among variables. Such a study enables researchers to predict one variable on the basis of their knowledge of another but not to draw a conclusion about a cause-effect relationship.

Descriptive study. A research study that describes situations. Such a study enables researchers to draw conclusions about the current state of affairs but not about correlational or cause-effect relationships.

Educational psychology. A discipline encompassing psychological principles and theories related to learning, motivation, child and adolescent development, individual and group differences, and psychological assessment, especially as these topics relate to classroom practice.

Elaboration. A cognitive process in which learners expand on new information based on what they already know.

Experimental study (experiment). A research study that involves the manipulation of one variable to determine its possible effect on another variable. It enables researchers to draw conclusions about cause-effect relationships.

Inclusion. The practice of educating all students, including those with severe and multiple disabilities, in neighborhood schools and general education classrooms.

Pedagogical content knowledge. Knowledge about effective methods of teaching a specific content area.

Principle. A description of how one variable influences another variable. It evolves when similar research studies yield similar results time after time.

Students with special needs. Students who are different enough from their peers that they require specially adapted instructional materials and practices.

Theory. An organized body of concepts and principles developed to explain certain phenomena; a description of possible underlying mechanisms to explain why certain principles are true.

Treatment group. A group of people in a research study who are given a particular experimental treatment (e.g., a particular method of instruction).

Visual-spatial thinking. The ability to imagine and mentally manipulate two- and three-dimensional figures.

Here is an additional glossary item if your instructor has assigned Appendix A:

Correlation coefficient. A statistic that indicates the nature of the relationship between two variables.

Application Exercise #1: Drawing Conclusions from Research Studies

From which of the following research studies can we draw conclusions about cause-effect relationships?

1. A biology teacher is teaching her students the hierarchy that biologists use to classify living things: kingdom, phylum, class, order, family, genus, and species. She wants to find out if the sentence "King Philip comes over for good spaghetti"—a sentence with words that begin with the same letters as the words in the hierarchy (K P C O F G S)—will help her students remember the hierarchy. She makes two handouts describing the classification hierarchy; both handouts are the same, except that one includes the "King Philip" sentence and one does not. She shuffles the two handouts together in a pile and distributes one handout to each student in her class. The following day, she finds that students who have been given the "King Philip" sentence remember the hierarchy more accurately.

2. Many of the boys in the town of Greenwood play soccer in the local recreational soccer program. Greenwood has no equivalent program for girls' soccer. The physical education teacher at Greenwood Elementary School believes that the boys' soccer skills are superior to those of the girls and suspects that the boys' greater experience playing soccer has made the difference. To test his hypothesis, the teacher develops a test of soccer skills that he can score objectively, and he finds that, yes, the boys do have better soccer skills.

3. A junior high social studies teacher finds that some of her students can easily remember the ideas she presents, yet others have trouble remembering information from one day to the next. She suspects that the students who have better memories for class material are those who are taking more complete notes in class. She collects students' notebooks one day and finds that students who are doing well in class take twice as many notes as students who are doing poorly.

4. Thirty fifth graders are learning how to add, subtract, multiply, and divide fractions by means of instructional computer software. The students are each given a computer disk that enables them to load the software on a personal computer in the school's computer lab; they then progress at their own pace through the computer program. The program gives them many practice problems that they can solve directly on the computer; it also provides immediate feedback about their solutions. Unbeknownst to anyone, some of the students have received faulty software: rather than receiving feedback after every problem they solve, they get feedback after every third problem. These students learn how to work with fractions more slowly than do students who get feedback about every problem they solve.

5. Ms. Santos notices that some of her students get exceptionally tense when they take tests in her class, and these students tend to get lower test scores than their classmates. With the assistance of a local college professor, Ms. Santos has each student take a mock classroom test while being hooked up to a biofeedback machine. She finds that students who get low test scores show signs of greater physiological stress than students who get high scores.

6.   Ms. Randall's class has fifteen copies each of the first and second editions of the same geography textbook. In the second edition, the main idea in each paragraph is emphasized with italics; otherwise, the second edition is exactly the same as the first. To distribute the textbooks as fairly as possible, Ms. Randall chooses the students who will receive each edition by drawing names out of a hat. She doesn't tell her students that some of them will have an advantage over others, however. Two weeks later, she finds that students reading the second edition perform better on their first geography quiz.

7.   Children from low-income families who participate in a Head Start preschool program before they begin kindergarten do better in school than children who have not participated in Head Start.

8.   An educational psychologist videotapes 20 high school history teachers in action for a period of four weeks. He then codes each teacher statement into one of three categories: presenting new information, asking a question, or giving instructions. He finds that when teachers ask more questions in class, students are more likely to do well on the districtwide history achievement test given later that year.

9.   Mr. Hughes's students are packed into his tiny classroom like sardines. He wants to discourage cheating in such tight quarters, so when he develops his first multiple-choice test, he constructs two different forms of the test. Both forms have the same test items. However, on one form of the test, the easiest items are at the beginning; on the other form, the most difficult items appear first. Mr. Hughes distributes the two forms of the test to his students in a random fashion. As he is scoring the test papers that night, he discovers that students who had the easiest items at the beginning have done better on the test overall than students who had the most difficult items first.

10.   As part of a districtwide evaluation for merit pay, a school principal observes each of her teachers in action for an entire school day and then writes an evaluation of his or her classroom performance. In looking over the completed evaluations, she discovers that she has evaluated teachers with a Master of Arts degree more highly than teachers with only a Bachelor of Arts degree.

Answers to Application Exercise #1

1. Cause-effect. We can conclude that knowledge of the sentence influenced memory for the hierarchy. The teacher is manipulating students' access or nonaccess to the "King Philip" sentence. The handouts are the same in every way *except* for the sentence, and the teacher assigns students to the treatment and control groups in an essentially random fashion. (Now that the teacher has identified this cause-effect relationship, she should share the sentence with the students in the control group as well, so that *all* of her students can benefit from it.)

2. No cause-effect. We cannot conclude that the soccer program causes the difference between boys and girls. Girls and boys are likely to have other background differences as well; furthermore, we have not ruled out possible genetic differences between boys and girls. To determine the actual effect of the soccer program, we would have to have both boys and girls involved in the program and would also have to select the participants on a random basis—conditions that are probably not possible in this situation.

3. No cause-effect. We cannot conclude that note taking leads to better memory for class material. The two groups of students are likely to be different in other ways besides note taking; for example, the higher-achieving students may be more interested in the subject matter than their classmates, or they may be more motivated to get good grades.

4. Cause-effect. We can conclude that more frequent feedback leads to faster learning. The two versions of software are identical except for the amount of feedback they give. The computer disks appear to have been distributed in a random fashion, so that those students receiving the faulty software are similar, on average, to those receiving error-free software.

5. No cause-effect. We cannot conclude that tension influences test performance. The high scorers and low scorers may be different in additional ways; for example, the high scorers might know the material better and so, as a result, are less tense during the test.

6. Cause-effect. We can conclude that having the main ideas emphasized in the textbook facilitates learning. The textbooks are identical in every way except for the italics, and the two groups of students have been chosen randomly. (Now that Ms. Randall knows there is a difference, she underlines the main ideas in each copy of the first edition so that all her students have equivalent instructional materials.)

7. No cause-effect. The study does not necessarily lead to the conclusion that Head Start promotes later school achievement. The Head Start participants might be different from nonparticipants in a number of ways; for example, they may have parents who are more concerned about school achievement.

8. No cause-effect. We cannot conclude that asking questions promotes achievement in history. The teachers may be different in other ways besides their question-asking; for example, those who ask more questions may be more enthusiastic instructors or have higher expectations for student performance.

9. Cause-effect. We can conclude that placing easier items at the beginning of the test facilitates test performance. Everything about the tests is the same except for the order of the items, and students receiving each form of the test have been selected randomly.

10. No cause-effect. We cannot conclude that an advanced degree leads to better performance in the classroom. The teachers with an M.A. are likely to be different from those with a B.A. in several ways. For example, they are probably older and more experienced than their less educated colleagues. They may also be more motivated to improve their teaching.

Sample Test Questions

Items marked with a "1)" on the left-hand side are lower-level questions that assess your general knowledge and understanding of the material. Items marked with a "2)" on the left-hand side are higher-level questions that assess your ability to apply what you have learned to a new situation.

Multiple-Choice

1) 1. Considering research findings described in the textbook, identify the only *true* statement among the statements below.

    a. In most cases, students quickly change their erroneous beliefs about the world once they hear more accurate explanations.

    b. As early as second grade, boys begin to demonstrate noticeably higher achievement in mathematics than girls.

    c. Students are most likely to learn when they are quite anxious about their classroom performance.

    d. Students who take notes on class material are more likely to remember it later on.

2) 2. Which one of the following conclusions can be drawn only from an *experimental* study?

    a. Teachers can help students understand classroom material better when they occasionally stop to ask questions that students must answer.

    b. Students who elaborate on classroom material remember it better than those who don't.

    c. Teachers who have higher expectations for their students have students who actually do achieve at higher levels.

    d. Older children think more logically than younger children.

2) 3. Three of the following are principles of learning. Which one is a *theory* rather than a principle?

    a. Students learn more quickly when they get consistent feedback about right and wrong answers.

    b. Visual aids are effective instructional tools because they help students form visual images of classroom material.

    c. Cooperative learning activities help students form friendships with classmates of different cultural backgrounds.

    d. Students who study for one hour each day for five days remember more than students who study for five hours all at once.

2) 4. The textbook describes how you are likely to develop as a teacher. Which one of the following common sayings best summarizes the textbook's description of teacher development?

    a. Beauty is in the eye of the beholder.

    b. A rolling stone gathers no moss.

    c. Turn the other cheek.

    d. Practice makes perfect.

2)   5.   Which one of the following best illustrates *inclusion* as educators use the term?

      a.   Ashley, who has a severe and highly contagious case of hepatitis, is home-schooled by a special tutor provided by the school district.

      b.   Brian, a sixth grader who has exceptionally poor reading skills, is in a class especially designed for students with learning disabilities.

      c.   Carol, who is blind, is in the regular classroom all day long; she has her reading materials tape-recorded or printed in Braille.

      d.   Darren, a ten-year-old with mental retardation, spends most of each day with a special education teacher, but he joins a regular second-grade class for art and music.

Essay

1)   6.   Explain how descriptive studies, correlational studies, and experimental studies are different from one another, and give a concrete example of a research question that each type of study might address.

2)   7.   A researcher finds that students who are physically aggressive at school are more likely to have abusive parents than students who are not aggressive. The researcher concludes that child abuse causes aggressive behavior. Is this conclusion warranted? Why or why not?

Answers to Sample Test Questions

1. d—Only this alternative is consistent with research findings presented in the textbook's discussion of the OOPS test. (See the answers to items 2, 4, 6, and 8 of the OOPS.)

2. a—A cause-effect relationship is implied here: Teacher questions promote greater student learning. The other three alternatives describe relationships among two variables but do not propose that one variable causes another. (See the section "Drawing Conclusions from Psychological and Educational Research.")

3. b—A visual image is an internal, mental phenomenon used to explain the effectiveness of visual aids. (See the section "Using Principles and Theories in Classroom Decision Making.")

4. d—Development of teaching expertise is most likely to come with practice and further education (see the section "Developing as a Teacher").

5. c—Inclusion is the practice of educating all students, even those with special educational needs, within a general education setting for most or all of the school day (see the section "Looking Ahead to the Following Chapters").

6. The three types of studies are described in the section "Drawing Conclusions from Psychological and Educational Research." Table 1.1 presents several examples of research questions that can be answered by each type of study. You can use three of these questions in your response, but better still, you can identify new examples.

7. The conclusion is *not* warranted. The researcher has conducted a correlational study, rather than an experimental study, and therefore has not ruled out other possible explanations for the differences in aggressiveness. (For example, perhaps impoverished living conditions are the cause of both child abuse and aggression.) See the section "Drawing Conclusions from Psychological and Educational Research," focusing especially on the subsection "A Cautionary Note."

Chapter 2

COGNITIVE AND LINGUISTIC DEVELOPMENT

Chapter Summary

Children develop skills and abilities in a somewhat predictable sequence, although not always at the same rate, and their development is a function of both hereditary and environmental factors. The brain continues to develop throughout childhood and adolescence. Although maturation plays a central role in the brain's development, many synapses form as a result of children's and adolescents' learning experiences.

In Jean Piaget's theory of cognitive development, two complementary processes—assimilation and accommodation—provide the mechanisms through which children develop and learn. Children often encounter challenges in their physical and social environments; as they work to address these challenges, they acquire increasingly logical and sophisticated thinking capabilities. Piaget proposed that cognitive development can best be characterized as a progression through four stages: sensorimotor, preoperational, concrete operations, and formal operations. Recent researchers sometimes find evidence that contradicts Piaget's assertions (e.g., some characteristics appear earlier than Piaget proposed, and others appear later). Nevertheless, the four stages give us a rough idea of the ages at which we can expect to see various logical thinking capabilities emerge.

In Piaget's theory, the focus is largely on how children acquire logical thinking capabilities *on their own*. In contrast, Lev Vygotsky proposed that adults and other competent individuals actively nurture particular ways of thinking about the world. In Vygotsky's view, children's mental processes have their roots in social processes (formal instruction, informal guidance, discussions, arguments, and so on), which children gradually *internalize* and can eventually use independently of other people. Vygotsky further proposed that children benefit most from tasks that they can perform only with the assistance of others—that is, tasks within their *zone of proximal development*. Many contemporary theorists have embraced and expanded on Vygotsky's ideas. For instance, they have offered a variety of strategies for supporting (*scaffolding*) students' efforts in challenging activities, and they argue that instruction is often most effective when it shows students how to *think about* as well as *do* a particular task.

A third perspective of cognitive development, information processing theory, focuses on how specific cognitive processes and abilities change over time. For instance, children become increasingly able to focus their attention on an assigned task, use increasingly sophisticated learning strategies, and become more metacognitively aware of what they actually know and how they can learn most effectively. Information processing theorists believe that cognitive development can best be characterized in terms of many gradual *trends*, rather than in terms of discrete stages.

Language capabilities— vocabulary, syntax, listening comprehension, oral communication, metalinguistic awareness—continue to develop throughout the school years. Learning a second language further enhances metalinguistic awareness and has the additional advantage of promoting greater understanding and appreciation of other cultures.

Several themes recur throughout the chapter's discussion of cognitive and linguistic development. (1) Children think in qualitatively different ways at different ages. (2) Children do not passively absorb information from the environment; instead, they actively construct their knowledge and understandings. (3) Knowledge and skills developed in the early years provide the foundation, and are sometimes essential prerequisites, for later acquisitions. (4) Challenging tasks and situations promote the development of more sophisticated abilities. (5) Social interaction with both adults and peers is essential for cognitive development.

Common Student Beliefs and Misconceptions Related to Chapter Content

Listed below are a number of commonly held beliefs that may interfere with an accurate understanding of cognitive and linguistic development. As you read Chapter 2, be on the lookout for evidence that contradicts these ideas:

1. Some future teachers believe that they only need to know the developmental characteristics of the particular age group at which they will be teaching. In reality, effective teachers know how learners develop *throughout* the K-12 school years and use that knowledge to promote their own students' development.

2. Most people typically use the word *maturation* in a different sense than developmentalists use the term (see the section "Basic Principles of Human Development" for developmentalists' meaning of the word).

3. Many students who have previously studied Piaget's theory believe that his four stages of cognitive development are accurate descriptions of how children think and behave at various ages.

4. Most people typically use the word *egocentrism* to mean "self-centeredness"—a meaning very different from Piaget's meanings of the term (see the discussions of *preoperational egocentrism* and *formal operational egocentrism* in the section "Piaget's Stages of Cognitive Development").

CHAPTER OUTLINE	FOCUS QUESTIONS
BASIC PRINCIPLES OF HUMAN DEVELOPMENT	• What general principles are common across many aspects of child and adolescent development? • What do all stage theories have in common? • What do developmentalists mean by *maturation*? by *temperament*? by *sensitive period*? How is each of these a function of heredity?
ROLE OF THE BRAIN IN COGNITIVE DEVELOPMENT	• How have various theorists interpreted current findings in neurological research?

PIAGET'S THEORY OF COGNITIVE DEVELOPMENT
 	
    Piaget's Basic Assumptions
    Piaget's Stages of Cognitive Development
    Current Perspectives on Piaget's Theory
	• What assumptions underlie Piaget's theory of cognitive development? What roles do *assimilation*, *accommodation*, and *equilibration* play in development? What implications do Piaget's assumptions have for classroom practice?
	
	• What characteristics are associated with each of Piaget's four stages? What strengths and weaknesses do children have at each stage?
	
	• What form does *egocentrism* take during the preoperational stage? What form does it take during the formal operational stage?
	
	• Which characteristics of the concrete operational and formal operational stages are especially relevant to mathematics and science instruction?
	
	• What forms of reasoning are you likely to see in students at the grade level you will be teaching? What implications do these reasoning capabilities have for your own teaching?
	
	• What does recent research tell us about the strengths and weaknesses of Piaget's theory?

CHAPTER OUTLINE	FOCUS QUESTIONS

VYGOTSKY'S THEORY OF COGNITIVE DEVELOPMENT
 	
    Vygotsky's Basic Assumptions
    Current Perspectives on Vygotsky's Theory
	• What assumptions underlie Vygotsky's theory of cognitive development? What role does *internalization* play in development? What implications do Vygotsky's assumptions have for classroom practice?
	
	• In what ways do thought and language become interdependent? From Vygotsky's perspective, what function do self-talk and inner speech play?
	
	• Describe Vygotsky's *zone of proximal development (ZPD)* in your own words. Think of tasks that are likely to be in the ZPD of the students you will be teaching.
	
	• What do contemporary theorists mean by *guided participation* and *apprenticeships*?
	
	• What is a *cognitive apprenticeship*? In what specific way is it "cognitive"?
	
	• What is *scaffolding*? How does it change over time? Can you think of a new example of this concept?

AN INFORMATION PROCESSING VIEW OF COGNITIVE DEVELOPMENT
 	
    Attention
    Learning Strategies
    Knowledge
    Metacognition
	• How is information processing theorists' notion of *trends* in cognitive development different from Piaget's notion of discrete stages?
	
	• As children develop, what changes do we see in attention, learning strategies, knowledge, and metacognition? What implications do these developmental changes have for teaching children of different ages?
	
	• From the perspective of information processing theory, what strengths and weaknesses are students likely to have at the grade level you will be teaching?

CHAPTER OUTLINE	FOCUS QUESTIONS

LINGUISTIC DEVELOPMENT
 	
    Theoretical Perspectives on Language Development
 	
    Trends in Language Development
 	
    Learning a Second Language
	• Why do theorists believe that both heredity and environment play roles in language development?
	
	• In what ways do students' receptive and expressive language capabilities change during the school years? What abilities are students likely to have at the grade level you will be teaching?
	
	• What are *undergeneralization, overgeneralization,* and *overregularization*? Think of a new example of each of these phenomena.
	
	• What can teachers do to promote students' language development? How can they promote *metalinguistic awareness*?
	
	• What are the advantages of learning a second language? When is immersion more effective? When is bilingual education more effective?

CONSIDERING DIVERSITY IN COGNITIVE AND LINGUISTIC DEVELOPMENT Accommodating Students with Special Needs	• How are your students likely to differ from one another in cognitive and linguistic development? • How can teachers adapt instruction to promote the cognitive and linguistic development of students with special needs?

THE BIG PICTURE
 	
    Developmental Principles in the Classroom
 	
    Cognitive Development
 	
    Linguistic Development
 	
    General Themes in Cognitive and Linguistic
    Development
	• What are the common themes that characterize both cognitive and linguistic development? Identify specific places where each theme appears in the chapter.

Supplementary Reading

Your instructor may assign Supplementary Reading #2, "Physical Development Across Childhood and Adolescence," which appears in the final section of this *Study Guide and Reader*.

Using the CD *Simulations in Educational Psychology and Research*

"The Pendulum Experiment" on the *Simulations in Educational Psychology and Research* CD is a hands-on activity similar to the "Pendulum Problem" Experiencing Firsthand exercise presented in the textbook.

Chapter Glossary

Accommodation. In Piaget's theory, dealing with a new event by either modifying an existing scheme or forming a new one.

Actual developmental level. In Vygotsky's theory, the extent to which one can successfully perform a task independently.

Apprenticeship. A situation in which a learner works intensively with an expert to learn how to accomplish complex tasks.

Assimilation. In Piaget's theory, dealing with a new event in a way that is consistent with an existing scheme.

Bilingual education. An approach to second-language instruction in which students are instructed in academic subject areas in their native language while simultaneously being taught to speak and write in the second language. The amount of instruction delivered in the native language decreases as students become more proficient in the second language.

Cognitive apprenticeship. A mentorship in which a teacher and a student work together to accomplish a challenging task or solve a difficult problem; in the process, the teacher provides guidance about how to think about the task or problem.

Cognitive processes. The ways in which one thinks about (processes) information.

Concrete operations stage. Piaget's third stage of cognitive development, in which adultlike logic appears but is limited to concrete reality.

Conservation. The realization that if nothing is added or taken away, amount (e.g., number, mass) stays the same regardless of any alterations in shape or arrangement.

Constructivism. A theoretical perspective that proposes that learners construct a body of knowledge from their experiences—knowledge that may or may not be an accurate representation of external reality. Adherents to this perspective are called **constructivists**.

Cortex. The upper part of the brain; site of conscious and higher-level thinking processes.

Deductive reasoning. Drawing a logical inference about something that must be true, given other information that has already been presented as true.

Developmental milestone. The appearance of a new, developmentally more advanced behavior.

Dialect. A form of English (or other language) characteristic of a particular region or ethnic group.

Disequilibrium. In Piaget's theory, an inability to explain new events by using existing schemes.

Egocentric speech. Speaking without taking the perspective and knowledge of the listener into account.

Elaboration. A cognitive process in which learners expand on new information based on what they already know.

Equilibration. In Piaget's theory, the movement from equilibrium to disequilibrium and back to equilibrium—a process that promotes the development of more complex forms of thought and knowledge.

Equilibrium. In Piaget's theory, a state of being able to explain new events by using existing schemes.

Expressive language. The ability to communicate effectively through speaking and writing.

Formal operational egocentrism. The inability of individuals in Piaget's formal operations stage to separate their own abstract logic from the perspectives of others and from practical considerations.

Formal operations stage. Piaget's fourth and final stage of cognitive development, in which logical reasoning processes are applied to abstract ideas as well as to concrete objects.

Guided participation. Giving a child the necessary guidance and support to perform an activity in the adult world.

Immersion. An approach to second-language instruction in which students hear and speak that language almost exclusively within the classroom.

Inner speech. "Talking" to oneself mentally rather than aloud.

Internalization. In Vygotsky's theory, the process through which social activities evolve into mental activities.

Irreversibility. An inability to recognize that certain processes can be undone, or reversed.

Knowledge base. One's knowledge about specific topics and the world in general.

Learning strategy. One or more cognitive processes used intentionally for a particular learning task.

Level of potential development. In Vygotsky's theory, the extent to which one can successfully execute a task with the assistance of a more competent individual.

Limited English proficiency (LEP). A limited ability to understand and communicate in oral or written English, usually because English is not one's native language.

Maturation. The unfolding of genetically controlled changes as a child develops.

Metacognition. One's knowledge and beliefs about one's own cognitive processes, and one's resulting attempts to regulate those cognitive processes to maximize learning and memory.

Metalinguistic awareness. The extent to which one is able to think about the nature of language.

Multiple classification. The recognition that objects may belong to several categories simultaneously.

Neuron. A cell in the brain or another part of the nervous system that transmits information to other cells.

Object permanence. The realization that objects continue to exist even after they are removed from view.

Operations. In Piaget's theory, organized and integrated systems of thought processes.

Organization. A cognitive process in which learners find connections (e.g., by forming categories, identifying hierarchies, determining cause-effect relationships) among the various pieces of information they need to learn.

Overgeneralization. An overly broad meaning for a word that includes some situations where the word is not appropriate.

Overregularization. Applying syntactical rules in situations where those rules don't apply.

Pragmatics. Knowledge about the culture-specific social conventions guiding verbal interactions.

Preoperational egocentrism. In Piaget's theory, the inability of children in the preoperational stage to view situations from another person's perspective.

Preoperational stage. Piaget's second stage of cognitive development, in which children can think about objects beyond their immediate view but do not yet reason in logical, adultlike ways.

Proportional reasoning. The ability to understand proportions (e.g., fractions, decimals, ratios) and use them effectively in mathematical problem solving.

Receptive language. The ability to understand the language that one hears or reads.

Rehearsal. A cognitive process in which information is repeated over and over as a possible way of learning and remembering it.

Reversibility. The ability to recognize that certain processes can be undone, or reversed.

Scaffolding. A support mechanism, provided by a more competent individual, that helps a learner successfully perform a task within his or her zone of proximal development.

Scheme. In Piaget's theory, an organized group of similar actions or thoughts.

Self-talk. Talking to oneself as a way of guiding oneself through a task; also known as *private speech*.

Semantics. The meanings of words and word combinations.

Sensitive period. An age range during which a certain aspect of a child's development is especially susceptible to environmental conditions.

Sensorimotor stage. Piaget's first stage of cognitive development, in which schemes are based on behaviors and perceptions.

Separation and control of variables. The ability to test one variable at a time while holding all other variables constant.

Single classification. The ability to classify objects in only one way at any given point in time.

Sociocultural perspective. A theoretical perspective that emphasizes the importance of society and culture for promoting cognitive development.

Stage theory. A theory that depicts development as a series of relatively discrete periods (or **stages**), with relatively slow growth within each stage and more rapid growth during the transition from one stage to another.

Symbolic thinking. The ability to represent and think about external objects and events in one's head.

Synapse. A junction between two neurons that allows messages to be transmitted from one to the other.

Syntax. The set of rules that one uses (often unconsciously) to put words together into sentences.

Temperament. A genetic predisposition to respond in particular ways to one's physical and social environments.

Transductive reasoning. Making a mental leap from one specific thing to another, such as identifying one event as the cause of another simply because the two events occur close together in time.

Undergeneralization. An overly restricted meaning for a word that excludes some situations to which the word does, in fact, apply.

Universals (in development). The similar patterns we see in how children change over time regardless of the specific environment in which they are raised.

Zone of proximal development (ZPD). In Vygotsky's theory, the range of tasks between one's actual developmental level and one's level of potential development—that is, the range of tasks that one cannot yet perform independently but can perform with the help and guidance of others.

Following are additional glossary items if your instructor has assigned Supplementary Reading #2:

Fine motor skills. Small, precise movements of particular parts of the body, especially the hands.

Gross motor skills. Large movements of the body that permit locomotion around the environment.

Growth spurt. Rapid increase in height and weight during puberty.

Menarche. First menstrual period in an adolescent female.

Puberty. Physiological changes that occur during adolescence and lead to reproductive maturation.

Spermarche. First ejaculation in an adolescent male.

Application Exercise #2: Recognizing a Student's Zone of Proximal Development

Which of the following students are working within their *zone of proximal development*? Defend your choices.

1. An elementary physical education teacher is teaching her second graders the basics of soccer. She describes the different positions that team members might play and explains the specific roles that players in each position have. She breaks the class into two teams of eleven players each and assigns each student a specific position on the field. Yet once the ball is in motion, everyone on the field immediately flocks to it, resulting in a game of "magnet" ball.

2. Selena is learning how to play the trumpet. She still has trouble with some of the high notes but does better when her teacher reminds her what she needs to do.

3. When Mr. Marino asks his fifth graders to write a short story, they seem to be at a loss for ideas. But when he suggests that they write a "Just So" story explaining why the elephant has such a big trunk or why the giraffe has such a long neck, they are each able to write a story with a main character, plot, conflict, and resolution.

4. Julian can locate virtually any place on the globe if he knows its latitude and longitude.

5. An art teacher demonstrates how to paint with watercolors and then walks around the room to watch his students work. He offers guidance when he sees someone having trouble creating new colors or keeping different colors from running together on the paper.

6. Regina is quite adept at simple algebra problems. While her classmates are solving for x on paper, she arrives at the correct answer in her head.

7. A fourth-grade teacher asks his students to read an article in a recent issue of *Time* magazine. He describes the main point of the article before his students begin reading it, and he gives them several questions that they should try to answer as they read. Even so, his students are unable to understand what they are reading.

8. In her unit on genetics, a high school science teacher has students working with fruit flies. Because the students are initially confused about what they are supposed to do, she writes specific instructions on the chalkboard and then circulates around the room to assist students who are having trouble identifying males and females correctly.

Answers to Application Exercise #2

1. No. Even with reasonable guidance and assistance, the students are unable to play their respective positions.

2. Yes. Selena plays the high notes successfully only with her teacher's assistance.

3. Yes. The students can write a short story successfully only when Mr. Marino structures the task for them and gives them some ideas about characters and plots.

4. No. Using latitude and longitude is obviously an easy task for Julian, because he needs no help from anyone else.

5. Yes. The students are sometimes having trouble with watercolor technique and therefore benefit from their teacher's assistance.

6. No. Regina is solving the problems quickly and easily, without help from anyone else.

7. No. Even with their teacher's advance summary and focus questions, they are unable to comprehend the article.

8. Yes. The students are able to proceed only with their teacher's instructions, and some of them are having difficulty sex-typing the flies without her assistance.

Application Exercise #3: Identifying Typical and Atypical Behaviors

In the following scenarios, which students are exhibiting behaviors typical for their age-group, and which ones are not? Justify your choices on the basis of Piaget's theory, information processing theory, or research findings related to language development.

1. When a fourth-grade teacher describes decimals, her students are totally confused. She tries several different ways of teaching the concept *decimal,* but without success.

2. A high school freshman is very distractible in class. Any little noise seems to draw her attention away from what she is supposed to be doing.

3. A first grader asserts that a lobster can't possibly be an animal because it doesn't have fur.

4. A second grader living in an inner-city ghetto comes to school upset about a neighbor who was killed in a drive-by shooting the night before. "The world would be a much better place if it didn't have guns," she says despondently.

5. In a high school physics lab, students are instructed to design and conduct an experiment to determine whether or not *weight* affects the speed at which something falls. As the students compare the speed with which objects of different weights fall, they are careful to use objects that are similar in size and shape, and they make sure that they drop all of them from the same height at exactly the same time.

6. A group of kindergartners sit quietly and politely as the school principal describes the procedure they should follow during a fire drill, but many of them are unable to describe the procedure themselves after the principal leaves the room.

7. A third-grade class is learning about Columbus's first trip across the Atlantic Ocean. Although the teacher has said nothing about what Columbus and his crew must have been thinking and feeling after weeks on the open sea, Ophelia raises her hand and asks, "Weren't they all really scared that they might never see land again?"

8. A seventh-grade teacher gives her students a five-page reading assignment in their social studies textbook; the following day, she gives them a quiz over what they have read. She is pleased at her students' excellent performance on the quiz and asks them what they did when they read and studied the assignment. The strategies they describe are similar to things she did when she studied as a college student.

9. Six-year-old Marianne sees a mother rabbit run into its hole and thinks that, because the mother no longer exists, her babies must now be orphans with no one to take care of them.

10. A fifth grader studies his spelling words by repeating the letters of each word over and over again.

11. The Sudbury High School and Pine Grove High School ice hockey teams are playing for the regional championship. When Sudbury's star player is sent to the penalty box for five minutes, the Pine Grove coach shouts, "All right, men! Let's make hay while the sun shines!" The team members realize that the coach's statement has nothing to do with making hay, that instead it means that they should try to score a goal while they have the advantage.

12. Five-year-old Ethan watches his teacher pour poster paint from a tall, thin jar into a short, wide aluminum cup so that Ethan can dip his brush into the paint more easily. The teacher asks if there is the same amount of paint in the cup as there had been in the jar. Ethan says yes, although he cannot explain why he thinks so.

13. When a teacher asks his seventh-grade class why the sun doesn't fall down from the sky, Elliott replies in all seriousness, "Because it's yellow."

14. Five preschoolers are working on an art project at the same table; they have only two pairs of scissors and one bottle of glue to share among them. Martin wants to keep the glue and one pair of scissors to himself; he doesn't understand why he must let the other children use them as well.

15. A fourth-grade class is studying different denominations of money and has learned what pennies, nickels, dimes, and quarters are worth. As the students watch, the teacher places ten nickels in a stack and spreads another ten nickels all around on the floor. "Which set of nickels would you rather have—the ten nickels stacked up or the ten nickels spread apart?" Louise says she would rather have the ten nickels stacked up because there are more of them.

16. Fifteen-year-old Nancy asserts that if the United Nations took a strong stand on dealing with world hunger, no child would ever go hungry again.

17. Maria is surprised to discover that her kindergarten teacher has children of his own. "You can't be a daddy, " she says. "You're a teacher."

18. Ten-year-old Kevin doesn't understand how $54 \div 6 = 9$ is the opposite of $9 \times 6 = 54$.

19. A ninth grader studies three hours for her geography test and thinks she knows the material well. Her low test score the following day indicates that she doesn't understand it at all.

20. A first-grade teacher places fifteen different objects on his desk and asks his students to look at them carefully. He says, "I'm going to cover these up in just a few seconds. How many things do you think you will be able to remember a few minutes from now?" His students confidently agree that they will be able to remember almost all of the objects. As it turns out, they can remember an average of only seven objects apiece.

21. When a second grader hears her teacher say, "The soldier was shot by the old woman," she thinks that the soldier did the shooting.

22. In his history class, a high school senior writes, "Cortez took a great deal of gold from the Aztecs, although he was exceptionally greedy." He does not understand that he is using the word *although* incorrectly here.

23. On Monday morning, five-year-old Susan tells her teacher what she did over the weekend. "We drove to the McAllisters' farm and rode Betsy." When her teacher explains that she doesn't know the McAllisters and wonders what kind of animal Betsy is, Susan becomes annoyed at her teacher's ignorance about these things.

24. An eighth grader writes, "John Wesley Powell *goed* down the Grand Canyon in a canoe."

Answers to Application Exercise #3

1. Typical. Decimals are proportions. From Piaget's perspective, proportional thinking doesn't appear until formal operations, when children are, on average, about eleven or twelve. More recent researchers have substantiated Piaget's claim.

2. Not typical. Information processing research tells us that, although children are easily distracted during the early elementary years, they become increasingly able to focus their attention as they grow older.

3. Typical. Young children often have too restricted a meaning of the word *animal*—an instance of undergeneralization.

4. Not typical. From Piaget's perspective, reasoning about contrary-to-fact ideas does not appear until the formal operations stage.

5. Typical. The students are demonstrating separation and control of variables, a characteristic of Piaget's formal operational stage.

6. Typical. Young children often think that being a "good listener" merely means sitting still and being quiet; they do not necessarily realize that listening also involves understanding and remembering what the speaker says.

7. Not typical. Ophelia is demonstrating elaboration: She is going beyond the information her teacher has actually presented. Elaboration, at least when used intentionally as a learning strategy, is rare before early adolescence.

8. Not typical. Students become increasingly knowledgeable about effective study strategies throughout the high school years. Seventh graders use relatively ineffective strategies compared to those that high school and college students are likely to use.

9. Not typical. Object permanence—recognizing that things continue to exist even when they disappear from sight—develops before the age of two, during Piaget's sensorimotor stage.

10. Typical. Rehearsal is a commonly used learning strategy during the later elementary school years.

11. Typical. Most high school students can look beyond the literal meanings of spoken messages and understand the figurative nature of common expressions and proverbs.

12. Typical. Children in the later years of Piaget's preoperational stage can sometimes think logically, but they are often unable to explain their reasoning.

13. Not typical. Thinking that the sun's color is responsible for its continuing presence in the sky is an example of transductive reasoning, which is common only during Piaget's preoperational stage.

14. Typical. Egocentrism, the inability to view the world from another person's perspective, is common during Piaget's preoperational stage.

15. Not typical. Conservation of number appears in early concrete operations, sometime around six or seven years of age.

16. Typical. Idealism is common among adolescents in Piaget's formal operations stage, but their idealistic beliefs may not be realistically accomplishable.

17. Typical. Children in Piaget's preoperational stage often have difficulty classifying things as belonging to two or more categories at the same time.

18. Not typical. Reversibility appears early in Piaget's concrete operations stage, sometime around six or seven years of age.

19. Typical. Many students overestimate what they have learned, even at the high school level.

20. Typical. Children in the early elementary grades tend to be overly optimistic about how much they will be able to remember.

21. Typical. Children in the early elementary grades often have difficulty interpreting passive sentences correctly.

22. Not typical. Children as old as twelve have trouble using connectives such as *although* correctly, but a high school senior should not have such difficulty.

23. Typical. Egocentric speech—speaking as if other people already know the things you're talking about—is common during Piaget's preoperational stage.

24. Not typical. Applying the *-ed* rule to irregular verbs—an instance of overregularization—is common in the early elementary years but unusual in adolescence.

Application Exercise #4: Identifying Developmentally Appropriate Teaching Practices

Which of the following teaching practices are appropriate for the age level of the students, and which are not? Defend your choices.

1.   Nathan temporarily forgets the answer to 9 – 6, so his third-grade teacher gives him a hint by saying, "Three plus six equal nine, so nine minus six must equal. . . ."

2.   In an attempt to foster creativity, a first-grade teacher divides her class into five groups and gives each one a creative activity to pursue (writing a play, making an invention, composing a song, and so on). She allots a two-hour period for this activity, then pulls the class back together to find out what everyone has accomplished.

3.   A high school physical education teacher describes the steps that students should take when they execute a difficult dismount from the parallel bars. As students begin practicing the dismount, the teacher encourages them to repeat the steps to themselves as they proceed.

4.   A middle school offers a class in introductory Russian that sixth and seventh graders may take as an elective.

5.   An eleventh-grade mathematics teacher asks students to solve for x in problems such as this:
$$3/7 = 12/x$$

6.   A third-grade teacher asks students to consider what might have happened if Columbus had not sailed to the New World in 1492.

7.   When giving his high school students their evening's reading assignment, Mr. Rodriguez provides a list of questions that they should be able to answer when they have finished.

8.   An eighth-grade science teacher describes how biologists often divide forms of animal life into two categories: vertebrates and invertebrates.

9.   A music teacher has her second-grade students performing in a Halloween play tomorrow. Marnie plays the lead character—an absentminded ghost—but still doesn't know most of her lines. "Don't worry, Ms. Jackson, I'll have Dad read them to me once tonight, so I'll be sure to remember them tomorrow." Ms. Jackson calls Marnie's father to make sure that he *will* read Marnie her lines at least once.

10.   A high school science teacher asks students in a chemistry lab to find out whether water boils sooner if more heat is applied. He gives them the equipment they need and shows them how to use it safely, but he provides no additional guidance about how to approach the task.

11.   Ms. James explains what her first graders should do at each of the four learning centers around the classroom this morning. Even though she thinks she has explained the procedures clearly, she encourages students to ask questions if they are unsure about what to do next.

12.   A fourth-grade teacher gives a short lecture explaining how the Rocky Mountains were formed by forces pushing upward from within the earth.

13.   A middle school language arts teacher encourages students to study their new vocabulary words by repeating the definitions over and over to themselves.

Answers to Application Exercise #4

1. Appropriate. Within the framework of Piaget's theory, most third graders should be in the concrete operations stage and so should be capable of reversibility.

2. Not appropriate. Young children are easily distracted and therefore have trouble focusing their attention on any one thing for very long. Students in each group will inevitably be distracted by the things that other groups are saying and doing.

3. Appropriate. According to Vygotsky, self-talk is not limited to young children; it is common for people of any age when they are performing a difficult task for the first time.

4. Appropriate. There is no hard and fast rule about when to begin studying a second language.

5. Appropriate. Research indicates that proportional thinking emerges in early adolescence. Within the framework of Piaget's theory, eleventh graders should be in the formal operations stage and so should be capable of proportional thought.

6. Not appropriate. From Piaget's perspective, students in the elementary grades are not yet capable of reasoning about ideas that are contrary to fact.

7. Appropriate. Students of all ages, even those in high school, often think they have learned things that they really haven't learned. By giving students questions they must answer from their reading assignment, Mr. Rodriguez is providing them with a way of testing themselves to find out what they actually do and do not understand.

8. Appropriate. According to Vygotsky, teachers should convey how culture interprets the world, and the terms *vertebrate* and *invertebrate* are examples of such cultural interpretation. Furthermore, from Piaget's perspective, eighth graders (who are typically at least thirteen years old) are capable of both multiple classification and abstract thought.

9. Not appropriate. Young children tend to overestimate how much they will be able to remember. One time through is probably insufficient even for an adult, let alone for a second grader, but Marnie is undoubtedly unaware of this fact.

10. Appropriate. From Piaget's perspective, high school students are capable of formal operational thought and so should be able to separate and control variables. They should be able to demonstrate the effect of more or less heat while keeping other variables (size and shape of container, amount of water, etc.) constant.

11. Appropriate. Many children in the early elementary grades don't realize they should ask questions when they don't understand. Ms. James is trying to teach them that asking questions is perfectly acceptable.

12. Not appropriate. The teacher is describing processes that students have never directly observed; thus, the ideas he is presenting are somewhat abstract. Fourth graders tend to have difficulty with strictly abstract ideas.

13. Not appropriate. Rehearsal is a commonly used learning strategy in the elementary grades. But older students are capable of elaboration, which is a more effective strategy.

Answers to Selected Margin Notes

Note: Some of the margin notes scattered throughout the textbook ask you to elaborate on what you're learning. When the items in the margins have definite right answers, I will provide the answers here in the *Study Guide and Reader*.

- Page 31: *Recall our earlier discussion of the importance of separating and controlling variables in experimental research (Chapter 1).*

    In an experimental study, the experimenter manipulates (i.e., controls) one variable at a time in order to observe its effect on a second variable. Other possibly influential factors are separated out and held constant so that the manipulated variable must, by process of elimination, be the cause of any changes observed in that second variable.

- Page 45: *Might you see better performance in "low-ability" students if you encourage them to work with a topic they know a lot about?*

    Yes, you should see better performance in these students when they have a rich knowledge base to which they can relate school subject matter.

Sample Test Questions

Items marked with a "**1**)" on the left-hand side are lower-level questions that assess your general knowledge and understanding of the material. Items marked with a "**2**)" on the left-hand side are higher-level questions that assess your ability to apply what you have learned to a new situation.

Multiple-Choice

2)   1.   Irene knows how to count to 10. She counts the coins she has in her pocket (2 quarters, 5 dimes, and 3 nickels) and says, "I have 10 cents." From Piaget's perspective, Irene is:

     a. Accommodating the counting task to the fact that the different coins have different values

     b. Assimilating the counting task to the way she has counted objects in the past

     c. Experiencing disequilibrium about how to count money

     d. Showing insufficient physiological maturation to perform the task correctly

2)   2.   Roy gets confused when his science teacher talks about a gas freezing at –100° Fahrenheit. "How can you have *minus* degrees, Ms. Lewis? Temperature can't be less than zero." Roy is showing _____, indicating that he may not yet have made the transition to Piaget's _____ stage.

     a. single classification; concrete operational

     b. multiple classification; formal operational

     c. dependence on concrete reality; concrete operational

     d. dependence on concrete reality; formal operational

2)   3.   Which one of the following is the best example of *scaffolding*?

     a. Before her beginning saxophone students start to play "Jingle Bells," Ms. Arnold reminds them where each finger should be on their instruments.

     b. Mr. Baker gives a detailed lecture about the events leading up to the Gulf War.

     c. Mr. Christian has his students write a ten-page research paper on the African country of their own choosing.

     d. Ms. DiCicco equips her kindergarten classroom with a variety of art supplies that students can use during free time.

2)   4.   Imagine that you and your students have certain opinions about issues being addressed in an upcoming election and that you all agree to communicate your opinions by writing a group letter to the editor of the local newspaper. Together you brainstorm strategies for expressing your thoughts in a logical and persuasive manner, and then you translate the best strategy into an outline of the major points that you, as a class, want to make in the letter. In doing these things with your students, you demonstrate the value of both brainstorming and outlining as strategies for developing a persuasive essay. Your approach can best be described as:

     a. Presenting a task outside students' zone of proximal development

     b. The process of equilibration

     c. Helping students separate and control variables

     d. A cognitive apprenticeship

1) 5. The following statements describe the development of information processing abilities as children progress through the school years. Three of the statements are accurate. Which one is *not*?

    a. Older children are more likely to be aware of what they do and do not know as they study.

    b. Children develop more effective learning strategies as they move into the junior high school and high school years.

    c. Older children are more likely than younger children to overestimate how much they can remember from something they've read or studied.

    d. As they grow older, children are more likely to find interrelationships among the various things they learn.

2) 6. Which one of the following statements illustrates *undergeneralization* as psychologists define the term?

    a. "Christopher Columbus sailed to the New World, where he found the Pilgrims already living at Plymouth."

    b. "An igloo can't be a house because houses are always made of wood or bricks."

    c. "A sea horse must be a mammal, because all horses are mammals."

    d. "He runned all the way to school, then turned around and runned all the way home again."

Essay

2) 7. Using Piaget's perspective of cognitive development, describe a *strength* and a *weakness* of children's logical thinking in each of these three stages: the preoperational stage, the concrete operational stage, and the formal operational stage. To illustrate your discussion, give specific examples of how children in each stage are likely to think or behave.

1) 8. Explain what psychologists mean by the terms *receptive language* and *expressive language*. Provide two concrete examples of how students' receptive language skills continue to develop during the school years; also provide two concrete examples of how their expressive language skills continue to develop during the school years.

Answers to Sample Test Questions

1. b—Irene is showing assimilation: She is dealing with a new situation in a way that is consistent with something she already knows how to do (see the section "Piaget's Basic Assumptions").

2. d—Roy is unable to comprehend the concept of a negative number—an abstract concept that has little basis in concrete reality. Roy's inability to deal with abstract ideas indicates that he has not yet made the transition to formal operations (see the discussion of Piaget's formal operations stage).

3. a—Ms. Arnold is providing guidance to help her students perform a complex task successfully. (See the discussion of scaffolding in the section "Current Perspectives on Vygotsky's Theory.")

4. d—In a cognitive apprenticeship, a teacher and one or more students work together to accomplish a challenging task. In the process, the teacher models effective ways to think about the task. (Cognitive apprenticeships are discussed in the section "Current Perspectives on Vygotsky's Theory.")

5. c—The reverse is true: Younger children are more likely to overestimate what they will be able to remember. They become increasingly more accurate as they grow older. (See the section on metacognition in "An Information Processing View of Cognitive Development.")

6. b—The speaker has too narrow a definition of the concept *house*. (Undergeneralization is defined and illustrated in the discussion of vocabulary development in "Trends in Language Development.")

7. Strengths and weaknesses of each stage can be found in "Piaget's Stages of Cognitive Development" (be sure to look at Tables 2.1 and 2.2). Your response to this question should include at least three concrete examples to illustrate your discussion, with at least one example for each of the three stages you have described. You can use some of the examples presented in the pages listed above, or better still, you can use examples of your own.

8. Receptive language is the ability to understand spoken and printed language; thus, it involves both listening and reading. Expressive language is the ability to communicate one's thoughts effectively; it includes both speaking and writing. Developmental changes in students' receptive and expressive language skills are identified throughout the section "Trends in Language Development."

Chapter 3

PERSONAL, SOCIAL, AND MORAL DEVELOPMENT

Chapter Summary

Students' personal characteristics and behavior patterns are the result of many things, including biological predispositions, parental childrearing styles, cultural expectations, and peer influences. Schools and teachers are important factors in students' personal, social, and moral development. For example, teachers often act as socialization agents, teaching children and adolescents to control their impulses, follow directions, work independently, cooperate with classmates, and so on. Furthermore, school is, for most students, the primary context in which to interact with peers and acquire social skills.

As students progress through childhood and adolescence, they form and continually modify perceptions of themselves; for instance, they acquire beliefs about their general characteristics and abilities (self-concept), develop opinions and feelings about their value and worth (self-esteem), learn the specific things they can and cannot do (self-efficacy), and eventually construct a definition of who they are as people, what things they find important, and what goals they hope to accomplish (identity). Students derive such self-perceptions not only from their prior experiences (e.g., their successes and failures) but also from the behaviors of others. As teachers, we must provide the support our students need to be successful and give them feedback that engenders optimism about future accomplishments. We must also consider students' age level; for example, if we consider Erikson's psychosocial stages, then we should (1) support preschoolers in their efforts to initiate activities, (2) encourage elementary school students to produce things and praise them for their accomplishments, and (3) provide opportunities for secondary school students to explore various career options and a variety of social and political belief systems.

Productive peer relationships are critical for optimal social and emotional development. Peers provide a testing ground for emerging social skills, offer support and comfort in times of trouble or uncertainty, and are influential socialization agents. Furthermore, peers provide opportunities for students to take others' perspectives, draw conclusions about others' motives and intentions, and identify effective solutions to interpersonal problems. Most students have friends that provide companionship and entertainment; particularly in adolescence, friends may provide advice and comfort as well. In the middle school and high school years, students may also become part of larger social groups—perhaps cliques, subcultures, or gangs. At the same time, some students are consistently rejected or neglected by their classmates, and these students may especially need teachers' friendship and support.

Many peers encourage appropriate and prosocial interpersonal skills, but some endorse antisocial and other counterproductive behaviors. Furthermore, some students may have difficulty interpreting social cues correctly or may have few effective social skills. As teachers, then, we may sometimes need to monitor and guide students' interpersonal interactions and take active steps to promote communication and interaction across diverse ethnic, socioeconomic, and linguistic groups, as well as between students with and without disabilities.

As children move through the grade levels, most acquire a definite sense of right and wrong, such that they behave in accordance with internal standards for behavior rather than act solely out of self-interest. This developmental progression is the result of many things, including increasing capacities for abstract thought and empathy, an evolving appreciation for human rights and others' welfare, and ongoing encounters with moral dilemmas and problems. Even at the high school level, however, students do not always take the moral high road, as personal needs and self-interests almost invariably enter into their moral decision making to some degree. As teachers, we can help students develop more advanced moral reasoning and increasingly prosocial behavior by giving them reasons why certain behaviors are unacceptable, encouraging them to recognize how others feel in various situations, exposing them to models of moral behavior, challenging their thinking with moral issues, and providing opportunities for community service and other prosocial behavior.

Some students face exceptional challenges in their lives (e.g., family problems, violence, drug addiction) that may affect their personal, social, and moral development. Students' cultural and ethnic backgrounds also affect their personal, social, and moral development; for example, some students' sense of identity may include pride in their ethnic heritage, and their sense of morality is likely to reflect the values of their local community. Students with special needs may need additional support to enhance their self-esteem, social skills, and moral development.

Four themes appear repeatedly in the chapter's discussion of personal, social, and moral development. (1) Students need standards for acceptable behavior as well as reasons why some behaviors are unacceptable. (2) Social interaction provides the impetus for many personal, social, and moral advancements. (3) Students need a warm, supportive environment in which they feel comfortable expressing their views and get positive feedback for their successes. (4) Just as students construct their knowledge and understandings of the world around them (see Chapter 2), so, too, do they construct their own beliefs about themselves, interpersonal relationships, and morality.

Common Student Beliefs and Misconceptions Related to Chapter Content

Below are several beliefs that college students often have before studying personal, social, and moral development—misconceptions that may interfere with an accurate understanding of what they read. As you read Chapter 3, be on the lookout for evidence that contradicts these common misconceptions:

1. Some students think of *socialization* in terms of socializing with their friends. Developmentalists' meaning for this term is quite different (see the section "Effects of Culture").

2. Some students confuse the term *authoritative* with the term *authoritarian*, which has a very different meaning. To discover the difference, read Supplementary Reading #3, "Parenting Styles and Children's Behavior," located near the end of this *Study Guide and Reader*.

3. Many students believe that to promote the development of positive self-concepts, we must never give negative feedback.

4. Some students equate morality with religion or in some other way have a limited view of what morality encompasses. As a result, they may believe that morals and morality have no place in the schools.

CHAPTER OUTLINE	FOCUS QUESTIONS
INFLUENCE OF HEREDITY AND ENVIRONMENT ON PERSONAL, SOCIAL, AND MORAL DEVELOPMENT Temperamental Differences Effects of Parenting Effects of Culture Peer Influences	• What is *temperament*? Give examples of temperamental differences you might see in the classroom. • What children's behaviors are associated with different parenting styles? How might children's temperaments affect their parents' disciplinary methods? • What do developmentalists mean by the term *socialization*? What kinds of behaviors might a culture socialize? • What kinds of behaviors do teachers typically socialize in students? Why are such behaviors important for students over the long run?
DEVELOPMENT OF A SENSE OF SELF Factors Influencing the Development of Self-Views Developmental Changes in Students' Self-Views	• Distinguish among *self-concept*, *self-esteem*, and *self-efficacy*. What effect do such self-views have on behavior? • What factors influence the development of students' self-views? What implications do these factors have for classroom practice? • In what ways do students' self-perceptions change during the school years? How are we likely to see the concepts *imaginary audience*, *personal fable*, and *identity* reflected in students' behavior? At what ages are we most likely to see each of these phenomena? • Summarize the nature of Erikson's eight stages of psychosocial development. What weaknesses in Erikson's theory have critics identified? • Considering developmental changes in students' self-views, as well as Erikson's psychosocial stages, characterize the age group(s) with whom you may eventually be working. Identify some age-appropriate strategies for the age group(s).

CHAPTER OUTLINE	FOCUS QUESTIONS

sOCIAL DEVELOPMENT
 	
   Peer Relationships
 	
   Social Cognition
 	
   Fostering Social Skills
 	
   Promoting Social Interaction Among Diverse Groups
	• What important roles do peers play in children's development? How do peer relationships change during the school years?
	
	• Explain the nature of *friendships*, *cliques*, *subcultures*, and *gangs*.
	
	• How do students' romantic relationships tend to change over the course of adolescence?
	
	• Summarize the characteristics of popular, rejected, and neglected students.
	
	• What is *social cognition*? How does it affect students' interpersonal relationships?
	
	• How does perspective-taking ability change with age? How can teachers promote perspective taking?
	
	• What various forms can aggression take? What factors seem to contribute to aggressive behavior?
	
	• How can teachers help students develop more effective social skills? How can they promote interaction among diverse groups?

MORAL AND PROSOCIAL DEVELOPMENT
 	
   Development of Moral Reasoning: Kohlberg's Theory
 	
   Possible Gender Differences in Moral Reasoning: Gilligan's Theory
 	
   Emotional Components of Moral Development
 	
   Determinants of Moral Behavior
 	
   Promoting Moral Development in the Classroom
	• What is a moral dilemma? Can you think of moral dilemmas that might arise in your own classroom?
	
	• How do individuals at each of Kohlberg's three levels and six stages reason about moral issues? According to Kohlberg, what factors affect a person's progression to the next higher stage? What strengths and weaknesses have researchers found in Kohlberg's theory?
	
	• In what way does Gilligan think males and females reason differently?
	
	• What emotions reflect moral development?
	
	• In Eisenberg's view, how do empathy and prosocial reasoning change with age?
	
	• What factors affect students' inclination to behave morally and prosocially?
	
	• What classroom strategies are apt to promote students' moral development?

CHAPTER OUTLINE	FOCUS QUESTIONS
CONSIDERING DIVERSITY IN PERSONAL, SOCIAL, AND MORAL DEVELOPMENT Accommodating Students with Special Needs	• What cultural and ethnic differences might we see in students' personal, social, and moral development? • In what ways might students with special educational needs be different from their classmates? How can teachers accommodate such differences?

THE BIG PICTURE
 	
    Personal Development
 	
    Social Development
 	
    Moral Development
 	
    Characteristics of Different Age-Groups
 	
    General Themes in Personal, Social, and Moral Development
	• Summarize the personal, social, and moral characteristics of the age group(s) with whom you hope to work.
	
	• What four themes are evident throughout the discussion of personal, social, and moral development?

Supplementary Reading

Your instructor may assign Supplementary Reading #3, "Parenting Styles and Children's Behavior," which appears in the final section of this *Study Guide and Reader*.

Using the Compact Disk

"Assessing Moral Reasoning" on the *Simulations in Educational Psychology and Research* CD is a hands-on activity similar to the "Heinz's Dilemma" Experiencing Firsthand exercise presented in the textbook.

Chapter Glossary

Aggressive behavior. Action intentionally taken to hurt another, either physically or psychologically.

Attachment. A strong, affectionate bond formed between a child and another individual (e.g., a parent); usually formed early in the child's life.

Authoritative parenting. A parenting style characterized by emotional warmth, high expectations and standards for behavior, consistent enforcement of rules, explanations of the reasons behind these rules, and the inclusion of children in decision making.

Clique. Moderately stable friendship group of perhaps three to ten members.

Conventional morality. Acceptance of society's conventions regarding right and wrong; behaving to please others or to live up to society's expectations for appropriate behavior.

Culture shock. A sense of confusion that occurs when a student encounters a culture with very different expectations for behavior than the expectations with which the student has been raised.

Empathy. Experiencing the same feelings as someone in unfortunate circumstances.

Ethnic identity. Awareness of one's membership in a particular ethnic or cultural group, and willingness to adopt certain behaviors characteristic of that group.

Gang. A cohesive social group characterized by initiation rites, distinctive colors and symbols, territorial orientation, and feuds with rival groups.

Guilt. The feeling of discomfort that individuals experience when they know that they have caused someone else pain or distress.

Hostile attributional bias. A tendency to interpret others' behaviors (especially ambiguous ones) as reflecting hostile or aggressive intentions.

Identity. A self-constructed definition of who a person thinks he or she is and what things are important in life.

Imaginary audience. The belief that one is the center of attention in any social situation.

Induction. A method for encouraging moral development in which one explains why a certain behavior is unacceptable, often with a focus on the pain or distress that someone has caused another.

Moral dilemma. A situation in which there is no clear-cut answer regarding the morally correct thing to do.

Neglected students. Students whom peers rarely select as people they would either really like or really *not* like to do something with.

Norms. Society's rules for acceptable and unacceptable behavior. (Note that we will use the term differently when we talk about assessment in Chapters 15 and 16.)

Peer pressure. A phenomenon whereby a student's peers strongly encourage some behaviors and discourage others.

Personal fable. The belief that one is completely unlike anyone else and so cannot be understood by other individuals.

Perspective taking. The ability to look at a situation from someone else's viewpoint.

Popular students. Students whom many peers like and perceive to be kind and trustworthy.

Postconventional morality. Behaving in accordance with one's own, self-developed, abstract principles regarding right and wrong.

Preconventional morality. A lack of internalized standards about right and wrong; making decisions based on what is best for oneself, without regard for others' needs and feelings.

Proactive aggression. Deliberate aggression against another as a means of obtaining a desired goal.

Prosocial behavior. Behavior directed toward promoting the well-being of someone else.

Reactive aggression. An aggressive response to frustration or provocation.

Rejected students. Students whom many peers identify as being undesirable social partners.

Roles. Patterns of behavior acceptable for individuals having different functions within a society.

Self-concept. One's perceptions of, and beliefs about, oneself.

Self-efficacy. The belief that one is capable of executing certain behaviors or reaching certain goals.

Self-esteem. Judgments and beliefs about one's own general value and worth.

Shame. A feeling of embarrassment or humiliation that children feel after failing to meet the standards for moral behavior that adults have set.

Social cognition. Considering how other people are likely to think, act, and react.

Socialization. The process of molding a child's behavior to fit the norms and roles of the child's society.

Social skills. Behaviors that enable a person to interact effectively with others.

Subculture. A group that resists the ways of the dominant culture and adopts its own norms for behavior.

Sympathy. A feeling of sorrow or concern for another person's problems or distress.

Temperament. A genetic predisposition to respond in particular ways to one's physical and social environments.

Here are additional glossary items if your instructor has assigned Supplementary Reading #3:

Authoritarian parenting style. A parenting style characterized by rigid rules and expectations for behavior that children are expected to obey without question.

Authoritative parenting. A parenting style characterized by emotional warmth, high expectations and standards for behavior, consistent enforcement of rules, explanations regarding the reasons behind these rules, and the inclusion of children in decision making.

Parenting style. The general pattern of behaviors that a parent uses to raise his or her children.

Permissive parenting style. A parenting style characterized by emotional warmth but few expectations or standards for children's behavior.

Uninvolved parenting style. A parenting style characterized by a lack of emotional support and a lack of standards regarding appropriate behavior.

Application Exercise #5: Identifying Typical and Atypical Behaviors

Of the students described below, which ones are exhibiting behaviors typical for their age group, and which ones are not? Justify your decisions on the basis of theories and/or research findings described in Chapter 3.

1.   When Larry gets a poor grade in his high school math class, he quickly jumps to the conclusion that he is not a good student—that he probably won't do well in any of his other classes (in science, Spanish, physical education, etc.) either.

2.   Roger, a sixth grader, gets visibly angry when he sees several "skinheads" taunt an African-American classmate. "Racism is wrong," he says. "Everyone on this planet is equal. We are all entitled to human dignity and the respect of our fellow human beings."

3.   When a fifth grader tells six-year-old Emmy that it's OK to punch a classmate in the stomach, Emmy replies, "No, it's not. It's not nice to hurt other kids."

4.   Fifteen-year-old Linda is obviously quite upset about something. When her teacher tries to find out what's wrong, Linda replies, "I need to talk to my best friend Tara. No one else can possibly understand."

5.   Several of the boys in Mr. Woodward's second-grade class are worried about the fact that they don't yet know what they want to be when they grow up.

6.   A third grader thinks that it's OK to copy someone else's math homework as long as she doesn't get caught in the act.

7.   Many of the students at Piedmont Junior High School try to dress and act like the students they label as the "popular" ones.

8.   A high school senior is depressed most of the time. "I'm no good at anything," she tells her teacher day after day.

9.   Many of the second-grade boys at Sunrise Elementary School have begun to wear the same style of clothing (white T-shirts, tight-fitting black jeans, and black hooded sweatshirts) and to use distinctive words (e.g., *dude*, *bodacious*, *bogus*) frequently in their speech.

10. Fourteen-year-old Ramon refuses to go to school after he chips two front teeth in an ice hockey accident. "Everyone will laugh at me until I get these fixed," he laments.

11. Six-year-old Sasha spends much of her time at school daydreaming about Brad Pitt, a well-known and handsome movie star.

12. A class of fourth graders is discussing the plight of homeless children. They readily acknowledge that these children might not have enough to eat and must often be very cold at night. However, they believe that the best course of action that these children can take is to get a job of some sort (for example, selling flowers on the street) rather than going to school.

13. Tom and Mary have been a "couple" for more than two years, and now, in their senior year, they have become sexually intimate.

14. Even though all the ninth graders at Harrison High School must take a required health class, many of them ignore the teacher's remarks about the dangers of unprotected sex. "I won't get pregnant," one girl says to a classmate, "and AIDS is something that only poor people get."

15. Chip is well known for his obnoxious behavior in the school lunchroom at Monroe Junior High. He delights in knocking other students' lunch trays onto the floor, thereby making the lunches inedible. When Ms. McCartney confronts Chip about his behavior, he shows no understanding that his classmates will have to go hungry for the rest of the day.

Answers to Application Exercise #5

1. Not typical. Students usually make distinctions among various aspects of themselves. This is especially true at the high school level, when they are likely to realize that they may be more capable in some disciplines than in others.

2. Not typical. From Kohlberg's perspective, Roger is showing postconventional moral reasoning—something that is rare before college.

3. Typical. Although Kohlberg proposed that young children are primarily concerned about consequences for themselves, other researchers have found that even preschoolers recognize that some behaviors, especially those that are harmful or unfair to others, are inherently wrong.

4. Typical. High school students often have close, intimate friends with whom they share their innermost thoughts. They may also exhibit a *personal fable*—a belief that they are completely unique and no one else (certainly not a teacher) has ever had the feelings or problems that they themselves have.

5. Not typical. Such behavior characterizes Erikson's stage of Identity versus Role Confusion, which in Erikson's view doesn't emerge until adolescence. More recently, researchers have found that even by the high school years, only a small minority of students have begun to think seriously about careers and other lifelong goals.

6. Typical. Most elementary students are in Kohlberg's preconventional level of moral reasoning: They define right and wrong behavior in terms of its consequences.

7. Typical. Peer influences are the strongest during the junior high school years.

8. Not typical. Although self-esteem drops temporarily when students make the transition to junior high school, most older adolescents have positive self-concepts and self-esteem. If the student is seriously and chronically depressed, the teacher should consult with the school counselor or psychologist and be on the lookout for signs that the student may be contemplating suicide (see the section on "Emotional and Behavioral Disorders" in Chapter 5 of the textbook).

9. Not typical. Affiliation with a particular subculture is most common in adolescence.

10. Typical. Ramon is exhibiting a phenomenon known as the *imaginary audience*—the belief that everyone's attention is focused entirely on him. The imaginary audience is most prevalent in early adolescence.

11. Not typical. Such romantic crushes are most common during the middle school years.

12. Typical. From Eisenberg's perspective, these students are showing a superficial "needs of others" orientation (Level 2). Such prosocial behavior is typical of many students in the elementary grades.

13. Typical. While we may or may not condone such behavior, we must be aware that many older adolescents are sexually active.

14. Typical. Characteristic of the personal fable so common during adolescence is a belief that one is invulnerable to life's normal risks.

15. Not typical. From Selman's perspective, Chip is showing egocentric perspective taking (Level 0). Such behavior is common in preschool and the early elementary years; however, most junior high school students are at Level 3 or 4.

Application Exercise #6: Identifying Developmentally Appropriate Teaching Practices

Which of the following teacher behaviors are appropriate for the age level of the students, and which are not? Defend your decisions based on the principles, theories, and research findings described in Chapter 3.

1. Early in the school year, a kindergarten teacher explains that students should raise their hands and wait to be called on when they want to speak. He also insists that students follow these instructions; for example, he ignores students when they speak out of turn.

2. A junior high school student asserts that skipping school occasionally is OK because her older brother says that it is. Mr. Castaneda tells her that going to school is one of our society's rules and that society will function more smoothly when its citizens know how to read and write.

3. A kindergarten teacher tries to motivate Wayne to print his lowercase letters more neatly. She tells him, "Look at how your letters compare to Jeremy's. See how his are neat and yours are messy?"

4. As Ms. Ferguson teaches her high school English class how to write a good resumé, she reminds them, "Now that you are sophomores, most of you should have a good idea about what you'll be doing after you graduate."

5. Early in the school year, a second-grade teacher tells her students that they must never take things from another student's plastic storage box, or "cubby," without that student's permission. She also tells them what the consequence will be if this rule is disobeyed.

6. Madison Elementary School is having its annual open house for parents tonight. In preparation for the event, Mr. Brock has his students put some of their best papers in a folder on their desks for their parents to see. He also has students' numerous art projects hanging on the walls.

7. A high school driver education teacher warns his students, "Be sure to stay within the speed limit. After all, there may be a traffic officer lurking in wait when you least expect one."

8. Before his first-grade class walks to the local park for a picnic lunch, Mr. Brillhart reminds the children that littering is not right because it makes the world an uglier place for others to live in.

9. When a classmate accidentally brushes by her in the hallway, ten-year-old Lucy explodes in anger and shouts, "Just you wait! I'll get you back after school!" Knowing that such incidents are typical for Lucy, Ms. Bergeron finds time to speak with her about how she misinterpreted the classmate's intentions. She also arranges for Lucy to meet with the school counselor to address her aggressive tendencies.

Answers to Application Exercise #6

1. Appropriate. Teachers play an important role in the socialization of children; they teach them some of the behaviors they will need in adult society.

2. Appropriate. The student is reasoning at Kohlberg's Stage 3, looking to an authority figure (her older brother) for guidance about what's right and wrong. Mr. Castaneda is using Stage 4 reasoning (law and order)—something that she should be able to understand and that may therefore promote the development of more mature moral reasoning.

3. Not appropriate. For many children, the first year of school is an unsettling one that leads to a temporary drop in self-concept. Comparisons with other students, especially if those comparisons are unfavorable ones, are apt to be counterproductive.

4. Not appropriate. Although Erikson proposed that identity issues are usually resolved in adolescence, more recent evidence indicates that most high school students have not yet begun to think seriously about the role they want to play in adult society.

5. Appropriate. From Kohlberg's perspective, second graders are reasoning at a preconventional level: They are concerned primarily about what the consequences of their actions will be.

6. Appropriate. According to Erikson, elementary students are in the Industry versus Inferiority stage—one in which they seek recognition for the things they produce.

7. Not appropriate. From Kohlberg's perspective, most high school students reason at the conventional level—they define right and wrong in terms of meeting someone's approval (Stage 3) or obeying society's rules (Stage 4). By focusing on the potential consequences of speeding, the teacher is using preconventional reasoning with these students. Ideally, he should be presenting reasons for following the speed limit that reflect reasoning one stage above where students are (i.e., Stage 4 reasoning for some and Stage 5 reasoning for others).

8. Not appropriate. From Kohlberg's perspective, Mr. Brillhart's first graders are probably reasoning at the preconventional level and so are concerned primarily about the consequences of their actions. From Selman's perspective, they are apt to be at Level 1 (subjective perspective taking), so they will view the needs of others in an overly simplistic fashion.

9. Appropriate. Lucy is exhibiting a *hostile attributional bias*, a tendency to interpret ambiguous interpersonal behaviors as reflecting aggressive intentions. Active intervention is often necessary to promote more socially beneficial interpretations.

Answers to Selected Margin Notes

- Page 67: *Have you ever heard a student say something that threatens a classmate's self-esteem? How might a teacher intervene in such a situation?*

  There is no single right or wrong answer to this question. However, if some students are continually behaving in ways that undermine another student's self-esteem, then teacher intervention is definitely in order. One strategy would be to use induction (see the discussion of this concept in the section "Promoting Moral Development in the Classroom") to help the culprits understand the effects of their thoughtless behavior. A second strategy would be to address any of the "victim's" characteristics or behaviors that lend themselves to ridicule (e.g., if the student is consistently being ridiculed for being dirty or smelly, then instruction in hygiene and/or needed hygienic supplies might be provided).

- Page 78: *Think back to our discussion of self-concept. What do Michelle's behaviors tell us about her self-perceptions of social competence?*

  Students tend to behave in ways that are consistent with their beliefs about themselves. Michelle apparently has a poor sense of social competence—a belief that is probably perpetuated by her lack of friends and the frequent insults she receives from others. Thus, she acts as if she isn't likely to make friends in any new social interaction, and so she hurls insults before anyone else can say a word.

- Page 79: *How is Selman's Level 0 similar to Piaget's preoperational stage of cognitive development?*

  Both are characterized by an inability to see a situation from any perspective except one's own; Piaget called this phenomenon *egocentrism*.

- Page 88: *Why is this level called preconventional?*

  People at this level are not yet considering society's conventions and norms for appropriate behavior.

- Page 92: *In what ways is Eisenberg's Level 3 similar to Kohlberg's Stage 3?*

  Both Eisenberg's Level 3 and Kohlberg's Stage 3 involve doing the "right" thing in order to gain someone else's approval. Furthermore, both involve fairly conventional, stereotypical ideas of acceptable behavior.

Sample Test Questions

Items marked with a "**1**)" on the left-hand side are lower-level questions that assess your general knowledge and understanding of the material. Items marked with a "**2**)" on the left-hand side are higher-level questions that assess your ability to apply what you have learned to a new situation.

Multiple-Choice

1)   1.   If you wanted to model your teaching style on *authoritative parenting*, you would be most likely to:
- a. Focus attention on students' academic achievement, without regard for any personal or emotional problems that they might bring with them to the classroom.
- b. Establish strict rules for classroom behavior and refuse to tolerate any objections to these rules.
- c. Explain why the rules you've established will help students learn more effectively.
- d. Let students make most of their own choices about what they will do on any given school day.

1)   2.   Socialization is best defined as the process through which children:
- a. Acquire such personality characteristics as friendliness or shyness
- b. Learn how to get along with others
- c. Learn what is acceptable behavior in their society
- d. Learn to appreciate being with other people

2)   3.   Three of the following teachers are likely to enhance their students' self-concepts and self-esteem. Which one is *least* likely to do so?
- a. Mr. Alvaro teaches students a technique that enables them to solve their geometry proofs more successfully.
- b. Ms. Berkowitz holds a class spelling bee to see which student is the best speller in the class.
- c. Ms. Caruso teaches her students how to do the butterfly stroke in swimming.
- d. Mr. Davidson uses a role-playing activity to help his students develop better interpersonal skills.

2)   4.   Which one of the following is the best reflection of an *imaginary audience*?
- a. Annette thinks that none of her friends can possibly understand how badly she feels about not having a date for the homecoming dance.
- b. Betsy doesn't like working in cooperative groups because she often has trouble understanding new concepts and doesn't want her classmates to think she's stupid.
- c. Christa doesn't think she could ever become a teacher because she doesn't like speaking in front of groups.
- d. Darlene is convinced that everyone in school has noticed that one of her ears sticks out more than the other.

1) 5. Eisenberg's theory of prosocial reasoning proposes that as children grow older, they:
   a. Become increasingly concerned about helping others in need
   b. Acquire a more positive self-concept regarding their social competence
   c. Develop more abstract notions about right and wrong
   d. Become increasingly aware of the thoughts and feelings that motivate their own behaviors

2) 6. Which one of the following statements is an example of *induction* as developmental theorists define the term?
   a. "When you shout out the answers to my questions, you prevent anyone else from answering them."
   b. "Under no circumstances will cheating be tolerated in this classroom."
   c. "As soon as everyone has settled down, you can all go to lunch."
   d. "Someone spilled blue paint all over the floor without telling me, and I think I know who that 'someone' is."

Essay

1) 7. Imagine that you have just begun a new teaching job. You soon discover that most of the students in your class belong to one of two ethnic groups, that the two groups rarely interact with each another, and that most interactions that *do* occur between the groups are hostile rather than friendly. Keeping the textbook's discussion of social development in mind, use three short paragraphs to describe three different strategies that you and your teaching colleagues might use to promote more appropriate and productive interactions between the two groups.

2) 8. Isaac says that stealing someone else's lunch money is OK as long as he doesn't get caught.
   a. In which one of Kohlberg's stages of moral reasoning does Isaac appear to be? Justify your choice.
   b. How might a teacher promote Isaac's development to a more advanced stage of moral reasoning? Describe three different strategies that are consistent either with Kohlberg's theory or with research findings.

Answers to Sample Test Questions

1. c—The behaviors that authoritative parents exhibit are described in the section "Effects of Parenting." An authoritative teacher would behave in a similar fashion.

2. c—Socialization is the process of shaping a child's behavior to fit society's norms and rules (see the section "Effects of Culture").

3. b—Competition is usually *not* recommended as a way of promoting a positive self-concept (see the section "Factors Influencing the Development of Self-Views," especially the subsection "Behaviors of Others").

4. d—The concept *imaginary audience* refers to the belief that oneself is the center of everybody else's attention. (See the discussion of early adolescence in "Developmental Changes in Students' Self-Views.")

5. a—This trend is clearly seen in Table 3.3.

6. a—Induction is giving students reasons why a behavior is unacceptable (see the section "Promoting Moral Development in the Classroom").

7. Strategies that you might use are described in the sections "Fostering Social Skills" and "Promoting Social Interaction Among Diverse Groups."

8. a. Isaac is in Kohlberg's Stage 1: He will do anything he can get away with and has no recognition of anyone else's needs (see Table 3.2).
    b. Four possible strategies are these (you would need to identify only three):
        *   Presenting reasoning one stage above a student's own reasoning (in Isaac's case, presenting reasoning at Stage 2)
        *   Explaining why stealing is unacceptable (induction)
        *   Modeling moral behavior (e.g., returning money that someone else has lost)
        *   Asking students to wrestle with moral issues and dilemmas (e.g., a dilemma about a boy who cannot afford lunch money and sees a wealthy classmate leave her lunch money unattended)

        The first strategy is described in the discussion of *disequilibrium* in the section "Factors Affecting Progression Through Kohlberg's Stages." The last three strategies are described in the section "Promoting Moral Development in the Classroom."

Chapter 4

INDIVIDUAL AND GROUP DIFFERENCES

Chapter Summary

The students in any single classroom will be diverse in terms of both individual differences (e.g., those based on intelligence or creativity) and group differences (e.g., those based on ethnicity, gender, or socioeconomic status). While it is helpful to be aware of such differences, we must be careful not to jump too quickly to conclusions about how individual students are likely to perform in the classroom. There is considerable individual variability within any group and a great deal of overlap between any two groups. Furthermore, unwarranted teacher expectations can have adverse effects on students' short-term achievement and long-term development (more about this point in Chapter 12).

Intelligence involves adaptive behavior and may manifest itself differently in different cultures. Many psychologists believe that intelligence is a single entity (a *general factor*, or *g*) that influences students' learning and performance across a wide variety of tasks and subject areas; this belief is reflected in the widespread use of IQ scores as general estimates of academic ability. But other theorists (e.g., Gardner, Sternberg) propose that intelligence consists of many, somewhat independent abilities and therefore cannot be accurately reflected in a single IQ score. Furthermore, there is a growing conviction that people are more likely to behave "intelligently" when they have physical and social support systems (e.g., computers, cooperative groups) to help them in their efforts; in other words, intelligence can be *distributed*. In general, one's environment has a significant effect on intelligence and intelligent behavior; as teachers, we must remember that intelligence can change over time, especially during the early years.

Creativity is new and original behavior producing an appropriate and productive result; it is probably a combination of many thinking processes and behaviors that reflect themselves differently in different situations and content areas. We are likely to see more creative behavior when we show students that we value creativity, focus their attention on internal rather than external rewards, promote mastery of the subject matter, and encourage risk taking.

For students from ethnic minority groups, there is often some degree of cultural mismatch between the home and school environments. We may see cultural differences in language and dialect, sociolinguistic conventions, cooperation, private versus public performance, eye contact, conceptions of time, familiarity with various types of questions, family relationships and expectations, and world views. All students benefit when we promote increased awareness of cultural differences and foster social interaction among students from diverse ethnic groups.

Males and females have very similar academic abilities, but they differ somewhat in motivation, self-esteem, explanations for success and failure, expectations for themselves, and interpersonal relationships. Many gender differences appear to be largely the result of the differing environmental conditions that boys and girls experience as they develop. As teachers, we should hold equally high expectations for both boys and girls and make sure that both genders have equal educational opportunities.

Factors such as poor nutrition, emotional stress, limited access to early academic experiences, low aspirations, and homelessness may all contribute to the generally lower achievement of students from low-income families. As teachers, we can help such students succeed in the classroom by providing the academic and emotional support they need and by building on students' many strengths.

Students at risk are those with a high probability of failing to acquire the minimum academic skills necessary for success in the adult world; they may graduate from high school without having learned to read or write, or they may drop out before graduation. To help such students succeed at school, we should identify them as early as possible, make the curriculum relevant to their needs, provide support for their academic success, and encourage greater involvement in school activities.

Common Student Beliefs and Misconceptions Related to Chapter Content

Below are several beliefs and misconceptions that college students often have before they study individual and group differences—beliefs and misconceptions that can interfere with an accurate understanding of the information they encounter in a textbook. As you read Chapter 4, be on the lookout for evidence that contradicts these commonly held ideas:

1. When average differences among groups are described, many people think of these differences as being much larger than they really are. For example, when they hear about gender differences in verbal ability or mathematics, they might think that most boys are better than most girls, or vice versa.

2. Some people think that intelligence is almost entirely inherited. Others believe that intelligence is exclusively the result of environmental factors.

3. Many people think of IQ scores as permanent characteristics, much as eye color and skin tone are.

4. Some people believe that IQ tests have no usefulness in school settings.

5. Some people see no advantage in acknowledging or accommodating cultural differences. Others acknowledge the importance of taking culture into account yet have difficulty looking beyond the "blinders" of their own cultural assumptions and values to consider some of the very basic ways in which people from other cultures might view the world differently than they do.

6. Some people believe that they were raised in a truly gender-equitable environment, even though research indicates that there are almost always differences in how parents treat their sons versus their daughters.

CHAPTER OUTLINE	FOCUS QUESTIONS
introductory paragraphs	• What are *individual differences*? *group differences*?
KEEPING INDIVIDUAL AND GROUP DIFFERENCES IN PERSPECTIVE	• What general principles does the textbook present regarding individual and group differences? What implications do these principles have for teachers?

INTELLIGENCE
   Measuring Intelligence
   How Theorists Conceptualize Intelligence
   Heredity, Environment, and Group Differences
   Being Optimistic About Students' Potential
	• What characteristics tend to be associated with intelligent behavior?
	
	• What kinds of test items are often found on intelligence tests?
	
	• Which IQ scores appear frequently? Which appear infrequently? How are IQ scores related to school achievement?
	
	• What limitations do intelligence tests have?
	
	• Why did Spearman believe that a general factor (*g*) underlies intelligence? What alternatives to the notion of *g* do Gardner and Sternberg offer?
	
	• What do theorists mean by *distributed intelligence*? What implications does this concept have for classroom practice?
	
	• What evidence exists to support the idea that both heredity and the environment contribute to intelligence?

CREATIVITY Fostering Creativity in the Classroom	• What is creativity? • Describe *divergent thinking*, and give an example. • Is creativity a single entity? How consistently do students exhibit creativity across different domains? • How can teachers foster creativity in the classroom?

CHAPTER OUTLINE	FOCUS QUESTIONS
CULTURAL AND ETHNIC DIFFERENCES Navigating Different Cultures at Home and at School Examples of Ethnic Diversity Creating a More Multicultural Classroom Environment	• What is a *culture*? What is an *ethnic group*? • What conditions can contribute to a cultural mismatch between home and school? • What cultural differences sometimes exist among students of different ethnic groups? In your own words, define *sociolinguistic conventions*, *wait time*, and *negative wait time*. • What can teachers do to maximize the classroom success of students from diverse ethnic backgrounds? • What strategies can teachers use to create a more multicultural classroom environment?
GENDER DIFFERENCES Origins of Gender Differences	• In what ways are boys and girls similar? In what ways are they different? • What environmental factors contribute to gender differences? • How can teachers make education more equitable for both boys and girls?
SOCIOECONOMIC DIFFERENCES Factors Interfering with School Success Working with Homeless Students Fostering Resilience Building on Students' Strengths	• What factors contribute to the generally lower school success of students from low-SES backgrounds? How can teachers counteract some of these factors? • What strategies are especially useful when working with homeless students? • What is *resilience*, and how can teachers foster it?
STUDENTS AT RISK Characteristics of Students at Risk Why Students Drop Out Helping Students at Risk Stay in School	• To which students does the term *at risk* refer? What characteristics do such students often exhibit? • For what reasons do students drop out prior to high school graduation? • What strategies can teachers use to help at-risk students be successful in school?
TAKING INDIVIDUAL AND GROUP DIFFERENCES INTO ACCOUNT Accommodating Students with Special Needs	• What individual and group differences should teachers consider as they work with students who have special educational needs?

CHAPTER OUTLINE	FOCUS QUESTIONS

THE BIG PICTURE
   Individual Differences
   Group Differences
   Students at Risk
	• What general principles can guide teachers as they take individual and group differences into account?

Chapter Glossary

African American dialect. A dialect of some African American communities that includes some pronunciations, grammatical constructions, and idioms different from those of Standard English.

Automaticity. The ability to respond quickly and efficiently while mentally processing or physically performing a task.

Convergent thinking. Pulling several pieces of information together to draw a conclusion or solve a problem.

Creativity. New and original behavior that yields an appropriate and productive result.

Cultural mismatch. A situation in which a child's home culture and the school culture hold conflicting expectations for the child's behavior.

Culture. Behaviors and belief systems of a particular social group.

Dialect. A form of English (or other language) characteristic of a particular region or ethnic group.

Distributed intelligence. The idea that people are more likely to act "intelligently" when they have physical and/or social support systems to assist them.

Divergent thinking. Taking a single idea in many different directions.

Equity (in instruction). Instruction without favoritism or bias toward particular individuals or groups of students.

Ethnic group. A group of people with a common set of values, beliefs, and behaviors. The group's roots either precede the creation of, or are external to, the country in which the group resides.

g. The theoretical notion that intelligence includes a *general factor* that influences people's ability to learn in a wide variety of content domains.

Group differences. Consistently observed differences, on average, among certain groups of individuals.

Higher-level question. A question that requires students to do something new with information they have learned—for example, to apply, analyze, synthesize, or evaluate it.

Individual differences. The ways in which people of the same age are different from one another.

Intelligence. The ability to modify and adjust one's behaviors in order to accomplish new tasks successfully. It involves many different mental processes, and its nature may vary, depending on the culture in which one lives.

Intelligence test. A general measure of current cognitive functioning, used primarily to predict academic achievement over the short run.

IQ score. A score on an intelligence test. It is determined by comparing one's performance on the test with the performance of others in the same age-group (see Chapter 15 of the textbook for a more in-depth description).

Multicultural education. Education that integrates the perspectives and experiences of numerous cultural groups throughout the curriculum.

Negative wait time. The tendency to interrupt someone who has not yet finished speaking.

Resilient students. Students who succeed in school despite exceptional hardships in their home lives.

Socioeconomic status (SES). One's general social and economic standing in society, encompassing such variables as family income, occupation, and level of education.

Sociolinguistic conventions. Specific language-related behaviors that appear in some cultures or ethnic groups but not in others.

Standard English. The form of English generally considered acceptable at school, as reflected in textbooks, grammar instruction, and so on.

Stereotype. A rigid, simplistic, and erroneous caricature of a particular group of people.

Students at risk. Students who have a high probability of failing to acquire the minimal academic skills necessary for success in the adult world.

Wait time. The length of time a teacher pauses, either after asking a question or hearing a student's comment, before saying something else.

Application Exercise #7: Identifying Typical Group Differences

Which of the situations below are consistent with what we know about gender, ethnic, and socioeconomic differences, and which are not? Defend your decisions.

1. When Mr. Russo asks his sophomore science students to raise their hands if they are planning to pursue a career in science, five students show an interest—Edith, Marilyn, Samantha, Rita, and Justin.

2. Carlos, a boy of Mexican American heritage, is beginning to work on his book report. "I'm going to see if I can do this better than anyone else in the class," he tells his teacher.

3. When teaching a unit on basketball in her physical education class, Ms. Martinez finds that boys who have trouble making a basket say that they need to try harder and practice more. In contrast, girls who have difficulty say that they were never very good at sports and so aren't likely to be so now.

4. Michael is an African American boy who lives in South Carolina. When his kindergarten teacher asks him, "What is this?" while pointing to a picture of a dog or a horse, Michael seems confused about how to respond. This puzzles his teacher, because she knows that he has seen numerous dogs and horses and is well aware of what they are called.

5. All of the girls in Ms. Tate's ninth-grade mathematics class are proud of their friend Margaret, because she is clearly the smartest student in the class.

6. Mr. Friedman notices that the three Navajo students in his class never volunteer answers when he asks questions.

7. A high school counselor looks at the mathematics achievement records (class grades and test scores) of next year's senior class and selects the top 20 students for an advanced mathematics class. The class consists of 18 males and 2 females.

8. Harold is one of five children in a single-parent family living in a local public housing complex. He often seems stressed out; for example, he is easily frustrated and has a quick temper.

9. At the annual Great Plains Regional High School field day, a favorite event is the buffalo chip throwing contest. The winner and four runners-up are all boys.

10. Ms. Jost gently scolds a Native American student named Felicia for coming to class late. Felicia looks Ms. Jost directly in the eye and appears to be listening closely.

11. A high school teacher notices that in the senior class, the girls tend to have closer, more intimate relationships with one another than the boys do.

12. When Mr. Jones asks an African American student named Joyce where her friend Wilma is, Joyce replies, "Oh, she be comin' late today."

13. Mary and Bob are partners in chemistry lab. Mary usually takes charge of the pair's activities, and Bob sits back and watches.

14. An African American student won't answer when her teacher asks her what her father does for a living.

Answers to Application Exercise #7

1. Not consistent. We would expect most of the students interested in a science career to be boys. By high school, boys are more confident than girls about their ability to succeed in science. Furthermore, gender stereotypes influence the career choices that many students make, and science is traditionally thought to be a "masculine" discipline. (Keep in mind, however, that males and females probably have similar *ability* to succeed in science.)

2. Not consistent. Children raised in most Hispanic communities are more accustomed to working cooperatively than competitively.

3. Consistent. Males tend to blame their failures on a lack of effort, whereas females tend to blame their failures on a lack of ability. This gender difference is most often found in traditionally "male" activities.

4. Consistent. In some African American communities in the southeastern United States, parents are more likely to ask their children questions involving comparisons (e.g., "What's that like?"), rather than questions involving labels. Michael may be unaccustomed to answering "What is this?" questions about things that he already knows.

5. Not consistent. Students are more likely to ridicule or avoid students who engage in traditionally counterstereotypical behaviors.

6. Consistent. The question/answer sessions so typical in many classrooms are unlike the experiences Native American students usually have in their local communities. Furthermore, many of these students have learned to allow a certain amount of wait time before responding to an adult's question—wait time that may be nonexistent in Mr. Friedman's classroom.

7. Not consistent. Any gender differences in mathematics achievement are quite small during the K-12 years. We would expect a more equal representation of males and females in the class.

8. Consistent. High stress levels are common in children of lower-SES families.

9. Consistent. After puberty, males tend to be stronger than females (in large part because of their increased testosterone levels).

10. Not consistent. Native American students are more likely to look down when an adult speaks to them, usually as a way of showing respect.

11. Consistent. Girls tend to be more affiliative than boys.

12. Consistent. African American students raised in some parts of the country often speak a dialect other than Standard English. A statement such as Joyce's is grammatically correct within the context of that dialect.

13. Not consistent. When boys and girls are paired together, the boys usually take the more active role.

14. Consistent. Children in some African American communities are taught not to answer questions about their families and home life.

Answers to Selected Margin Notes

- Page 107: *When might it be appropriate for a teacher to use intelligence test results? What potential dangers are there in relying solely on IQ scores as a measure of students' abilities?*

    IQ scores are one source of information that teachers can use to help them select instructional materials and activities appropriate for every child. However, such scores should be used *only* within the context of other data about each student. Intelligence tests do not assess every aspect of intelligent behavior, and students may be quite capable in ways that a single test score does not reflect. IQ scores, especially when used in isolation from other information, may lead a teacher to form unwarranted expectations about a student's future classroom performance.

- Page 112: *What implications does such environmental support have for the development of intelligence? Use Vygotsky's concept of zone of proximal development to answer this question.*

    In Vygotsky's view, tasks that students can accomplish only with outside support (tasks within students' zone of proximal development) are more likely to promote cognitive development than tasks that students can already do independently.

- Page 122: *Why do you think some teachers encourage competition among their students?*

    To my knowledge, no research has been conducted to answer this question. I suspect that many teachers believe that competition will motivate their students. As you will discover when you read Chapter 12, most students do *not* find competition motivating.

- Page 135: *What are possible reasons why some students don't participate in their school's extracurricular activities?*

    Here are several possibilities (you can probably think of others as well):
    - They feel intimidated by the "popular" students who dominate those activities, or else they lack confidence that they will be accepted by those students.
    - Their friends don't participate in the activities.
    - They lack the athletic abilities and skills necessary for team sports.
    - They find the activities irrelevant to their own interests.
    - They have no means of transportation for getting to school earlier than usual or getting home later than usual.
    - They have jobs or family commitments after school.

Sample Test Questions

Items marked with a "**1**)" on the left-hand side are lower-level questions that assess your general knowledge and understanding of the material. Items marked with a "**2**)" on the left-hand side are higher-level questions that assess your ability to apply what you have learned to a new situation.

Multiple-Choice

2) 1. Franklin is a fourth grader who has just obtained a score of 110 on an intelligence test. Which one of the following is a correct interpretation of his score?

    a. Franklin is showing below-average performance for a fourth grader.

    b. Franklin has done better on the test than most students his age.

    c. Franklin should probably be moved to the next higher grade level.

    d. Franklin is beginning to understand school material at an abstract level.

2) 2. Martha has trouble reading, and she is a bit clumsy when it comes to sports and athletics. However, she does well in her math classes, and she is quite popular among her classmates. Which view of intelligence is best reflected in Martha's pattern of strengths and weaknesses?

    a. Sternberg's triarchic theory

    b. Gardner's multiple intelligences

    c. Spearman's concept of *g*

    d. The notion of distributed intelligence

1) 3. Three of the following are accurate statements about the differences between boys and girls. Which one is *not* accurate?

    a. Boys are more motivated than girls to achieve in areas that are stereotypically masculine.

    b. Boys are likely to think their academic failures are due to insufficient effort; girls are more likely to think the same failures are due to a lack of ability.

    c. Boys show greater inherited athletic ability than girls as early as preschool.

    d. Girls form closer friendships than boys do.

1) 4. Three of the following statements are consistent with the textbook's description of students from low-SES backgrounds. Which statement is *not*?

    a. Students from low-SES backgrounds have less exposure to television than students from middle-income families.

    b. Students from low-SES backgrounds are less likely to have been read to as young children.

    c. Students from low-SES backgrounds are likely to have a less healthful diet than is true for other students.

    d. Students from low-SES backgrounds are often "stressed out" about circumstances at home.

2) 5. Three of the students below show warning signs for being at risk. Which student is *least* likely to be at risk?

    a. Andrea is absent from school about two days out of every five.

    b. Bill is still in sixth grade, even though he is almost fourteen years old.

    c. Connie has been getting low grades since elementary school, and her reading comprehension skills are poor.

    d. Dwayne has spent so much time at practice for the football and basketball teams that his grades have dropped considerably.

Essay

1) 6. Drawing on research findings presented in the textbook, identify at least four ways that students from diverse cultural backgrounds may have difficulty adjusting to a traditional classroom in our country.

1) 7. Explain what psychologists mean when they refer to students as being *at risk*. Describe three strategies you might use to help students at risk.

Answers to Sample Test Questions

1. b—With a score of 110, Franklin has done better than 74.8 percent of the students in his age group (see Figure 4.2 in the section "Measuring Intelligence").

2. b—Martha appears to have high logical-mathematical and interpersonal intelligence, but lower linguistic and bodily-kinesthetic intelligence (see Table 4.2 in the section "Gardner's Theory of Multiple Intelligences").

3. c—Before puberty, boys and girls have similar physiological capabilities (see Table 4.3 in the section "Gender Differences").

4. a—The other three alternatives are consistent with the discussion of socioeconomic differences (beginning on textbook page 131). Television viewing habits are not discussed in the textbook, and in fact there is no evidence to indicate that children from low-income families watch less television than other children do. Most families at all income levels have television sets.

5. d—Students at risk engage in few if any extracurricular activities. By participating in school sports, Dwayne is showing psychological attachment to his school. (See the section "Characteristics of Students at Risk.")

6. Characteristics of certain cultural groups that may influence classroom performance are described in the section "Examples of Ethnic Diversity." Your response should describe at least four of these.

7. Students at risk are those with a high probability of failing to acquire the minimal academic skills (reading, writing, spelling, math, etc.) necessary for success in the adult world. Strategies for keeping these students in school include the following (your response should include at least three of them):
    • Identify students at risk as early as possible.
    • Create a warm, supportive school and classroom atmosphere.
    • Make the curriculum relevant to students' lives and needs.
    • Communicate high expectations for academic success.
    • Provide extra academic support.
    • Show students that they are the ones who have made success possible.
    • Encourage and facilitate identification with school.

Chapter 5

STUDENTS WITH SPECIAL EDUCATIONAL NEEDS

Chapter Summary

This chapter describes students with special needs—those who are different enough from their classmates that they require specially adapted instructional materials and practices to help them maximize their school success. Increasingly, students with special needs are being educated in general education classrooms for part or all of the school day. Such students often show greater academic achievement, better self-concepts, and more appropriate social skills than students with special needs who are educated in self-contained classrooms or separate facilities. In the United States, inclusive practices are encouraged by the Individuals with Disabilities Education Act (IDEA), which mandates that public schools: (1) provide a free and appropriate education for any student identified as having one or more disabilities; (2) evaluate the student accurately, thoroughly, and without discrimination; (3) provide as typical an educational experience as possible for the student; (4) develop and implement an individualized education program (IEP) that addresses the student's unique needs; and (5) ensure due process in decision making.

Despite some disadvantages of assigning categories and labels to students with special needs, several factors contribute to their continuing use: (a) Students within a particular category often share characteristics that point to specific instructional strategies, (b) numerous professional organizations and journals have sprung up to promote the interests and advancement of students in particular categories, and (c) in the United States, federal funds are available to support special educational services only for students who have been identified as having a particular disabling condition. Although students within any single category often have similar characteristics and needs, we must be careful not to overgeneralize about how best to help each student.

Chapter 5 identifies three groups of students with specific cognitive or academic difficulties. Students with *learning disabilities* often have average or above-average overall scores on intelligence tests but experience difficulty with one or more specific cognitive processing skills. Students with *attention-deficit hyperactivity disorder* (ADHD) either have trouble focusing and maintaining their attention or act in a hyperactive, impulsive fashion; some students with ADHD exhibit both inattention and hyperactive, impulsive behavior. Students with *speech and communication disorders* have abnormalities in speech or language comprehension that significantly interfere with classroom performance. To some extent, instructional strategies must be tailored to students' specific difficulty areas. Yet several strategies are applicable to many of these students: providing sufficient scaffolding to maximize the likelihood of students' classroom success, clearly communicating expectations for students' classroom performance, and enhancing students' self-confidence and motivation with regard to academic tasks.

The chapter identifies two groups of students with social or behavioral problems. Students with *emotional or behavioral disorders* exhibit either externalizing behaviors (e.g., aggression, defiance) or internalizing behaviors (e.g., depression, withdrawal from social interaction) that significantly interfere with classroom learning and performance. Students with *autism* have marked impairments in social interaction and communication, repetitive behaviors, and narrowly focused interests; such characteristics may be due to an abnormal sensitivity to environmental stimuli. Both groups are likely to benefit from training in interpersonal skills. They may also perform more successfully in a structured environment in which desired behaviors are clearly identified and consequences for desired and undesired behaviors are consistently administered.

Many students with general delays in cognitive and social functioning are officially identified as having *mental retardation*, a condition characterized by low general intellectual functioning and deficits in adaptive behavior. Strategies for working effectively with such students include pacing instruction more slowly than usual, explaining tasks concretely and in very specific terms, and encouraging independent and self-reliant behaviors.

Students with physical and sensory challenges include those with *physical and health impairments* (conditions that result in reduced energy, alertness, or muscle control), *visual impairments*, *hearing loss*, and *severe and multiple disabilities*. Although our instructional strategies will depend to a great extent on students' specific challenges, strategies beneficial to most students with physical and sensory challenges include maximizing access to general educational opportunities, making use of technological innovations that can facilitate communication and learning, and providing assistance only when students really need it.

Students identified as being *gifted* often require special educational services to meet their full potential. We must be open-minded about how we identify such students, keeping in mind that giftedness may reflect itself differently in different cultures. Strategies for promoting the achievement of students with gifts and talents include forming study groups of students with similar abilities, teaching complex cognitive skills within the context of various academic subject areas, and providing opportunities for independent study.

Numerous educational strategies apply to virtually all students with special needs. For instance, we should: (1) obtain as much information as possible about each student; (2) consult and collaborate with specialists; (3) communicate regularly with parents; (4) hold the same expectations for a special needs student that we hold for other students (to the extent that is reasonable); (5) identify prerequisite knowledge and skills that a student, perhaps because of a disability, may not have acquired; (6) be flexible in approaches to instruction; (7) include students in educational decision making; and (8) facilitate students' social integration into the classroom.

Common Student Beliefs and Misconceptions Related to Chapter Content

Below are four misconceptions that college students often have about students with special needs—misconceptions that may interfere with an accurate understanding of what they read in their textbooks. As you read Chapter 5, be on the lookout for evidence that contradicts these common misconceptions:

1. Some people believe that the labels assigned to various disabilities (e.g., *learning disability*) always reflect permanent, lifelong conditions.

2. Some people who are studying to become regular classroom teachers think that they will rarely, if ever, have students with special educational needs (e.g., those with mental retardation or those with emotional and behavioral disorders) in their classrooms.

3. Many people believe that autism is primarily an emotional disorder. In fact, the characteristics associated with autism are probably due to cognitive factors (e.g., an undersensitivity or oversensitivity to sensory stimulation).

4. Some people believe that students who are gifted don't need special educational services.

CHAPTER OUTLINE	FOCUS QUESTIONS
EDUCATING STUDENTS WITH SPECIAL NEEDS IN GENERAL EDUCATION CLASSROOMS Historical Overview of the Inclusion Movement Public Law 94-142: The Individuals with Disabilities Education Act (IDEA) Is Inclusion in the Best Interest of Students? The Current Conception of Inclusion	• How has the education of students with special needs changed over the past century? • In the United States, what rights does the Individuals with Disabilities Education Act (IDEA) ensure for students with special needs? What implications do these rights have for teachers? • What is an IEP, and what are its components? • In what ways do students with special needs benefit from being educated in general education classrooms?
GENERAL CATEGORIES OF STUDENTS WITH SPECIAL NEEDS Using People-First Language An Overall Organizational Scheme	• What problems are associated with categorizing special needs? What are the advantages in categorizing them? • What is *people-first language*? Why is it recommended?
STUDENTS WITH SPECIFIC COGNITIVE OR ACADEMIC DIFFICULTIES Learning Disabilities Attention-Deficit Hyperactivity Disorder (ADHD) Speech and Communication Disorders General Recommendations for Students with Specific Cognitive or Academic Difficulties	• What are *learning disabilities*, and how might they affect students' academic achievement? • What is *attention-deficit hyperactivity disorder*? What characteristics are associated with ADHD? • What are *speech and communication disorders*? How might they affect students' classroom performance? • How can teachers enhance the learning and achievement of students with various cognitive or academic difficulties?
STUDENTS WITH SOCIAL OR BEHAVIORAL PROBLEMS Emotional and Behavioral Disorders Autism General Recommendations for Students with Social or Behavioral Problems	• What are *emotional and behavioral disorders*? How are the characteristics associated with such disorders apt to affect academic achievement? • Distinguish between *externalizing* and *internalizing* behaviors. • How is *autism* different from an emotional or behavioral disorder? What characteristics are often seen in students with this disability? • How can teachers facilitate classroom success for students with emotional and behavioral disorders? for students with autism?

CHAPTER OUTLINE	FOCUS QUESTIONS
STUDENTS WITH GENERAL DELAYS IN COGNITIVE AND SOCIAL FUNCTIONING Mental Retardation	• What criteria are used to identify students with *mental retardation*? How can teachers accommodate the specific academic and social needs of these students?

STUDENTS WITH PHYSICAL AND SENSORY CHALLENGES
 	
    Physical and Health Impairments
    Visual Impairments
    Hearing Loss
    Severe and Multiple Disabilities
    General Recommendations for Students with
      Physical and Sensory Challenges
	• What conditions characterize students with *physical and health impairments, visual impairments, hearing loss,* and *severe and multiple disabilities*? What other characteristics might students in each of these categories have?
	
	• How can teachers enhance the learning and achievement of students with various physical and sensory challenges? What strategies are useful with *all* of these students?

STUDENTS WITH ADVANCED COGNITIVE DEVELOPMENT Giftedness	• In what areas might students show exceptional talent? Why is giftedness so difficult to pin down? • What characteristics and abilities do students who are gifted tend to have? • What strategies can teachers use to enhance the learning and achievement of students who are gifted?
CONSIDERING DIVERSITY WHEN IDENTIFYING AND ADDRESSING SPECIAL NEEDS	• What groups tend to be overrepresented among students identified as having special needs? What are some possible explanations for such disproportionate representation?

THE BIG PICTURE
 	
    Inclusion
    Categories of Students with Special Needs
    Strategies for Helping All Students with Special
      Needs
	• What general strategies can teachers use to adapt instruction more effectively to the needs of all students?

Chapter Glossary

Adaptive behavior. Behavior related to daily living skills and appropriate conduct in social situations; a deficit in adaptive behavior is used as a criterion for identifying students with mental retardation.

Attention-deficit hyperactivity disorder (ADHD). A category of special needs marked either by inattention or by both hyperactivity and impulsive behavior (or by all three of these); such characteristics probably have a biological origin.

Autism. A category of special needs characterized by impaired social interaction and communication, repetitive behaviors, restricted interests, and a strong need for a predictable environment; underlying the condition may be either an undersensitivity or an oversensitivity to sensory stimulation.

Cooperative teaching. A general education teacher and special education teacher collaborating to teach all students in a class, including students both with and without special educational needs, throughout the school day.

Emotional and behavioral disorders. A category of special needs characterized by behaviors or emotional states that are present over a substantial period of time and significantly disrupt students' academic learning and performance.

Externalizing behavior. A symptom of an emotional or behavioral disorder that has direct or indirect effects on other people (e.g., aggression, disobedience, stealing).

Giftedness. A category of special needs characterized by unusually high ability in one or more areas, to the point where students require special educational services to help them meet their full potential.

Hearing loss. A category of special needs characterized by malfunctions of the ear or associated nerves that interfere with the perception of sounds within the frequency range of normal human speech.

Inclusion. The practice of educating all students, including those with severe and multiple disabilities, in neighborhood schools and general education classrooms.

Individualized education program (IEP). A written description of an appropriate instructional program for a student with special needs. In the United States, an IEP is mandated by the Individuals with Disabilities Education Act (IDEA) for all students with disabilities.

Individuals with Disabilities Education Act (IDEA). U.S. legislation granting educational rights to people with cognitive, emotional, or physical disabilities from birth until age 21; it guarantees a free and appropriate education, fair and nondiscriminatory evaluation, education in the least restrictive environment, an individualized education program, and due process.

Internalizing behavior. A symptom of an emotional or behavioral disorder that primarily affects the student with the disorder, with little or no effect on others (e.g., anxiety, depression).

Learning disabilities. A category of special needs characterized by lower academic achievement than would be predicted from students' IQ scores and a deficiency in one or more specific cognitive processes.

Least restrictive environment. The most typical and standard educational environment that can reasonably meet a student's needs.

Mainstreaming. The practice of having students with special needs join general education classrooms primarily when their abilities enabled them to participate in normally scheduled activities as successfully as other students.

Mental retardation. A category of special needs characterized by significantly below-average general intelligence and deficits in adaptive behavior.

Mnemonic. A special memory aid or trick designed to help students learn and remember a specific piece of information.

People-first language. Language in which a student's disability is identified *after* the student (e.g., "student with a learning disability" rather than "learning disabled student").

Physical and health impairments. A category of special needs characterized by general physical or medical conditions (usually long-term) that interfere with students' school performance to such an extent that special instruction, curricular materials, equipment, or facilities are necessary.

Savant syndrome. A syndrome characterized by an extraordinary ability to perform a specific task despite difficulty in other aspects of mental functioning; occasionally observed in students with autism.

Self-contained class. A class in which students with special needs are educated as a group apart from other students.

Severe and multiple disabilities. A category of special needs in which students have two or more disabilities, the combination of which requires significant adaptations and highly specialized services in students' educational programs.

Speech and communication disorders. A category of special needs characterized by impairments in spoken language or language comprehension that significantly interfere with students' classroom performance.

Students with special needs. Students who are different enough from their peers that they require specially adapted instructional materials and practices.

Visual impairments. A category of special needs characterized by malfunctions of the eyes or optic nerves that prevent students from seeing normally even with corrective lenses.

Application Exercise #8: Identifying Special Needs

Identify the special need that each of the following students is most likely to have.

1. Meghan must be supervised closely during recess. She picks fights with other students, especially those younger than herself, and she has no real friends. Meghan's father has a history of alcoholism and becomes violent when he gets drunk.

2. Even with his thick glasses, Ronald has trouble reading what his teacher writes on the board. He squints while looking at his textbooks and often misreads words that he should be able to recognize.

3. Although Rachel is a fifth grader, her knowledge and skills are more typical of a first grader, and she seems happiest playing with children who are several years younger than herself. One of her fifth-grade classmates says that she "acts silly, like my little brother."

4. As a junior high school student, Matthew plays the trombone in the school orchestra and is a standout on the cross-country team. He does quite well in math but is having difficulty in his history, geography, and English classes, all of which require a fair amount of reading. His mother reports that he spends at least three hours doing homework every night but often finds his assignments difficult and frustrating.

5. Calvin's performance on school tasks is inconsistent. Curiously, he usually does better on challenging tasks than on easy ones. He has many friends at school, although they describe him as being a bit pompous, because he sometimes uses words that they don't understand— words like *venerable*, *capricious*, and *anachronism*.

6. Nadine tires easily and must rest often. She visits the school nurse twice a day for her medication, and she often stays in the nurse's office to take a short nap. Participating in the regular physical education program is out of the question, because Nadine doesn't have the endurance to keep up with her classmates.

7. Harlan's written work—homework assignments, compositions, and exams—reveals a young man with a great deal of academic potential. However, Harlan is extremely quiet in class; when his teacher calls on him, he has trouble putting his thoughts into words.

8. As a middle school student, Sandra has trouble paying attention in class for more than five minutes at a time. She is exceptionally hyperactive for her age; for example, she gets out of her seat frequently and talks incessantly to those around her. Her parents say she has always been this way; they have taken her to several specialists over the years, but none has been able to pinpoint a physical or emotional source for her behavior.

9. Valerie does exceptionally well on exams; in fact, she often has the highest score in the class. Yet during class sessions, she never says a word unless she is specifically called on, even though she converses readily with her friends in other situations. On several occasions in class, her teacher has asked Valerie questions that he knows she can answer correctly, but she says nothing and acts as if she's forgotten everything she has learned.

10. Candace rarely talks in her first-grade class and prefers to spend most of her time alone. She is often preoccupied with the pencils in her pencil box.

11. Luis seems extremely depressed much of the time. He frequently describes himself as a "complete zero." He spends his study hall time writing poems that usually depict despair, destruction, and death.

Answers to Application Exercise #8

1. Meghan's difficulty interacting appropriately with others and establishing any long-term interpersonal relationships suggests a possible *emotional or behavior disorder*.

2. Ronald has a *visual impairment*.

3. Although we don't know anything about what Rachel's performance on an intelligence test might be, low achievement in all areas of the school curriculum and social behaviors inappropriate for her age group are indicative of *mental retardation*.

4. Matthew's uneven record in academic achievement and his particular difficulty with reading indicate a possible *learning disability*.

5. Calvin's behavior indicates possible *giftedness*. His poor performance on easy tasks is probably due to boredom rather than to a lack of ability.

6. Nadine has a *physical or health impairment* that may require special educational services (e.g., in physical education) to meet her needs.

7. Harlan's difficulty with spoken language indicates a possible *speech or communication disorder*.

8. Sandra's behaviors are consistent with *attention-deficit hyperactivity disorder*.

9. Valerie is showing signs of *giftedness* but may be trying to hide her ability from her peers.

10. Candace's lack of social interaction and communication, combined with her unusual interest in certain objects, indicates possible *autism*.

11. Long-term depression indicates an *emotional or behavioral disorder*. The teacher should worry that Luis might be contemplating suicide and immediately contact the school psychologist or counselor.

Answers to Selected Margin Notes

- Page 145: *What additional concerns might people have had about self-contained classes?*
  They may have had any number of concerns, including these:
  - Students were not getting the "normal" school experiences that would maximize academic and social development.
  - Students in self-contained classrooms had few if any opportunities to interact and form friendships with nondisabled peers.
  - Expectations for students may have been lower in self-contained classrooms and the curriculum watered down accordingly.
  - Special class placement might adversely affect students' self-esteem.

- Page 146: *Why is it important for parents to be included in the multidisciplinary team?*
  For one thing, parents often have useful information and observations about their child that can provide a more complete and accurate understanding of his/her strengths and weaknesses. Second, it is often advantageous to coordinate strategies being implemented at school with things parents are doing at home. And third, an instructional program is most likely to be effective when the child's parents are fully supportive of a teacher's efforts.

- Page 148: *Why do you think students placed in regular classrooms often have more appropriate classroom behavior? Why do you think they may have better self-concepts and more positive attitudes about school?*
  By being in a general education classroom, they are probably getting the message that they are, to some extent, like everyone else rather than "different" in some way. Furthermore, they are more likely to see models of appropriate classroom behavior than they would if they were in, say, a self-contained class for students with emotional and behavioral problems. And perhaps most important, their teachers are more likely to hold high expectations for both their academic achievement and their classroom behavior.

- Page 150: *Why do you think it is so difficult to define some categories of special needs?*
  Although students may be similar in some ways, they are likely to be very different in others.

- Page 161: *Why are [students with emotional and behavioral problems] so often disliked by their classmates?*
  They often interact with their peers in inappropriate and perhaps counterproductive ways.

- Page 167: *Based on this information, does Steven meet the two criteria for mental retardation presented earlier?*
  The evidence for the first criterion (significantly below-average general intelligence) is shaky at best: Only IQ scores are used. There is no evidence relative to the second criterion (deficits in adaptive behavior).

- Page 178: *Why else might some individuals oppose special services for students who are gifted?*
  We can only speculate as to why some people might be opposed to gifted education. One possible concern is that special services for gifted programs might divert funds and personnel that might otherwise be devoted to other students. Another possibility is that when some students are given special services for the gifted and others are not, the latter are essentially being told that they have lower ability than some of their classmates.

Sample Test Questions

Items marked with a "**1**)" on the left-hand side are lower-level questions that assess your general knowledge and understanding of the material. Items marked with a "**2**)" on the left-hand side are higher-level questions that assess your ability to apply what you have learned to a new situation.

Multiple-Choice

1)   1.   In the United States, three of the following are mandated by Public Law 94-142 (IDEA). Which one is *not* mandated by this legislation?

     a. Special educational services must be provided for gifted students as well as for students with cognitive, emotional, and physical disabilities.

     b. Students with special needs must be educated in the most "typical" school environment that can meet their specific needs.

     c. Decisions about the best program for a student with special needs should be made only after a fair evaluation of all available information.

     d. The instructional program developed for a student with special needs must be described in terms of the specific objectives to be accomplished and the methods by which those objectives will be achieved.

2)   2.   Which one of the following students is most likely to be identified as having a *learning disability*?

     a. Alan gets tired very easily and must often stop to rest in the middle of an assignment.

     b. Barbara has trouble reading despite a score of 110 on a recent intelligence test.

     c. Carl prefers to play with younger children and demonstrates low achievement in all areas of the school curriculum.

     d. Dolly often stutters when she's called on in class.

1)   3.   Some students with emotional or behavioral disorders exhibit one or more of the following behaviors. Which one is an *internalizing behavior*?

     a. Stealing other people's possessions

     b. Setting fires

     c. Refusing to interact with peers

     d. Hitting and biting other people

2)   4.   Students with mental retardation have deficits in *adaptive behavior*. Which one of the following is the best example of such deficits?

     a. Angela thoroughly enjoys studying math and science but has little interest in other topics.

     b. At least once a week, Beth threatens to commit suicide.

     c. Craig's attention is easily drawn to bright objects and loud noises.

     d. David has trouble remembering and following normal classroom routines.

1)   5.   Experts recommend three of the following strategies for teaching students who are gifted. Which strategy do they *not* necessarily recommend?

         a. Identifying mentors who can teach students specialized skills

         b. Forming study groups of students with similar abilities

         c. Focusing instruction on the areas in which students are weakest

         d. Providing opportunities for independent study

Essay

1)   6.   Why are students with special educational needs often included in general education classrooms for most or all of the school day? Describe three distinct benefits that inclusion may have.

1)   7.   The textbook identifies a number of strategies that are applicable to most or all students with special educational needs. Describe three of these strategies, and illustrate each one with a concrete example of what a teacher might do.

Answers to Sample Test Questions

1. a—PL 94-142 does not address the special educational needs of gifted students. The categories addressed by IDEA are listed in the section "Public Law 94-142."

2. b—Students with learning disabilities have difficulty with one or more cognitive processes even though they often have average or above-average intelligence (see the section "Learning Disabilities").

3. c—An internalizing behavior primarily affects the student with the disorder (see the section "Emotional and Behavioral Disorders"). The other three alternatives are externalizing behaviors, which affect other people as well.

4. d—Students with mental retardation may have difficulty with self-direction (following a schedule, completing required tasks, etc.) See Figure 5.4 in the section "Mental Retardation."

5. c—Much of the instruction for gifted students is aimed at challenging them and helping them develop their special talents further (see the subsection "Adapting Instruction" within the larger section "Giftedness").

6. Inclusion has benefits for students both with and without disabilities. Several advantages are listed in the section "Is Inclusion in the Best Interest of Students?"

7. Your response should describe three of the strategies presented in "The Big Picture" section near the end of the chapter. It should also include a specific example of how a teacher might carry out each strategy.

Chapter 6

LEARNING AND COGNITIVE PROCESSES

Chapter Summary

Theorists define learning as a relatively permanent change due to experience. Behaviorists describe learning in terms of the observable responses that people make and the environmental stimuli that influence how those responses change over time. Cognitive psychologists describe it in terms of such internal mental processes as attention, memory, and problem solving. Social cognitive theorists build on elements of both behaviorism and cognitive psychology as they describe what and how people learn by observing and imitating those around them. Each of the three perspectives—behaviorism, cognitive psychology, and social cognitive theory—has numerous implications for classroom practice.

Cognitive psychologists suggest that learners often process the same situation in idiosyncratic ways, in part because they all draw on unique bodies of knowledge and experiences to understand and interpret the situation. Most cognitive psychologists propose that learning does not involve absorbing information directly from the environment; instead, it involves constructing one's own understanding of the world. The things that students do mentally with classroom subject matter will determine how effectively they learn and remember it.

The term *memory* refers to learners' ability to "save" things (mentally) that they have previously learned. *Storage* refers to the acquisition of new information, and *encoding* involves changing that information in some way as it is stored. *Retrieval* is the process of "finding" previously stored information when it is needed.

Many cognitive theorists propose that human memory has three components. The *sensory register* provides temporary storage for incoming information, holding new input for two or three seconds at most. By paying attention to information, learners move it to *working memory*, where they actively think about and make sense of it. Attention and working memory have a limited capacity; hence, our students can pay attention to and think about only a limited amount of information at any one time. The third component—*long-term memory*—has an extremely large capacity and an indefinitely long duration.

Both information (*declarative knowledge*) and skills (*procedural knowledge*) are stored in long-term memory. To store information effectively, learners should engage in meaningful learning, organization, elaboration, or visual imagery. To learn a new skill effectively, learners may, in many situations, first have to store it in a declarative form (e.g., as a list of steps to be followed) and then practice it over time, gradually gaining greater competence as they do so. Strategies for helping students process and learn classroom subject matter include showing how it relates to prior knowledge, presenting it in an organized fashion, asking students to draw inferences, providing many opportunities for practice, and providing mnemonics for seemingly "meaningless" pairs and lists.

Retrieving information from long-term memory appears to be a process of following pathways of associations. Students' attempts at retrieving what they have learned are more likely to be successful if students have learned classroom subject matter to mastery and connected it with numerous other things they know, if they use it frequently, and if relevant retrieval cues are present in their environment. Increasing wait time—in other words, giving students more time to respond to the questions and comments of others—promotes greater retrieval and enhances students' overall academic performance.

Students' cognitive processes will differ, in part, as a function of their cultural backgrounds, English proficiency, and any special educational needs that they might have. At one time or another, all students are likely to have difficulty processing and learning classroom subject matter. By considering and fostering the specific cognitive processes involved in effective learning, teachers can help *all* students achieve classroom success.

Common Student Beliefs and Misconceptions Related to Chapter Content

Below are several beliefs that college students often have before studying cognitive psychology— beliefs that may interfere with an accurate understanding of what they read. As you read Chapter 6, be on the lookout for evidence that contradicts these common beliefs:

1. Some students believe that we don't necessarily have to *think about* the information we receive—that mere exposure to the information is enough.

2. Many students have the misconception that something remembered for a few days or weeks and then forgotten has been in short-term memory rather than long-term memory. In fact, psychologists conceptualize short-term memory—more often called *working memory* in recent years—as an entity that typically holds information for *less than a minute*. Information that is retained for significantly longer than a minute has been stored in long-term memory.

3. Some students believe that rote memorization—repeating something over and over without really thinking about it—is an effective way to learn.

4. Some students think of *rehearsal* only in terms of practicing lines in a play or oral presentation. Cognitive psychologists' meaning of this term is quite different.

CHAPTER OUTLINE	FOCUS QUESTIONS
LOOKING AT LEARNING FROM DIFFERENT PERSPECTIVES Learning as a Change in Behavior Learning as a Change in Mental Associations Learning and the Brain Keeping an Open Mind About Theories of Learning	• In what two ways is learning commonly defined? With which learning theories is each definition associated? • Why did behaviorists propose that the study of learning should focus exclusively on stimuli and responses? How have cognitive psychologists responded to behaviorists' concern about the study of nonobservable, mental phenomena (i.e., thinking)? • What does contemporary brain research tell us about the nature of learning? What does it *not* tell us?
BASIC ASSUMPTIONS OF COGNITIVE PSYCHOLOGY	• What basic assumptions underlie cognitive psychology? What implications does each assumption have for teaching practice? • Why do many cognitive psychologists believe that learning often involves a process of construction?
BASIC TERMINOLOGY IN COGNITIVE PSYCHOLOGY	• What do cognitive psychologists mean by the terms *memory, storage, encoding,* and *retrieval*? Can you think of a new example of each one of these?
A MODEL OF HUMAN MEMORY The Nature of the Sensory Register Moving Information to Working Memory: The Role of Attention The Nature of Working (Short-Term) Memory Moving Information to Long-Term Memory: Connecting New Information with Prior Knowledge The Nature of Long-Term Memory Critiquing the Three-Component Model	• What roles do the sensory register, working memory, and long-term memory play in learning? How much capacity does each component have? How long does information stored in each component last? • What role does attention play in the memory system? How can teachers encourage students to pay attention? • Which aspects of the memory system have a limited capacity? What implications does this limited capacity have for classroom instruction? • At what point in the memory system do students connect new information with existing knowledge? • What alternative view of memory have some theorists offered?

CHAPTER OUTLINE	FOCUS QUESTIONS

LONG-TERM MEMORY STORAGE
  The Various Forms of Knowledge
  How Declarative Knowledge Is Learned
  How Procedural Knowledge Is Learned
  Prior Knowledge and Working Memory in Long-Term Memory Storage
  Using Mnemonics in the Absence of Relevant Prior Knowledge
	• What different forms does knowledge take? Why are multiple encodings of a single piece of information beneficial?
	
	• What long-term memory storage processes may be involved in acquiring declarative knowledge? Describe these processes in your own words, and think of a new example of each one.
	
	• Which long-term memory storage processes are clearly effective? Which one is relatively ineffective, and why?
	
	• What three conditions are necessary for meaningful learning to occur? What implications do these conditions have for classroom instruction?
	
	• What processes may be involved in acquiring procedural knowledge? How can teachers help students learn new skills?
	
	• Why does students' prior knowledge affect their ability to store new information effectively?
	
	• When are mnemonics most useful? Describe *verbal mediation,* the *keyword method,* and a *superimposed meaningful structure.* Use each of these techniques to help you remember something in one of your college classes.

LONG-TERM MEMORY RETRIEVAL
  The Nature of Long-Term Memory Retrieval
  Factors Affecting Retrieval
  Why People Sometimes Forget
	• How do cognitive psychologists think that retrieval of information from long-term memory occurs? What conditions facilitate retrieval, and why?
	
	• What teaching strategies can facilitate retrieval of previously learned information and skills?
	
	• What are five different reasons why students may "forget" classroom subject matter? With these reasons in mind, identify several teaching strategies that can minimize the chances that students will forget important material.

CHAPTER OUTLINE	FOCUS QUESTIONS
GIVING STUDENTS TIME TO PROCESS: EFFECTS OF INCREASING WAIT TIME	• What do theorists mean by *wait time*? After what two events are teachers "waiting"? • How much wait time do teachers typically allow? How much time appears to be beneficial? • When wait time increases, what changes are seen in students' behavior? in teachers' behavior?

ACCOMMODATING DIVERSITY IN COGNITIVE PROCESSES
 	
    Facilitating Cognitive Processing in Students with
    Special Needs
	• How might students' cognitive processes differ as a function of ethnic differences? How might they differ as a function of special needs?

THE BIG PICTURE
 	
    Effective Cognitive Processes
 	
    Encouraging Effective Cognitive Processes in the
    Classroom
	• Summarize what you've learned about the nature of human memory and effective storage processes.
	
	• What general implications does our current understanding of human memory have for classroom practice?

Chapter Glossary

Activation. The degree to which a particular piece of information in memory is currently being attended to and mentally processed.

Attention. The focusing of mental processes on particular environmental stimuli.

Automaticity. The ability to respond quickly and efficiently while mentally processing or physically performing a task.

Behaviorism. A theoretical perspective in which learning and behavior are described and explained in terms of stimulus-response relationships. Adherents to this perspective are called **behaviorists**.

Cognitive psychology. A theoretical perspective that focuses on the mental processes underlying human learning and behavior. Adherents to this perspective are sometimes called **cognitivists**.

Construction. A mental process in which a learner takes many separate pieces of information and uses them to build an overall understanding or interpretation of an event.

Constructivism. A theoretical perspective that proposes that learners construct a body of knowledge from their experiences—knowledge that may or may not be an accurate representation of external reality. Adherents to this perspective are called **constructivists**.

Cortex. The upper part of the brain; site of conscious and higher-level thinking processes.

Decay. A hypothesized weakening over time of information stored in long-term memory, especially if the information is used infrequently or not at all.

Declarative knowledge. Knowledge related to "what is," to the nature of how things are, were, or will be.

Elaboration. A cognitive process in which learners expand on new information based on what they already know.

Encoding. Changing the format of new information as it is being stored in memory.

Failure to store. One's failure to mentally process information in ways that promote its storage in long-term memory.

Inability to retrieve. Failing to locate information that currently exists in long-term memory.

Information processing theory. A theoretical perspective that focuses on the specific ways in which individuals mentally think about and "process" the information they receive.

Interference. A phenomenon whereby something stored in long-term memory inhibits one's ability to remember something else correctly.

Keyword method. A mnemonic technique in which an association is made between two ideas by forming a visual image of one or more concrete objects (**keywords**) that either sound similar to, or symbolically represent, those ideas.

Knowledge base. One's knowledge about specific topics and the world in general.

Learning. A relatively permanent change, due to experience, in either behavior or mental associations.

Long-term memory. The component of memory that holds knowledge and skills for a relatively long period of time.

Maintenance rehearsal. See *rehearsal*.

Meaningful learning. A cognitive process in which learners relate new information to the things they already know.

Meaningful learning set. An attitude that one can make sense of the information one is studying.

Memory. A learner's ability to save something (mentally) that he or she has previously learned, *or* the mental "location" where such information is saved.

Mnemonic. A special memory aid or trick designed to help students learn and remember a specific piece of information.

Neuron. A cell in the brain or another part of the nervous system that transmits information to other cells.

Organization. A cognitive process in which learners find connections (e.g., by forming categories, identifying hierarchies, determining cause-effect relationships) among the various pieces of information they need to learn.

Procedural knowledge. Knowledge concerning how to do something.

Recall task. A memory task in which one must retrieve information in its entirety from long-term memory.

Recognition task. A memory task in which one must identify correct information among irrelevant information or incorrect statements.

Reconstruction error. Constructing a logical but incorrect "memory" by using information retrieved from long-term memory plus one's general knowledge and beliefs about the world.

Rehearsal. A cognitive process in which information is repeated over and over as a possible way of learning and remembering it. When it is used to maintain information in working memory, it is called *maintenance rehearsal.*

Response (R). A specific behavior that an individual exhibits.

Retrieval. The process of "finding" information previously stored in memory.

Retrieval cue. A hint about where to "look" for a piece of information in long-term memory.

Rote learning. Learning information primarily through verbatim repetition, without attaching any meaning to it.

Sensory register. A component of memory that holds incoming information in an unanalyzed form for a very brief period of time (probably less than a second for visual input and two or three seconds for auditory input).

Social cognitive theory. A theoretical perspective in which learning by observing others is the focus of study.

Stimulus (S) (pl. stimuli). A specific object or event that influences an individual's learning or behavior.

Storage. The process of "putting" new information into memory.

Superimposed meaningful structure. A familiar shape, word, sentence, poem, or story imposed on information to make it easier to recall; used as a *mnemonic.*

Synapse. A junction between two neurons that allows messages to be transmitted from one to the other.

Verbal mediator. A word or phrase that forms a logical connection or "bridge" between two pieces of information; used as a *mnemonic.*

Visual imagery. The process of forming mental pictures of objects or ideas.

Wait time. The length of time a teacher pauses, either after asking a question or hearing a student's comment, before saying something else.

Working memory. A component of memory that holds and processes a limited amount of information; also known as *short-term memory.* The duration of information stored in working memory is probably about five to twenty seconds.

Application Exercise #9: Analyzing Cognitive Processes

Identify the cognitive processes and/or components of memory involved in each of the following.

1.   When Michelle reads about the assassination of Martin Luther King, Jr., she associates it with the racist attitudes that many people have toward African Americans.

2.   Alex remembers that Juneau is the capital of Alaska by thinking, *"D'you know* the capital of *Alaska?"*

3.   Walt studies his spelling words by writing each one three times in a row.

4.   Candace is studying her multiplication tables, including 6 × 9 = 54 and 7 × 8 = 56. When she is multiplying 7 and 8 on a homework assignment, she erroneously writes "54."

5.   Dominic's physical education teacher is demonstrating how to dribble a basketball past an opponent. Dominic thinks to himself, "Aha! To keep the ball away from my opponent, I need to move the ball as unpredictably as I can."

6.   As her teacher reads the first chapter of *Stuart Little,* Juanita tries to imagine the little mouse washing himself in a human-size bathroom sink.

7.   Just before a mathematics quiz, Frank looks at the formula for computing the area of a circle ($A = \pi r^2$) one last time. He repeats the formula to himself until he receives his exam sheet, at which point he quickly writes it down in the margin so he won't forget it.

8.   When Kevin's teacher asks him, "In the biological classification system, in which class do we find spiders?" Kevin's mind goes blank. Later, he and his friend Joey are talking about old movies, and Joey mentions *Arachnophobia* as one of his all-time favorites. Suddenly Kevin remembers the answer to his teacher's question—arachnids.

9.   James remembers that *le chien* is French for "the dog" by picturing a dog with a big *chain* around its neck.

10. As his teacher explains how *The Scarlet Letter* reflects the values of Puritan New England, Joel is thinking about the fight that he had with his best friend at lunch.

11. When the music teacher asks, "Which operas did Mozart write?" her students cannot remember a single one. She gives them a hint: "One of his operas involves a wedding." At this point, Tom immediately shouts out, *"The Marriage of Figaro!"*

12. Gail is reading about the American Revolution. To help herself remember what she is reading, Gail lists the various events that occurred before and during the war on a piece of paper; she then draws arrows to indicate possible cause-effect relationships among them.

13. Once a week, Suzanne reviews the vocabulary words she has learned in Spanish I this year.

14. Ben is reading a college-level textbook that he is having trouble understanding. "Surely I can make sense of this if I work at it a while," he thinks to himself.

15. Rhonda remembers the biological classification system—kingdom, phylum, class, order, family, genus, species—by remembering "King Philip comes over for good spaghetti."

Answers to Application Exercise #9

1. Michelle is engaging in *meaningful learning*. She is understanding King's assassination in terms of something she already knows—racism.

2. Alex is using a mnemonic—*verbal mediation*—to connect Juneau ("d'you know") to Alaska.

3. Walt is using *rehearsal* in an attempt to store how the words are spelled.

4. Candace may be suffering from *interference*—she is confusing the answer to 6×9 with the answer to 7×8.

5. Dominic is engaging in *elaboration*. The teacher did not specifically say that one should dribble the ball unpredictably, but Dominic is inferring so from the teacher's behavior.

6. Juanita is storing part of the story as a *visual image*.

7. Frank is engaging in *maintenance rehearsal*, a process that will keep the formula in his working memory until he has a chance to write it down.

8. In class, Kevin is suffering from an *inability to retrieve* the word *arachnid*. Later, the movie title provides him the *retrieval cue* he needs.

9. James is using the *keyword* mnemonic to make the connection between *le chien* and "the dog."

10. The teacher's explanation is not getting beyond Joel's *sensory register* because he isn't *paying attention*.

11. The teacher provides a *retrieval cue* that enables Tom to retrieve one of Mozart's operas.

12. By identifying the connections among events, Gail is *organizing* the material.

13. Suzanne apparently knows that occasional review will enhance her ability to *retrieve* those words when she needs them.

14. Ben has a *meaningful learning set*—an intention to learn something at a meaningful level.

15. Rhonda is using a *superimposed meaningful structure* to help her remember the list.

Application Exercise #10: Identifying Effective Classroom Practices

Decide whether each of the following teaching practices is consistent with cognitive psychology's principles of learning, and why.

1.   Mr. Hendricks asks his students to multiply 623 × 59 in their heads.

2.   As Ms. Ziolkowski describes how Japanese culture is different from our own, she occasionally stops to ask students a question for them to think about and answer.

3.   Even though Mr. Stolte's students are now studying multiplication and division, he occasionally has them do problems requiring addition and subtraction.

4.   Ms. Tipton warns Sam, an avid reader, that he may be reading too much. She tells him, "I'm afraid that your mind will get so cluttered with the things you read that you won't have room in your brain for the things you need to learn in school."

5.   Before beginning a lesson on mammals, Ms. Thomas asks, "How many of you have pets at home? How many have dogs? cats? fish? birds? lizards? Can you think of ways in which all of these animals are alike?"

6.   Ms. Durocher teaches in a Boston suburb, close to where many early events of the American Revolution took place. When she begins to talk about the revolution in a history lesson, she describes each local event as it comes to her mind.

7.   Mr. Urquhart reminds his students, "All eyes should be on me as I explain tonight's homework assignment."

8.   Mr. Palermo's class has just read Nathaniel Hawthorne's *The Scarlet Letter*. "I don't think Hester Prynne did anything wrong," says Karen. Mr. Palermo waits several seconds to see if other students agree or disagree before sharing his own opinion about Hester's behavior.

9.   As Mr. Gotthardt describes World War II's D-Day, he passes around pictures from an old issue of *Life* magazine that show Allied troops landing at Omaha Beach.

10. Mr. Davis says, "Now that we know the properties of acids, what things might acids help us do?"

11. Ms. Gibbs is preparing her students for a standardized achievement test they will be taking next Monday. "Listen closely and put this in your short-term memories," she advises them. "Be sure to get a good night's sleep and eat a good breakfast before you come to school that day."

12. Mr. Li's class is studying South America. He has them study a different aspect of the continent each month—the topography in September, the culture in October, major cities in November, economics in December, and so on—so that they won't get all these things confused.

13. Mr. Nakamura wants his students to be as relaxed as possible while he describes a difficult concept, so he gives them paper and crayons so that they can doodle as he talks.

14. Ms. Ellis is showing members of the high school majorette squad how to do a butterfly spin. "You hold the baton in the middle and keep your arm out straight," she says. "You move the large end and then the small end of the baton *over* your arm. With the next spin, you move both the large end and small end *under* your arm. Then over, over, and under, under. As the baton goes up, your arm goes down, and vice versa. See?" Ms. Ellis has the students practice the spin in slow motion and encourages them to say "Over, over, under, under" as they do so.

15. Ms. Montgomery says, "OK, students, we've studied a number of basic elements, including aluminum, boron, calcium, carbon, copper, iodine, iron, potassium, silicon, tin, and zinc. Let's classify them into two groups—metals and nonmetals."

16. To keep her students' attention, Ms. Peterson engages in a rapid-fire presentation of facts they need to know.

17. When scoring her students' physics tests, Ms. Tobias gives credit only when students describe things exactly as presented in the book. This way, she can score their answers consistently and fairly.

18. Mr. Joslin isn't pleased with the geography textbook he must use with his students; he thinks that it presents far too many details about each region that the class will be studying. So before he assigns each chapter, he tells his students what parts they should focus on as they read.

19. Ms. Freitag has her second graders practice reading commonly used English words over and over again. Such practice sometimes involves responding to flash cards, but more often, it involves reading many short stories that include the words.

20. Mr. Sheehan says, "Now that we have studied three simple machines—levers, wedges, and pulleys—who can tell me what kind of machine an axe is?" When the students don't raise their hands immediately, he tells them, "An axe is a wedge."

21. Ms. Sanderson tells students in her French class that they can remember that *marcher* means "to walk" by thinking about "marching."

22. Mr. Wolfe is reviewing yesterday's discussion of poetry. "What do we call the word for a poem's rhythmic pattern?" When no one responds after several seconds, he says, "See if you can remember. It begins with the letter *M*." At that point several students shout out, "Meter!"

23. Ms. Flanagan is trying to give her students an idea of how long humans have populated the earth. She tells them, "Think of the earth's history as being a 24-hour day. Human beings have only been in existence between 11:59 p.m. and midnight."

Answers to Application Exercise #10

1. Not consistent. Such a problem would probably exceed the limits of students' working memory capacity.

2. Consistent. Her questions may serve one or more of several purposes—to keep students' attention, check for possible misinterpretations, and promote elaboration.

3. Consistent. Occasional review of things already learned will promote better retrieval over the long run.

4. Not consistent. Long-term memory has a capacity that is, for all intents and purposes, unlimited in capacity. Furthermore, a rich knowledge base facilitates meaningful learning and elaboration.

5. Consistent. Ms. Thomas activates students' prior knowledge about mammals before beginning the lesson, thereby promoting connections between the information she will present and the things that students already know.

6. Not consistent. If Ms. Durocher wants her students to understand how various events of the revolution were interrelated, she should make their relationships clear. A stream-of-consciousness presentation will not help students organize the information she presents.

7. Consistent. Although eye contact alone does not guarantee that students will pay attention, it does increase the likelihood that they will.

8. Consistent. Mr. Palermo is allowing wait time after a student's response—something that should promote greater student participation.

9. Consistent. The pictures should help students form visual images that can supplement what they read and hear about the invasion.

10. Consistent. By asking students to apply what they have learned, he is promoting elaboration.

11. Not consistent. Short-term (working) memory lasts a few seconds, not a few days.

12. Not consistent. Students can probably better understand South America if they see how its various characteristics are related. They will have difficulty interrelating (organizing) all they learn if they study different characteristics at different times.

13. Not consistent. Students may be paying more attention to their artwork than to Mr. Nakamura's explanation.

14. Consistent. By encouraging students to practice the spin and repeat the steps to themselves, she is helping them convert declarative knowledge into procedural knowledge.

15. Consistent. She is helping students organize what they have learned.

16. Not consistent. She is probably exceeding students' working memory capacity, in which case they won't be able to process or remember everything they hear. Furthermore, the rapid-fire presentation probably will not give students the time they need to make sense of what they're hearing; in other words, they won't be able to engage in meaningful learning or elaboration.

17. Not consistent. She is encouraging rote learning rather than meaningful learning.

18. Consistent. People can process only so much information in a certain amount of time, so they must often be selective about what they learn. Mr. Joslin is helping them select important information.

19. Consistent. By having the students read the words over and over again, she is helping them learn to recognize common English words to a level of automaticity. Given the limited capacity of working memory, students are more likely to comprehend the things they read if word recognition is automatic.

20. Not consistent. Mr. Sheehan is probably allowing insufficient wait time to retrieve and/or construct an answer.

21. Consistent. She is helping students make the connection between *marcher* and "walk" by providing a verbal mediator.

22. Consistent. He allows students several seconds to retrieve the answer, but they are unable to do so. The letter *M* provides a retrieval cue that focuses their search of long-term memory.

23. Consistent. She is using an analogy to help students relate the incomprehensible length of the earth's history to something they already know.

Answers to Selected Margin Notes

- Page 189: *From a teacher's perspective, what are the potential advantages of defining learning as a change in behavior? as a change in mental associations?*

  By defining learning as a change in behavior, teachers can specify ahead of time exactly what they want students to be able to do. Furthermore, they can easily observe the extent to which learning is taking place. By defining learning as a change in mental associations, teachers are more likely to identify important connections that students should make; they are also more likely to consider the role that students' prior knowledge must play in new classroom learning tasks. (You may have identified additional advantages of either definition.)

- Page 190: *Can you think of examples of how scientists in other disciplines have drawn inferences about unobservable phenomena?*

  Inference drawing is hardly unique to psychology. For example, chemists developed the concepts *molecule* and *atom* to explain chemical reactions long before such tiny entities were ever observed. Similarly, astronomers have developed the notion of *black hole* solely from the patterns of light and dark that reach their high-powered telescopes.

- Page 198: *Do you see why this process is called maintenance rehearsal?*

  Maintenance rehearsal *maintains* information in working memory indefinitely.

- Page 205: *If meaningful learning relies on relevant prior knowledge, what are the implications for teaching students from diverse cultural backgrounds?*

  Students from different cultural backgrounds are likely to have the same *amount* of background knowledge (because students in any single classroom are usually similar in age and so have had a similar number of experiences), but they may be less familiar with aspects of mainstream culture and so have less background related to a traditional school curriculum. Thus, it is important to determine what knowledge these students do and do not have and to build upon the things that they already know.

- Page 211: *Which of these strategies remind you of Vygotsky's theory of cognitive development?*

  When students repeat the steps over and over to themselves, they are engaging in *self-talk*. When teachers verbalize their thoughts during a complex task, they demonstrate effective ways of thinking about and analyzing the task (see the discussions of *internalization* and *cognitive apprenticeship*).

- Page 212: *Do you now see why Kanesha had such difficulty remembering the coccyx, ulna, sacrum, clavicle, and patella?*

  She had no knowledge that would help her understand why these bones have the names that they do.

- Page 216: *What kinds of assessment procedures are most likely to encourage automaticity? What kinds are least likely to encourage it?*

  Assessing basic knowledge and skills *frequently* should promote automaticity because it provides numerous opportunities for practice. In some cases, such assessment might involve asking students to do something as quickly as they can (e.g., asking them to write the answers to 100 basic addition facts within five minutes); in other cases, it might involve asking them to use basic skills within the context of more complex, and perhaps more authentic, activities. In contrast, assessing knowledge and skills *in*frequently, and allowing unlimited time to respond to questions and tasks—while quite appropriate in certain situations—is unlikely to promote automaticity.

Sample Test Questions

Items marked with a "**1**)" on the left-hand side are lower-level questions that assess your general knowledge and understanding of the material. Items marked with a "**2**)" on the left-hand side are higher-level questions that assess your ability to apply what you have learned to a new situation.

Multiple-Choice

2) 1. In which one of the following situations would a *behaviorist* be most likely to say that learning has taken place?
   a. Ruth starts writing her short stories in cursive letters after she studies cursive writing in school.
   b. Matt finally figures out the logic behind a particular geometry proof.
   c. Lucius feels both anger and sadness when he reads about the Holocaust.
   d. JaNeane suddenly realizes that the expression "Look before you leap" isn't necessarily meant to be taken literally.

2) 2. Thursday night, Jennifer studies for a test on Friday morning. She remembers the material quite accurately on Friday and gets an A on the test. However, when she takes a review test two weeks later, she can no longer remember that same material. How far in Jennifer's memory did the material get?
   a. It reached her sensory register.
   b. It reached her working memory.
   c. It reached her long-term memory.
   d. It never got into her memory at all.

2) 3. After her French teacher says, "Merci beaucoup," Henrietta repeats the phrase and then immediately turns to talk to her friend. How far in Henrietta's memory did the material get?
   a. It reached her sensory register.
   b. It reached her working memory.
   c. It reached her long-term memory.
   d. It never got into her memory at all.

2) 4. Justin is trying to learn information in his textbook. His eyes are focused on the words in front of him, but he is thinking about the fishing trip he has planned for this weekend. How far in Justin's memory did the material get?
   a. It reached his sensory register.
   b. It reached his working memory.
   c. It reached his long-term memory.
   d. It never got into his memory at all.

2)   5.   In which situation is a student most clearly *elaborating* on new information?

       a. Gloria thinks, "Hmm, World War I ended on November 11. That's my friend Cecily's birthday."

       b. Martin thinks, "I see that many California cities have Spanish names. So early settlers in California were probably Spanish."

       c. Francine says to herself, "The capital of South Dakota is Pierre. Pierre, South Dakota. Pierre, South Dakota. Pierre, South Dakota."

       d. Neil says, "The first ten elements in the periodic table are hydrogen, helium, lithium, beryllium, boron, carbon, nitrogen, oxygen, fluorine, and neon. Let's see if I can remember all ten in the correct order."

2)   6.   Mr. Wang wants his physical education students to learn how to dribble a basketball so well that they can perform the skill almost without thinking. In other words, he wants them to learn the task to a level of *automaticity*. Which one of the following strategies will best help his students achieve that goal?

       a. Tell students how important it is for them to learn to dribble.

       b. Explain the logic behind dribbling it one way rather than another.

       c. Demonstrate dribbling while students observe.

       d. Give students a lot of practice dribbling.

Essay

1)   7.   According to the textbook, three conditions are necessary for meaningful learning to occur. Describe these three conditions, and identify a teaching strategy that you might use to make sure each condition is present while students are learning.

2)   8.   The nine planets of the solar system, in order of their distance from the sun, are Mercury, Venus, Earth, Mars, Jupiter, Saturn, Uranus, Neptune, and Pluto. Develop a mnemonic for remembering this list using a *superimposed meaningful structure*.

<u>Answers to Sample Test Questions</u>

1. a—Only Ruth is demonstrating a change in behavior (see the section "Learning as a Change in Behavior"). The other three situations involve nonobservable, mental phenomena.

2. c—Because Jennifer remembered the material from one day to the next, it was in her long-term memory. The duration of working memory is less than a minute; the duration of the sensory register is only a second or two. (See the section "The Nature of the Sensory Register.")

3. b—Henrietta had to pay attention in order to repeat the phrase, so she stored it in working memory. But because she immediately turned to talk to her friend, she probably didn't process it sufficiently to store it in long-term memory. (See the section "Moving Information to Long-Term Memory.")

4. a—Everything sensed is stored in the sensory register. But because Justin is not giving his *mental* attention to the page, he is not storing the words in his working memory. (See the section "Moving Information to Working Memory.")

5. b—Martin is the only one going beyond the information itself—in this case, by drawing an inference. (Gloria is relating the information to something she already knows—the process of meaningful learning—but is not extending the new information in any way.) See the discussion of elaboration in the section "How Declarative Knowledge Is Learned."

6. d—Automaticity develops primarily through repetition and practice (see the section "Factors Affecting Retrieval").

7. The three conditions—a meaningful learning set, relevant prior knowledge, and awareness of the relevance of that knowledge—are described in the section "Meaningful Learning." Examples of strategies that you might use to promote each one are these:
    *   <u>A meaningful set</u>: Insist that students explain things in their own words rather than verbatim from a textbook.
    *   <u>Relevant prior knowledge</u>: Begin instruction with what students already know and proceed from there.
    *   <u>Awareness of the relevance of prior knowledge</u>: Draw an analogy between a new idea or concept and a personal experience students have previously had.

8. A superimposed meaningful structure (described in the section "Using Mnemonics in the Absence of Relevant Prior Knowledge") is a word, phrase, sentence, or the like, that represents a list of items. In this case, we might use a sentence such as this one: "<u>M</u>y <u>v</u>ery <u>e</u>ager <u>m</u>other just <u>s</u>ent <u>u</u>s <u>n</u>ew <u>p</u>etunias." The first letters of each word correspond to the planets in terms of their relative distance from the sun.

Chapter 7

KNOWLEDGE CONSTRUCTION

Chapter Summary

Many cognitive psychologists believe that individuals *construct* knowledge from their experience rather than simply absorb it in the form presented to them; the resulting "reality" they perceive is not necessarily identical to the reality of the external world. Constructive processes may occur either when information is first received (during long-term memory storage) or when it is later recalled (during long-term memory retrieval).

Some theorists describe the processes by which people construct their own personal understandings of the world; this perspective is sometimes called *individual constructivism*. Other theorists focus more on people's collective efforts to impose meaning on the world around them; this perspective is often called *social constructivism*. Social constructivists suggest that students benefit from interacting frequently with one another as they study and try to master classroom subject matter. Interactive methods of instruction have several advantages. They encourage students to clarify, organize, and elaborate on what they have learned sufficiently that they can explain it to their peers. Furthermore, when students present conflicting ideas, they must reexamine their own perspectives and perhaps revise their views to achieve a more accurate and complete understanding of the topic at hand. And active discussions of classroom topics provide a means through which students can observe and ultimately acquire higher-level thinking skills and metacognitive strategies.

People organize what they learn in a variety of ways. A *concept* provides a way of mentally grouping or categorizing objects or events. Students truly understand a concept when they know its defining features and can accurately identify both positive and negative instances. We can help our students learn concepts more effectively by giving definitions, presenting numerous and varied positive and negative instances, and asking students to generate their own examples.

Schemas are organized bodies of knowledge about specific topics; *scripts* are schemas that involve a predictable sequence of events. Schemas and scripts often enable learners to fill in missing details and thereby to understand classroom subject matter more completely. Some schemas and scripts are culture-specific—a point to keep in mind when teaching students from diverse cultural backgrounds.

Personal theories are general belief systems about the world; they include numerous concepts and the interrelationships among them. Students' personal theories can provide guidance in concept learning. At the same time, they may include many misconceptions that interfere with students' learning of academic subject matter.

As teachers, we can help students construct accurate interpretations of the world around them by (1) providing opportunities for them to experiment with the physical world, (2) presenting others'

98

interpretations of various phenomena (e.g., through the concepts and principles of academic disciplines, or through art and literature), (3) emphasizing conceptual understanding, (4) promoting classroom dialogue, (5) using authentic activities, and (6) creating a community of learners in which teacher and students actively and cooperatively work to help one another learn.

Students' misconceptions often persist despite instruction regarding more accurate explanations. We are more likely to promote conceptual change when we (1) determine what misconceptions students have before instruction, (2) show students that their existing beliefs are inadequate, (3) motivate them to develop a more accurate understanding of the topic in question, and (4) monitor their written work, as well as their questions and comments in class, for any especially persistent misconceptions.

Different students are likely to interpret classroom events and subject matter differently, in part because they each bring diverse experiences and knowledge bases into play when trying to make sense of the things they see and hear. We can increase our students' multicultural awareness by promoting *multiple constructions* of the same situation—by encouraging them to look at events from the perspectives of different groups. At the same time, we must be on the lookout for counterproductive constructions that some of our students (including those with special needs) may derive from their classroom experiences.

Common Student Beliefs and Misconceptions Related to Chapter Content

Listed below are three commonly held beliefs that may interfere with an accurate understanding of processes related to knowledge construction. As you read Chapter 7, be on the lookout for evidence that contradicts these ideas:

1. Many people erroneously think that knowledge is absorbed exactly as it is received, so that what is stored in memory is an accurate representation of the world.
2. Some people may believe that an especially vivid memory of an event must certainly be an accurate recollection of the event.
3. Many people think that an individual's misconception about the world will quickly disappear once a correct explanation is presented; they don't realize that misconceptions are often quite resistant to change.

CHAPTER OUTLINE	FOCUS QUESTIONS

CONSTRUCTIVE PROCESSES IN LEARNING AND MEMORY
 	
    Construction in Storage
 	
    Construction in Retrieval
	• How is the process of construction involved in storage? How is it involved in retrieval?
	
	• What is individual constructivism? Speculate about implications that this perspective might have for classroom practice.

KNOWLEDGE CONSTRUCTION AS A SOCIAL PROCESS Benefits of Group Meaning-Making in the Classroom	• How might the social construction of knowledge occur at a single point in time? How might it occur over a long period? • In what ways does student dialogue promote learning? What additional benefits can group projects and discussions have?

ORGANIZING KNOWLEDGE
 	
    Concepts
 	
    Schemas and Scripts
 	
    Personal Theories
	• What is a *concept*? In what ways do undergeneralization and overgeneralization reflect incomplete concept learning?
	
	• Explain how students' knowledge of concepts might take the form of *feature lists, prototypes,* and *exemplars*. With these ideas in mind, identify several strategies for teaching concepts.
	
	• What are *schemas* and *scripts*? How do they influence learners' construction of meaning?
	
	• How do students' *personal theories* influence learning?

WHEN KNOWLEDGE CONSTRUCTION GOES AWRY: ORIGINS AND EFFECTS OF MISCONCEPTIONS	• What misconceptions about the world are students likely to have? • How do misconceptions affect learning?

PROMOTING EFFECTIVE KNOWLEDGE CONSTRUCTION
 	
    Providing Opportunities for Experimentation
 	
    Presenting the Ideas of Others
 	
    Emphasizing Conceptual Understanding
 	
    Using Authentic Activities
 	
    Promoting Dialogue
 	
    Creating a Community of Learners
	• What strategies do cognitive psychologists recommend for helping students construct accurate understandings? Explain why each of these strategies is likely to be effective.
	
	• What is an *authentic activity*? Think of examples of authentic activities that you might use for the subject matter you will be teaching.
	
	• What is a *community of learners*? What forms might it take? What advantages might it have?

CHAPTER OUTLINE	FOCUS QUESTIONS
PROMOTING CONCEPTUAL CHANGE	• Why might a student often retain misconceptions despite instruction that contradicts them? • What is *conceptual change*? Under what conditions is it most likely to occur? What implications do these conditions have for promoting conceptual change in the classroom?
CONSIDERING DIVERSITY IN CONSTRUCTIVE PROCESSES 　Accommodating Students with Special Needs	• Why might students from different backgrounds sometimes form different interpretations of the same situation? • What characteristics of students with special needs have implications for knowledge construction? How can teachers facilitate more effective knowledge construction for these students?
THE BIG PICTURE 　Constructive Processes 　Organizing Knowledge 　Promoting Knowledge Construction and Conceptual 　　Change	• Summarize what you've learned about constructive processes, ways of organizing knowledge, and conceptual change.

Using the Compact Disk

Two activities on the *Simulations in Educational Psychology and Research* CD are relevant to this chapter:

• "Bartlett's Ghosts" is similar to the "War of the Ghosts" Experiencing Firsthand exercise presented in the textbook.

• "Intuitive Physics" illustrates principles related to misconceptions and presents recommendations for promoting conceptual change.

Chapter Glossary

Authentic activity. A classroom activity similar to one students are likely to encounter in the outside world.

Community of learners. A classroom in which teacher and students actively and collaboratively work to help one another learn.

Concept. A mental grouping of objects or events that have something in common.

Conceptual change. Revising one's knowledge and understanding of a topic in response to new information about that topic.

Conceptual understanding. Knowledge acquired in an integrated and meaningful fashion.

Correlational feature. A characteristic present in many positive instances of a concept but not essential for concept membership.

Defining feature. A characteristic that must be present in all positive instances of a concept.

Distributed cognition. A process whereby people think about an issue or problem together, sharing ideas and working collaboratively to draw conclusions or develop solutions.

Exemplar. A specific example that is an important part of a learner's general knowledge and understanding of a concept. Several exemplars taken together give the learner a sense of the variability that exists within any category of objects or events.

Individual constructivism. A theoretical perspective that focuses on how people, as individuals, construct meaning from the events around them.

Misconception. Previously learned but incorrect information.

Negative instance. A nonexample of a concept.

Overgeneralization. An overly broad meaning for a word that includes some situations where the word is not appropriate; an overly broad view of what objects or events a concept includes.

Personal theory. A self-constructed explanation for one's observations about a particular aspect of the world; it may or may not be consistent with generally accepted explanations of scientific phenomena.

Positive instance. A specific example of a concept.

Prototype. A mental representation of a "typical" positive instance of a concept.

Reconstruction error. Constructing a logical but incorrect "memory" by using information retrieved from long-term memory plus one's general knowledge and beliefs about the world.

Salience. In concept learning, the degree to which a particular feature or characteristic is obvious and easily noticeable.

Schema. In contemporary cognitive psychology, an organized body of knowledge about a specific topic.

Script. A schema that involves a predictable sequence of events related to a common activity.

Social constructivism. A theoretical perspective that focuses on people's collective efforts to impose meaning on the world.

Undergeneralization. An overly restricted meaning for a word that excludes some situations to which the word does, in fact, apply; an overly narrow view of what objects or events a concept includes.

Application Exercise #11: Analyzing Constructive Processes

Explain each of the following situations using concepts or principles related to knowledge construction:

1. James is trying to remember how to spell the word *permanent*. He can remember the first four letters (p-e-r-m) and the last four letters (n-e-n-t), but he's not sure what the middle vowel is. He correctly decides that the middle vowel must be an *a* based on how the word is pronounced.

2. As a third-grade teacher begins to read *Black Beauty* to her class, eight-year-old Casey pictures the main character—a horse—with a shiny coat, flowing mane, and long black tail.

3. Ms. Forbes explains that objects are buoyant in water when they are, on average, less dense than the water they displace. Yvonne misinterprets the teacher's statement as confirming something she already "knows": Light things float and heavy things sink.

4. Several students get together to read and interpret William Shakespeare's *Julius Caesar*. One student describes the benefits of the group discussion this way: "I like hearing my friends' ideas about what the characters are really trying to say. Shakespeare isn't always an easy guy to understand, you know."

5. When asked to explain who a *nurse* is, five-year-old Jeremy says, "The lady who's nice to you at the doctor's office."

6. As students in Nadia's band class are warming up to play their instruments, an announcement comes over the school intercom. Nadia catches bits and pieces of the announcement—she hears "Student Council" and "Thursday"—and guesses that the Student Council must be meeting Thursday after school.

7. Mr. Holder shows his sixth graders a large map of Africa and explains how the Nile River flows north to the Mediterranean Sea. Although his students hear what he says, his comment doesn't really "register" with many of them. In a class discussion a few days later, Paul describes the river as running south, *away* from the Mediterranean. "No, Paul," Linda volunteers, "I used to think that that was true. But rivers must run *toward* the sea, not away from it. So the Nile must run north."

8. When asked to explain the various phases of the moon (new moon, half moon, etc.), Misty explains that the earth casts its shadow on the moon during most of the month, and that sunlight has an unimpeded path to the moon only for the full moon. Misty illustrates her explanation by drawing several diagrams on the chalkboard. In fact, Misty's explanation is incorrect: The earth comes between the sun and the moon only rarely, during a lunar eclipse.

9. Maureen remembers this "fact" from a previous lesson about the French Revolution: "Marie Antoinette had her head chopped off because she couldn't bear Henry VIII any children."

10. Sam reads a story about a family going to a fast-food restaurant for lunch. The story never mentions that the family members order and pay for their meals at the counter before they sit down. Nevertheless, Sam assumes that they do these things.

11. When asked to explain what a *musical instrument* is, Ronetta answers, "Well, let's see, it could be a trumpet, or a violin, or a xylophone, or ... I guess that's all I can think of." Her teacher asks, "Are drums musical instruments?" "No," Ronetta responds, "a drum isn't an instrument."

Answers to Application Exercise #11

1. James is demonstrating *construction in retrieval*. He combines the letters that he can actually remember with other information that he has (i.e., how the word is pronounced) to construct a reasonable (and, in this case, accurate) guess about how the word is spelled.

2. Casey is constructing a visual image of Black Beauty based on his knowledge (perhaps in the form of a *schema*) of what horses typically look like.

3. Yvonne is imposing a *misconception* on what the teacher is saying and so learns something that is not completely accurate. Even a very heavy object (e.g., a metal battleship) will float if its average density is less than that of the water it displaces.

4. Learners can sometimes construct meaning more effectively when they work together to make sense of a situation—a process consistent with the *social constructivist* view of knowledge construction.

5. Jeremy apparently has a better understanding of the *correlational features* of a nurse (e.g., female, kindness) than of the *defining features* (health care professional).

6. Nadia is demonstrating *construction during storage*: She must construct meaning from incomplete information.

7. Paul's *misconception* that rivers always run south prevails over Mr. Holder's statement that the Nile flows north. In contrast, Linda has undergone *conceptual change* and now realizes that rivers must flow downhill toward the sea.

8. Misty has a *personal theory* about the phases of the moon—a theory that includes several concepts and their interrelationships.

9. Maureen combines things she recalls from French history (Marie Antoinette and her encounter with the guillotine) with a piece of English history (Henry VIII and his treatment of wives), thus showing *reconstruction error* in what she remembers.

10. Sam uses her knowledge of typical procedures at a fast-food restaurant—a *script*—to fill in details that the story leaves out.

11. Ronetta's knowledge of the concept *instrument* appears to be based more on a few *exemplars* (trumpet, violin, xylophone) than on defining features. Furthermore, she *undergeneralizes* when she excludes drums.

Application Exercise #12: Identifying Effective Classroom Practices

Decide whether each of the following teaching practices is consistent with principles of learning related to knowledge construction, and *why*.

1. Ms. Forbes discovers that, despite instruction to the contrary, Yvonne still believes that heavy objects cannot possibly float. "What will happen when I put a heavy casserole dish in a sink full of water?" Ms. Forbes asks her. "It will sink, of course," Yvonne replies. Ms. Forbes places such a casserole dish in water to show her that it floats.

2. Mr. Goldberg's class has already learned that insects have three body parts, six legs, wings, and antennae. Then he says, "Let's take a look at a picture of a wasp. See? It has all the parts that insects have, so it must be an insect."

3. In a unit on clouds, Ms. Lavoie shows a picture of a cloud and says, "One type of cloud is a cumulonimbus cloud. Here is what a typical cumulonimbus cloud looks like." She then moves on to a discussion of cumulus clouds.

4. In her French class, Ms. Malnati makes sure that her students have frequent opportunities to converse with one another in French.

5. Mr. Huang is teaching a unit on buoyancy and asks his students why it's easier to swim in salt water. Marla replies, "It's easier because the salt holds you up." Mr. Huang realizes that her understanding of buoyancy isn't quite right, but he lets it go because he figures that a more correct understanding will evolve over time.

6. Mr. Sawyer has his middle school students read a short story about a Bar Mitzvah. Knowing that many of his students are not Jewish, he first describes what a typical Bar Mitzvah is like.

7. Mr. Rochelle knows that he needs to move quickly if he's going to cover all the material that he has planned for his pre-calculus students. So he introduces two or three new topics or procedures each day, giving his students homework problems every night that allow them to review and practice the things they are studying in class.

8. After a hard practice session after school, Coach DiStephano calls the members of the girls' soccer team together and asks them to discuss and debate various strategies for defeating the Westview Warriors—a team whose defense has a reputation for being almost impenetrable—in next Saturday's game.

9. Mr. Robichaud decides that his geology students will learn general principles of geology most effectively if they discover everything for themselves, so he dispenses with a textbook for his class and devotes class time almost entirely to hands-on experiences with rocks.

10. As Ms. Valentine describes an upcoming quiz in her language arts class, she tells her students, "Yesterday I gave you a list of definitions for the week's new vocabulary words. As long as you learn those definitions, you should be in good shape for the quiz."

11. As Mr. Paige's class studies the topic of weather, different groups of students conduct research on different topics (cloud formation, hurricanes, the effects of high- and low-pressure systems, the effects of the Gulf Stream, the meanings of meteorological symbols, etc.). Mr. Paige gives the groups guidance about how to proceed in their research but makes it clear that he has limited knowledge about the topics they are studying. After a couple weeks of research, students in each group teach their classmates what they have learned.

Answers to Application Exercise #12

1. Consistent. When she sees that Yvonne is holding fast to her misconception that heavy objects cannot float, Ms. Forbes presents a phenomenon that contradicts Yvonne's belief—a recommended strategy for promoting *conceptual change*.

2. Consistent. Mr. Goldberg is asking students to use something they already know to interpret new information. Furthermore, he is focusing their attention on the *defining features* of insects.

3. Not consistent. Ms. Lavoie provides a *prototype* of a cumulonimbus cloud, but she does nothing else to help students learn the concept. Ms. Lavoie should also identify defining features and present several positive instances of cumulonimbus clouds. Furthermore, she should show students some negative instances, so that they learn what a cumulonimbus cloud is *not*.

4. Consistent. Conducting a conversation in French is an example of an *authentic activity*—one in which students use what they have learned in a real-world task.

5. Not consistent. Students are unlikely to correct their *misconceptions* if they get no feedback that their beliefs are incorrect.

6. Consistent. Mr. Sawyer is providing a *script* that should help his students make sense of the story.

7. Not consistent. Mr. Rochelle is probably moving too quickly through the material for students to develop a *conceptual understanding* of the mathematical concepts and procedures that they are studying.

8. Consistent. *Dialogue* among students is often an effective way of promoting knowledge construction. In this situation, dialogue may be especially useful as a means of helping the girls clarify their own thinking about how to play soccer strategically; it should also expose the girls to perspectives that may be more useful than their own.

9. Not consistent. Although experimentation is one effective way of promoting knowledge construction, the students can probably learn only so much from "experimenting" with rocks. Another effective way of promoting knowledge construction is to expose students to how others have tried to make sense of the world—an idea that has emerged from *social constructivism*. A textbook provides one means through which students can encounter the ideas (e.g., concepts, principles) that others have developed to help them understand the nature of rocks.

10. Not consistent. The vocabulary words are, in essence, *concepts* that she wants her students to learn. She is encouraging the students only to learn definitions, perhaps at a rote level; there is no guarantee that students will relate these words to anything else they know. Ms. Valentine should use other strategies that facilitate concept learning. For instance, she might ask students to use each word in a sentence (thereby having them generate their own examples), or she might have them explain how each word relates to other words (concepts) in their vocabularies.

11. Consistent. Mr. Paige has created a community of learners in his classroom.

Answers to Selected Margin Notes

- Page 230: *Skillful readers often skip some of the words on the page and yet understand what they read quite accurately. How is this possible?*

  Using the letters and words that they've read, as well as context cues (what the topic of the reading passage is about, what they expect the author will say, etc.) and their prior knowledge, they can construct a reasonable interpretation of what the text is probably trying to communicate.

- Page 231: *What implications does the notion of reconstruction error have for the credibility of eyewitness testimony?*

  Eyewitness testimony is sometimes an inaccurate representation of what actually happened (Buckhout, 1974; Lindsay, 1993; Loftus, 1991, 1992). People's descriptions of the crime may vary considerably, depending on prior knowledge about the individuals involved, expectations about what typically happens in such a situation, and additional information presented at a later time.

- Page 235: *Are definitions likely to be effective when students learn them by rote? Why or why not?*

  Learning definitions by rote is unlikely to be effective. When students learn a definition in a word-for-word fashion, they may not relate the concept and its meaning to anything else in their knowledge base. As a result, they may not realize that objects or events with which they are familiar are positive instances of that concept.

- Page 238: *What is a typical script for a trip to the grocery store? to the movies? to a fast-food restaurant?*

  Going to the grocery store often includes parking in the parking lot, getting a grocery cart, going up and down the aisles putting desired items in the cart, waiting in line at the check-out counter, paying for the groceries, and using the cart to take the purchased items to your car. Going to the movies often includes waiting in line, purchasing a ticket, buying popcorn or a soft drink, sitting down in the theater, watching previews and commercials, and watching the movie. Going to a fast-food restaurant usually involves waiting in line at the counter while looking at the menu items, telling the cashier what you want, paying for what you've ordered, waiting at the counter until the food is handed to you on a tray, carrying the tray to a table, sitting down and eating, and disposing of trash and leftovers in a trash bin.

- Page 243: *Unfortunately, the researchers didn't eliminate other possible explanations for their results. Besides teacher-prescribed vs. self-chosen procedures, what other differences between the two groups might account for the study's results?*

  Additional differences between the two groups included these:
  - Raising rabbits versus raising goldfish
  - Raising pets at school versus raising them at home
  - Sharing responsibility for pet care at school versus doing it alone at home

  You may have identified additional differences as well.

Sample Test Questions

Items marked with a "1)" on the left-hand side are lower-level questions that assess your general knowledge and understanding of the material. Items marked with a "2)" on the left-hand side are higher-level questions that assess your ability to apply what you have learned to a new situation.

Multiple-Choice

2) 1. John learns that the capital of South Dakota is Pierre. A few days later, as he is trying to recall this information, he thinks for a while and then finally says, "Oh, I remember now. It's Perry." Which one of the following statements best explains John's error?

    a. John uses his script for state capitals to develop a logical conclusion as to what South Dakota's capital must be.

    b. John is exhibiting construction during retrieval; he remembers parts of the capital city's name and then fills in the rest.

    c. John has developed an incorrect schema for Pierre.

    d. John has undergone conceptual change between the time when he first learned the information and the time when he has to remember it.

2) 2. Ms. Eisenstadt wants her students to understand what a *dribble* is in basketball. Given what we know about effective concept learning, her best strategy would be to:

    a. Show them the correct way to dribble a ball

    b. Show them how *not* to dribble a ball

    c. Show them both what dribbling is and what it isn't

    d. Keep it simple by bouncing the ball just twice in a row

2) 3. For which one of the following concepts would a definition be *most* helpful to students?

    a. *invertebrate*

    b. *green*

    c. *duck*

    d. *pencil*

2) 4. Margaret says that the earth is flat. When her teacher tells her that the earth is round, Margaret pictures a world shaped like a pancake—both round *and* flat. From the perspective of cognitive psychology, how can we best explain Margaret's error?

    a. People's working memories are insufficient to hold two complex pieces of information simultaneously.

    b. People rarely learn effectively when they must encode verbal input in a visual form.

    c. People's prior beliefs affect their interpretations of new information.

    d. People must pay attention in order to learn.

2) 5. Which one of the following is the best example of an *authentic activity*?

    a. Spelling words aloud before a spelling test

    b. Reading the "chapter objectives" at the beginning of a textbook chapter

    c. Doing mathematics word problems

    d. Drawing a map of the school building

1) 6. Which one of the following best characterizes a *community of learners*?
   a. Students take turns lecturing to the rest of the class.
   b. At the beginning of each week, students vote on the topics they will study that week.
   c. Different students become experts on different topics and then share their expertise with their classmates.
   d. Students "buy" and "sell" what they have learned in much the same way that people in the outside world buy and sell goods they've grown or manufactured.

1) 7. If we apply the idea of knowledge construction to an understanding of students from diverse cultural backgrounds, we are most likely to say that:
   a. Different students interpret their experiences differently because they have different knowledge bases and schemas from which to draw.
   b. Students from some cultures are likely to interpret classroom material at face value, whereas students from other cultures are likely to derive abstract, underlying ideas from that same material.
   c. Some cultures value cooperation more than others, and students from "cooperative" cultures are the only students who are likely to engage in the social construction of knowledge.
   d. Students from some cultures are more likely to have had exposure to authentic activities than students from other cultures.

Essay

2) 8. Explain the difference between a concept's *defining features* and *correlational features*. Illustrate your discussion by identifying two defining features and two correlational features of the concept *beach*.

1) 9. Using principles of cognitive psychology, explain why students' misconceptions are often so resistant to change.

1) 10. Imagine that you are a new teacher. You discover that your students have several misconceptions about the subject matter your class will be studying over the next few weeks. Describe three different strategies you might use to help your students correct those misconceptions. Base your response on the textbook's discussion of promoting conceptual change.

Answers to Sample Test Questions

1. b—John remembers part of what he is trying to retrieve—the beginning *P* and the *err* in the middle—and uses those letters to construct a logical, although incorrect, city name. See the section "Construction in Retrieval."

2. c—Concepts are learned more effectively when students see both positive and negative instances. (See the section "Concepts as Feature Lists.")

3. a—Definitions are most helpful when a concept's defining features are not obvious. In the case of *invertebrate,* the defining feature "lack of a backbone" isn't readily apparent. (See the section "Concepts as Feature Lists.")

4. c—Margaret interprets her teacher's statement that the world is round in light of her own misconception that the world is flat (see the section "When Knowledge Construction Goes Awry"). Note that you need to draw on information from both Chapter 6 and Chapter 7 to answer this question.

5. d—Drawing a map is the alternative most similar to something one might eventually do in an out-of-school context. Authentic activities are described in the section "Promoting Effective Knowledge Construction."

6. c—In a community of learners, students serve as resources for one another, and they often become experts on particular topics (see the description of a community of learners in the section "Promoting Effective Knowledge Construction").

7. a—The textbook's description of cultural differences in knowledge construction is most consistent with this alternative (see "Considering Diversity in Constructive Processes"). No evidence exists to support the other three alternatives.

8. Defining features must be present in all positive instances of the concept. Correlational features are present in many positive instances but are not essential for concept membership. (See the explanations of both terms in the section "Concepts as Feature Lists") Two defining features of *beach* are sand and proximity to a large body of water. Correlational features of *beach* include waves, seaweed, shells, swimmers, sunbathers, lifeguards, and beach umbrellas; you may have identified other correlational features as well.

9. The essence of your answer should be that students often interpret new information within the context of what they already know. You should include at least one of these concepts in your response: *rote learning, meaningful learning, elaboration,* or *construction.* (See "When Knowledge Construction Goes Awry.")

10. You can find several strategies in the section "Promoting Conceptual Change." Your response should include at least three of these strategies.

Chapter 8

HIGHER-LEVEL THINKING SKILLS

Chapter Summary

By *higher-level thinking skills*, we mean the more complex ways that human beings think and learn. Four general higher-level thinking skills are described in this chapter: metacognition, transfer, problem solving, and critical thinking.

Metacognition includes both the beliefs that students have about their own cognitive processes and their attempts to regulate those processes to maximize learning and memory. Many study strategies involve metacognition. Examples of study strategies that researchers have found to be particularly effective are identifying and focusing on important information, taking notes, retrieving relevant prior knowledge, organizing, elaborating, summarizing, and monitoring comprehension.

Many students of all ages have misconceptions about how they can best learn and remember information; in other words, they are metacognitively naive. Several factors affect their use of effective strategies, including their prior knowledge about the topic they are studying, their previous comprehension monitoring (which has enabled them to determine how effective their existing strategies have been), their beliefs about the nature of knowledge and learning (i.e., their *epistemological beliefs*), and explicit training in study strategies. In addition to teaching academic content, we should concurrently teach students effective strategies for studying that content and give them sufficient practice and scaffolding to ensure their success in using such strategies. Ultimately, we must help our students discover that school is more than just a place for learning isolated facts in a rote fashion.

Transfer occurs when something learned in one situation either helps (for positive transfer) or hinders (for negative transfer) learning or performance in another situation. Transfer is more likely to occur when relevant information and skills are retrieved in the transfer situation. Unfortunately, much information and many skills are acquired in specific contexts (a phenomenon known as *situated cognition*), decreasing the likelihood that students will retrieve them outside of those contexts. We can do many things to help students apply what they learn in school to new situations; for instance, we can explore topics in depth rather than superficially, show students the many ways in which classroom material can be applied, and give them numerous opportunities to practice using that material, especially in real-world tasks.

Problem solving is one form of transfer. Schools more frequently teach students how to solve well-defined problems, rather than ill-defined ones, yet real-world problems are often ill-defined in nature. We can help students become more effective problem solvers in a number of ways: by teaching algorithms and heuristics relevant to various problem situations, helping students understand the meaning and rationale underlying particular problem-solving procedures, providing practice in dealing with and defining ill-defined problems, and promoting automaticity for fundamental knowledge and skills.

Critical thinking involves evaluating information in terms of its accuracy and worth. It takes a variety of forms, depending on the situation; for instance, it may involve analyzing persuasive arguments, determining whether data support a particular conclusion, or choosing the best of several alternatives. As teachers, we should encourage and model a certain amount of intellectual skepticism, provide many opportunities for students to engage in critical analysis of classroom subject matter, and ask questions that guide students in their analyses.

Whether students engage in higher-level thinking depends not only on their knowledge and abilities but also on their *dispositions*—their general inclinations to approach tasks in particular ways. Examples of dispositions are a meaningful learning set, curiosity about puzzling events, persistence in the face of obstacles, and willingness to use errors to improve future performance. To some degree, dispositions are a function of motivation (a topic discussed in Chapters 11 and 12). Yet as teachers, we can also encourage dispositions essential for higher-level thinking processes by modeling such processes ourselves and making them an important part of classroom activities.

Students will exhibit considerable diversity in their higher-level thinking skills. For example, students from diverse cultural backgrounds, although they may have developed effective problem-solving strategies within the contexts of their own home and neighborhood environments, may have difficulty transferring what they've learned to more formal classroom tasks involving similar skills. And many students with special needs may have acquired few if any effective study strategies and so may need considerable scaffolding in their early attempts at using such strategies.

Several general strategies may be useful for promoting higher-level thinking skills: (1) emphasizing meaningful learning and conceptual understanding, (2) teaching higher-level skills within the context of specific topics, (3) communicating that our "knowledge" about the world is dynamic and ever-changing, (4) regularly scheduling group discussions and projects that require higher-level skills, (5) using authentic activities to promote transfer of thinking skills to the real world, (6) fostering dispositions to use higher-level skills, and (7) incorporating higher-level thinking into assessment tasks.

Common Student Beliefs and Misconceptions Related to Chapter Content

Below are three misconceptions that college students often have before reading about higher-level thinking processes—misconceptions that may interfere with an accurate understanding of what they read. As you read Chapter 8, be on the lookout for evidence that contradicts these common misconceptions:

1. Many people believe that children and adolescents naturally know how to learn classroom material—that effective learning and study strategies don't need to be taught.

2. Some people believe that note taking interferes with learning.

3. Many people believe that general mental "exercise" improves the mind.

CHAPTER OUTLINE	FOCUS QUESTIONS
THE NATURE OF HIGHER-LEVEL THINKING	• How are higher-level questions different from lower-level ones?

METACOGNITION AND STUDY STRATEGIES
    Effective Study Strategies
    Factors Affecting Strategy Use
	• What is *metacognition*? What knowledge and abilities does it include? Why is it especially important at the upper grade levels?
	
	• What study strategies does research indicate to be effective? Are there special circumstances under which each strategy is more or less effective?
	
	• Assess your own use of effective study strategies. (For your convenience, a copy of Table 8.1 in the textbook is duplicated in this chapter of the *Study Guide and Reader*.
	
	• Why do students often have trouble identifying important information? How can teachers help them identify it more accurately?
	
	• What functions does note taking serve? What kinds of notes are most effective?
	
	• How does a *concept map* facilitate learning?
	
	• Describe how a teacher might use *elaborative interrogation* to promote elaboration.
	
	• What is *comprehension monitoring*? How does self-questioning promote this process? What happens when students don't monitor comprehension as they read and study?
	
	• What factors influence the extent to which students use effective study strategies?
	
	• What components does study skills training often include? How can teachers help students develop more effective learning strategies?

CHAPTER OUTLINE	FOCUS QUESTIONS

TRANSFER
   Basic Concepts in Transfer
   Factors Affecting Transfer
   Importance of Retrieval in Transfer
	• What is transfer? How are positive and negative transfer different? How are specific and general transfer different? Think of new examples of each of these concepts.
	
	• What is the *formal discipline* view of transfer? What common teaching practices are based on this notion? What is the current status of this perspective?
	
	• What do theorists mean by *situated cognition*? What implications does this concept have for classroom practice?
	
	• What factors promote transfer? What implications do these factors have for classroom practice?
	
	• Explain the role that *retrieval* plays in transfer.

PROBLEM SOLVING
   Basic Concepts in Problem Solving
   Cognitive Factors Affecting Problem Solving
   Using Computer Technology to Promote Effective Problem Solving
	• How are well-defined and ill-defined problems different? Think of examples of each kind of problem in your own life.
	
	• What are *algorithms* and *heuristics*? Think of examples of each of these concepts.
	
	• What cognitive factors affect problem solving? What implications does each factor have for facilitating problem solving in the classroom?
	
	• What is a *mental set*? Why does it sometimes interfere with effective problem solving?
	
	• How might you use computer technology to foster problem solving at the grade level(s) at which you hope to be teaching?

CRITICAL THINKING	• What is *critical thinking*? What forms might it take? • How can teachers promote critical thinking in the classroom?
THE ROLE OF DISPOSITIONS IN HIGHER-LEVEL THINKING	• What is a *disposition*? Give examples of how dispositions might be reflected in students' behavior. • Why do students sometimes *not* have the dispositions that lead to higher-level thinking?

CHAPTER OUTLINE	FOCUS QUESTIONS
CONSIDERING DIVERSITY IN HIGHER-LEVEL THINKING PROCESSES Accommodating Students with Special Needs	• How do students' backgrounds affect their use of higher-level thinking skills? • To what extent do students with various kinds of special needs exhibit higher-level thinking skills? How can *metacognitive scaffolding* facilitate their use of effective learning strategies?
THE BIG PICTURE General Strategies for Promoting Higher-Level Thinking Skills	• In what way are complex cognitive processes related to intelligence? • What general strategies can teachers use to promote higher-level thinking skills?

Supplementary Reading

Your instructor may assign Supplementary Reading #8, "Learning in the Content Areas," which appears in the final section of this *Study Guide and Reader*.

Using the Compact Disk

"Intuitive Physics" on the *Simulations in Educational Psychology and Research* CD is relevant to the textbook's discussion of transfer.

"Assessment in the Balance" on the *Simulations in Educational Psychology and Research* CD is relevant to the textbook's discussion of problem solving.

Which Study Strategies Do You Use, and When?

Here is a copy of Table 8.1 in your textbook. You may wish to fill it out here rather than in your textbook.

Study Strategy	In which classes or subjects do you use this strategy frequently?	In which classes or subjects might you benefit from using this strategy more often?	What factors affect your ability to use this strategy successfully?
Identifying important information			
Taking notes			
Retrieving relevant prior knowledge			
Organizing			
Elaborating			
Summarizing			
Monitoring comprehension			

Chapter Glossary

Algorithm. A prescribed sequence of steps guaranteeing a correct problem solution.

Comprehension monitoring. The process of checking oneself to make sure one understands the things being read or heard.

Concept map. A diagram of concepts within an instructional unit and the interrelationships among them.

Critical thinking. Evaluating the accuracy and worth of information or arguments.

Disposition. A general inclination to approach and think about a task in a particular way.

Elaborative interrogation. A study strategy in which students develop and answer knowledge-expanding (elaborative) questions about the material they are trying to learn.

Epistemological beliefs. One's beliefs about the nature of knowledge and knowledge acquisition.

Formal discipline. A view of transfer that postulates that the study of rigorous subjects enhances one's ability to learn other, unrelated things.

General transfer. An instance of transfer in which the original learning task and the transfer task do not overlap in content.

Heuristic. A general problem-solving strategy that may or may not yield a problem solution.

Higher-level question. A question that requires students to do something new with information they have learned—for example, to apply, analyze, synthesize, or evaluate it.

Higher-level thinking. Thought that involves going beyond information specifically learned (e.g., application, analysis, synthesis, evaluation).

Ill-defined problem. A problem in which the desired goal is unclear, information needed to solve the problem is missing, and/or several possible solutions to the problem exist.

Illusion of knowing. Thinking one knows something that one actually does not know.

Lower-level question. A question that requires students to express what they have learned in essentially the same way they learned it—for example, by reciting a textbook's definition of a concept or describing an application their teacher presented in class.

Mental set. Encoding a problem in a way that excludes potential problem solutions.

Metacognition. One's knowledge and beliefs about one's own cognitive processes, and one's resulting attempts to regulate those cognitive processes to maximize learning and memory.

Metacognitive scaffolding. A support structure that guides students in their use of metacognitive strategies.

Negative transfer. A phenomenon whereby something learned at one time interferes with learning or performance at a later time.

Positive transfer. A phenomenon whereby something learned at one time facilitates learning or performance at a later time.

Self-questioning. The process of asking oneself questions as a way of checking one's understanding of a topic.

Situated cognition. Knowledge and thinking skills that are acquired and used primarily within certain contexts, with limited if any transfer to other contexts.

Specific transfer. An instance of transfer in which the original learning task and the transfer task overlap in content.

Transfer. A phenomenon whereby something that an individual has learned at one time affects how the individual learns or performs in a later situation.

Well-defined problem. A problem in which the goal is clearly stated, all information needed to solve the problem is present, and only one correct answer exists.

Here are additional glossary items if your instructor has assigned Supplementary Reading #8:

Benchmark lesson or experiment. Lesson or experiment that begins a new unit by illustrating the issues that the unit will address.

Confirmation bias. A tendency to look for evidence that confirms a hypothesis and to ignore evidence that contradicts the hypothesis.

Emergent literacy. Knowledge and skills that lay a foundation for reading and writing; typically develops in the preschool years as a result of early experiences with oral and written language.

Model. In science, knowledge of the components of a particular scientific entity and the interrelationships among those components.

Personal theory. A self-constructed explanation for one's observations about a particular aspect of the world; it may or may not be consistent with generally accepted explanations of scientific phenomena.

Phonological awareness. The ability to hear the distinct sounds (phonemes) within a word.

Theory. An organized body of concepts and principles developed to explain certain phenomena; a description of possible underlying mechanisms to explain why certain principles are true.

Whole language instruction. An approach to teaching reading and writing in which basic skills are taught solely within the context of authentic reading and writing tasks.

Word decoding. In reading, identifying the sounds associated with a word's letters and then determining what the word probably is.

Application Exercise #13: Facilitating Effective Study Strategy Use

Which of the following techniques are likely to promote more effective study strategies, and which are not? Defend your choices.

1. Ms. Randolph reminds her seventh graders that they should be taking notes in class today. Then, throughout the class session, she identifies specific concepts and ideas that they should include in their notes.

2. To simplify her history lessons, Ms. Benn presents historians' depictions of historical events as fact rather than as the educated guesses they often are.

3. Mr. Rangel begins a unit on mountains by telling his class, "Before we look at how mountains are formed, I want you to try to erase from your memories anything you think you already know about mountains. Let's all begin as blank slates on this subject and start totally from scratch."

4. Ms. Salé gives students questions they should ask themselves tonight as they read the chapter on cell division.

5. During the last five minutes of class each day, Mr. Benedetti has students take out a sheet of paper and write a brief summary of the day's lesson.

6. Mr. Murphy recommends that a struggling student take a study skills course during the summer when she is not distracted by her regular school schedule. In this two-week course, a variety of strategies will be described, and a specific example of how each strategy might be used will be presented.

7. At the beginning of a lecture on World War II, Mr. Quesenberry says, "There are two things you should learn from today's class: why the United States entered the war and what influence its involvement had on the war's final outcome."

Answers to Application Exercise #13

1. Will promote better strategies. Generally speaking, note taking promotes learning. Students' class notes are most likely to be helpful when they include the main ideas presented in class. Seventh graders have probably not had much prior experience taking notes and may be at a loss about what things they should be writing down. By telling them what things are important to include, Ms. Randolph is providing scaffolding that should enable them to develop a good set of notes.

2. Will not promote better strategies. Her approach is apt to foster the *epistemological belief* that knowledge involves having clear-cut answers rather than understanding the complex, sometimes ambiguous nature of history. Such a belief may, in turn, promote superficial memorization strategies rather than true attempts to make sense of the material.

3. Will not promote better strategies. Students are more effective learners when they relate new information to what they already know. Mr. Rangel is urging them *not* to make such meaningful connections.

4. Will promote better strategies. Questions can help focus students' attention on the things that are important for them to learn. Questions also provide a means through which students can monitor their comprehension. After reading the chapter, the students should be able to answer Ms. Salé's questions. If they cannot do so, they will know that they haven't yet learned the things they need to learn from the chapter.

5. Will promote better strategies. Summarizing is an effective study strategy. It helps students identify important ideas and the interrelationships among them.

6. Will not promote better strategies. Students learn study skills more effectively when they encounter them within the context of specific academic subject areas and when they have numerous opportunities to practice using those skills.

7. Will promote better strategies. Providing objectives for a lesson helps students identify the important ideas to be gleaned from the lesson.

Application Exercise #14: Predicting Transfer and Problem Solving

For each of the following situations, decide whether successful transfer or problem solving is likely to occur. Justify your decisions on the basis of the principles and theories of transfer and problem solving described in Chapter 8.

1. When Clarence learns about the law of inertia in his science class, it suddenly makes sense to him why his father's motor boat continues to move forward after the engine is turned off.

2. Mr. Montey teaches students in his middle school math class how to calculate the area of a triangle (area = 1/2 base × height). He presents an example of how to use the formula with a triangle that has a base of 4 centimeters and a height of 7 centimeters and makes sure that all his students arrive at the correct answer of 14 square centimeters. He then proceeds to a discussion of how to calculate a triangle's perimeter.

3. Mr. Swetzig dictates this algebra problem and asks students to solve for x in their heads:
$$x^4 + x^3 + 4x^2 + 2x = 84$$

4. Ryan has been studying Spanish for three years now. He is hoping that his knowledge of Spanish will help him learn Italian when he goes on a student exchange program to Rome this summer.

5. A one-semester high school psychology course is designed to give students an introduction to the field of psychology—to physiological psychology, perception, child development, human learning, social psychology, individual differences, industrial psychology, and so on.

6. Janice is learning how to sew cuffs on the sleeves of the shirt she is making in her "life skills" class. She realizes that the process is very similar to sewing on a collar—something she already knows how to do.

7. Teresa studies the state capitals until she knows them all at a level of automaticity.

8. When Peter's mother asks him what he is learning in history, he says, "A bunch of stuff. It's all just history."

9. In a unit on softball, Ms. Warren teaches her students to keep their eye on the ball as it comes toward the bat and to swing the bat out to meet the ball. She is hoping that her students will use the same strategy when they begin the tennis unit in two weeks.

10. In her woodworking class, Lucy learns how to use a miter box to cut 45° angles for the corners of a picture frame she is working on. Next week, she will need to use the miter box again when Mr. Nesbitt shows the class how to frame a doorway.

11. Vanessa studies computer programming, hoping that it will help her think more logically in her other classes.

12. Heath memorizes the formula $E = mc^2$ and recites it perfectly. He knows that E stands for energy and m stands for mass, although he's not sure what c refers to.

<u>Answers to Application Exercise #14</u>

1. Likely. Clarence is learning the law of inertia in a meaningful fashion, because he is relating it to something he already knows.

2. Not likely. Students are more likely to transfer information they have learned when they have *numerous* examples and opportunities to practice using the information.

3. Not likely. Students will probably have insufficient working memory capacity to remember the entire problem as they simultaneously try to solve it.

4. Likely. Spanish and Italian are languages with common roots and similar vocabulary. Transfer is more likely to occur when the previously learned information (in this case, Spanish) and the knowledge to be learned in the transfer situation (in this case, Italian) are obviously similar.

5. Not likely. The course provides superficial coverage of many topics. Transfer is more likely to occur when students study a specific topic in depth.

6. Likely. Janice is retrieving relevant knowledge at the time she needs it.

7. Not likely. Although thorough learning facilitates transfer, students are more likely to transfer general principles than specific facts. The state capitals are specific facts that have little applicability to anything else.

8. Not likely. Peter is thinking of the subject matter as something that is *context-bound*—as being a part of history but nothing else. He isn't relating the subject matter to anything else he knows.

9. Likely. The behaviors involved in both situations (keeping one's eye on an approaching ball and swinging to meet it) are similar.

10. Likely. Both tasks require cutting 45-degree angles to form corners and so are clearly similar. Furthermore, the second task will occur soon after the first task.

11. Not likely. The logic that one uses in computer programming is not necessarily the same logic that one uses in other disciplines. Vanessa is basing her assumption on the notion of *formal discipline*—the idea that studying rigorous subjects strengthens the mind. Most psychologists have rejected this view of transfer.

12. Not likely. Students are unlikely to apply things they learn in a meaningless fashion.

Answers to Selected Margin Notes

- Page 263: *Do such prompts remind you of the concept of scaffolding?*
  They should. *Scaffolding* is a support structure that enables students to perform a difficult task successfully. Scaffolding sometimes involves providing hints about how the task should be done (see Chapter 2).

- Page 265: *Does this approach also remind you of scaffolding?*
  Modeling effective strategies and giving guidance about how to use them are additional forms that scaffolding may take (see Chapter 2).

- Page 269: *As you read a textbook, when is the information in working memory? in long-term memory? With your answers in mind, explain why students should monitor their comprehension both as they read and also at a later time.*
  Information is in working memory as soon as you pay attention to it and remains there as long as you continue to think about it actively. If you process it in some way beyond just paying attention to it, it will be stored in long-term memory within a few seconds. If you monitor your comprehension of the information as you are learning it, you are considering it while it is still in working memory—where it probably won't last very long—and you are likely to be overly optimistic about how well you know it (Nelson & Dunlosky, 1991; Weaver & Kelemen, 1997). If you monitor your comprehension at a later point in time, you are assessing your ability to retrieve it effectively from long-term memory, which is what you will need to be able to do over the long run.

- Page 278: *What implications does this idea [promoting knowledge and skills that are context-free] have for classroom assessment practices?*
  Some activities should ask students to apply classroom subject matter in a wide variety of situations, including real-life tasks and problems.

- Page 284: *How could you use algebra to solve this problem?*
  Let x be the number of pigs and $21 - x$ be the number of chickens. Because the pigs have four legs each and the chickens have two legs each, the total number of pig legs is $4x$ and the total number of chicken legs is $2(21 - x)$. The total number of legs is 60, so:
  $$4x + 2(21 - x) = 60$$
  Solving for x, we find that $2x + 42 = 60$, so $2x = 18$ and $x = 9$ (the number of pigs). The number of chickens is $21 - 9$, or 12.

- Page 288: *Such instructional strategies are more likely to be helpful for average-ability rather than high-ability students. Why might this be so?*
  Davidson and Sternberg (1998) suggest that high-ability students have already developed effective metacognitive processes on their own.

- Page 290: *How might the teacher have modified the activity to increase its authentic nature?*
  One simple way would have been to ask that students find an actual subtraction problem in their lives. Alternatively, the teacher might have presented a realistic classroom decision making situation that required problem solving; students could then write a word problem that described the situation and the question to be answered.

- **Page 293**: *Can you identify the two errors in the student's calculations?* (This is a question within the photo caption.)

    She miscalculated the sum of the ten scores (the scores add up to 700, not 710), and she forgot to divide by 10 (the total number of test scores). Thus, the mean of the scores is 70.

Sample Test Questions

Items marked with a "**1**)" on the left-hand side are lower-level questions that assess your general knowledge and understanding of the material. Items marked with a "**2**)" on the left-hand side are higher-level questions that assess your ability to apply what you have learned to a new situation.

Multiple-Choice

2)   1.   Which one of the following statements reflects an *epistemological belief*?
   a. "If I can't make sense of something right away, I'll never make sense of it at all."
   b. "I'll do my homework first, and then I'll treat myself by watching a video."
   c. "It takes the sun's rays seven minutes to reach the earth. That's amazing!"
   d. "Why is it that people at the South Pole don't fall into outer space?"

1)   2.   Three of the following statements are consistent with what research tells us about study skills training. Which one is *not*?
   a. Students should focus on learning just one specific study strategy very, very well.
   b. Students should have lots of practice applying the study strategies they learn.
   c. Students must have high self-efficacy that they can succeed in the classroom before they will use the strategies they are taught.
   d. Students should be given reasons why a study strategy is helpful.

2)   3.   In which of the following situations is *negative transfer* occurring?
   a. A student who has used a typewriter for many years discovers that the letters are in the same places on a computer keyboard.
   b. A student who is studying Portuguese finds many similarities in vocabulary and grammar with the Spanish she already knows.
   c. A middle school student has tests in science and language arts this week.
   d. After learning to add two fractions by simply adding their numerators, a student begins to multiply fractions in a similar fashion, getting an incorrect result.

2)   4.   Three of the following teachers are using strategies that should facilitate students' ability to transfer the things that they are learning. Which teacher is *not* using a strategy that should promote transfer?
   a. Ms. Arons has members of her soccer team practice shooting at the goal during the warm-up period before a game.
   b. Mr. Bartoli makes sure his students have mastered addition before he moves on to subtraction.
   c. Mr. Chen shows students many different examples of volcanic mountains (Mount St. Helens, Mount Rainier, Mount Vesuvius, etc.).
   d. Ms. Drew tells students in her sociology class that many principles of sociology are very different from those of psychology.

1)   5.   Three of the following strategies should promote effective problem solving. Which one will *not*?
   a. Help students understand the logic behind mathematical procedures.
   b. Make sure that students master each topic before moving to the next one.
   c. Have students practice mathematical principles on just one or two particularly vivid examples.
   d. Teach students general principles more than specific facts.

1)   6.   Only one of the following is *always* found in critical thinking. Which one?
   a. Separating and controlling variables
   b. Evaluating information or arguments
   c. Visual-spatial thinking
   d. Algorithmic problem solving

Essay

1)   7.   Define *comprehension monitoring,* and explain why students who engage in comprehension monitoring learn more successfully than those who do not.

2)   8.   Steven wants to become a surgeon. His teacher urges him to take computer programming to develop his logical thinking skills for medical school. Is the teacher's reasoning accurate? Why or why not?

Answers to Sample Test Questions

1. a—Epistemological beliefs are beliefs about the nature of knowledge and knowledge acquisition (see the section "Factors Affecting Strategy Use"). The first statement reflects the speaker's belief that learning occurs either quickly or not at all.

2. a—Study strategies training is more effective when students learn a variety of strategies rather than just one (see Table 8.2 in the textbook).

3. d—Negative transfer occurs when knowledge or skills learned in one situation are applied inappropriately in another situation (see the section "Basic Concepts in Transfer").

4. d—Ms. Drew is stressing the differences between sociology and psychology. Students are more likely to show transfer from one situation to another when they are aware of the similarities between the two (see the section "Factors Affecting Transfer").

5. c—Problem solving is one form of transfer, and students are more likely to transfer what they learn when they have numerous examples and opportunities to practice (see the sections "Factors Affecting Transfer" and "Depth and Integration of Knowledge Relevant to the Problem").

6. b—By definition, critical thinking involves evaluating information or arguments in terms of their accuracy and worth (see the section "Critical Thinking").

7. Comprehension monitoring is a process of periodically checking one's own understanding during a learning activity (e.g., reading, studying). Students who engage in comprehension monitoring know when they haven't fully learned something and so can take steps to remediate their incomplete knowledge. (See the discussion of comprehension monitoring in the section "Effective Study Strategies.")

8. The teacher is incorrect. Learning in one situation is unlikely to facilitate learning and performance in another situation if the information and cognitive processes required in the two situations are very different. In Steven's case, the logical thinking skills necessary for computer programming and those necessary for medical school are not necessarily the same. The teacher's reasoning is an example of the formal discipline perspective of transfer—a perspective that has largely been discredited (see the section "Specific Versus General Transfer").

Chapter 9

BEHAVIORIST VIEWS OF LEARNING

Chapter Summary

Behaviorists focus on the role that the environment (i.e., stimuli) plays in bringing about changes in behavior (i.e., responses). It is clear from behaviorist principles that the classroom environments we create have a significant effect on students' learning and behavior.

Classical conditioning is one way through which people acquire responses (often emotional in nature) to stimuli in the environment. Classical conditioning occurs when (a) one stimulus (the unconditioned stimulus) already elicits a particular response (the unconditioned response), and (b) that stimulus is presented in conjunction with another stimulus, usually on several occasions. Under these circumstances, the second (conditioned) stimulus begins to elicit a (conditioned) response as well. As teachers, we should strive to create a classroom environment that conditions pleasure and relaxation responses to academic tasks, not an environment that elicits fear and anxiety.

Operant conditioning occurs when a learner's response is followed by a reinforcing stimulus, thereby increasing the likelihood that the learner will repeat the response. We can increase the frequency of appropriate and productive student behaviors by reinforcing those behaviors whenever they occur or by gradually reinforcing closer and closer approximations to those behaviors (in other words, by *shaping* them). Furthermore, we should describe desired behaviors clearly, individualize reinforcers according to students' preferences, and make response-consequence contingencies explicit and consistent. We must also be careful that we *don't* reinforce undesirable or counterproductive student behaviors.

Students' behaviors are influenced not only by the consequences of those behaviors but also by antecedent events. For instance, once students have learned a response to a particular stimulus, they will tend to make the same response to similar stimuli (i.e., they will *generalize*). Seemingly similar situations may sometimes call for very different responses, however; in such situations, it is important to help students *discriminate* between occasions when particular behaviors are and are not appropriate, perhaps by providing cues regarding the responses we expect them to make. It is important, too, that we put students in situations in which desired behaviors are most likely to occur (i.e., that we create *setting events*) and that we engage students in easy tasks that will lead naturally to more difficult and challenging ones (through the phenomenon of *behavioral momentum*).

Behaviorist principles offer several strategies for reducing and possibly eliminating nonproductive or counterproductive classroom behaviors. As teachers, we might remove the consequences that reinforce an unwanted behavior (resulting in the behavior's *extinction*), *cue* students about inappropriate behavior, or reinforce responses that are *incompatible* with those we wish to eliminate. In some situations, we may need to *punish* students for inappropriate behaviors, particularly when those behaviors interfere significantly with classroom learning or jeopardize students' physical safety or psychological well-being. Yet we should think of punishment as a last resort and abide by strict guidelines in its use, keeping in mind that consequences such as physical punishment, public humiliation, and out-of-school suspension are neither effective nor in students' long-term best interests.

Ideally, desired behaviors are most likely to continue when they lead to such intrinsically reinforcing consequences as feelings of mastery or pride. When intrinsic reinforcement seems unlikely, we can instead maintain productive behaviors over the long run by reinforcing them on an intermittent basis.

Applied behavior analysis, functional analysis, and positive behavioral support are three approaches through which we can apply behaviorist principles in a systematic fashion. Research indicates that such techniques are often effective in promoting greater academic success and more appropriate classroom behavior.

Students will have different histories of reinforcement and different experiences with the various stimuli in the classroom; hence, they will inevitably have different reactions to the same tasks and situations. Some students with special needs will exhibit counterproductive classroom behaviors; behaviorist principles may be especially useful in working with such students.

Behaviorist techniques are most applicable when students have the *ability* to behave appropriately. When cognitive factors interfere with learning or behavior, however, behaviorist approaches alone may be ineffective. Furthermore, we must be careful that we don't provide extrinsic reinforcement unnecessarily; in doing so, we may encourage students to do things *quickly* rather than *well*, and we may undermine any intrinsic reinforcers that are currently operating.

Common Student Beliefs and Misconceptions Related to Chapter Content

Below are several misconceptions that college students often have before studying behaviorist views of learning—misconceptions that may interfere with an accurate understanding of what they read. As you read Chapter 10, be on the lookout for evidence that contradicts these common beliefs:

1. Some students, especially if they have previously encountered only early behaviorist perspectives (e.g., Pavlov's work with dogs, Skinner's work with pigeons), may believe that behaviorists focus primarily on animal learning and that behaviorist research has little relevance to how children learn in the classroom.

2. Some students erroneously think that a *reinforcer* is always a concrete object.

3. Future teachers often use the term *reinforce* to mean giving learners additional information or providing additional experiences related to a topic (e.g., "We can reinforce children's knowledge of math facts by giving them lots of practice"). They then confuse this meaning of the term with the behaviorist meaning.

4. Many students think that *negative reinforcement* is a synonym for *punishment*.

5. Many future teachers say that punishment is something that a teacher should never use, yet they recommend other strategies for reducing inappropriate behavior (e.g., "imposing consequences") that, for all intents and purposes, mean the same thing as punishment.

CHAPTER OUTLINE	FOCUS QUESTIONS
BASIC ASSUMPTIONS OF BEHAVIORISM	• What basic assumptions underlie behaviorist views of learning? • What do behaviorists mean by the term *contiguity*?

CLASSICAL CONDITIONING
    Classical Conditioning of Emotional Responses
    Generalization
    Extinction
	• How did Pavlov's dog demonstrate *learning* as behaviorists define the term? Analyze Pavlov's experiment using classical conditioning terminology.
	
	• Explain classical conditioning in your own words. Identify examples of responses *you* may have learned through classical conditioning.
	
	• Explain how a person might learn an emotional response to a particular situation through classical conditioning.
	
	• What is *generalization* in classical conditioning? What is *extinction*? Think of new examples of these phenomena.
	
	• From the perspective of classical conditioning, how can teachers help reduce students' anxiety about school activities and classroom subject matter?

CHAPTER OUTLINE	FOCUS QUESTIONS

OPERANT CONDITIONING
 	
    Contrasting Classical and Operant Conditioning
 	
    Reinforcement in the Classroom
 	
    Using Reinforcement Effectively
	• State the basic principle of operant conditioning in your own words.
	
	• How is operant conditioning different from classical conditioning?
	
	• Why do behaviorists use the term *reinforcer* instead of *reward*?
	
	• Explain the difference between *primary reinforcers* and *secondary reinforcers*. Give examples of each.
	
	• What is *positive reinforcement*? What various forms does it take? Describe the difference between extrinsic reinforcers and intrinsic reinforcers.
	
	• What is *negative reinforcement*? What effect does it have on the behavior it follows? How is it different from punishment?
	
	• How important is *immediate* reinforcement, and at what ages is it most important? How can teachers foster *delay of gratification*?
	
	• What role does *motivation* play in operant conditioning?
	
	• What guidelines does the textbook offer for using reinforcement in the classroom?
	
	• What is a *terminal behavior*? Why is it advantageous to specify the terminal behavior in advance?
	
	• Describe the nature of a *token economy*.
	
	• What is a *group contingency*? What effects can it have?
	
	• What is a *contingency contract*? What are its essential components?

CHAPTER OUTLINE	FOCUS QUESTIONS
SHAPING NEW BEHAVIORS	• Describe *shaping* in your own words. Can you think of a new example of this process?
EFFECTS OF ANTECEDENT STIMULI AND RESPONSES Cueing Setting Events Generalization Discrimination Behavioral Momentum	• What is *cueing*? What is a *setting event*? What is *behavioral momentum*? How can teachers apply each of these concepts to encourage desired classroom behaviors? • How does generalization occur within the context of operant conditioning? How does discrimination occur?
REDUCING AND ELIMINATING UNDESIRABLE BEHAVIORS Extinction Cueing Inappropriate Behaviors Reinforcing Incompatible Behaviors Punishment	• Compare extinction in operant conditioning to extinction in classical conditioning. • Describe how teachers can use *extinction, cueing, reinforcement of incompatible behavior,* and *punishment* to discourage inappropriate behavior. • Why is extinction not always effective as a means of reducing undesirable behavior? • What forms can punishment take? What kinds of punishment are recommended in classroom settings, and what kinds are not? What guidelines should teachers follow if they believe that they have no alternative but to punish students for misbehavior?
MAINTAINING DESIRABLE BEHAVIORS OVER THE LONG RUN Promoting Intrinsic Reinforcement Using Intermittent Reinforcement	• How can teachers encourage students to continue making desired responses over the long run? • What is *intermittent reinforcement*? How does it affect learning? How does it affect extinction?

CHAPTER OUTLINE	FOCUS QUESTIONS
ADDRESSING ESPECIALLY DIFFICULT CLASSROOM BEHAVIORS Applied Behavior Analysis Functional Analysis and Positive Behavioral Support	• What strategies does *applied behavior analysis* include? What strategies do *functional analysis* and *positive behavioral support* include? What does research tell us about the effectiveness of these approaches?
CONSIDERING DIVERSITY IN STUDENT BEHAVIORS Accommodating Students with Special Needs	• Using a behaviorist point of view, explain why different students respond in different ways to the same situations. • What behaviorist principles can teachers use to help students with special needs achieve academic and social success?
STRENGTHS AND POTENTIAL LIMITATIONS OF BEHAVIORAL APPROACHES	• In what situations are behaviorist techniques most helpful? When are they less useful? • What are potential disadvantages of using extrinsic reinforcement in the classroom?
THE BIG PICTURE	• Summarize the behaviorist approach to learning and teaching.

Chapter Glossary

Activity reinforcer. An opportunity to engage in a favorite activity.

Antecedent response. A response that increases the likelihood that another, particular response will follow.

Antecedent stimulus. A stimulus that increases the likelihood that a particular response will follow.

Applied behavior analysis (ABA). The systematic application of behaviorist principles in educational and therapeutic settings; sometimes known as *behavior modification*.

Backup reinforcer. A reinforcer that a student can "purchase" with one or more tokens earned in a token economy.

Baseline. The frequency of a response before operant conditioning takes place.

Behavioral momentum. An increased tendency for an individual to make a particular response immediately after making similar responses.

Behaviorism. A theoretical perspective in which learning and behavior are described and explained in terms of stimulus-response relationships. Adherents to this perspective are called **behaviorists**.

Classical conditioning. A form of learning whereby a new, involuntary response is acquired as a result of two stimuli being presented at the same time.

Concrete reinforcer. A reinforcer that can be touched.

Conditioned response (CR). A response that, through classical conditioning, begins to be elicited by a particular stimulus.

Conditioned stimulus (CS). A stimulus that, through classical conditioning, begins to elicit a particular response.

Conditioning. Another word for learning; commonly used by behaviorists.

Contiguity. The occurrence of two or more events at the same time. **Contiguous** is the adjective used to refer to events having contiguity.

Contingency. A situation in which one event happens only after another event has already occurred. One event is **contingent** on another's prior occurrence.

Contingency contract. A formal agreement between a teacher and a student that identifies behaviors the student will exhibit and the reinforcers that will follow those behaviors.

Continuous reinforcement. Reinforcing a response every time it occurs.

Cueing. A teacher's use of signals to indicate that a particular behavior is desired or that a particular behavior should stop.

Delay of gratification. The ability to forego small, immediate reinforcers in order to obtain larger ones later on.

Discrimination. A phenomenon in operant conditioning whereby an individual learns that a response is reinforced in the presence of one stimulus but not in the presence of another, similar stimulus.

Extinction. In classical conditioning, the eventual disappearance of a conditioned response as a result of the conditioned stimulus being repeatedly presented alone (i.e., in the absence of the

134

unconditioned stimulus). In operant conditioning, the eventual disappearance of a response that is no longer being reinforced.

Extrinsic reinforcer. A reinforcer that comes from the outside environment, rather than from within the individual.

Functional analysis. Examining a student's inappropriate behavior, as well as its antecedents and consequences, to determine the function(s) that the behavior might serve for the student.

Generalization. A phenomenon in both classical conditioning and operant conditioning whereby an individual learns a response to a particular stimulus and then makes the same response in the presence of similar stimuli.

Group contingency. A situation in which everyone in a group must make a particular response before reinforcement occurs.

Incompatible behaviors. Two or more behaviors that cannot be performed simultaneously.

In-school suspension. A form of punishment in which a student is placed in a quiet, boring room within the school building. It often lasts one or more school days and involves close adult supervision.

Intermittent reinforcement. Reinforcing a response only occasionally, with some occurrences of the response going unreinforced.

Intrinsic reinforcer. A reinforcer provided by oneself or inherent in the task being performed.

Logical consequence. A consequence that follows logically from a student's misbehavior; in other words, the punishment fits the crime.

Negative reinforcement. A consequence that brings about the increase of a behavior through the removal (rather than the presentation) of a stimulus.

Neutral stimulus. A stimulus that does not elicit any particular response.

Operant conditioning. A form of learning whereby a response increases in frequency as a result of its being followed by reinforcement.

Positive behavioral support. A modification of traditional applied behavior analysis that includes identifying the purpose that an undesirable behavior serves for a student and providing an alternative way for the student to achieve the same purpose.

Positive feedback. A message that an answer is correct or a task has been well done.

Positive reinforcement. A consequence that brings about the increase of a behavior through the presentation (rather than removal) of a stimulus.

Premack principle. A phenomenon whereby individuals do less-preferred activities in order to engage in more-preferred activities.

Presentation punishment. A form of punishment involving the presentation of a new stimulus, presumably one that an individual finds unpleasant.

Primary reinforcer. A stimulus that satisfies a basic physiological need.

Psychological punishment. Any consequence that seriously threatens a student's self-concept and self-esteem.

Punishment. A consequence that decreases the frequency of the response it follows.

Reinforcement. The act of following a particular response with a reinforcer and thereby increasing the frequency of that response.

Reinforcer. A consequence (stimulus) of a response that leads to an increased frequency of that response.

Removal punishment. A form of punishment involving the removal of an existing stimulus, presumably one that an individual views as desirable and doesn't want to lose.

Response (R). A specific behavior that an individual exhibits.

Response cost. The loss either of a previously earned reinforcer or of an opportunity to obtain reinforcement.

Secondary reinforcer. A stimulus that becomes reinforcing over time through its association with another reinforcer.

Setting event. In behaviorism, a complex environmental condition in which a particular behavior is most likely to occur.

Shaping. A process of reinforcing successively closer and closer approximations of a desired terminal behavior.

Social reinforcer. A gesture or sign that one person gives another to communicate positive regard.

Stimulus (S) (pl. stimuli). A specific object or event that influences an individual's learning or behavior.

Terminal behavior. The form and frequency of a desired response that a teacher or other practitioner is shaping through operant conditioning.

Time-out. A procedure whereby a misbehaving student is placed in a dull, boring situation with no opportunity to interact with others and no opportunity to obtain reinforcement.

Token economy. A technique whereby desired behaviors are reinforced by tokens, reinforcers that students can use to "purchase" a variety of other reinforcers.

Unconditioned response (UCR). A response that, without prior learning, is elicited by a particular stimulus.

Unconditioned stimulus (UCS). A stimulus that, without prior learning, elicits a particular response.

Verbal reprimand. A scolding for inappropriate behavior.

Application Exercise #15: Recognizing Examples of Classical and Operant Conditioning

In each of the following situations, a response is being learned through either classical or operant conditioning. Decide which form of conditioning is occurring in each case. If classical conditioning is taking place, identify the UCS, UCR, CS, and CR. If operant conditioning is taking place, identify the response, the reinforcer, and, if applicable, the antecedent stimulus.

1.   Lindsey's mother has told Lindsey that she must do her homework every day before she can get together with her friends. Lindsey finds that by doing her homework quickly (although not necessarily carefully or accurately), she can spend more time at the mall with Mayesha and Heather.

2.   When it's time for his fourth graders to go to lunch, Mr. Linnebur lets each row of students line up only when the entire row is quiet. Mr. Linnebur finds that he rarely has discipline problems at lunch time if he uses this procedure.

3.   When Rhonda plugs in the oscilloscope in physics lab, an electrical short in the instrument gives her a nasty shock and she quickly pulls her hand away. Rhonda refuses to touch the oscilloscope in the lab after that. In fact, she is reluctant to handle any of the lab's electrical equipment.

4.   Ms. Fiscus praises John when he reads the word *cat* correctly. Sometimes, however, he reads the word *car* as "cat"; he receives no praise from Ms. Fiscus when he does so. Eventually he learns to tell the difference between *cat* and *car*.

5.   In history class, Ms. Swanson gets angry about Tom's poor test performance and humiliates him in front of his classmates. This humiliation creates bad feelings in Tom—feelings about Ms. Swanson as well as about her behavior.

6.   Will usually turns in lengthy assignments several days early so he doesn't have to worry about them anymore.

7.   Shannon's friend lends her a novel by Stephen King. Although Shannon doesn't usually spend much time reading, she finds this novel exciting and fun to read. When she finishes it, she begins to borrow other Stephen King novels from the library and reads them from cover to cover.

8.   In his attempts to get Ms. Steinberg's attention, Josh tries talking loudly at inappropriate times. This strategy works for a while, because Ms. Steinberg admonishes him sternly for his outbursts. However, Ms. Steinberg eventually decides that it would be better to ignore Josh's disruptive behavior rather than to reprimand him. At this point, Josh discovers that he can continue to get a rise out of his teacher only when he throws an occasional obscenity into his outspoken remarks.

Answers to Application Exercise #15

1. Operant conditioning. Doing her homework quickly (the response) is reinforced by being able to spend time with her friends (the reinforcer). The *Premack principle* is operating here.

2. Operant conditioning. Sitting quietly (the response) is followed by being allowed to get in line for lunch (the reinforcer). A *group contingency* is in effect here, because everyone in the row must be quiet before the reinforcer is presented.

3. Classical conditioning. The shock (UCS) leads to an immediate withdrawal of the hand (UCR). By being associated with the shock, the oscilloscope (CS) begins to elicit an avoidance response (CR) as well. Rhonda is also *generalizing* this conditioned response to other equipment in the lab.

4. Operant conditioning. Saying "cat" (the response) is followed by praise (the reinforcer). John begins to *discriminate* between the stimuli *cat* and *car*.

5. Classical conditioning. The humiliation (UCS) elicits bad feelings (UCR). Because Ms. Swanson is associated with the humiliation, she becomes a CS that elicits similar bad feelings (CR).

6. Operant conditioning. Completing assignments early (the response) leads to a reduction in worry (a *negative reinforcer*).

7. Operant conditioning. Reading (the response) is reinforced by excitement and enjoyment (an *intrinsic reinforcer*). The reading response *generalizes* to other novels by Stephen King.

8. Operant conditioning. Talking out of turn (the response) is followed by Ms. Steinberg's attention (the reinforcer). Ms. Steinberg is attempting to *extinguish* Josh's behavior by ignoring him. By continuing to reinforce those statements that contain undesirable words, however, she is actually *shaping* Josh's inappropriate remarks.

Application Exercise #16: Identifying Effective Classroom Practices

From a behaviorist perspective, which of the following teaching strategies are likely to be effective and which are not? Using behaviorist terminology, develop a rationale for each of your decisions.

1. A reading teacher has several students who are at risk for dropping out of high school. She finds reading materials that relate to each student's particular interests (football, fashion, auto mechanics, and so on).

2. Mr. Turiel tells his students, "As soon as you complete your multiplication tables, you can go to one of the learning centers you all enjoy so much."

3. Hoping to boost Yvette's self-confidence, Mr. Evans praises her when she finally passes one of his tests, even though he knows that she cheated on the test.

4. In a unit on genetics, Mr. Lima has students separate fruit flies by gender. He explains that the females have more stripes on their abdomen than the males do and that the males have bristle-like "combs" on their front legs. He walks around the room as students work and gives them positive feedback when they are separating the flies correctly.

5. Ronny clearly wants to be "Mr. Cool" in Ms. LaBranche's middle school science class. It seems as if he provokes Ms. LaBranche just to gain the admiration of his friends. In an attempt to encourage more productive behavior, Ms. LaBranche begins praising Ronny every time she sees him on task.

6. Later in the school year, Ms. LaBranche finds that Ronny is quite a comedian and enjoys making his classmates laugh. Furthermore, she discovers that Ronny can often create very clever jokes out of classroom subject matter. She takes Ronny aside one day and says, "I'll make a deal with you, Ronny. If you can stay on task throughout class each day, I'll give you the last few minutes of the period to tell two or three jokes. Two conditions, however: The jokes have to relate to whatever topic we've been studying that day, and they must not hurt anyone's feelings."

7. Kathy is a third grader with a history of counterproductive social behavior; she insults, teases, and ridicules other students almost daily. Over a period of several weeks, Mr. Puzio meets with Kathy twice a week after school to teach her more appropriate ways of interacting with her classmates. Every time Kathy displays her newly learned interactive skills with another child, Mr. Puzio catches her eye and smiles at her.

8. In his instrumental music class, Mr. Salazar praises his students no matter how well they play their instruments, even if they don't show any signs of improvement over a period of several weeks.

9. As Mr. Pacheco takes his first graders on a nature walk through a local park, he asks them to pick up any litter that they find along the trail. The children develop quite an enthusiasm for the task and proudly show him some of the trash they are finding. When the class returns to

school, Mr. Pacheco looks at his watch and says, "Hmm, we got back earlier than I thought we would. Before we go inside, let's pick up some of the litter we see on the playground."

10. At lunch time on the first day of school, Ms. Denton has her first graders line up to get ready to go to the cafeteria. "Remember what I told you earlier, children," she says. "We need to walk *quietly* down the hall so we don't disturb children in other classrooms."

11. In a unit on golf in her physical education classes, Ms. McDaniels is teaching her students how to swing a golf club. She begins by praising them for using good form even when they miss the ball altogether. Eventually she praises them only when they use good form *and* hit the ball, and then only when, by swinging the club appropriately, they hit the ball a reasonable distance and in the proper direction.

12. After recess, Ms. Yancey's fifth graders are having trouble settling down. She tells them, "Okay, you can have another ten minutes to talk among yourselves, but then you need to get back to work on your book reports."

13. Laura rarely turns in the homework that Ms. Jonassen assigns. One day Laura *does* turn in her homework, but Ms. Jonassen is not aware of the fact until that evening, when she is grading her students' papers. The following day, Ms. Jonassen makes sure to give Laura positive feedback by telling her, "Nice work yesterday."

14. At the beginning of the school year, Mr. Kelsey gives free time at the end of each day to students who finish their in-class assignments on time. Once his students are regularly completing their assignments in a timely manner, he continues to reinforce this behavior on occasion but more frequently makes free time contingent on other desired responses.

15. Susan often blurts out answers in class, to the point where she usually dominates class discussions. To help Susan control her outspokenness, Mr. Krick develops a contingency contract for her. He meets with her after school to describe its contents; he then asks her to sign it.

Answers to Application Exercise #16

1. Effective. The students will be learning new things about topics of interest to them as they read, so reading behavior will be *intrinsically reinforced*.

2. Effective. Mr. Turiel is reinforcing completion of the multiplication tables with a desired activity. In other words, he is using the *Premack principle*.

3. Not effective. Mr. Evans is reinforcing an undesirable behavior—cheating.

4. Effective. Mr. Lima is reinforcing desired behavior by giving positive feedback. Furthermore, he is teaching students to *discriminate* between two different stimuli by reinforcing different responses to each one.

5. Not effective. Not all students find praise reinforcing. Because Ronny is trying to maintain his "cool" image, he is unlikely to appreciate Ms. LaBranche's well-intended words.

6. Effective. Ms. LaBranche has identified a new behavior that serves the same purpose as Ronny's disruptive behavior: to gain the admiration of classmates. This strategy is often used in *positive behavioral support*.

7. Effective. Mr. Puzio is using *continuous reinforcement* to increase appropriate behavior.

8. Not effective. Ideally, Mr. Salazar should be reinforcing closer and closer approximations to the desired behavior: playing a musical instrument competently. In other words, he should be *shaping* students' behavior. By continuing to reinforce the same behavior week after week, he is giving students no reason to improve.

9. Effective. Mr. Pacheco is taking advantage of *behavioral momentum*: The students are more likely to make desired responses after they have already been making similar responses.

10. Effective. Ms. Denton is *cueing* appropriate behavior.

11. Effective. Ms. McDaniels starts by reinforcing something her students can do and then *shapes* more skillful behavior over time.

12. Not effective. Ms. Yancey is reinforcing undesirable behavior (e.g., being noisy and hyperactive) by allowing students to talk with one another for an additional 10 minutes.

13. Not effective. Ideally, reinforcement should be immediate, particularly if students have difficulty delaying gratification. Furthermore, when Ms. Jonassen finally *does* reinforce Laura, she does not indicate what response is specifically being reinforced.

14. Effective. Mr. Kelsey switches from *continuous reinforcement* to *intermittent reinforcement* of a desired response (finishing assignments on time) as a way of maintaining this response over the long run.

15. Not effective. Effective contingency contracts are those that a teacher and student develop *together*, agreeing on both the desired behaviors and the reinforcers that will be contingent on those behaviors.

Answers to Selected Margin Notes

- Page 300: *Is this "blank slate" assumption inconsistent with anything you've read in earlier chapters?*

  It's inconsistent with many theorists' belief that some developmental changes occur as a result of maturation—the gradual unfolding of genetically controlled characteristics (see Chapter 2)—and the idea that children inherit temperamental differences in how they respond to the world (see Chapters 2 and 3). It's also inconsistent with the assumption that some disabilities have genetic origins (see Chapter 5).

- Page 304: *Do you remember the earlier example of learning to respond negatively to an instructor's scowl? Can you explain your learning from the perspective of classical conditioning?*

  The question is referring to the first example under the bullet "Learning is most likely to take place when stimuli and responses occur close together in time." Because the D– grade already gives you a bad feeling in your stomach, we can say that the bad grade is an unconditioned stimulus (UCS) that elicits the unconditioned response (UCR) of feeling uncomfortable. The teacher's scowl occurs in conjunction with the UCS. When the scowl itself elicits the uncomfortable feeling, it has become a conditioned stimulus (CS) and the feeling in response to it alone (i.e., in the absence of the D–) has become a conditioned response (CR).

- Page 306: *How is the concept of contingency different from contiguity?*

  Contiguity exists when two or more events occur at the same time. Contingency exists when one event happens *only* after another event occurs.

- Page 307: *Recall that behaviorists focus on stimuli and responses. Which of these is reinforcement: a stimulus or a response?*

  Reinforcement is a stimulus; it has an impact on a person's responses.

- Page 309: *How might you determine which reinforcers are most effective for your students?*

  You can ask students or their parents. (Keep in mind, however, that children do not always have a good sense of which consequences are truly reinforcing for them; Northup, 2000.) You can also observe students to see what kinds of consequences students consistently seek out.

- Page 309: *What stimulus is removed in each case? What response is being reinforced as a result?*

  1. Electric shock is being removed. Pressing the bar is being reinforced.
  2. Worry is being removed. Finishing the assignment is being reinforced.
  3. Confusion is being removed. Procrastinating on the assignment is being reinforced.
  4. The noise and rowdiness are being removed. Yelling is being reinforced.

- Page 310: *Can you use the concept of working memory to explain why immediate reinforcement might be better than delayed reinforcement?*

  Immediate feedback may be more effective because both the performed behavior and the feedback are in working memory at the same time and so can be connected (e.g., Anderson, 1987).

- Page 315: *How might you use shaping to teach an 8-year-old to write in cursive? a 12-year-old to swing a baseball bat? an aggressive high school student to behave prosocially?*
  - Writing in cursive: Teachers frequently use shaping to teach cursive writing. They may begin by having students trace cursive letters that have been lightly written between two horizontal lines. They may then present only part of a letter, having students trace that part and then complete the letter. Over a period of time, students copy rather than trace the letters, write the letters from memory, write the letters from memory between smaller and smaller lines, and eventually write the letters on unlined paper.
  - Swinging a baseball bat: One possibility is to begin with "T-ball," where the child swings and hits a stationary ball placed at the appropriate height on a plastic stand. After the child masters hitting the ball off the batting tee, the ball can be thrown from a short distance, then from a longer one, and so on. An alternative approach is to begin with a very large ball and then gradually decrease the size of the ball that the child needs to hit.
  - Teaching prosocial behavior: You should begin by identifying and reinforcing a behavior that the student already exhibits frequently—one that, although perhaps not prosocial, is at least nonaggressive. Once this behavior is occurring frequently, you can selectively reinforce only a more "prosocial" form of the behavior, and then a more desirable form of *that* behavior, and so on, until eventually truly prosocial behavior is occurring regularly.

- Page 315: *How are the concepts of cueing and retrieval cues similar? How are they different?*
  Both serve as reminders. Cueing reminds a student of appropriate behavior, whereas a retrieval cue helps a student recall previously learned information.

- Page 318: *How is extinction similar in classical and operant conditioning? How is it different?*
  In both cases, extinction involves a gradual reduction in the frequency of a response when the circumstances that originally led to conditioning are no longer present. In classical conditioning, extinction occurs when the conditioned stimulus (something that appears *before* the response) is repeatedly experienced in the absence of the unconditioned stimulus. In operant conditioning, extinction occurs when reinforcement no longer is presented *after* the response.

- Page 322: *Can you explain how release from a time-out situation is negative reinforcement?*
  An unpleasant (boring) situation is removed contingent on the student's engaging in appropriate behavior (e.g., being calm and quiet) rather than inappropriate behavior.

- Page 325: *One statement in this paragraph is based on the concept of shaping. Another reflects the concept of scaffolding. Can you identify each of these statements?*
  Providing extrinsic reinforcement for little improvements is shaping. Breaking down a complex task into smaller pieces is a form of scaffolding.

- Page 325: *Which form of reinforcement, continuous or intermittent, would you use to teach your students to persist at difficult tasks?*
  Intermittent reinforcement is preferable, because it makes a response more resistant to extinction. With an intermittent schedule, students are essentially learning that not every response is going to pay off, but that some responses eventually *will* pay off.

- Page 326: *Can you think of other possible reasons for the success of behaviorist techniques?* Because the desired terminal behavior is identified at the very beginning, students' efforts can be directed toward a particular goal. Furthermore, the frequent success (i.e., reinforcement) that students experience is likely to increase their self-confidence (or *self-efficacy*, as we will call it in social cognitive theory) that they can do something successfully. There are undoubtedly other possible explanations as well.

- Page 328: *In a number of places throughout the chapter I have sneaked unobservable phenomena (e.g., thoughts, feelings) into my description of behaviorist principles. Can you find some places where I have done so?*
  Here are a few places where I have done so (there are many others as well):
  - At the beginning of the section "Classical Conditioning," I refer to Alan's *anxiety* whenever he is up at bat. Later in that section, I say that Brenda *feels happy* when she hears a song.
  - In the section "Primary Versus Secondary Reinforcers," I say that not everyone *appreciates* secondary reinforcers.
  - In the section "Positive Versus Negative Reinforcement," I define an activity reinforcer as an opportunity to engage in a *favorite* activity, and I talk about *intrinsic* reinforcers. Later, in the discussion of negative reinforcement, I say that Rhonda no longer has to *worry* about her assignment.
  - In the section "Punishment," I describe removal punishment as involving a stimulus that a person finds *desirable* and doesn't *want* to lose.
  - In the section "Using Intermittent Reinforcement," I say that it may take Maria longer to *realize* that she is no longer being reinforced.

Sample Test Questions

Items marked with a "1)" on the left-hand side are lower-level questions that assess your general knowledge and understanding of the material. Items marked with a "2)" on the left-hand side are higher-level questions that assess your ability to apply what you have learned to a new situation.

Multiple-Choice

1)   1. Three of the assumptions below characterize behaviorist views of learning. Which one is *not* an assumption that behaviorists make?
   - a. People are most likely to make connections between a stimulus and a response when the two occur close together in time.
   - b. Rats and people often learn in similar ways.
   - c. Thinking processes cannot be observed and so cannot be studied scientifically.
   - d. People rarely learn anything when the stimuli around them are unpleasant.

2)   2. Three of the following are examples of operant conditioning. Which one is *not*?
   - a. When Alice's teacher praises her in class for her fine oral report, Alice is embarrassed and vows never to act so smart in front of her friends again.
   - b. When Bart changes the way he throws the javelin, he finds that it goes farther than it ever has before, and so he continues to use the new technique.
   - c. When Cordell tells a funny joke, his classmates all laugh. Cordell soon becomes the class clown, telling jokes at every opportunity.
   - d. When Donna discovers that she can leave physical education class early by complaining about a stomachache, she begins to get these "stomachaches" about once a week.

2)   3. Which one of the following is an example of *negative reinforcement*?
   - a. Eric's friends think he's cool because he has the audacity to swear in class.
   - b. Ophelia completes her English paper two days early so she won't have it hanging over her head anymore.
   - c. Timothy's teacher scolds him when she finds a copy of *Playboy* hidden behind the textbook he's supposed to be reading.
   - d. Myra gets the attention of all the boys when she wears tight, skimpy outfits to school.

2)   4. Raymond discovers that he gets better grades on his history tests when he studies a little bit every night than when he tries to cram at the last minute. Raymond starts applying the same strategy to his biology and geography classes as well. From the perspective of operant conditioning, Raymond is demonstrating:
   - a. Generalization
   - b. Baseline behavior
   - c. Shaping
   - d. Discrimination

1)   5.   Three of the following practices are consistent with the textbook's guidelines for using punishment to reduce inappropriate behavior. Which one is *not* consistent with these guidelines?

  a.   Teach more appropriate behavior as well.

  b.   Give reasons why the punished behavior cannot be tolerated.

  c.   Let students know in advance what behaviors will be punished, and how.

  d.   Assign extra classwork when students have been especially disruptive.

2)   6.   Sally has trouble sitting still in class. Mr. Torrentino begins praising Sally every time she sits quietly for a reasonable period of time. He notices improvement in Sally's classroom behavior and so continues reinforcing Sally in this fashion in the weeks that follow. By Thanksgiving, Sally is behaving as well as her classmates, so Mr. Torrentino concludes that he no longer has to reinforce her for sitting still. Soon after this, Sally's behavior begins to deteriorate, and by January she is back to her old, restless self. From an operant conditioning perspective, what should Mr. Torrentino *definitely* have done differently in this situation?

  a.   He should have taught Sally to discriminate between situations in which sitting still was and was not appropriate.

  b.   He should have punished her for getting out of her seat and for other similarly "restless" behaviors.

  c.   He should have continued to reinforce her for sitting quietly on an intermittent basis.

  d.   He should have used a reinforcer other than praise.

Essay

2)   7.   Miriam was badly beaten by an aggressive classmate in the school corridor yesterday, and now she does not want to go to school. Explain this situation in terms of *classical conditioning*. Identify the UCS, UCR, CS, and CR.

2)   8.   You want to teach Leon to catch a baseball. Describe how you might use *shaping* to teach this skill. Specify:

  a.   An appropriate terminal behavior

  b.   A reinforcer you might reasonably use

  c.   The specific steps you would take during the shaping process

Answers to Sample Test Questions

1. d—People often learn from unpleasant stimuli. For examples, see the section "Classical Conditioning of Emotional Responses."

2. a—Operant conditioning always leads to an increase in the reinforced behavior (see the basic principle of operant conditioning presented at the beginning of the section "Operant Conditioning"). Alice probably won't increase her "acting smart" behavior. The teacher's praise is not reinforcing for Alice; instead, it appears to be punishing.

3. b—By completing her paper, Ophelia gets rid of something unpleasant: She no longer has the assignment hanging over her head. See the discussion of negative reinforcement in the section "Reinforcement in the Classroom."

4. a—Raymond learns to make a response in the presence of one stimulus (history classes) and begins to demonstrate the same response in the presence of similar stimuli (other classes). The section "Effects of Antecedent Stimuli and Responses" describes generalization within the context of operant conditioning.

5. d—Extra classwork is usually *not* recommended as classroom punishment because it communicates the message that schoolwork is unpleasant (see the section "Ineffective Forms of Punishment").

6. c—When reinforcement stops, extinction often occurs. An intermittent schedule of reinforcement makes a learned response more resistant to extinction once reinforcement finally *does* stop (e.g., at the end of the school year). See the section "Maintaining Desirable Behaviors over the Long Run."

7. The beating (or the pain associated with it) was an unconditioned stimulus (UCS) that elicited an unconditioned response (UCR) of fear or anxiety. School was associated with the beating, so it has become a conditioned stimulus (CS) that elicits fear as well. Miriam's fear of school is therefore a conditioned response (CR). See the section "Classical Conditioning" for other examples.

8. a. The desired end result is catching a baseball regularly. You should describe this terminal behavior in specific, concrete, and observable terms (see the section "Using Reinforcement Effectively"). For example, you might say that Leon will catch 90 percent of the pitches thrown to him from a distance of 20 feet.
   b. The reinforcer should be something that is definitely reinforcing for Leon. If Leon truly wants to learn how to play baseball, his success at catching the ball should be reinforcement enough. Otherwise, you might use positive feedback, praise, points that are accumulated and eventually exchanged for a small prize, etc. You need to identify only one reinforcer here, but be sure to explain why you think it will be effective in this situation.
   c. Shaping is a process of reinforcing closer and closer approximations to the desired terminal behavior (see the section "Shaping New Behaviors"). There are several possible approaches that you might take to shape Leon's "catching" behavior. For example, you might begin with a very large ball and then gradually reduce the size of the ball Leon must catch. Or you might first pitch the ball to Leon from only a few feet away, gradually increasing your distance as he shows greater success. Your approach might even use a combination of decreasing ball size and increasing distance. Whatever you do, you should change the nature of the response you reinforce over time, and you should make sure that Leon demonstrates mastery of each new behavior before you proceed to the next one.

Chapter 10

SOCIAL COGNITIVE VIEWS OF LEARNING

Chapter Summary

Social cognitive theory focuses on the ways that people learn by observing others. Social cognitive theorists believe that both environmental conditions (e.g., the consequences of behavior, the presence of models) and personal variables (e.g., goals, expectations, self-efficacy) influence learning and behavior. In addition to creating a classroom environment conducive to learning, then, we must also foster those personal characteristics that will enable students to achieve academic success.

Social cognitive theorists' beliefs about how reinforcement influences learning and behavior are quite different from those of behaviorists. From a social cognitive perspective, reinforcement and punishment affect learning indirectly rather than directly, and consequences to one student vicariously influence the behaviors of others as well. Students who observe a classmate being reinforced or punished for a particular behavior may conclude that engaging in that behavior will yield similar consequences for themselves. Furthermore, the nonoccurrence of expected reinforcement is punishing, and the nonoccurrence of expected punishment is reinforcing. As teachers, we should recognize that the consequences of students' behaviors are likely to influence the expectations that students form, the ways in which they process information, and the choices that they make.

Students learn from both live and symbolic models. We should provide numerous opportunities for our students to observe us and others demonstrating important skills; we can also expose our students to exemplary characters portrayed in books, films, and other media. Four processes are necessary for modeling to occur: *attention* to the model, *retention* (memory) of what the model does, capacity for *motor reproduction* of the modeled behavior, and *motivation* to exhibit the modeled behavior. We should make sure that all four factors are present when we use modeling as an instructional technique.

Students are more likely to engage and persist in certain activities when they believe that they can be successful—that is, when they have high *self-efficacy*. We can promote greater self-efficacy in students by having them observe successful peer models, assuring them that they too can succeed, and giving them many opportunities to experience success working either as individuals or as part of a group.

As children and adolescents grow older, most of them become increasingly self-regulating; for example, they begin to set standards and goals for themselves, and they monitor, guide, evaluate, and reinforce their own behavior. Principles of self-regulation can be applied not only to behavior, but to learning and problem solving as well. We can promote the development of self-regulation by having students set some of their own goals, teaching them to guide their own performance through self-instructions and self-regulated problem-solving strategies, helping them monitor and evaluate their efforts accurately, encouraging them to reinforce themselves for good work, and, eventually, assigning activities in which students study and learn with little or no teacher assistance.

Environment, behavior, and personal characteristics all interact with one another in their effects on learning—a three-way interdependence known as *reciprocal causation*. As teachers, we must recognize that the environment we create affects both the behaviors that students exhibit and the personal factors that influence their learning. Those behaviors and personal factors will, in turn, influence the future classroom environment that students experience.

Students often benefit more from models who are similar to themselves in cultural background, socioeconomic status, gender, and (if applicable) disability. Students with special needs will often be among those who need the greatest support in developing self-regulation strategies.

The three theoretical perspectives of learning that we have examined—cognitive psychology, behaviorism, and social cognitive learning—differ somewhat regarding such issues as reinforcement, cognition, control, and educational implications. As teachers, we must recognize that all three perspectives have useful applications for classroom practice.

Common Student Beliefs and Misconceptions Related to Chapter Content

Below are two ideas that sometimes interfere with college students' ability to understand the things that they read about social cognitive theory. As you read Chapter 11, be on the lookout for evidence that contradicts these ideas:

1. Some students think that modeling always involves a real person demonstrating a behavior. In fact, models can also be fictional characters in books, films, television shows, or other media (see the discussion of *symbolic models* at the beginning of the section "Modeling").

2. In the discussion of operant conditioning in Chapter 9, you learned about the concept of *extinction,* whereby a response decreases in frequency when it is no longer being reinforced. Social cognitive theorists have a very different view of what happens when reinforcement no longer occurs—a view that involves *expectations*.

CHAPTER OUTLINE	FOCUS QUESTIONS
BASIC ASSUMPTIONS OF SOCIAL COGNITIVE THEORY	• What general assumptions underlie social cognitive theory?
THE SOCIAL COGNITIVE VIEW OF REINFORCEMENT AND PUNISHMENT Expectations Vicarious Experiences Cognitive Processing Choice of Behavior Nonoccurrence of Expected Consequences	• From a social cognitive perspective, in what ways do reinforcement and punishment affect learning and behavior? • What are *vicarious reinforcement* and *vicarious punishment*? Think of examples of these phenomena in your own life. • What is an *incentive*? Why is it not necessarily the same as a reinforcer? • What happens when the expected consequences of behavior (either reinforcement or punishment) don't occur?
MODELING How Modeling Affects Behavior Characteristics of Effective Models Helping Students Learn from Models	• What's the difference between a *live model* and a *symbolic model*? • Describe the four effects of modeling—*observational learning, response facilitation, response inhibition,* and *response disinhibition*—in your own words. • What characteristics do effective models often have? Why do students imitate some behaviors but not others? • What four conditions are essential for learning from models? What implications do these conditions have for teachers?
SELF-EFFICACY How Self-Efficacy Affects Behavior Factors in the Development of Self-Efficacy	• What is *self-efficacy*? How is it different from *self-concept*? What effects does it have on behavior and learning? • What experiences contribute to either high or low self-efficacy? What strategies can teachers use to enhance students' self-efficacy? • What is *collective self-efficacy*? What implications does it have for classroom practice?

CHAPTER OUTLINE	FOCUS QUESTIONS
SELF-REGULATION Self-Regulated Behavior Self-Regulated Learning Self-Regulated Problem Solving	• What do social cognitive theorists mean by the term *self-regulation*? • What is *self-regulated behavior*? What roles do standards and goals play in such behavior? What roles do *self-monitoring, self-instructions, self-evaluation,* and *self-imposed contingencies* play? How can teachers promote self-regulated behavior? • What does *self-regulated learning* involve? Why is it so important, and how can teachers foster it? • How can teachers promote more appropriate social behaviors through *self-regulated problem solving*?
RECIPROCAL CAUSATION	• Describe *reciprocal causation* in your own words. Identify several ways in which each of the three factors in reciprocal causation—environment, behavior, and person—affects the other two.
CONSIDERING DIVERSITY FROM A SOCIAL COGNITIVE PERSPECTIVE Using Diverse Models to Promote Success and Self-Efficacy Promoting Self-Regulation in Students with Special Needs	• Why do students benefit from observing models who are similar to themselves? • What concepts and principles from social cognitive theory are especially useful in understanding and helping students with special needs?
THE BIG PICTURE Unifying Ideas in Social Cognitive Theory Comparing the Three Perspectives of Learning	• What central ideas characterize social cognitive theory? • How are cognitive psychology, behaviorism, and social cognitive theory similar? How are they different?

Chapter Glossary

Collective self-efficacy. People's beliefs about their ability to be successful when they work together on a task.

Incentive. A hoped-for, but not certain, consequence of behavior.

Intrinsic motivation. The internal desire to perform a particular task.

Live model. An individual whose behavior is observed "in the flesh."

Mediation training. Training that involves teaching students how to mediate conflicts among classmates by asking opposing sides to express their differing viewpoints and then work together to devise a reasonable resolution.

Observational learning effect. Occurs when an observer acquires a new behavior after watching someone else demonstrate it.

Reciprocal causation. The interdependence of environment, behavior, and personal variables as these three factors influence learning.

Resilient self-efficacy. The belief that one can perform a task successfully after experiencing setbacks; includes the belief that effort and perseverance are essential for success.

Response disinhibition effect. Occurs when an observer displays a previously forbidden or punished behavior more frequently after seeing someone else exhibit that behavior without adverse consequences.

Response facilitation effect. Occurs when an observer displays a previously learned behavior more frequently after seeing someone else being reinforced for that behavior.

Response inhibition effect. Occurs when an observer displays a previously learned behavior less frequently after seeing someone else being punished for that behavior.

Self-efficacy. The belief that one can execute certain behaviors or reach certain goals.

Self-evaluation. The process of evaluating one's own performance or behavior.

Self-imposed contingencies. Contingencies that students provide for themselves; the self-reinforcements and self-punishments that follow various behaviors.

Self-instructions. Instructions that students give themselves as they perform a complex behavior.

Self-monitoring. The process of observing and recording one's own behavior.

Self-regulated behavior. Engaging in self-chosen behaviors that lead to the accomplishment of personally chosen standards and goals.

Self-regulated learning. Regulating one's own cognitive processes to learn successfully; includes goal setting, planning, attention control, use of effective learning strategies, self-monitoring, and self-evaluation.

Self-regulated problem-solving strategy. A strategy that helps students solve their own interpersonal problems.

Self-regulation. The process of setting standards and goals for oneself and engaging in cognitive processes and behaviors that lead to the accomplishment of those standards and goals.

Social cognitive theory. A theoretical perspective in which learning by observing others is the focus of study.

Symbolic model. A real or fictional character portrayed in the media (television, books, etc.) that influences an observer's behavior.

Vicarious punishment. A phenomenon whereby a response decreases in frequency when another (observed) person is punished for that response.

Vicarious reinforcement. A phenomenon whereby a response increases in frequency when another (observed) person is reinforced for that response.

Application Exercise #17: Applying Principles of Social Cognitive Theory

Using social cognitive theory, explain what is happening in each of the following situations.

1. During the first week of his French I class, Mr. Rizzo says, "Repeat after me—*Le crayon rouge est sur la table vert.*" His students are all motivated to do well in French; however, they have trouble repeating the sentence because they can't remember what he said.

2. Max is making a sketch of a sports car. He stops to scrutinize his work and discovers that the front hood is the wrong shape. He erases the front end of his car and draws it again.

3. Erin is working extremely hard in her science class in the hopes that she will get an A from Mr. Richards—someone who has a reputation for being a tough grader.

4. Sylvia is trying to teach Wendy how to do a cartwheel. Sylvia performs several cartwheels in slow motion so that Wendy can see all the steps involved. Then she says, "You can do it, I know you can!" Wendy makes at least 20 unsuccessful attempts and eventually gives up. "I don't think I'll ever be able to do a cartwheel," she says dejectedly.

5. Rhea completes her research paper exactly as Mr. O'Brien has said it should be done. Yet Mr. O'Brien does not give Rhea full credit for the assignment because all the references in her bibliography are more than ten years old. Rhea is angry and frustrated because Mr. O'Brien never mentioned that the bibliography had to include things published within the last ten years.

6. Mickey thinks that if he can get elected as president of the student council, he will have a better shot at getting into a good college.

7. Ms. Wing wants the girls in her high school physical education class to develop better muscle tone. She invites Jim Davidson, a weight trainer at the local conditioning center, to come and demonstrate appropriate use of the school's weight machines. The girls pay little attention to what he is doing, thinking that weight training is mostly for men, not women.

8. Gina notices that a girl who makes the cheerleading squad immediately becomes more "popular" at school. Gina wants to be popular too, so she tries out for cheerleading the following year.

9. Martin frequently inserts inappropriate four-letter words into the comments that he makes in Ms. Zimmerman's class. Jason learned never to say such words in his previous classes, but apparently they're OK in Ms. Zimmerman's room. Jason begins to use them liberally whenever he speaks in class.

10. In Ms. Reese's math class, Melissa quickly gives up on problems she cannot immediately solve. When Ms. Reese expresses her concern, Melissa's response is, "I'm just no good at math, so why even try?"

11. Serena has always been a straight-A student. When she gets her first B *ever* in the second semester of her senior year, she bursts into tears. Her friends don't understand it; after all, Serena has already been accepted at the college of her choice, and a single B certainly won't change that fact.

12. Ms. Smith ridicules Jerry for asking a "stupid" question in class. After this, no one in class has the nerve to ask questions when something is confusing or unclear.

13. Mr. Saber discovers that his students feel much more confident about solving challenging problems when they work in small groups rather than alone.

Answers to Application Exercise #17

1. *Modeling* is unlikely to occur unless four conditions—attention, retention, motor reproduction, and motivation—are all present. In this situation, *retention* is missing: Students can't remember the modeled behavior.

2. *Self-regulation* includes both *self-monitoring* (e.g., looking at the product one has created) and *self-evaluation* (e.g., determining whether the product meets one's standards).

3. Erin is working for an *incentive*—a hoped-for, but not guaranteed, reinforcer for her efforts.

4. Sylvia is *modeling* a cartwheel for Wendy. Wendy's *self-efficacy* is temporarily enhanced by Sylvia's message, but that self-efficacy soon decreases when Wendy's efforts repeatedly result in failure.

5. Here we see the *nonoccurrence of expected reinforcement*— a form of punishment in social cognitive theory.

6. Mickey has an *expectation* that a particular behavior will be reinforced.

7. The girls are unlikely to model the behavior because they do not believe it is *"gender-appropriate" behavior* for females.

8. When Gina sees someone else be reinforced with "popularity," she experiences *vicarious reinforcement* for becoming a cheerleader.

9. The *nonoccurrence of expected punishment* is reinforcing to Jason. Here we see *response disinhibition:* A behavior that has previously been forbidden is being exhibited by a model (Martin) without adverse consequences.

10. People with low *self-efficacy* exert little effort and give up quickly when they experience failure.

11. As people become increasingly self-regulated, they begin to set *standards* for their own behavior and judge themselves unfavorably when they don't meet those standards.

12. When they see their classmate being ridiculed for asking a question, the students experience *vicarious punishment*.

13. The students have *collective self-efficacy:* They believe that they can be successful if they work together.

Application Exercise #18: Identifying Effective Classroom Practices

From the perspective of social cognitive theory, which of the following teaching behaviors are likely to be effective, and which are not? Defend your choices.

1. Mr. Warner tells Brad, "I know you've never wrestled before, but with practice you can become a successful wrestler. Come on, let's see what you're made of."   Mr. Warner pairs Brad with a stronger, more experienced wrestler who consistently pins him to the mat as the two boys practice over the next hour and a half.

2. It is December 20th, the day before school closes for a two-week vacation. Mr. Reagan's junior high school science students are restless, as their minds are on the upcoming holiday season. Nevertheless, Mr. Reagan is already three weeks behind in the schedule he has planned for the school year and believes he must make good use of this last day. In preparation for the day's lesson, he tells his class, "Today I will demonstrate how to use a microscope correctly. You will all be using microscopes in your lab session the first day you get back from vacation."

3. During a unit on tennis, Ms. Sommarstrom sees Marcy execute an especially good serve. "Excellent form on that serve," she tells Marcy in earshot of her classmates.

4. Mr. Tuttle tells his high school students many tales about the things he did as a teenager—driving recklessly on city streets, playing practical jokes on local merchants, drinking heavily, and experimenting with marijuana. "I regret it all," he says. "Looking back, I wish I'd taken my high school education more seriously than I did."

5. Belinda often cracks her knuckles in class, and her classmates find the behavior very annoying. Mr. Chi takes Belinda aside and explains the problem, but she responds, "Oh, Mr. Chi, I don't crack my knuckles *that* much." Because Belinda clearly has little awareness of how frequently she exhibits the distracting behavior, Mr. Chi asks her to record each instance of knuckle cracking on a piece of graph paper for the next five days.

6. As Ms. Etsitty shows her third graders how to write a lowercase cursive *b,* she says the words, "Up, down, around, and out."

7. During a cooperative learning activity, Mr. Sanchez reminds his students, "Remember, you will each be individually tested on the things you are learning as a group, so you should make sure that each and every one of you is learning the material. As an extra bonus, if any group gets an average of 90 percent on the test, all group members will get an additional three percentage points."

8. The day after Halloween, Ms. Levensohn's first graders are all a bit hyperactive. After an exasperating morning, Ms. Levensohn warns them, "If anybody in this room makes so much as a single peep in the next five minutes, the entire class will stay in during recess and work on the math assignment we didn't finish today." Jared immediately burps, and several students around him laugh. Ms. Levensohn thinks that her class might settle down after everyone has had a chance to run around outside for a while, so when the recess bell rings, she tells them to get on their jackets and line up by the outside door.

9. Ms. Struthers wants to promote self-regulation in her second graders, so she asks them to set their own goals regarding the number of spelling words they will each learn every week. Some students are saying that they will learn only one new word each week, even though they are clearly capable of learning many more than that on a weekly basis. Nevertheless, Ms. Struthers allows them to work toward these simple, easily achievable goals as a way of enhancing their self-efficacy about spelling.

10. In her high school literature class, comprised almost entirely of African American students, Ms. Orlando has been assigning classic English and American novels (e.g., Charles Dickens's *A Tale of Two Cities*, John Steinbeck's *The Grapes of Wrath*). She discovers that the students have trouble "getting into" these books: They often begin to read them but rarely finish. When she switches to literature that portrays African Americans (e.g., Zora Neale Hurston's *Their Eyes Were Watching God*, Alice Walker's *The Color Purple*), her students are not only more eager to read but also more inspired by the strong characters they read about.

11. Mr. Masterson is concerned about Sheri, a girl in his sophomore English class who is quite capable of doing challenging academic assignments but prefers to spend all her time attending social functions rather than doing her homework. Mr. Masterson wants to provide a good role model for Sheri, so he develops a homework assignment that students should do in groups of three. He includes Sheri in a group with two extremely conscientious, although relatively unpopular, students. Sheri expresses her dismay that she will be working with "geeks." Nevertheless, Mr. Masterson hopes that Sheri will begin to imitate some of the academic behaviors that the other two group members exhibit.

12. Scott tells Ms. Robinson, "I know I'm not reading my history book each night the way I'm supposed to, but I turn the television on as soon as I get home from school every day, and somehow I can never tear myself away from it except to eat dinner. I feel so guilty not doing my homework, but I don't seem to have any willpower." Ms. Robinson suggests to him, "Your reading assignments are usually only about ten pages apiece. When you get home from school every day, read the first five pages of your assignment *first*, then reward yourself by letting yourself watch TV. After dinner, read the last five pages, and reward yourself again. Think of your favorite television shows as a reward for a job well done. That way, you won't have that guilt trip when you watch them."

Answers to Application Exercise #18

1. Not effective. The effects of *others' messages* on self-efficacy are short-lived unless a student's efforts eventually lead to success. Brad is achieving no success in this situation.

2. Not effective. Mr. Reagan is unlikely to have all four conditions essential for successful *modeling* to occur. At a minimum, he probably won't have his students' *attention*. Furthermore, they may have little *motivation* to learn, and they will probably have difficulty with *retention* of the things he shows them.

3. Effective, provided that public praise is reinforcing for Marcy. Marcy is being directly reinforced, and other students are experiencing *vicarious reinforcement* for such a serve.

4. Not effective. Through the stories of his wild teenage years, Mr. Tuttle—who, as a teacher, can potentially be a very powerful model—is modeling inappropriate behavior.

5. Effective. Mr. Chi is helping Belinda engage in *self-monitoring*—an important step on the road to self-regulated behavior.

6. Effective. By teaching students instructions that they can give themselves as they perform a new task, Ms. Etsitty is facilitating the *retention* component of modeling.

7. Effective. Mr. Sanchez is making the contingency between behavior and consequences clear. Furthermore, he is providing an *incentive* (bonus points) for students to help one another learn.

8. Not effective. The *nonoccurrence of threatened punishment* reinforces the noisy behavior. Ms. Levensohn should identify a consequence she can realistically carry out when undesirable behavior occurs. Furthermore, having students miss recess is probably *not* a good idea at the first grade level (see the discussion of punishment Chapter 9).

9. Not effective. Although encouraging students to set their own goals promotes *self-regulation*, such goals should be challenging ones rather than ones that can be achieved easily. Accomplishing easy tasks does little, if anything, to enhance self-efficacy.

10. Effective. Ms. Orlando is exposing her students to positive role models—in particular, to *symbolic models*. Models are more likely to be effective when students perceive their behaviors to be relevant to their own situations. Presumably, Ms. Orlando's students are perceiving African American models as being more relevant to their own lives than the characters in Dickens's and Steinbeck's novels.

11. Not effective. The other two members of Sheri's group do not possess two important characteristics of effective models: They have little prestige in Sheri's eyes, and they are exhibiting behaviors that Sheri will probably think are irrelevant to her own situation.

12. Effective. Ms. Robinson is encouraging *self-reinforcement* for appropriate behavior. Self-reinforcement is often effective when students are motivated to change their own behavior.

Answers to Selected Margin Notes

- Page 340: *Why is this called the disinhibition effect?*

    A response that was previously inhibited (because it has been punished in the past) is no longer being inhibited.

- Page 340: *How are the response facilitation and response disinhibition effects similar? How are they different?*

    Both involve an increase in behavior. But only the response disinhibition effect involves a *previously forbidden* behavior.

- Page 347: *What factors in Nathan's situation may have contributed to his low self-efficacy for learning French?*

    At least two factors—the failure of his friends and his belief that learning a foreign language is a "girl" thing—are definitely contributing to his low self-efficacy. In addition, Nathan may have had previous failures in learning a language that have led him to conclude that he is "no good" at this kind of thing.

- Page 350: *Students from low-income families typically set low goals for themselves in terms of career aspirations. Can you explain this fact in light of the discussion here?*

    The standards and goals that people adopt for themselves are often modeled after those of the people around them. Students from low-income families are probably exposed to more people with low expectations for themselves than to people with high self-expectations.

- Page 352: *Can you relate steps 3, 4, and 5 to Vygotsky's notions of self-talk and inner speech (Chapter 2)?*

    Vygotsky proposed that children guide themselves through a new task by talking themselves through the task, doing so first out loud (*self-talk*) and eventually in an internal, mental fashion (*inner speech*).

- Page 357: *What theoretical perspective does Becky's comment about "having a conversation with myself, an inner dialogue" remind you of?*

    Becky's inner dialogue should remind you of Vygotsky's notion that social processes (e.g., conversations) evolve into mental processes. It should also remind you of his concepts of *self-talk* and *inner speech*.

Sample Test Questions

Items marked with a "**1**)" on the left-hand side are lower-level questions that assess your general knowledge and understanding of the material. Items marked with a "**2**)" on the left-hand side are higher-level questions that assess your ability to apply what you have learned to a new situation.

Multiple-Choice

1) 1. Three of the following are assumptions that underlie social cognitive theory. Which one is *not* an assumption that social cognitive theorists make?

    a. As people develop, they begin to take control of their own behavior, rather than be influenced solely by environmental events.

    b. People will learn something only if reinforcing or punishing consequences follow their behavior.

    c. People set goals for themselves and strive to achieve their goals.

    d. Learning doesn't always result in an immediate behavior change.

2) 2. Which one of the following is an example of *vicarious reinforcement*?

    a. Abigail sees the flash of a knife blade in Wade's pocket and is angry that Wade would violate school policy by bringing a weapon to class.

    b. Bernice does an excellent job on her science fair project, but she doesn't get feedback about her performance until several days after the science fair is over.

    c. Chad sees Jason cheat on a test and then later get an A on that test, whereas Chad himself receives only a C. Chad starts cheating on exams after that.

    d. Douglas reads as much as he can about life under the sea because he wants to be a marine biologist someday.

2) 3. Janice sees Mark drinking a soft drink in Ms. Murray's class. "Geez, Mark," she whispers to him after class, "taking drinks to class is against school rules. Aren't you afraid that you'll get caught?" Mark replies that he's been bringing drinks to class all year and Ms. Murray has never told him to stop; usually she doesn't even notice what he's doing. Janice begins bringing her own drink to class after that. Which one of the following effects of modeling does this situation illustrate?

    a. Response retention

    b. Response facilitation

    c. Response inhibition

    d. Response disinhibition

2) 4. Which one of the following students is most clearly demonstrating *self-regulated behavior* as social cognitive theorists define the term?

    a. Antonio can type all 26 letters without looking at the keyboard.

    b. Bonnie behaves herself in class so that she can get the free time her teacher has promised for good behavior.

    c. Claude gets around the school building all by himself even though he is blind.

    d. Dana is quite proud of herself when she can finally do a handstand on her own.

1) 5. *Mediation training* involves teaching students to:
   a. Give themselves instructions as they perform difficult tasks
   b. Help their classmates solve interpersonal conflicts
   c. Anticipate the consequences of their behaviors
   d. Remember the behaviors that their teachers demonstrate

1) 6. Which one of the following statements best reflects social cognitive theorists' concept of *reciprocal causation*?
   a. Not only are students' behaviors influenced by environmental circumstances, but those behaviors also change the environment that students later experience.
   b. Students are more likely to engage in a particular behavior when they see others being reinforced for that behavior.
   c. Students can learn only when they are paying attention to the things that happen around them.
   d. Students are more likely to engage in a particular activity when they believe that they can be successful at that activity.

Essay

2) 7. Imagine that, as a high school teacher, you want students to learn how to conduct themselves during a job interview. You decide to *model* the behaviors you want your students to learn (looking the interviewer in the eye, describing one's job-related experience and capabilities with confidence, etc.). Explain how, as you model effective interviewing techniques, you would take into account the four essential processes involved in modeling.

1) 8. Explain what psychologists mean by the term *self-efficacy*. Then describe three different strategies that social cognitive theorists believe can enhance students' self-efficacy about classroom tasks.

Answers to Sample Test Questions

1. b—Reinforcement and punishment have several indirect effects on learning. However, learning can also occur in their absence. (See the last bulleted item in the section "Basic Assumptions of Social Cognitive Theory.")

2. c—Chad's cheating behavior increases as a result of seeing Jason reinforced for cheating. Vicarious reinforcement is described in the section "Vicarious Experiences."

3. d—Janice begins to engage in a previously forbidden behavior when she sees Mark engage in that behavior without adverse consequences. (See the description of response disinhibition in the section "How Modeling Affects Behavior.")

4. d—As social cognitive theorists define the term, self-regulation involves a number of processes, including goal setting, self-monitoring, self-instructions, self-evaluation, and self-imposed contingencies (see the section "Self-Regulated Behavior"). Of the four alternatives, only *d* clearly reflects one of these processes. More specifically, Dana's pride in her accomplishment is an example of a *self-imposed contingency*—in this case, self-reinforcement.

5. b—In mediation training, students learn to help one another resolve interpersonal problems (see the section "Self-Regulated Problem Solving").

6. a—Reciprocal causation is the belief that three factors—environment, behavior, and personal characteristics—all influence one another (see the section "Reciprocal Causation"). Alternative *a* describes the influence that two of these factors—environment and behavior—have on each other. The other three alternatives describe effects that are one-way rather than reciprocal (e.g., alternative *b* describes the effect of an environmental event on behavior).

7. Your response should include one or more strategies for:
   • Capturing and maintaining students' *attention*
   • Helping students remember the behaviors you model (*retention*)
   • Making sure your students are physically capable of the behaviors you model (*motor reproduction*)
   • Promoting students' *motivation* for learning the interviewing skills you are teaching them
   Relevant strategies are presented in the section "Helping Students Learn from Models."

8. Self-efficacy is a person's belief that he or she is capable of executing certain behaviors or reaching certain goals. Social cognitive theorists propose that one's own prior successes, messages from others, others' successes (especially the successes of peers), and successes of one's group can all enhance self-efficacy (see the section "Factors in the Development of Self-Efficacy"). The strategies you describe should reflect at least two of these four factors.

Chapter 11

MOTIVATION AND AFFECT

Chapter Summary

Motivation energizes, directs, and sustains behavior. It influences learning and behavior in several ways: It focuses learners' attention on particular goals, instigates behaviors that help learners achieve those goals, influences what and how learners cognitively process information, determines the specific consequences that are likely to be reinforcing, and ultimately leads to higher achievement.

Intrinsic motivation arises from conditions within students themselves or from factors inherent in the task being performed. Extrinsic motivation is based on factors external to students and unrelated to the task at hand. We are especially likely to see the positive effects of motivation when our students are intrinsically rather than extrinsically motivated. Yet intrinsic motivation to master academic subject matter tends to decline as students move through the grade levels; increasingly, students learn and achieve in the classroom as a means to another end (e.g., getting high grades), rather than as an end in itself.

Psychologists have approached the topic of motivation in four major ways. *Trait theorists* propose that motivation takes the form of relatively enduring personality characteristics, such as achievement motivation, need for affiliation, and need for approval. Many *behaviorists* propose that people behave to obtain reinforcing outcomes, and perhaps also to avoid punishing ones. *Social cognitive theorists'* notions of motivation rest on principles related to goals, expectations, and self-efficacy. *Cognitive theorists*, as you might guess, focus on the cognitive processes that underlie motivation; for example, they suggest that people are often motivated to resolve perceived discrepancies in the environment, and they consider how people's interpretations of events and consequences affect future choices and actions.

All human beings probably share certain basic needs, but psychologists do not always agree about what those needs might be. One early theorist, Abraham Maslow, suggested that people are intrinsically motivated (in his words, they strive for self-actualization) only after more fundamental needs—physiological needs and the needs for safety, love and belonging, and esteem—have already been satisfied. More recently, some theorists have suggested that people have a need to protect their sense of competence; that is, they have a need for *self-worth*. Other theorists have proposed that a *need for relatedness*—to feel socially connected and obtain the love and respect of others—is also universal.

Sometimes learning and cognitive processing are emotionally charged—a phenomenon known as hot cognition. In general, students will learn and remember more when they become involved in classroom subject matter emotionally as well as cognitively.

A small amount of anxiety often facilitates performance, but a great deal of anxiety typically debilitates it, especially when difficult tasks are involved. Many circumstances trigger anxiety, including unfamiliar situations, threats to self-esteem, and, for many students, the transition from elementary to secondary school. In most cases, we should strive to keep our students' anxiety at a low or moderate level—for example, by clearly communicating expectations for performance and ensuring that students have a good chance of succeeding in classroom activities.

Students will differ considerably in the motives they exhibit in the classroom; for example, some may engage in *self-handicapping*, whereby they paradoxically undermine their own performance as a way of protecting their sense of self-worth. To some extent, motivation is related to ethnicity and gender; for example, students from different ethnic groups may satisfy their needs for relatedness in different ways, and girls tend to have a higher need for affiliation than boys. Some students with special needs may also show different motivational patterns than their classmates.

Common Student Beliefs and Misconceptions Related to Chapter Content

Below are three misconceptions that college students often have before studying the topic of human motivation—misconceptions that may interfere with an accurate understanding of what they read. As you read Chapter 11, be on the lookout for evidence that contradicts these common beliefs:

1. Some people think of motivation as residing totally within a learner (i.e., you're either motivated to do something or you're not). In fact, classroom practices have a significant influence on students' motivation.

2. Some people think of *achievement motivation* as a general characteristic that applies to all aspects of a student's life, rather than as a characteristic that is somewhat specific to a particular task or situation.

3. Many people believe that even small amounts of anxiety are detrimental to learning and classroom performance.

CHAPTER OUTLINE	FOCUS QUESTIONS
THE NATURE OF MOTIVATION 　How Motivation Affects Learning and Behavior 　Intrinsic Versus Extrinsic Motivation	• What do psychologists mean by the term *motivation*? What do they mean by *situated motivation*? • What effects does motivation have on learning and behavior? • Distinguish between *extrinsic motivation* and *intrinsic motivation*? Why is it often more desirable to have students who are *in*trinsically motivated?
THEORETICAL PERSPECTIVES OF MOTIVATION 　The Trait Perspective 　The Behaviorist Perspective 　The Social Cognitive Perspective 　The Cognitive Perspective	• Summarize each of the four theoretical perspectives of motivation. • What is *achievement motivation*? How have theorists' conceptualizations of it changed over time?
WHAT BASIC NEEDS DO PEOPLE HAVE? 　Self-Worth 　Relatedness	• What five groups of needs does Maslow's hierarchy include? What implications does Maslow's hierarchy have for classroom practice? • Describe the concept of *self-worth*. How does *self-handicapping* enable some students to protect their sense of self-worth? • Describe the *need for relatedness*. In what various ways might this need be reflected in students' behavior at school? • What behaviors are often seen in students with a high *need for affiliation*? What behaviors are often associated with a high *need for approval*?

CHAPTER OUTLINE	FOCUS QUESTIONS
AFFECT AND ITS EFFECTS Hot Cognition Anxiety	• What is *hot cognition*? How does it affect learning and memory? • What is *anxiety*? How are *state anxiety* and *trait anxiety* different? How are *facilitating anxiety* and *debilitating anxiety* different? What particular effects does debilitating anxiety have? • What are some possible sources of anxiety for students? With these sources in mind, identify several strategies for keeping students' anxiety at a productive level.
ADDRESSING DIVERSITY IN MOTIVATION AND AFFECT Accommodating Students with Special Needs	• What ethnic, gender, and socioeconomic differences might we see in students' motivation? • What motivational characteristics might students with various special needs have? How can teachers accommodate those characteristics?
THE BIG PICTURE Guiding Principles	• What general suggestions does the textbook offer for motivating students in the classroom?

Supplementary Reading

Your instructor may assign Supplementary Reading #4, "Maslow's Hierarchy of Needs," which appears in the final section of this *Study Guide and Reader*.

Chapter Glossary

Achievement motivation. The need for excellence for its own sake, without regard for any external rewards that one's accomplishments might bring.

Affect. The feelings and emotions that an individual brings to bear on a task.

Anxiety. A feeling of uneasiness and apprehension concerning a situation with an uncertain outcome.

Challenge. A situation in which a person believes that he or she can probably succeed with sufficient effort.

Debilitating anxiety. Anxiety that interferes with performance. A high level of anxiety is likely to be debilitating.

Drive. A motivational state in which something necessary for optimal functioning (food, water, etc.) is missing.

Extrinsic motivation. Motivation promoted by factors external to the individual and unrelated to the task being performed.

Facilitating anxiety. Anxiety that enhances performance. Relatively low levels of anxiety are usually facilitating.

Hot cognition. Learning or cognitive processing that is emotionally charged.

Intrinsic motivation. The internal desire to perform a particular task.

Motivation. A state that energizes, directs, and sustains behavior.

Need for affiliation. The tendency to seek out friendly relationships with others.

Need for approval. A desire to gain the approval and acceptance of others.

Need for relatedness. The need to feel socially connected to others, as well as to secure their love and respect.

Self-handicapping. Undermining one's own success, often as a way of protecting one's sense of self-worth when being asked to perform difficult tasks.

Self-worth. Beliefs about one's own general ability to deal effectively with the environment.

Situated motivation. A phenomenon whereby aspects of one's immediate environment enhance one's motivation to learn particular things or behave in particular ways.

State anxiety. A temporary feeling of anxiety elicited by a threatening situation.

Threat. A situation in which people believe that they have little or no chance of success.

Trait anxiety. A pattern of responding with anxiety even in nonthreatening situations.

Trait theory of motivation. A theoretical perspective portraying motivation as involving enduring personality characteristics that people have to a greater or lesser extent.

Here are additional glossary items if your instructor has assigned Supplementary Reading #4:

Deficiency need. In Maslow's hierarchy, a need that results from something a person lacks.

Growth need. In Maslow's hierarchy, a need that serves to enhance a person's growth and development and is never completely satisfied.

Self-actualization. The tendency for human beings to enhance themselves and fulfill their potential—to strive toward becoming everything that they are capable of becoming.

Application Exercise #19: Analyzing Motivational States

Explain each of the following student behaviors using concepts and principles of motivation presented in Chapter 11.

1. At the end of the summer, Herschel has mixed feelings about returning to school. He isn't crazy about having to get up early each morning to catch the bus, but he is eager to reconnect with friends he hasn't seen in three months.

2. Because Ramona loves animals, she has decided to become a veterinarian, and so she takes a lot of biology and chemistry in high school with her long-term plans for vet school in mind.

3. Billy is continually asking his teacher to look at the progress he's making on his Popsicle-stick rendition of Fort Ticonderoga, even though it's clear that he knows what he's doing and doesn't need any guidance.

4. Inez is so up-tight during her oral presentation on sickle-cell anemia that she forgets many of the things she wanted to say about the disease.

5. Harry's class has just begun reading C. S. Lewis's *The Lion, the Witch and the Wardrobe*, and the teacher has asked the students to read the first two chapters by Monday. Harry finds the characters and plot so captivating that he spends most of Saturday reading the book, and he finishes the final chapter on Sunday afternoon.

6. Even though he wants to do well on his history final, Luke waits until late the night before the test to begin studying, and he arrives at class the following morning on a marijuana "high."

7. Tanya enjoys mathematics, but she also knows that she will make her parents happy if she brings home good grades in math.

8. In a unit on developing nations, students in a middle school social studies class feel very sad when they see photographs of children with severe malnutrition. Weeks later, they still remember those children, even though they've forgotten many of the other things they've learned about developing nations.

9. Ginny's family rarely has any food in the house, so she often comes to school hungry in the morning. Whenever she can do so without being seen, she steals food from her classmates' lunchboxes.

10. Monica doesn't enjoy writing very much, but she signs up for a creative writing course because most of her friends will be in the class.

Answers to Application Exercise #19

1. Herschel's desire to see his friends reflects his *need for relatedness*. His desire to sleep later each morning may reflect a *physiological need*.

2. Motivation directs students toward particular *goals*. In this case, Ramona's love of animals leads her to work toward a degree in veterinary medicine.

3. Billy appears to have a high *need for approval*.

4. Inez has *debilitating anxiety*, which interferes with her ability to remember what she's learned about her topic.

5. Harry is showing *intrinsic motivation:* He is reading the book because it gives him pleasure, not because of any external rewards it might bring.

6. Luke appears to be engaging in *self-handicapping:* He's undermining his chances for success as a way of protecting his sense of *self-worth*.

7. Tanya is both *intrinsically* and *extrinsically* motivated to do well in math. The two forms of motivation are not necessarily incompatible.

8. Students are more likely to pay attention to and remember topics that are emotionally charged—a phenomenon known as *hot cognition*.

9. From the perspective of early behaviorists, Ginny is trying to address a *drive*, in this case hunger. From Maslow's perspective, Ginny is addressing her *physiological needs*.

10. Students with a high *need for affiliation* tend to prefer classes that enable them to be with their friends over classes that address their own interests.

<u>Application Exercise #20: Identifying Effective Classroom Practices</u>

Of the teaching strategies described below, which are consistent with principles and guidelines presented in Chapter 11, and which are not? Defend your decisions.

1.   Mr. O'Malley provides a sufficient variety of tasks and activities for his kindergartners so that virtually all students can find an area in which they can be exceptional.

2.   At the high school where Mr. Knobles teaches, classes are scheduled in a "block" format in which each class meets for two hours every other day. Mr. Knobles incorporates at least one activity into each class session that allows students to get up, move around, and release any pent-up energy.

3.   To motivate her students to prepare for an upcoming statewide achievement test, Ms. Murphy tells them, "This test is more important than anything else you'll do this school year. How well students at this school do on the test may affect how much money the state legislature gives to the school for next year. In fact, my teaching job's on the line here."

4.   Mr. Siegler acknowledges each student's birthday, congratulates students with special personal accomplishments during the year, and sends a card or personal note in times of illness or family tragedy.

5.   Mr. Simpson allows an unlimited number of retakes on each of his weekly quizzes so that students won't have any anxiety when they take the quizzes.

6.   Ms. Bunting makes all assignments voluntary in her high school physics class. "I'm hoping you will do them for the sheer joy of learning more about physics," she tells her students.

7.   During a discussion of developing countries in her fifth-grade class, Ms. Bacall explains how in some countries, children as young as nine or ten work long days in factories to support their families. "Sometimes these children must get up at five o'clock in the morning, ride their bicycles an hour or more to work, put in a ten- or twelve-hour day, and then ride their bikes home in the dark. Many of them work in toy factories making toys for children in wealthier countries, but they could never afford to buy such toys themselves. Can you imagine how you might feel if you were one of those children?"

8.   Mr. Endicott teaches ninth-grade science in a small school district where grades 1–8 are taught in four different elementary schools scattered around the district. To help his students better understand how high school will be different from elementary school, he begins the first day of class this way: "Here at the high school, our expectations are far more demanding than they are in the elementary schools. Look at the person sitting to your right. Now look at the person sitting to your left. Chances are that one of the three of you won't pass this course."

9.   Ms. Iwata, a third-grade teacher, gives awards to recognize special contributions or activities that might otherwise go unnoticed—for example, an award for a student who frequently serves as peacemaker on the playground and an award for a student who has helped her classmates improve skills or grades.

10.   Ms. Markstrom has regular and predictable procedures for how materials are handed out and collected and how assignments are to be completed.

Answers to Application Exercise #20

1. Consistent. Mr. O'Malley's strategy should enhance every student's sense of *self-worth*.

2. Consistent. Mr. Knobles is addressing students' *physiological needs*.

3. Not consistent. Ms. Murphy is probably generating *debilitating anxiety* in some (perhaps all) of her students.

4. Consistent. Mr. Siegler is addressing students' *need for relatedness*.

5. Not consistent. For most students, a small amount of anxiety facilitates performance. Students who are a little bit anxious about their performance will achieve at a higher level than students who have no anxiety whatsoever. (As you will discover in Chapter 13, an occasional retake of a classroom assessment may be appropriate in a mastery learning approach to instruction. Furthermore, as you will discover when you read Chapter 16, students should have some leeway to make mistakes without penalty. Nevertheless, *unlimited* retakes serve little purpose.)

6. Not consistent. Ms. Bunting is assuming that her students are intrinsically motivated to learn physics. While this may be true for some of her students, in general intrinsic motivation to learn school subject matter declines as students get older. Some of her students will probably do the assignments—and therefore master physics—only if those assignments are tied to other outcomes, such as grades.

7. Consistent. By evoking students' feelings about the subject matter, the teacher is promoting *hot cognition*—something that should help them remember the subject matter better.

8. Not consistent. Many students already find the transition from elementary to secondary school to be a source of considerable anxiety. Mr. Endicott's statement will almost certainly lead to *debilitating anxiety*.

9. Consistent. Ms. Iwata is enhancing students' sense of *self-worth*. Her awards may be especially beneficial for students who have trouble achieving success in more academic arenas.

10. Consistent. Ms. Markstrom is trying to keep students' anxiety levels down by communicating clear expectations for students' performance.

<u>Answers to Selected Margin Notes</u>

- Page 368: *How is situated motivation similar to situated cognition?*
  Both situated motivation and situated cognition occur only in a particular environmental context.

- Page 369: *Can you find each of these effects in the case study of Anya?*
  Each effect is reflected in the case study as follows:
  - <u>Goal-directed behavior</u>: Anya wants to become a professional artist.
  - <u>Effort and energy</u>: Anya draws at every available opportunity.
  - <u>Initiation and persistence</u>: At her own initiative, Anya adds drawings to notebooks, essays, and spelling quizzes, and she buries herself in each new drawing assignment.
  - <u>Cognitive processing</u>: Anya pays close attention in art class.
  - <u>Reinforcement</u>: Drawing is an intrinsically reinforcing activity for Anya.
  - <u>Improved performance</u>: Her teacher comments on her improvement over the course of the school year.

Sample Test Questions

Items marked with a "**1**)" on the left-hand side are lower-level questions that assess your general knowledge and understanding of the material. Items marked with a "**2**)" on the left-hand side are higher-level questions that assess your ability to apply what you have learned to a new situation.

Multiple-Choice

1) 1. Three of the following describe ways in which motivation often affects learning and behavior. Which one is *not* true about motivation's effects?

    a. Motivated students are more energetic.

    b. Motivated students are more likely to engage in meaningful learning.

    c. Highly motivated students are more likely to be persistent in the face of obstacles.

    d. Motivated students often work hard without any intrinsic or extrinsic reinforcers.

2) 2. Which one of the following is the clearest example of *self-handicapping*?

    a. Aimee prides herself on being the fastest runner on the middle school cross-country team.

    b. Brad can't wait to get home from school because he knows his mother has just rented one of his favorite video games.

    c. Carol really wants a part in the school musical, but the public audition makes her self-conscious, so she intentionally screws it up.

    d. David would really like to be a pilot, but he suspects that the Air Force Academy would never accept him because of his poor eyesight.

2) 3. Rita plans to visit Ecuador some day because that's where her cousins live. When she gets to junior high school, she finally has a chance to take Spanish—a language she will need when she travels to South America. But she decides to enroll in French instead so that she can be with her best friend. From this information, we can guess that Rita has a high need for:

    a. Affiliation

    b. Safety

    c. Self-actualization

    d. Approval

2) 4. Given what we know about the effects of anxiety on learning and performance, which one of the following boys is likely to learn most effectively from his biology teacher's lecture on insects and arachnids?

    a. Albert is very nervous because he has to give an oral report at the end of the class period.

    b. Ben would like to do well in this class, but it won't be the end of the world if he doesn't.

    c. Clark doesn't really care how he does in the class; he's a senior and has already been accepted by the college of his choice.

    d. Dwight is very worried that his teacher will give a pop quiz at the end of class, and he didn't do the reading last night.

Essay

1) 5. Psychologists often make a distinction between *intrinsic motivation* and *extrinsic motivation*.

    a. Describe the nature of these two forms of motivation, and give a concrete example of each one in action.

    b. Explain why intrinsic motivation is more desirable in the classroom.

1) 6. Explain what theorists mean by the *need for relatedness*, and describe at least three different ways in which we might see this need reflected in students' behavior.

Answers to Sample Test Questions

1. d—Motivation determines the kinds of consequences that students find reinforcing. Often, their efforts will be reinforced intrinsically rather than extrinsically, but they are unlikely to work for very long when they get no benefits whatsoever.

2. c—Carol is behaving in a way that undermines her chances of success. By not taking the audition seriously, she has a ready-made excuse for failing to get a part in the musical and so can protect her sense of self-worth.

3. a—Rita wants to be with her best friend as often as possible—behavior indicative of a strong need for affiliation. (See the discussion of the need for affiliation in the section "Individual Differences in the Need for Relatedness.")

4. b—A little anxiety is often facilitating, but a great deal is likely to be debilitating. Albert and Dwight appear to be overly anxious; Clark appears to have no anxiety at all. (See "How Anxiety Affects Classroom Performance.")

5. a. Intrinsic motivation is an internal desire to perform a particular task; it is due to factors within the individual or inherent in the task being performed. Extrinsic motivation is promoted by factors external to the individual and unrelated to the task being performed. Your response should include a concrete example of each of these concepts. (To illustrate, interest in a topic is a form of intrinsic motivation, and working on an assignment for the good grade one might receive is a form of extrinsic motivation.)
    b. Students are most likely to show the beneficial effects of motivation (persistence, effective cognitive processing, etc.) when they are intrinsically motivated to engage in classroom activities.

6. The need for relatedness is a fundamental need to feel socially connected and to secure the love and respect of others. It might show up in students' behavior in any of the following ways (your response should include at least three of the following behaviors or similar ones):
    *   Placing higher priority on social interaction than on getting schoolwork done
    *   Working to create a favorable impression for others (e.g., by dressing fashionably or acting "cool")
    *   Succumbing to peer pressure (e.g., "following the crowd")
    *   Showing concern for others' welfare
    *   Helping others with schoolwork
    *   Spending a lot of time with friends

Chapter 12

COGNITIVE FACTORS IN MOTIVATION

Chapter Summary

Just as motivation affects cognitive processes, so, too, do cognitive processes affect motivation. Such processes are the focus of this chapter. As teachers, we cannot realistically address either learning or motivation in isolation from the other.

Some motivation theorists believe that students are most likely to be intrinsically motivated when two conditions exist: (1) when they have high *self-efficacy* regarding their ability to succeed at classroom tasks, and (2) when they have a sense of *self-determination*—a sense that they have some control over the course that their lives will take. As teachers, we can promote students' self-efficacy by giving them competence-promoting feedback, helping them master challenging tasks, and defining success in terms of long-term improvement. We can promote a greater sense of self-determination by presenting rules and evaluations in an informational rather than controlling fashion, minimizing reliance on extrinsic reinforcers, and occasionally allowing students to make choices and be involved in classroom decision making.

Other theorists have proposed that motivation for performing a particular task depends on two subjective variables. First, students must have an expectation, or *expectancy*, that they will be successful; their expectations for success will depend not only on their own skill levels but also on such outside factors as the quality of instruction and the availability of resources and support. Second, students must *value* the task: They must believe that there are direct or indirect benefits to performing it—perhaps achieving a desired goal, looking "cool," or simply having fun. In some instances, growing children may begin to adopt the values of people around them—a phenomenon known as *internalized motivation*.

One form of intrinsic motivation is *interest*, which can take either of two forms. *Situational interest* is temporary and evoked by something in the immediate environment. *Personal interest* is more stable and resides within the individual. As teachers, we can often motivate students to study classroom subject matter by arousing curiosity and stimulating situational interest, as well as by capitalizing on individual personal interests.

Children and adolescents often have a wide variety of goals. Students who have *mastery goals* want to acquire additional knowledge or skills. Students who have *performance goals* either want to look competent in the eyes of others (a *performance-approach goal*) or else not to look incompetent (a *performance-avoidance goal*). The three goals are not necessarily mutually exclusive (a student might have two, or even all three), but generally speaking, students with mastery goals are more likely to recognize that competence comes only through effort and practice, choose activities that maximize their opportunities for learning, and use their errors constructively to improve future performance. Other common goals include *work-avoidance goals* (i.e., getting by with minimal effort), *social goals* (i.e., gaining and maintaining relationships with others), and career goals. Sometimes students are able to achieve two or more goals simultaneously; at other times, achieving one goal prevents them from satisfying others.

176

Attributions are the explanations students give for why they succeed or fail at tasks. Students may attribute events to causes that are (a) internal or external to themselves, (b) stable or unstable, and (c) controllable or uncontrollable. Attributions affect many aspects of behavior and cognition, including students' expectations for future success, expenditure of effort, help-seeking behavior, choice of activities, and, ultimately, classroom performance. As teachers, we can give students reasons for optimism about their future chances of success by attributing both their successes and their failures to factors they can control, including effort (if it has, in fact, influenced the outcome) and cognitive strategies. We should also attribute students' successes (but not failures) to a stable ability on which they can depend. Ultimately, we can promote an *I can do it* attitude (a *mastery orientation*) by facilitating students' success on classroom tasks, and especially on challenging ones.

Teachers often draw conclusions about their students early in the school year. Sometimes these conclusions are warranted, sometimes not. Furthermore, teacher's explanations (attributions) for students' successes and failures (e.g., whether they chalk up students' academic performance to intelligence, effort, or some other factor) influence their expectations for students' future performance. Premature and unwarranted expectations for students tend to be self-perpetuating; they influence teachers' behaviors toward students and ultimately also influence students' self-perceptions and academic achievement. We must remember that students' current deficiencies are not necessarily indicative of long-term difficulty, and we must be careful that we don't give inequitable treatment based on low expectations for performance. As teachers, we must use our knowledge of individual and group differences to help all of our students, including those with special educational needs, to achieve their maximum potential.

Common Student Beliefs and Misconceptions Related to Chapter Content

Below are two beliefs that college students sometimes have that may interfere with an accurate understanding of what they read about cognitive factors in motivation:

1. Some students believe that extrinsic reinforcers are *always* a good idea, when in some situations such reinforcers can actually *undermine* motivation.

2. Some students believe that focusing high school students' attention on grades and other criteria for college admissions is the best motivator. In fact, although high school students are often concerned about such issues, they will often learn more effectively if their primary goal is to master classroom subject matter rather than to get good grades.

CHAPTER OUTLINE	FOCUS QUESTIONS
THE INTERPLAY OF COGNITION AND MOTIVATION	• Using the opening case study, give two examples of how cognition affects motivation.

SELF-PERCEPTIONS AND INTRINSIC MOTIVATION
    Self-Efficacy
    Self-Determination
	• What two conditions do many theorists believe are essential for intrinsic motivation? What teaching strategies can promote each of these conditions?

EXPECTANCIES AND VALUES
    Internalizing the Values of Others
    Fostering Expectancies and Values in the Classroom
	• What factors affect *expectancy* for success?
	
	• Under what circumstances are students likely to *value* classroom topics? When are they *un*likely to value such topics?
	
	• Describe the process through which students might increasingly adopt the values of others.

INTEREST
    Situational Versus Personal Interest
    Promoting Interest in Classroom Subject Matter
	• Distinguish between *situational interest* and *personal interest*. What conditions are likely to promote each one?
	
	• Identify at least three different strategies you might use to generate interest in the subject(s) you expect to be teaching.

GOALS
    Mastery and Performance Goals
    Work-Avoidance Goals
    Social Goals
    Career Goals
    Capitalizing on Students' Goals
	• How are *mastery goals, performance-approach goals*, and *performance-avoidance goals* different? What characteristics and behaviors are associated with each type of goal?
	
	• What is a *work-avoidance goal*? How might it be reflected in students' behavior?
	
	• What forms might a *social goal* take?
	
	• What factors affect students' career goals?
	
	• How can teachers capitalize on students' goals in the classroom?

CHAPTER OUTLINE	FOCUS QUESTIONS
ATTRIBUTIONS: PERCEIVED CAUSES OF SUCCESS AND FAILURE Dimensions Underlying Students' Attributions How Attributions Influence Affect, Cognition, and Behavior Developmental Trends in Attributions Factors Influencing the Development of Attributions Mastery Orientation Versus Learned Helplessness	• What is an *attribution*? Along what dimensions do students' attributions differ? • To what factors do students tend to attribute their successes, and why? To what factors do they tend to attribute their failures, and why? • In what ways do attributions affect behavior and cognition? What specific effects do different kinds of attributions have? • How do students' attributions change with age? Distinguish between an *entity view* and an *incremental view* of intelligence. • What factors influence the development of attributions? What implications do these factors have for classroom practice? • What is a *mastery orientation*? What is *learned helplessness*? What characteristics are associated with each of these? What strategies can teachers use to foster a mastery orientation?
TEACHER EXPECTATIONS AND ATTRIBUTIONS How Expectations and Attributions Affect Classroom Performance Forming Productive Expectations and Attributions for Student Performance	• What kinds of explanations (attributions) do teachers often form for students' current classroom performance? How do such attributions affect teachers expectations for students' *future* performance? How do these attributions and expectations in turn affect teachers' and students' behaviors? • How can teachers guard against forming unnecessarily low expectations for students? • Under what circumstances do attributions to effort backfire? To what should a teacher attribute students' failures when students are already exerting considerable effort?

CHAPTER OUTLINE	FOCUS QUESTIONS
CONSIDERING DIVERSITY IN THE COGNITIVE ASPECTS OF MOTIVATION Ethnic Differences Gender Differences Socioeconomic Differences Accommodating Students with Special Needs	• What differences in students' motivation are associated with age? with ethnicity? with gender? with socioeconomic status? with special educational needs? What implications do such differences have for classroom practice?
THE BIG PICTURE General Principles of Motivation Revisiting the Four Theoretical Perspectives	• What general principles emerge from the discussion of motivation in Chapters 11 and 12? • Describe some ways in which each perspective of motivation identified in Chapter 11—trait, behaviorist, social cognitive, and cognitive— has entered into the discussion of motivation in Chapters 11 and 12.

Chapter Glossary

Attribution. An internally constructed causal explanation for one's success or failure.

Attribution theory. A theoretical perspective that focuses on people's attributions concerning the causes of events that befall them, as well as on the behaviors that result from such attributions.

Core goal. A long-term goal that drives much of what a person does.

Entity view of intelligence. A belief that intelligence is a "thing" that is relatively permanent and unchangeable.

Expectancy. In motivation theory, the belief that one will be successful in accomplishing a task or achieving a goal.

Incremental view of intelligence. The belief that intelligence can and does improve with effort and practice.

Interest. A feeling that a topic is intriguing or enticing.

Internalized motivation. The adoption of behaviors that others value, without regard for the external consequences of such behaviors.

Learned helplessness. A general belief that one is incapable of accomplishing tasks and has little or no control of the environment.

Learned industriousness. The recognition that one can succeed at some tasks only with effort, persistence, and well-chosen strategies.

Mastery goal. A desire to acquire additional knowledge or master new skills.

Mastery orientation. A general belief that one is capable of accomplishing challenging tasks.

Performance-approach goal. A desire to look good and receive favorable judgments from others.

Performance-avoidance goal. A desire not to look bad and receive unfavorable judgments from others.

Performance goal. A desire either to look good and receive favorable judgments from others, or else *not* to look bad and receive unfavorable judgments.

Personal interest. A long-term, relatively stable interest in a particular topic or activity.

Self-determination. A sense that one has some choice and control regarding the future course of one's life.

Self-efficacy. The belief that one is capable of executing certain behaviors or reaching certain goals.

Self-fulfilling prophecy. A situation in which one's expectations for an outcome either directly or indirectly lead to the expected result.

Situational interest. Interest evoked temporarily by something in the environment.

Work-avoidance goal. A desire to avoid having to perform classroom tasks or to complete them with only minimal effort.

<u>Application Exercise #21: Promoting Intrinsic Motivation</u>

Of the teaching strategies described below, which are likely to promote *intrinsic* motivation to learn or perform, and which are not? Defend your decisions.

1. Ms. McFalls looks at Jake's watercolor painting and tells him, "You've composed a well-balanced painting, and you have a fine eye for color. But it looks to me as if the different colors are bleeding together more than you want them to. Let me show you a strategy for keeping the bleeding to a minimum."

2. Mr. Welch tells his students, "Let's see which one of you can run fastest."

3. In a unit on percussion, Mr. Wyatt lets his second graders experiment with several different percussion instruments.

4. Mr. Chandler tells his students, "I'll give you ten minutes of free time at the end of the day if you complete your seatwork assignments before lunch."

5. Ms. Jaworski reminds her fourth graders how proud their parents will be if they bring home good report cards.

6. Mr. Scudder shows Joel how to do a lay-up shot in basketball. As Joel practices the shot, he finds that he gets more baskets than he had previously.

7. Ms. Ramirez has her high school students set their own deadlines for turning in the five small papers due during the semester, with the stipulation that they set the five deadlines at least one week apart from one another.

8. As her second graders line up to go to lunch, Ms. Woerner reminds them, "Remember, I shouldn't hear any of you talking on the way to the cafeteria."

9. Ms. Kauffman finds the colonial period of American history absolutely fascinating; her enthusiasm about this period is obvious to her students as she describes the people, places, and events of the times.

10. In a unit on vertebrates, Mr. Koropp has students each research a particular mammal, reptile, or amphibian of their own choosing until they become "experts" on that animal. He then has them teach whatever they've learned to several other students in small-group settings.

Answers to Application Exercise #21

1. Likely. Ms. McFalls is giving competence-promoting feedback, which should enhance self-efficacy.

2. Not likely. Mr. Welch is encouraging his students to compare themselves with others, rather than to focus on their own improvement.

3. Likely. One way to promote interest in school subject matter is to get students actively involved.

4. Not likely. Extrinsic reinforcement promotes extrinsic motivation rather than intrinsic motivation, particularly if students perceive it as a form of behavior control.

5. Not likely. Ms. Jaworski is focusing students' attention on a performance goal (looking good to others), rather than on a mastery goal. The focus is on external rather than internal consequences.

6. Likely. Success enhances self-efficacy, and self-efficacy enhances intrinsic motivation.

7. Likely. By giving students control over an aspect of classroom life, Mr. Ramirez is promoting a sense of self-determination, which should enhance intrinsic motivation.

8. Not likely. Ms. Woerner is presenting the instruction in a controlling, rather than informational, manner. This strategy may promote extrinsic motivation, but it won't promote intrinsic motivation.

9. Likely. One way teachers can promote interest (and hence intrinsic motivation) is to model their own interest in and enthusiasm for the subject matter.

10. Likely. Choices promote self-determination, and an opportunity to teach others what one has learned promotes interest.

Application Exercise #22: Characterizing Attributions

Below are statements that convey students' explanations for their own performance (items 1–4) or teachers' explanations for students' performance (items 5–9). Determine whether each statement reflects (a) an *internal* or *external* locus, (b) *stability* or *instability*, and (c) *controllability* or *uncontrollability*. For the last five (teacher) statements, focus on what the statement implies about the teacher's beliefs about locus, stability, and controllability for the *student*, not for the teacher.

1.   "That test was really picky and unfair!"

2.   "I know I can do this right eventually if I just keep working at it."

3.   "I've never been able to carry a tune. Must be in the genes: My sister can't carry one either."

4.   "Oh, no! Mr. Burns has scheduled my oral report for Friday the 13th, the most unlucky day of the year. I'm doomed!"

5.   "I think we should have Jason evaluated by the school psychologist. His reading is so poor that I think he may have a learning disability."

6.   "It's no wonder that Eric behaves as badly as he does. Look at the family he comes from!"

7.   "I don't know why I even bother coming to school every day. These kids aren't motivated to do *anything*!"

8.   "Concheta is an incredibly talented musician. I wouldn't be surprised if she won a Grammy someday."

9.   "I know you can do this if you just try a little harder."

<u>Answers to Application Exercise #22</u>

1. External, unstable (future tests might be better), uncontrollable

2. Internal, unstable, controllable

3. Internal, stable, uncontrollable

4. External, unstable (the bad luck is limited to a single day), uncontrollable

5. Internal, stable, uncontrollable

6. External, stable, uncontrollable

7. Internal, probably unstable (although this would depend on the teacher's beliefs about the stability of the students' motivation), controllable

8. Internal, stable, probably uncontrollable (although this would depend on whether the teacher things of talent as something that is the result of heredity or lots of practice)

9. Internal, unstable, controllable

Application Exercise #23: Identifying Effective Classroom Practices

Of the teaching strategies described below, which are consistent with guidelines presented in Chapter 12 for promoting students' motivation (either intrinsic or extrinsic), and which are not? Defend your decisions.

1. Ms. Proctor announces, "Vinnie's essay was by far the best essay in the class."

2. Mr. Murphy says, "The next lesson is not especially interesting, but it's important for you to learn. Let's see if we can all struggle through it together."

3. A mathematics teacher tells students, "Mathematics is important for many careers, including science, accounting, computer programming, business, nursing, construction, and sales."

4. An art teacher tells his students, "Here are the criteria I will be applying when I grade the sculptures you are working on now. These criteria are the kind that art associations often recommend for evaluating the work of professional artists."

5. On Monday, the coach of a cross-country team tells her students, "Each day this week we'll run the same five-mile course we ran last Friday. Try to cut down your running time a little bit each day. See if you can cut sixty seconds off last Friday's time by the end of the week."

6. Peggy has spent several hours each night working on assignments for her chemistry class, but she still doesn't understand the material. "Maybe you just need to try a little harder, Peggy," her teacher suggests.

7. Ms. Smith says, "I know you don't want to learn this stuff, but it's important to know."

8. David is frustrated that he is having more difficulty learning to read than most of his classmates. His teacher reminds him, "Many students have trouble learning to read at first, but with practice it gets easier and easier. Let's look at some of the books you were reading last September. See how simple they are compared to what you are reading now?"

9. Mr. Jakes likes to keep students challenged all day long. As soon as it's clear to him that they have mastered one task, he introduces a more difficult one.

10. In a unit on softball, Ms. Ralston tells Tim, "When you hit the ball, it always seems to go too far to the right, so it becomes a foul ball rather than a base hit. I think I can explain why it's always going in that direction."

11. When José attains the status of "first chair" in the trumpet section, his music teacher tells him, "You're a good musician, José. You seem to have some natural musical talent, and you have obviously been practicing very hard."

12. In his high school French class, Mr. Lord has students work in small groups to write and perform plays spoken entirely in French. Each group must base its play on a well-known movie, such as *Titanic*, *Casablanca*, or *Gone with the Wind*.

13. Ms. Bell tells her class, "In my classroom, I expect students to do their own work without conferring with others. What's most important in this world is what you can do *on your own*, not what you can do with the help of others."

Answers to Application Exercise #23

1. Not consistent. For one thing, teachers should keep a student's successes private and confidential unless they have the student's permission to do otherwise. Second, teachers should keep competition among students to a minimum. By telling the class that Vinnie has done better than everyone else, this teacher is creating a competitive atmosphere.

2. Not consistent. Teachers are more likely to motivate students when they model interest in the subject matter.

3. Consistent. One effective motivational strategy is to relate school subject matter to students' future needs.

4. Consistent. The teacher is making his expectations for student performance clear. Furthermore, he is explaining why his criteria are important ones to use. (See the discussion of *internalized motivation*.)

5. Consistent. The coach is encouraging students to strive for challenging yet achievable goals. She is also promoting self-comparison rather than comparison with others.

6. Not consistent. Attributing failure to insufficient effort is effective only when a student clearly *hasn't* exerted much effort. Peggy has already been trying very hard to succeed in chemistry.

7. Not consistent. Teachers should communicate their belief that students want to learn school subject matter.

8. Consistent. The teacher is defining success in terms of the progress David has made. She is also defining it as eventual rather than immediate mastery.

9. Not consistent. Ideally, challenging tasks should be balanced with easier ones. This way, students' occasional mistakes occur within the context of an overall pattern of success.

10. Consistent. The teacher is evaluating Tim's performance in a way that will help him improve.

11. Consistent. The teacher is attributing José's success to both high ability and a lot of effort.

12. Consistent. Mr. Lord is introducing variety, novelty, and make-believe into a classroom activity; all of these qualities promote interest in classroom subject matter.

13. Not consistent. From a motivational standpoint, Ms. Bell is not allowing students to address their social goals. (In addition, she seems unaware of the many benefits of group work and peer discussions; for example, see Chapters 7 and 13.)

Answers to Selected Margin Notes

- Page 404: *In which of these goal(s) do you see intrinsic motivation? In which do you see extrinsic motivation?*

   Mastery goals are a form of intrinsic motivation. Performance-approach and performance-avoidance goals reflect extrinsic motivation.

- Page 413: *How might learned industriousness be related to students' epistemological beliefs?*

   Students who believe that learning is a relatively rapid process give up quickly when they have to struggle to understand classroom material (see the description of epistemological beliefs in Chapter 8).

Sample Test Questions

Items marked with a "1)" on the left-hand side are lower-level questions that assess your general knowledge and understanding of the material. Items marked with a "2)" on the left-hand side are higher-level questions that assess your ability to apply what you have learned to a new situation.

Multiple-Choice

1)   1. According to motivation theorists, three of the following are significant factors in a student's *expectancy* for success in a particular activity. Which one is *not*?
   a. The teacher doesn't seem to have much expertise related to the activity.
   b. Performing the activity has direct or indirect benefits for the student.
   c. The activity is much more difficult than activities the student has previously performed successfully.
   d. Several "how-to" books about the activity are available on a nearby shelf.

2)   2. Which one of the following illustrates *situational interest*?
   a. Richard can't get his mind off the "really neat surprise" his teacher has promised for the end of the day.
   b. Ellen has a large collection of country-western music.
   c. Rodney reads everything he can about aerodynamics and hopes to become a designer of large aircraft when he grows up.
   d. Paula has always been intrigued by stories of ancient Egypt. She is especially fascinated with the Egyptians' method of mummifying their dead and has a couple of museum booklets she has purchased about mummification procedures.

2)   3. Which one of these students clearly has a *mastery goal* rather than a performance goal?
   a. Amanda wants to keep her 4.0 average so that she can get an academic scholarship at a good college.
   b. Barney knows how proud his parents will be if he is accepted into the National Honor Society.
   c. Candace is fascinated by the chapter about Ellis Island in her history book, because her grandparents were immigrants in the 1930s.
   d. Dave is hoping he'll play exceptionally well in tonight's basketball game so that he can get the admiration of a girl he has a crush on.

2)   4. Sharon studied very hard for a physics test but has gotten a D– on the test. Her teacher tells her that she probably would have done better if she'd just studied more. Given what we know from attribution theory, we can guess that Sharon will:
   a. Attribute her failure to a lack of effort
   b. Begin to use more effective study strategies
   c. Believe that performance on physics tests is all a matter of luck, so that she might do better next time even if she doesn't study
   d. Conclude that she doesn't have the ability to do well in physics

Essay

1) 5. Explain *self-determination* and its effects on motivation. Then describe three strategies you might use to enhance students' sense of self-determination.

2) 6. Explain each of the following student behaviors using *attribution theory*.

   a. Edie gets a low score on a history test and is angry at her teacher for writing such "unfair" questions. She overlooks the fact that most of her classmates have done quite well on the test.

   b. Wilbur thinks of himself as being good at math. In fact, he notes, high math ability runs in the family: His father is an accountant and his mother is a statistician. So he is confident that he will do well in the accelerated calculus course he is taking next year.

Answers to Sample Test Questions

1. b—Perception of an activity's benefits affect *value* rather than expectancy. Quality of instruction (*a*), difficulty of task (*c*), and availability of resources (*d*) all affect expectancy. (See the section "Expectancies and Values.")

2. a—Situational interest is provoked by something in the immediate environment. The other three alternatives reflect longer-term *personal interests*.

3. c—Candace's fascination with Ellis Island reflects her desire to acquire additional knowledge about the topic. The other three students are striving to look good and receive favorable judgments from others; in other words, they are striving for performance goals. (See the section "Mastery and Performance Goals.")

4. d—When students fail at a task at which they have expended a great deal of effort and are then told that they didn't try hard enough, they are apt to conclude that they don't have the ability to be successful at the task. (See the discussion following the "Carberry and Seville #2" exercise in the section "Forming Productive Expectations and Attributions for Student Performance.")

5. Students who have a sense of self-determination believe that they have some control over the course that their lives will take. Some motivation theorists believe that a sense of self-determination is an important factor (perhaps an essential one) affecting intrinsic motivation. The book offers the following strategies for fostering a sense of self-determination (your response should include at least three of them or justifiable alternatives):
   • Present rules and instructions in an informational rather than controlling manner.
   • Give students the chance to make choices.
   • Allow some autonomy in organized extracurricular activities.
   • Evaluate performance in a noncontrolling fashion.
   • Minimize reliance on extrinsic reinforcers.
   • Help students keep externally imposed constraints in proper perspective.

6. a. Students have a tendency to attribute their failures to such external causes as luck or the behavior of others. (See the section "Dimensions Underlying Students' Attributions.")
   b. When students attribute their success on a task to a stable factor such as high ability, they will anticipate continued success at that task. (See "How Attributions Influence Affect, Cognition, and Behavior.")

Chapter 13

INSTRUCTIONAL STRATEGIES

Chapter Summary

Effective teachers engage in considerable advance planning, and they continually evaluate and modify their plans as the school year progresses. They identify the goals (*instructional objectives*) that they would like their students to accomplish, conduct *task analyses* to break complex tasks into smaller and simpler components, and develop *lesson plans* that spell out activities they will use on a daily basis.

Some forms of instruction are *expository* in nature; that is, they present (expose) the information in essentially the same form that students are expected to learn it. *Lectures, textbooks,* and other explanatory materials are more effective when we apply basic principles of cognitive psychology—for example, when we show students how new material relates to their prior knowledge and when we help them encode ideas in multiple ways. *Mastery learning, direct instruction,* and *computer-based instruction* all provide structured contexts in which students learn and practice new information and skills and receive frequent feedback about how they are doing. The *Internet* provides a means for students to access information available from government offices, public institutions, private associations, and many other sources worldwide.

Hands-on approaches allow students to experience and practice applying classroom subject matter firsthand. In *discovery learning,* students develop an understanding of a particular topic by interacting with their physical or social environment; it is more likely to be successful when we provide a structure that nudges students toward desired discoveries and when students have the necessary prior knowledge and guidance for appropriately interpreting those discoveries. *In-class activities* can take a variety of forms—for example, completing drill-and-practice worksheets, writing short stories, or playing musical instruments—that vary considerably in purpose, scope, and the extent to which lower-level or higher-level skills are required. *Authentic activities* and *computer simulations* offer experiences similar to real-world tasks, while *computer tool applications* provide assistance with complex undertakings. *Homework* is useful for giving students practice with familiar material, introducing them to new yet simple topics, or encouraging application of classroom subject matter to situations and problems in students' lives outside of school.

Interactive and collaborative approaches use teacher-student and student-student interactions to foster greater understanding of academic topics and are often especially effective in fostering elaboration and other higher-level thinking skills. *Teacher questions* provide a means for assessing students' existing understandings and promoting more sophisticated ones. *Class discussions* and *technology-based discussions* provide arenas in which students can encounter multiple perspectives on complex or controversial topics. *Reciprocal teaching* encourages more sophisticated metacognition and study skills by modeling and providing practice in summarizing, questioning, clarifying, and predicting. In *cooperative learning,* students are rewarded for helping one another accomplish assigned tasks but are also individually accountable for achieving instructional objectives. *Peer tutoring* helps both the tutor and the student being tutored gain a better understanding of classroom subject matter. Both cooperative learning and peer tutoring are often more effective when students have a procedure or structure to follow.

Different instructional strategies are appropriate not only for different objectives but also for different students. Interactive and cooperative instructional strategies may be especially effective for females, as well as for students whose cultural backgrounds encourage cooperation rather than competition. Interactive strategies may also be invaluable in facilitating the cognitive and social development of students with special educational needs.

There is no single "best" instructional strategy. Ultimately, we must choose our strategies on the basis of our instructional objectives, the specific topics we are teaching, and the unique characteristics of the students in our classrooms.

Common Student Beliefs and Misconceptions Related to Chapter Content

Below are several misconceptions that future teachers often have about instruction. As you read Chapter 13, be on the lookout for evidence that contradicts these common beliefs:

1. Many future teachers think of planning, instruction, classroom management, and assessment as relatively separate aspects of teaching, rather than as the interdependent activities they truly are.

2. Some people think that there must be a single "best" approach to instruction. In reality, different instructional strategies are appropriate in different situations.

3. Some people believe that lecturing is rarely an effective teaching strategy. Others believe that one lecture is as good as another—that students can learn equally well regardless of how information is presented.

4. Some people have had bad experiences with cooperative learning and so are skeptical about its effectiveness.

5. Many people think that when one student tutors another, only the student being tutored benefits from the session.

CHAPTER OUTLINE	FOCUS QUESTIONS
OVERVIEW OF INSTRUCTIONAL STRATEGIES	• Distinguish between *teacher-directed* and *student-directed* instruction.

PLANNING FOR INSTRUCTION
   Identifying the Goals of Instruction
   Conducting a Task Analysis
   Developing a Lesson Plan
	• What are the advantages of instructional objectives from a teacher's perspective? What are the advantages from a student's perspective?
	
	• How are *standards* and *taxonomies* helpful in developing objectives? What kinds of behaviors are included in the cognitive, psychomotor, and affective domains?
	
	• What guidelines should teachers keep in mind as they develop instructional objectives?
	
	• In what situations are *short-term objectives* appropriate? When are *long-term objectives* appropriate?
	
	• What are the advantages of a *task analysis*? In your own words, describe behavioral analysis, subject matter analysis, and information processing analysis.
	
	• What components does a lesson plan typically have?

EXPOSITORY APPROACHES
   Lectures and Textbooks
   Mastery Learning
   Direct Instruction
   Computer-Based Instruction
   Online Research
	• What is *expository instruction*?
	
	• What strategies enhance the effectiveness of lectures and textbooks?
	
	• On what assumptions is *mastery learning* based? What are the typical elements of this approach, and in what situations is it most appropriate?
	
	• What is *direct instruction*? What activities does it typically include, and when is it most useful?
	
	• What forms does *computer-based instruction* take? What are its potential benefits?
	
	• Describe at least three ways you might use the Internet in the subject(s) you hope to be teaching.

CHAPTER OUTLINE	FOCUS QUESTIONS

HANDS-ON APPROACHES
    Discovery Learning
    In-Class Activities
    Computer Simulations and Applications
    Homework
    Authentic Activities
	• What is *discovery learning*? In what situations is it most useful and effective? What specific strategies can enhance the effectiveness of a discovery learning activity?
	
	• What forms might an in-class activity take? What strategies are useful for maximizing the benefits of in-class activities?
	
	• For what kinds of objectives might computer simulations and computer tool applications be appropriate?
	
	• What guidelines should teachers keep in mind when assigning homework?
	
	• What are *authentic activities*? What benefits might they have?

INTERACTIVE AND COLLABORATIVE APPROACHES
    Teacher Questions
    Class Discussions
    Reciprocal Teaching
    Technology-Based Discussions
    Cooperative Learning
    Peer Tutoring
	• What functions can teacher questions serve? What strategies can enhance their effectiveness?
	
	• What strategies are useful for facilitating class discussions?
	
	• What is *reciprocal teaching*? What learning strategies is it designed to promote? How can teachers scaffold a reciprocal teaching session?
	
	• Explain how a technology-based discussion might be set up.
	
	• Describe the nature of *cooperative learning*. What strategies are important for its success?
	
	• Describe the *jigsaw* technique and *scripted cooperation* as possible approaches to cooperative learning.
	
	• What are *base groups*? What functions might base groups serve in a classroom?
	
	• In what situations is *peer tutoring* useful? What are its potential benefits? How can teachers enhance the effectiveness of peer tutoring?

CHAPTER OUTLINE	FOCUS QUESTIONS

TAKING STUDENT DIVERSITY INTO ACCOUNT
   Considering Group Differences
   Accommodating Students with Special Needs
	• What student characteristics should teachers consider when choosing instructional strategies?
	
	• What instructional strategies may be especially suitable for students with special educational needs?
	
	• For what students might interactive and cooperative approaches to instruction be especially valuable?

THE BIG PICTURE	• For what types of objectives, lessons, and students are different instructional strategies most useful?

Supplementary Readings

Your instructor may assign one or both of these supplementary readings:

• Supplementary Reading #5, "Example of a Lesson Plan," which appears in the final section of this *Study Guide and Reader*.

• Supplementary Reading #6, "A Shocking Lesson," which appears in the final section of this *Study Guide and Reader*.

Chapter Glossary

Advance organizer. An introduction to a lesson that provides an overall organizational scheme for the lesson.

Affective domain. The domain of learning tasks that includes attitudes and values about the things one learns.

Base group. A cooperative learning group that works together for an entire semester or school year and provides a means through which students can be mutually supportive of one another's academic efforts and activities.

Bloom's taxonomy. A taxonomy in which six learning tasks, varying in degrees of complexity, are identified for the cognitive domain: knowledge, comprehension, application, analysis, synthesis, and evaluation.

Cognitive domain. The domain of learning tasks that includes knowledge of information, as well as ways of thinking about and using that information.

Computer-assisted instruction (CAI). Programmed instruction presented by means of a computer; it is one form of computer-based instruction.

Computer-based instruction (CBI). Instruction provided via computer technology.

Cooperative learning. An approach to instruction whereby students work with their classmates to achieve group goals and help one another learn.

Direct instruction. An approach to instruction that uses a variety of techniques (brief explanations, teacher questioning, rapid pacing, guided and independent practice) to promote learning of basic skills.

Discovery learning. An approach to instruction whereby students develop an understanding of a topic through firsthand interaction with the physical or social environment.

Distance learning. A situation in which learners receive technology-based instruction at a location physically separate from their instructor.

Expository instruction. An approach to instruction whereby information is presented in more or less the same form in which students are expected to learn it.

Higher-level question. A question that requires students to do something new with information they have learned—for example, to apply, analyze, synthesize, or evaluate it.

Hypermedia. A collection of computer-based instructional material, including both verbal text and such other media as pictures, sound, and animations. The material is interconnected in such a way that students can learn about one topic and then proceed to related topics of their own choosing.

Hypertext. A collection of computer-based verbal material that allows students to read about one topic and then proceed to related topics of their own choosing.

Instructional objective. A statement describing a final goal or outcome of instruction.

Jigsaw technique. An instructional technique in which instructional materials are divided among members of a cooperative learning group, with individual students being responsible for learning different material and then teaching that material to other group members.

Long-term objective. An objective that requires months or years of instruction and practice to be accomplished.

Lower-level question. A question that requires students to express what they have learned in essentially the same way they learned it—for example, by reciting a textbook's definition of a concept or describing an application their teacher presented in class.

Mastery learning. An approach to instruction whereby students learn one topic thoroughly before moving to a more difficult one.

Peer tutoring. An approach to instruction whereby students who have mastered a topic teach those who have not.

Prior knowledge activation. Reminding students of information they have already learned relative to a new topic.

Programmed instruction. An approach to instruction whereby students independently study a topic that has been broken into small, carefully sequenced segments.

Psychomotor domain. The domain of learning tasks that includes simple and complex physical movements and actions.

Reciprocal teaching. An approach to teaching reading and listening comprehension whereby students take turns asking teacherlike questions of their classmates.

Scripted cooperation. In cooperative learning, a technique in which cooperative groups follow a set of steps or "script" that guides members' verbal interactions.

Short-term objective. An objective that can typically be accomplished within the course of a single lesson or unit.

Signal. In expository instruction, a cue that lets students know that something is important to learn.

Standards. General statements regarding the knowledge and skills that students should achieve and the characteristics that their accomplishments should reflect.

Student-directed instruction. An approach to instruction in which students have considerable say in the issues they address and how to address them.

Task analysis. A process of identifying the specific knowledge and/or behaviors necessary to master a particular subject area or skill.

Teacher-directed instruction. An approach to instruction in which the teacher is largely in control of the course of the lesson.

Here are additional glossary items if your instructor has assigned Supplementary Reading #6:

Branching program. A form of programmed instruction in which students responding incorrectly to a question proceed to one or more remedial frames for further clarification or practice before continuing on with new information.

Computer-assisted instruction (CAI). Programmed instruction presented by means of a computer; it is one form of computer-based instruction.

Linear program. A form of programmed instruction in which all students proceed through the same sequence of instructional frames.

Programmed instruction (PI). An approach to instruction whereby students independently study a topic that has been broken into small, carefully sequenced segments.

Application Exercise #24: Applying Criteria Related to Instructional Objectives

Of the instructional objectives listed below, which ones are consistent with guidelines presented in the textbook, and which ones are not? Defend your choices. (For consistency's sake, all objectives are presented as imperatives.)

1. "Provide an introduction to the Vietnam War."

2. "Have opportunities to practice multiplication skills in real-world settings."

3. "Correctly spell at least 90% of the words on the district's spelling list for third graders."

4. "Teach the breast stroke."

5. "Change the oil and oil filter in an automobile engine correctly."

6. "Demonstrate library research skills; for example:
    • Locate books related to a particular topic.
    • Find articles about current events in newspapers and news magazines.
    • Use computer data bases to find books or articles written by a particular author."

7. "Investigate the life cycles of butterflies and moths."

8. "Run a mile in under eight minutes."

9. "Identify foods in each of the basic food groups."

10. "Know correct grammar."

Answers to Application Exercise #24

1. Not consistent. The objective focuses on what the teacher will do, not on what students will do.

2. Not consistent. No outcome is identified.

3. Consistent. The objective describes the outcome of instruction.

4. Not consistent. The objective focuses on what the teacher will do, not on what students will do.

5. Consistent. The objective describes the outcome of instruction.

6. Consistent. Complex skills can be described in general, abstract terms and illustrated with examples of behaviors that reflect those skills.

7. Not consistent. No outcome is identified.

8. Consistent. The objective describes the outcome of instruction.

9. Consistent. The objective describes the outcome of instruction.

10. Not consistent. The outcome is not described in a way that would enable us to determine whether students have *achieved* that outcome. A better objective might be "*Use* correct grammar," along with examples of behaviors that reflect this ability (e.g., "Show subject-verb agreement," "Use correct verb forms in past, present, and future tenses").

Application Exercise #25: Identifying Effective Instructional Strategies

Which of the following instructional strategies are consistent with information and guidelines presented in Chapter 13, and which are not? Justify your decisions.

1. As Ms. Horton talks about the characteristics of an insect, she uses a diagram that shows its six legs, three body parts, and antennae.

2. After her class reads several poems by Edgar Allan Poe, Ms. Marzano asks students to identify themes that underlie all of the poems. In the ensuing class discussion, it quickly becomes clear that her students are not likely to reach consensus about the poems. Therefore, she brings the discussion to a close after only a few minutes and turns to another topic.

3. Ms. Kruger urges her physics students to relate her lesson on *momentum* to their own personal experiences. She doesn't describe specific experiences that they might relate it to, however, because she knows that different students have different backgrounds.

4. Mr. Troyer has broken his sixth-grade mathematics curriculum into a sequence of small units. Students must show that they understand the material in each unit by getting a score of 90 percent or better on a unit test; at this point, they proceed to the next unit in the sequence. Mr. Troyer provides additional assistance and practice when students need it to attain a score of 90 percent.

5. Ms. Fornier divides her class into groups of four students apiece; each group will research the customs of a particular South American country. She instructs them, "In two weeks, your group must present a 15-minute report about its country to the rest of the class. Your best strategy as a group is to choose one person to give the report and then have the rest of the group help that student find and organize the information he or she needs to present."

6. Mr. Clooney is using a reciprocal teaching approach as he has his students read a chapter on bird migration. At one point, he asks Marie to pose a question about the information the group has just read.

7. When Ms. Kirkpatrick discovers that she has forgotten to bring the materials she needs for the class activity she has planned for the day, she quickly digs into her file cabinet and finds a lesson on another topic that can fill the same amount of time—a lesson that students in previous years have enjoyed very much.

8. When Mr. Young discovers that some of his students can use the Pythagorean theorem to solve geometry problems but others cannot yet use the theorem appropriately, he asks students who have achieved mastery to work with those who have not.

9. Mr. Kosmicki tells his students, "The growth of a glacier is like pancake batter being poured into a frying pan. As more and more substance is added to the middle, the edges spread farther and farther out."

10. Ms. Rogers tells her class, "Today we'll be studying the Industrial Revolution—why it occurred, what industries it involved, and what living conditions were like at the time."

11. To provide a challenge for her students, Ms. Iglesias assigns her algebra class several complex and difficult word problems. When she finds that even her brightest students are spending more time than she expected on the problems and still not arriving at any reasonable solutions, she says, "All right, then, let's make these problems your homework for tonight. The assignment will be worth the same as one of the tests I give you every Friday."

12. Mr. Epstein has his students learn about the geography of various Asian countries by means of a computer program. The computer presents information about each country in a single frame; when a student has finished reading the information presented in each frame, he or she presses the space bar to proceed to the next frame. After everyone has completed the program, Mr. Epstein gives his students a quiz to find out what they've learned.

13. Before introducing students to the concepts *acid* and *base,* Ms. Trussler makes several acids and bases available in the laboratory and allows students to explore their properties freely.

14. Ms. Shaklee conducts a cooperative learning exercise in which students meet in groups of three to learn about the three branches of the federal government—executive, legislative, and judicial. Each student in a group receives materials about a different branch of the government and must teach that information to the other two group members.

15. Mr. Goodsell's class often engages in lively debates about controversial topics. He notices that the same students tend to dominate every discussion and that other students speak rarely if at all. "Oh, well," he reasons, "we don't have time for *everyone* to speak."

16. Ms. Liu has her students work in pairs to study a reading assignment in their science textbook. She teaches the students to query one another about the material using such questions as "Can you explain . . . in your own words?" and "What might happen if . . . ?"

17. To check for students' understanding of ideas being discussed in class, Ms. Bush asks frequent questions of her students. Hoping to encourage automaticity in students' responding, she always calls on the student who raises his or her hand first.

18. Ms. McGill teaches her fourth graders the fundamentals of journalism within the context of having the class "publish" monthly issues of a school newspaper throughout the school year. She makes sure that, at one time or another, each student has the opportunity to serve as reporter, writer, editor, and desktop publisher.

19. After his middle school students have read a particular chapter in their textbook, Mr. Kelley asks, "Who can give us a short summary of the first section of the chapter?"

20. Ms. Jones has her students display their science projects on the class computer so that students can look at one another's work. Students can respond to their classmates' work by

submitting their questions and comments to a confidential "page" that only their teacher will be able to read.

21. Knowing that the lectures in his high school world studies class are usually packed full of information, Mr. Pease stops every ten minutes or so and gives his students a couple of minutes to compare notes and ask one another questions.

22. Mr. Vickarelli has his high school biology students explore human anatomy using a computer program that allows them to "travel" through and look at various parts of the body.

23. After the students in Mr. Maar's art class complete the sculptures on which they have been working for the past week or so, Mr. Maar asks them to evaluate their creations on the basis of several criteria.

24. Ms. Krump knows that the students in her high school world history class have probably not studied world history before now. To give them an overview of the subject, she has them spend the first few days of class exploring a hypermedia program that has been derived from a 20-volume encyclopedia of world history.

25. Mr. Marquis is teaching an advanced placement course—a course that may allow his high school seniors to earn college credit. To make the course as similar as possible to a "college experience," Mr. Marquis assigns 50 to 60 pages of reading each week. His students complain that they feel overwhelmed by the amount of reading material, and they ask for his guidance about the things they should focus on as they read. Mr. Marquis responds by saying, "I know your reading assignments are very challenging for you. But they will help you develop the study skills you will need for college next year."

26. Ms. Reese is teaching her students about *adverbs*. She begins the lesson by briefly reviewing the parts of speech the students have previously studied. She then says, "Today you'll learn what an adverb is. You'll also be able to find adverbs in a variety of sentences." She defines an adverb and gives several examples; after that, she presents some sentences on an overhead projector and asks students to identify the adverbs in the sentences. Once it is clear that the students have a good understanding of adverbs, she has them work independently at their desks to find adverbs in their storybooks and textbooks. As they do so, she circulates throughout the classroom to give guidance and feedback.

27. After a cooperative learning activity, Mr. Meader gives each group a written evaluation of how cooperatively and effectively he thinks the group has functioned.

Answers to Application Exercise #25

1. Consistent. Visual aids used to supplement expository instruction promote learning, perhaps by providing an additional way for students to encode the information being presented.

2. Not consistent. Classroom discussions often help students process classroom material more effectively and are especially useful for helping students explore complex or controversial topics.

3. Not consistent. Teachers need to describe specific relationships between new material and the things students already know. Ms. Kruger's students undoubtedly share common experiences that involve momentum. For example, all of them have probably been in a car that stopped suddenly and seen objects in the car continue to move forward. And many of them have probably been on roller skates and found it difficult to stop.

4. Consistent. Mr. Troyer's instruction has the basic elements of mastery learning—small and discrete units (presumably sequenced in a logical order), demonstration of mastery of one unit before proceeding to the next, and remedial activities for those who need them.

5. Not consistent. There is no individual accountability for learning. Only the group member who actually presents the information needs to learn it.

6. Consistent. In reciprocal teaching, a teacher gradually turns the responsibility of asking questions over to students.

7. Not consistent. Ms. Kirkpatrick is choosing an activity without consideration of what her instructional objectives are.

8. Consistent. Peer tutoring often enhances the academic achievement of both the students being tutored and the students doing the tutoring.

9. Consistent. Analogies are one way of helping students relate new information to what they already know.

10. Consistent. Ms. Rogers is presenting a brief advance organizer, something that should give students an overall structure for organizing the material she presents.

11. Not consistent. Homework assignments should involve tasks that students can accomplish with little if any assistance from others, and they should contribute only a minimal amount to students' final grades.

12. Not consistent. There is no advantage in presenting information on a computer screen when it could just as easily be presented in a textbook. Good educational computer programs provide numerous opportunities for students to make active responses—something that is often not possible through using textbooks alone.

13. Not consistent. Discovery learning is most effective when students already have some knowledge of the topic and are given some guidance and structure about how to proceed. (An additional problem here is that some of the chemicals, if improperly handled, might cause physiological damage, such as skin burns.)

14. Consistent. Ms. Shaklee is using the jigsaw technique; in the process, she is creating a situation in which group members must depend on one another for their learning.

15. Not consistent. Students benefit more from class discussions when they participate actively in the discussions (you might want to revisit the section "Benefits of Group Meaning-Making in the Classroom" in Chapter 7). Mr. Goodsell might consider using small-group discussions as a way of encouraging all students to participate.

16. Consistent. Peer tutoring sessions are often more effective when students have a particular structure to follow.

17. Not consistent. If the only students called on are those who raise their hands quickly, many students probably never have an opportunity to respond to questions. Instead, Ms. Bush should provide sufficient wait time for most or all students to develop answers to her questions. In addition, she can get greater student participation if she calls on different students each time or devises a means (e.g., "voting") through which all students can answer questions simultaneously.

18. Consistent. Ms. McGill is teaching journalism through an authentic activity.

19. Consistent. In expository instruction, summaries facilitate learning. By asking a student to provide the summary, Mr. Kelley is checking for students' understanding of the material. If the student summarizes the material inappropriately, Mr. Kelley might either call on another student or give his own summary of what he has discussed.

20. Not consistent. Ideally, students should be able to give one another feedback and build on one another's ideas; in this way, the group works together to construct a better understanding of the subject matter (see the section "Technology-Based Discussions"). In Ms. Jones's system, students communicate their reactions only to her, not to their classmates.

21. Consistent. Mr. Pease is giving students time to process the information he presents.

22. Consistent. When the "real thing" isn't possible, computer simulations can be a challenging and motivating alternative.

23. Consistent. One recommended strategy for in-class activities is to encourage students to reflect on and evaluate their own work.

24. Not consistent. Hypermedia is useful only if students have sufficient knowledge to impose an organization on what they are studying. Ms. Krump's students know little if anything about world history. The hypermedia program might be useful for specific topics later in the school year, but for now students may find the amount of information overwhelming and have trouble identifying the things they should focus on.

25. Not consistent. Whenever teachers must present a great deal of information through expository instruction, they should provide signals regarding what material is most important to study and learn.

26. Consistent. Ms. Reese's procedure includes many recommended components of direct instruction, including review of previously learned material, statement of the goals of a lesson, guided practice, and independent practice.

27. Not consistent. Cooperative groups should evaluate their *own* effectiveness (although perhaps with their teacher's assistance).

Answers to Selected Margin Notes

- Page 431: *Why is the third domain called affective?*
  Psychologists use the term *affect* to refer to feelings and emotions (see Chapter 12).

- Page 439: *Educational videos and field trips are two additional forms of expository instruction. What particular benefits might these forms of instruction have?*
  Videos and field trips enable students to encode information in multiple forms—perhaps verbally, visually, and auditorially. Field trips also provide concrete experiences to which students can relate classroom material. (You may have identified other benefits as well.)

- Page 446: *Which uses of computer technology just described are largely teacher-directed? Which are more student-directed?*
  Computer-assisted instruction and computer-based instruction are in most cases teacher-directed (the computer is the "teacher"). Hypertext, hypermedia, and surfing the Internet are more student-directed, in that students are largely in control of what they learn and in what order they learn it.

- Page 448: *Refer back to the discussion of cognitive apprenticeship in Chapter 2. How might such an apprenticeship incorporate discovery learning?*
  In a cognitive apprenticeship, a teacher and student work together to tackle a challenging task; such a task might include investigating a new phenomenon through exploration and identification of its properties. In the process, the teacher shares with the student how to *think about* the phenomenon being investigated (e.g., how to separate and control variables, how to analyze and interpret findings).

- Page 450: *How might Ms. Minichiello's "distant planet" activity in the opening case study help students learn?*
  Ms. Minichiello tells the students, "Imagine that your family ... decide[s] to travel to a distant planet. It's very expensive to travel there. You can only take *one* item, so pick the one item you would bring." By presenting this task, Ms. Minichiello is trying to help students understand just how great a distance the families were traveling given the modes of transportation and primitive "roads" at the time, and how few worldly goods the families would have room for. In other words, she is trying to promote meaningful learning.

- Page 453: *Why might some autonomy in homework be important?*
  Students need some opportunities for self-directed learning to acquire skills important for self-regulated learning (see the section "Self-Regulated Learning" in Chapter 10). Furthermore, autonomy promotes a sense of self-determination, an important (some would say essential) element of intrinsic motivation (see the section "Self-Determination" in Chapter 12).

- Page 460: *Can you explain the value of each [strategy] by relating it to effective memory storage processes?*
  The four strategies have effects such as these:
  - Summarizing: Summarizing requires students to identify and organize (i.e., find interrelationships among) the main ideas.

- Questioning: Depending on the types of questions being asked, questions can either facilitate comprehension monitoring or promote elaboration.
- Clarifying: By clarifying things they don't fully understand, students are better able to learn them in a meaningful, rather than rote, fashion.
- Predicting: By making predictions, students are drawing inferences from the things they have already learned (i.e., they are engaging in elaboration).

- Page 460: *Why is this approach called reciprocal teaching?*
  The students take turns serving as "teacher" for their classmates.

- Page 461: *Can you find at least one example each of summarizing, questioning, clarifying, and predicting in this dialogue? What strategies does the teacher use to elicit desired student responses?*
  Examples of each strategy are these:
  - Summarizing: Kam: The babies are born in the summer . . . The mother hides the babies in different places . . . To bring them food.
  - Questioning: Kam: How does she get the babies safe?
  - Clarifying: Milly: She needs to bring food. She probably leaves a twig or something.
  - Predicting: Milly: What she teaches her babies . . . like how to hop.
  The teacher models appropriate questions (e.g., "What would happen if the babies were born in the winter?"), guides the student "teacher" (e.g., "That's a good question to ask. Call on someone to answer that question."), and gives prompts (e.g., "And she visits them . . .").

- Page 461: *In what way does reciprocal teaching reflect a cognitive apprenticeship?*
  By modeling and encouraging question-asking, the teacher shows effective ways of thinking about what one is reading.

- Page 462: *Judging from the students' summary, what can we say about their epistemological beliefs related to anthropology?*
  The students recognize that as a discipline, anthropology is not necessarily fact; rather, it consists of varying perspectives that may or may not be correct. Furthermore, anthropological theories have greater or lesser usefulness in explaining the evidence that anthropologists gather.

- Page 468: *Why might teaching younger students a particular skill enhance tutors' self-regulation related to that skill? Explain this finding using Vygotsky's concept of internalization.*
  Biemiller, Shany, Inglis, and Meichenbaum (1998) suggest that it gives the tutor practice in guiding another person's attempts at a skill. In the process, the tutor also begins to internalize such guidance, thus being able to better guide and regulate his or her *own* performance of the skill. As Chapter 2 points out, Vygotsky suggests that many mental processes begin as social processes that are gradually internalized.

Sample Test Questions

Items marked with a "1)" on the left-hand side are lower-level questions that assess your general knowledge and understanding of the material. Items marked with a "2)" on the left-hand side are higher-level questions that assess your ability to apply what you have learned to a new situation.

Multiple-Choice

2)   1.   "Describe what a democracy is in your own words." This objective can best be classified as being at the _____ level of Bloom's taxonomy for the cognitive domain.
   a. synthesis
   b. knowledge
   c. comprehension
   d. application

2)   2.   Which one of the following teachers is conducting a *subject matter* task analysis?
   a. Ms. Archibeque divides an upcoming unit on meteorology into five smaller topics—fronts, wind, temperature, clouds, and precipitation—and arranges them in a logical sequence.
   b. Mr. Barnett wants his students to become better writers and stops to consider the things that he himself thinks about as he writes.
   c. Ms. Coopersmith identifies the specific skills that a student must learn to use a video camera correctly.
   d. Mr. Delaney considers what his students must do to become better note takers—skills such as organizing, elaborating, and identifying main ideas.

1)   3.   Which one of the following best illustrates a *signal* in expository instruction?
   a. Mr. Anders pauses every few minutes to give students a chance to ask questions.
   b. Ms. Beck reminds students that they need to read Chapter 5 before Friday.
   c. Before starting a lesson on gravity, Ms. Carson looks to make sure that everyone's eyes are focused on her.
   d. Mr. Drew writes important concepts on the chalkboard.

1)   4.   Three of the following are characteristic of a mastery learning approach to instruction. Which one is *not necessarily* a component of mastery learning?
   a. Students must master both lower-level and higher-level skills.
   b. Students proceed through a sequence of units arranged in a logical order.
   c. Students must demonstrate mastery of one topic before proceeding to the next.
   d. Students receive extra help when they need it.

1)   5.   Which one of the following strategies is most consistent with guidelines presented in the textbook regarding *discovery learning*?
   a. Allow at least 90 minutes for the activity.
   b. Give students some guidelines about how to proceed.
   c. Reinforce desired "discoveries."
   d. Conduct the activity before students have acquired any information about the topic under investigation.

2)   6.   Three of the following teachers are assigning homework in ways consistent with the textbook's guidelines. Which one is *not*?

     a. Mr. Andrew gives homework assignments for which his students will need little or no assistance from anyone else.

     b. Ms. Blair has her students read a few pages in their social studies textbook each night.

     c. Ms. Crawford tells students that their performance on homework will be worth 60 percent of their final grades.

     d. Mr. Delgado occasionally gives his students a voluntary homework assignment— one that they can either do or not do, as they prefer.

2)   7.   In which one of the following situations would *reciprocal teaching* be most appropriate?

     a. Mr. Arias wants his students to remember the techniques they learn in woodworking class.

     b. Ms. Broughton wants her students to learn to interact more appropriately with their classmates.

     c. Mr. Conway is concerned that his students don't remember much of what they read in their history textbooks.

     d. Ms. Danforth wants her students to develop more effective problem-solving skills.

1)   8.   Three of the following are accurate statements about cooperative learning. Which one is *not* accurate?

     a. Researchers find that it often promotes high academic achievement.

     b. Researchers find that it often promotes friendships across diverse groups.

     c. Researchers find that it is more effective when students are individually accountable for what they have learned.

     d. Researchers find that students work best when they can choose the other members of their group.

Essay

1)   9.   Whether you use regular classroom lectures or shorter and less formal descriptions and explanations, expository instruction will almost certainly be a teaching strategy that you use regularly. With research on expository instruction in mind, describe four *specific* strategies that you can use to help your students learn the information that you present through expository instruction.

2)   10.   Imagine that, as a teacher, you have three students in your class who have been identified as being gifted. Of the instructional strategies described in Chapter 13, identify *four* that might be particularly valuable for helping these students achieve at levels commensurate with their abilities. In four short paragraphs, briefly describe how you would implement each strategy and justify why you believe it would be especially suitable for gifted students.

Answers to Sample Test Questions

1. c—One indication of comprehension is the ability to translate an idea into one's own words (see Table 13.1).

2. a—A subject matter task analysis involves breaking the material to be taught into the specific topics and ideas that it includes. Alternatives *b* and *d* are examples of an information processing analysis, and alternative *c* is an example of a behavioral analysis. (See the section "Conducting a Task Analysis.")

3. d—Signals are the various techniques teachers use to let students know what things are most important for them to learn (see Table 13.2).

4. a—Mastery learning does not necessarily need to include both lower-level and higher-level skills. The other three alternatives are typical components of a mastery learning approach (see the section "Mastery Learning").

5. b—Students are most likely to benefit from a discovery learning session when the activity is structured to some extent (see the section "Discovery Learning").

6. c—The textbook suggests that teachers minimize the degree to which they use homework assignments to determine final class grades (see the section "Homework").

7. c—Reciprocal teaching is used primarily as a method of enhancing students' reading comprehension skills (see the section "Reciprocal Teaching").

8. d—Experts generally recommend that the teacher form the groups rather than let students form groups themselves (see the bulleted guidelines presented in the section "Cooperative Learning").

9. The four strategies you describe should be based on factors that have been shown to facilitate learning during expository instruction. A number of possibilities are presented in Table 13.2.

10. Possible responses to this question are presented in the bottom right-hand cell of Table 13.3. You might also consider the student characteristics described in Table 13.4. Your answer need not be restricted to the tables, however. Each of your four paragraphs should include a concrete description of a strategy you intend to use and a rationale as to why it's appropriate for gifted learners. You may also want to draw on the discussion of giftedness in Chapter 5 when answering this question.

Chapter 14

CREATING AND MAINTAINING
A PRODUCTIVE CLASSROOM ENVIRONMENT

Chapter Summary

Classroom management is a process of establishing and maintaining a classroom environment conducive to students' learning and achievement. As teachers, we want to create a classroom in which students are consistently engaged in classroom tasks and activities and in which few student behaviors interfere with those tasks and activities.

Several strategies are useful for establishing a productive classroom environment. In particular, we can (a) physically arrange the classroom in a way that facilitates our interactions with students and minimizes distractions, (b) create a classroom climate in which students have a sense of belonging and an intrinsic motivation to learn, (c) set reasonable limits for students' behavior, (d) plan classroom activities that encourage on-task behavior, (e) continually monitor what students are doing, and (f) modify our instructional strategies when they are clearly ineffective.

We are defining a *misbehavior* as a behavior that can potentially disrupt classroom learning and planned classroom activities. Some minor misbehaviors are usually best ignored, including those that probably won't be repeated, those that are unlikely to be imitated by other students, and those that occur only temporarily and within the context of unusual circumstances. Other minor infractions can be dealt with simply and quickly by cueing students about their inappropriate behaviors. Chronic misbehaviors that significantly interfere with student learning often require planned intervention. In some cases, we may be able to address a problem behavior successfully by having a discussion with the student about the situation. In other circumstances, we may find that self-regulating strategies or behaviorist approaches bring about improvement. We may sometimes find it desirable to discuss chronic and serious misbehaviors with a student's parents so that we can coordinate efforts and work toward a common solution.

As we plan for a productive classroom, we must consider the characteristics of the students we are likely to have in our classroom. Creating a warm, supportive atmosphere and a sense of community in the classroom may be especially important for students from diverse cultural backgrounds, students from lower socioeconomic groups, and students with special needs. As we deal with classroom misbehavior, we must be especially understanding when students exhibit behaviors that are the product of a particular cultural upbringing or the result of a specific disability.

We will be most effective when we work cooperatively with other teachers, other institutions, and parents to promote students' learning, development, and achievement. It is especially important that we keep in regular contact with parents, sharing information in both directions about the progress that students are making and coordinating efforts at school with those on the home front. We can keep the lines of communication open through a variety of mechanisms—

for instance, by scheduling parent-teacher conferences, sending notes home, making frequent telephone calls, and getting parents actively involved in school activities. We may need to make an extra effort to establish productive working relationships with those parents who, on the surface, seem reluctant to become involved in their children's education.

Common Student Beliefs and Misconceptions Related to Chapter Content

Below are two beliefs that future teachers sometimes have before studying concepts and principles related to classroom management; such beliefs may interfere with an accurate understanding of what they read. As you read Chapter 14, be on the lookout for evidence that contradicts these commonly held beliefs:

1. Some future teachers think that a well-managed classroom must invariably be one that is quiet and orderly.

2. Some future teachers think of teaching as an activity that occurs in relative isolation from other adults, rather than as an activity that involves frequent coordination with other teachers, community agencies, and parents.

CHAPTER OUTLINE	FOCUS QUESTIONS

CREATING AN ENVIRONMENT CONDUCIVE TO LEARNING
 	
  Arranging the Classroom
 	
  Creating an Effective Classroom Climate
 	
  Setting Limits
 	
  Planning Activities That Keep Students on Task
 	
  Monitoring What Students Are Doing
 	
  Modifying Instructional Strategies
	• What is a well-managed classroom?
	
	• What strategies do effective classroom managers use in terms of:
	  • Arranging the classroom?
	  • Creating a classroom climate?
	  • Setting limits?
	  • Planning classroom activities?
	  • Monitoring what students are doing?
	  • Modifying instruction?
	
	• How might you create a *sense of community* in your own classroom?
	
	• What rules and procedures might be appropriate for students at the grade level you will be teaching?
	
	• How can teachers strike a balance between giving students the easy tasks that are most likely to keep misbehaviors to a minimum and providing challenges that are most likely to promote cognitive growth?
	
	• How can teachers strike a balance between giving students enough structure that they know what is expected of them, yet not so much structure that higher-level thinking skills are stifled?
	
	• What is *withitness*? What purpose does it serve?
	
	• In what way do beginning teachers and expert teachers often think differently when their students engage in nonproductive classroom behavior?

CHAPTER OUTLINE	FOCUS QUESTIONS

DEALING WITH MISBEHAVIORS
 	
    Ignoring the Behavior
    Cueing the Student
    Discussing the Problem Privately with the Student
    Promoting Self-Regulation
    Using Behaviorist Approaches
    Conferring with Parents
	• How does the textbook define *misbehavior*?
	
	• Why are some misbehaviors best ignored?
	
	• What is *cueing*? When is it apt to be useful?
	
	• What are the advantages of discussing a problem behavior with a student? Why should such conversations be conducted in private?
	
	• What strategies can teachers use to promote self-regulation? In what situations are such strategies likely to be effective?
	
	• When are behaviorist approaches most useful? What specific strategies do these approaches include?
	
	• When is a conference with parents advisable?

TAKING STUDENT DIVERSITY INTO ACCOUNT
 	
    Creating a Supportive Climate
    Defining and Responding to Misbehaviors
    Accommodating Students with Special Needs
	• Why is a supportive classroom climate especially important when working with students from diverse ethnic backgrounds? Why is it important when working with students of low-SES families?
	
	• Why should students' cultural backgrounds be considered when addressing misbehaviors?
	
	• What classroom management strategies are particularly helpful when working with students with special needs?

COORDINATING EFFORTS WITH OTHERS
 	
    Working with Other Teachers
    Working with the Community at Large
    Working with Parents
	• What benefits result when teachers coordinate their efforts with one another?
	
	• What activities might "working with the community at large" involve?
	
	• What strategies can teachers use to communicate regularly with parents?
	
	• Why are some parents reluctant to become involved in their children's education? What strategies can teachers use to get them more involved?
	
	• What suggestions does the textbook offer for working successfully with parents?

CHAPTER OUTLINE	FOCUS QUESTIONS
THE BIG PICTURE	• Identify several strategies presented in the chapter that you think can best enable *you* to make a difference in the lives of your students.

Chapter Glossary

Classroom climate. The psychological atmosphere of the classroom.

Classroom management. Establishing and maintaining a classroom environment conducive to learning and achievement.

Collective self-efficacy. People's beliefs about their ability to be successful when they work together on a task.

Cueing. A teacher's use of signals to indicate that a particular behavior is desired or that a particular behavior should stop.

Misbehavior. An action that has the potential to disrupt students' learning and planned classroom activities.

Sense of community. A widely shared feeling that teacher and students have common goals, are mutually respectful and supportive of one another's efforts, and believe that everyone makes an important contribution to classroom learning.

Sense of school community. The sense that all faculty and students within a school are working together to help every student learn and succeed.

Withitness. The appearance that a teacher knows what all students are doing at all times.

Application Exercise #26: Identifying Effective Classroom Management Strategies

Which of the following teacher behaviors are effective classroom management strategies, and which are not? Justify your decisions.

1. Mr. Dayton wants to make sure his fifth graders enjoy every minute of the school day, so he turns all his lessons into games and other fun-filled activities. He also devotes the last 30 minutes of each school day to "fun time"—to nonacademic activities designed to leave students with a good feeling about school.

2. Mr. Adams acknowledges his students' birthdays (or half-birthdays, for those born in the summer months) with an "Adams Apple"—an apple with a birthday candle stuck in the top.

3. Ms. Schutz describes the three major assignments that students in her literature class must complete during the semester, and together she and her students come to an agreement about a reasonable due date for each assignment.

4. At the end of the third week of school, Ms. Jameson and her third graders discuss the procedures they have been using for daily activities—for starting the school day, going to lunch, getting ready to go home at the end of the day, and so on. Several students say that the procedure they use for going to lunch isn't fair, and so together the class develops a procedure that might work better.

5. Mr. Trenton knows that the first few months of junior high school are unsettling ones for many students, so he gives his classes free rein to do as they please during the first two weeks of school. After this, he sets rules for classroom behavior and begins to enforce them.

6. Ms. Camareri lets her students sit wherever they want in the classroom. She figures that the occasional off-task behavior that results when friends sit by one another (whispering, passing notes, etc.) is counterbalanced by the fact that their social needs are being met.

7. Mr. Mireles has a specific procedure that he wants his third graders to follow when they need to use the restroom or get a drink of water. He has a sign-out sheet by the door; his students write their names on the sheet whenever they must leave the classroom, as well as the times that they leave and return. Mr. Mireles has a limit on the number of times a student can leave the classroom for such "errands": twice in the morning and twice in the afternoon.

8. When Mr. Dembrowski must take a few minutes to help Stacey with a difficult math problem, he turns his chair so that he can simultaneously watch his other students working quietly at their desks.

9. Ms. Piper has discovered that Raymond has a very short attention span. She puts him at the back of the classroom, where he won't disturb other students with his frequent off-task behaviors.

10. Mr. Keegan sends his students to the school library, telling them each to look up a particular kind of mammal.

11. When Mr. Fortuna gives his class a paper-pencil test, he works quietly at his desk but scans the room often to see what his students are doing and whether anyone has any questions.

12. Ms. McFadden tells her high school science students, "Always use a pen with black ink when you complete assignments for this class. I simply will not accept assignments written in pencil or in other colors of ink."

13. Ms. Sanguedolce's middle school social studies students know that when they first get to class, they should take out their journals and write their reactions to an item described either in yesterday's newspaper or on last night's local television news program.

14. Mr. Burns gives his health class a general overview of a videotape they are about to see. After he does so, he enlists the help of four students to help him get the video equipment from the end of the hall and set it up at the front of the class.

15. On the first day of her Algebra II class, Ms. Yocum gives her students several problems that they should be able to do based on what they learned in Algebra I last year. She knows that these problems are especially challenging ones that will require a great deal of thought.

16. Mr. Winfrey tells his students, "It's important to follow this format when you do your math assignments so I can find your answers easily and give you credit when you've earned it."

Answers to Application Exercise #26

1. Not effective. The classroom should have a somewhat businesslike atmosphere. This is not to say that students cannot have fun in the classroom; however, it *is* to say that their energy should be focused on accomplishing instructional objectives.

2. Effective. The birthday apples show that Mr. Adams cares about his students as people.

3. Effective. This strategy gives students a sense of control over their classroom life and thereby promotes intrinsic motivation.

4. Effective. Ms. Jameson is getting students involved in decision making about classroom activities.

5. Not effective. The first few days of school are critical ones for communicating expectations for students' behavior. During the first two weeks of school, Mr. Trenton does not communicate any expectations for his students, nor does he create a businesslike atmosphere in his classroom.

6. Not effective. Students should be on task as much as possible; satisfying social needs, while important, is no substitute for classroom learning. A more effective strategy would be to allow friends to sit near one another only when they can stay on task if they do so.

7. Effective. Mr. Mireles's students don't have to ask permission every time they want to go to the restroom or drinking fountain. Therefore, they have a certain amount of control over an aspect of their school day.

8. Effective. Ideally, a teacher should be able to see what all students are doing at all times.

9. Not effective. It is better to seat inattentive students close to the teacher.

10. Not effective. Mr. Keegan has given his students very little structure for this task, and so they probably don't have a clear sense of what they are supposed to do.

11. Effective. Mr. Fortuna is demonstrating withitness.

12. Not effective. Ms. McFadden is presenting her requirement in a controlling manner. If she has a legitimate reason for requiring black ink from everyone, then she might instead say something like, "Black ink is easier for me to read. I can grade your work more consistently and fairly if you use black ink pens on all your assignments."

13. Effective. The procedure gives students something to do during a transition time.

14. Not effective. Mr. Burns is creating some "down time" in which students are not actively engaged in learning. He should have set up the equipment before class began.

15. Not effective. It is usually better to start out the year with relatively easy tasks and then introduce more challenging ones as the year goes on. Teachers are more likely to have behavior problems in their classrooms when the tasks that they assign are especially difficult ones for students.

16. Effective. Mr. Winfrey is describing a required procedure in an informational, rather than controlling, fashion.

Application Exercise #27: Dealing with Student Misbehaviors

For each of the following misbehaviors, decide which one of these strategies would probably be most appropriate, and defend your choices:
- Ignoring
- Cueing
- Private discussion with the student
- Self-regulation
- A behaviorist approach
- Parent conference

1. As her class takes a weekly quiz, Ms. Stewart notices Robert looking in the direction of Kevin's test paper. She suspects that he hasn't yet had a chance to decipher any of Kevin's responses.

2. Missy clicks her ballpoint pen constantly during class, to the point where the students around her are being distracted and annoyed. Over the past few weeks, Ms. Givens has repeatedly asked Missy to stop the behavior, but it continues unabated. Missy tells her teacher, "I know I should stop, Ms. Givens, but most of the time I don't even realize I'm doing it."

3. Although Jerri willingly completes tasks that she can do at her desk or in small cooperative groups, she consistently refuses when Mr. Baranski asks her to do anything that involves speaking in front of the entire class.

4. As he hurries past Melanie to get to his seat in French class, Lucas unintentionally knocks Melanie's loose-leaf notebook out of her hands. The notebook falls to the floor, and some of the pages fall out. Lucas is obviously embarrassed and offers to help put the notebook back together again. As a result of the disturbance, Ms. Winston must wait a couple of extra minutes before she can begin class.

5. Stanley throws the bat wildly whenever he hits the ball during baseball practice. Mr. Greene has repeatedly asked him to stop doing so because the flying bat poses a danger to other team members. Unfortunately, Stanley seems to have no interest in changing his behavior.

6. It's Halloween, and Mr. Ritchey's fourth graders have all brought their costumes to school so that they can dress up for the class Halloween party and school costume parade later in the day. The festivities don't start for another 30 minutes, so Mr. Ritchey has his students working in cooperative groups on a science project that is due next week. Unfortunately, the children are talking more about their costumes than about the science project, and their attention to the project disappears altogether when three of the children's parents come in with cookies and punch for the class party.

7. Heidi is physically aggressive toward her classmates whenever things don't go her way. Mr. Elliott has talked with her about her behavior several times but has seen little improvement in her behavior. Heidi seems to have little interest in changing how she interacts with other students.

8. During independent seatwork time, Oliver often talks to himself, distracting those around him. He wants to stop because he knows that his classmates make fun of him for his incessant chattiness to no one in particular. Yet Ms. Young's frequent reminders to work more quietly haven't made a difference.

9. Ms. Schweck finds Andrew sleeping in her class two or three times a week. When she speaks with Andrew about the problem, he tells her that he really enjoys her class and wishes he could stay awake. He says that he often has trouble falling asleep at night and so is quite tired in school the following day.

10. Keith is not contributing constructively to his cooperative group. Furthermore, he's doing everything he can to distract the rest of the group from getting its assigned task accomplished. The other group members have complained to Ms. McMartin and requested that she take him out of their group. Ms. McMartin doesn't want to do this, because she suspects that Keith will be a distracting influence no matter which group he's in; furthermore, she wants him to learn to work effectively in a group setting. She has spoken with Keith after class about the situation, but he clearly is not interested in learning or in helping his classmates learn.

11. Mr. Nouri has his students working in pairs on "brain teaser" mathematics word problems. He overhears one pair of students gossiping about a classmate rather than doing the assignment, although he doubts that anyone else in the classroom can hear their conversation.

12. Mr. Marzetta notices that Janie is doodling in her notebook during his explanation of the water cycle. He is surprised to find her doing so, because she is a good student who always performs well on assignments and quizzes.

13. Mary, who has mild mental retardation, is a member of Mr. Caro's third-grade classroom for most of the school day. Mr. Caro finds that when Mary goes to the pencil sharpener to sharpen a pencil, she sometimes gets distracted by things that are happening elsewhere in the classroom and forgets to return to her seat. Mr. Caro knows that Mary wants desperately to please him and is frustrated about her own forgetfulness. But his occasional little admonishments haven't helped.

14. Midway through the school year, Michael's classroom performance, which has previously been quite good, suddenly deteriorates to a consistent "D" level.

15. At the end of art class, Eric is so busy talking to someone else that he has forgotten to clean his pottery wheel.

Answers to Application Exercise #27

1. Cueing. Cheating interferes with students' learning. A simple cue will let Robert know that Ms. Stewart is aware of the behavior and wants it to stop.

2. Self-regulation. Missy is motivated to change her behavior. Ms. Givens might have Missy begin with self-monitoring, recording each click she catches herself making.

3. Private discussion. Jerri seems motivated to do well in school, as evidenced by her willingness to complete other tasks. Yet repeated cueing has not produced a change in her attitude toward public speaking tasks. By talking privately with Jerri, Mr. Baranski may be able to find out why she balks at such tasks.

4. Ignoring. Lucas didn't intend to knock the notebook to the floor, and the natural consequences of his action (feeling embarrassed and having to help Melanie pick things up) are probably sufficient to discourage him from being so careless in the future.

5. A behaviorist approach. The behavior has continued over a period of time, and Stanley has little motivation to change his habits. Reinforcement for putting the bat down appropriately combined with mild punishment for throwing the bat might be effective.

6. Ignoring. The children's off-task behavior is due to special circumstances and will not necessarily occur after today.

7. A behaviorist approach. Heidi's behavior is interfering with school activities and is potentially jeopardizing the safety of others. Cueing hasn't worked, and Heidi isn't motivated to change on her own. Mr. Elliott might try to extinguish or punish aggressive behavior (e.g., with time-out) and then teach and reinforce more appropriate behaviors. He might also try to determine if aggressive behavior serves some purpose for Heidi and, if so, teach her alternative ways of satisfying her needs.

8. Self-regulation. Oliver wants to change his behavior, yet cueing hasn't worked. Ms. Young might suggest self-monitoring along with self-reinforcement for working quietly.

9. Parent conference. A private discussion with the student has been ineffective, and the source of the problem appears to lie outside school walls.

10. A behaviorist approach. Keith's behavior is interfering with his own learning and that of other group members. Cueing hasn't worked, and he's not interested in changing his behavior. Using applied behavior analysis, Ms. McMartin might identify an effective reinforcer to encourage more productive behavior in cooperative learning activities. Or, using functional analysis and positive behavioral support, she might try to determine the purpose(s) that Keith's inappropriate behaviors serve for him and identify alternative behaviors that serve the same purpose(s) for Keith.

11. Cueing. The behavior is interfering with learning but may stop once the students know that Mr. Nouri is aware of what they are doing.

12. Ignoring. Janie's behavior does not appear to be interfering with her learning.

13. Self-regulation. Mary wants to change her behavior but doesn't know how. Mr. Caro might teach Mary some self-instructions (e.g., "Sharpen my pencil, then go back to my seat") that she can repeat to herself each time she goes to the pencil sharpener.

14. Private discussion. Michael's recent grades have presumably been sufficient to cue him that his performance is not what it should be, yet there has been no improvement. A sudden drop in motivation for no apparent reason warrants a private discussion to try to identify and remedy the problem.

15. Cueing. Eric simply needs a reminder about appropriate behavior.

Answers to Selected Margin Notes

- Page 481: *Is it possible to overmanage a classroom? If so, what might be the negative ramifications of doing so?*

  Teachers who present a lengthy list of rules and procedures for every imaginable situation and those who punish every conceivable misbehavior (no matter how minor) are probably overmanaging their classrooms. Such approaches are likely to (a) create an uncaring, threatening atmosphere and (b) reduce students' sense of control about classroom tasks.

- Page 483: *How might the teacher adapt the journal assignment for students who cannot yet read or write?*

  One strategy would be to have students tape their journal entries on a cassette recorder, with the teacher recording messages back to them. Another would be to have the students draw pictures of activities they have enjoyed either in class or at home; the teacher and the students could then spend a couple of minutes talking about the pictures. If students have some knowledge of letter-sound correspondences, the teacher might encourage them to label their pictures with a word or two using "best guess" spellings.

- Page 484: *In what sense do Eli, Jake, and Vanessa have control in Ms. Cornell's class? What might Ms. Cornell do to help them control their classroom lives in more productive ways?*

  They are "in control" in the sense that they can do almost anything they want to in Ms. Cornell's class. Strategies for promoting a sense of control while also maintaining some order in the classroom can be found in the sections "Giving Students a Sense of Control" and "Promoting Self-Regulation," as well as in Chapter 12's discussion of self-determination.

- Page 488: *Do you see parallels between authoritative parenting and the guidelines for setting limits described in this chapter?*

  Authoritative parents hold high expectations and standards for children's behavior, explain why some behaviors are acceptable and others are not, and include children in decision making. All of these characteristics are evident in the textbook's discussion of setting limits.

- Page 489: *With this point in mind, how might Ms. Cornell (in the opening case study) have gotten the year off to a better start?*

  Rather than begin a new curriculum on the first day of class, she might have begun with a few "get-to-know-one-another" activities and some academic tasks that involve a review of last year's curriculum.

- Page 490: *Can you relate this strategy to behavioral momentum?*

  Behavioral momentum is a phenomenon whereby people are more likely to make desired responses if they are already making similar responses. Keeping students busy during transition times maintains students' "momentum" regarding academic tasks.

- Page 494: *Can you relate ignoring to a specific concept in operant conditioning?*

  When a response is not reinforced in any way, *extinction* occurs.

- Page 494: *Why is ignoring not an effective strategy in Ms. Cornell's classroom?*

  Although Ms. Cornell is not reinforcing the misbehaviors of Eli, Jake, and Vanessa, classmates apparently *are* reinforcing the misbehaviors.

- Page 495: *From a motivational standpoint, how might private discussions with students be helpful?* (This question is part of the photo caption.)

  A discussion can provide an opportunity for teacher and student to work *together* to identify a solution; in this way, the student gains a sense of *self-determination* (see Chapter 12). Furthermore, meeting with the teacher may possibly enable the student to address his or her need for *relatedness* (see Chapter 11).

- Page 499: *What behaviorist techniques might Ms. Cornell use to help Eli, Jake, and Vanessa become more productive members of her classroom?*

  Reinforcing appropriate behaviors (if necessary, shaping such behaviors over a period of time), punishing inappropriate behaviors, and encouraging other students not to reinforce undesirable behaviors are three obvious strategies. Furthermore, Ms. Cornell should make response-consequence contingencies clear (e.g., she might use contingency contracts), and she should apply both reinforcement and punishment consistently. Using a positive behavioral support approach, Ms. Cornell might also determine the purpose that the students' misbehaviors serve (e.g., perhaps the three students crave attention) and identify alternative, more productive behaviors that can serve the same purpose.

- Page 499: *Social cognitive theorists also advocate following through with the consequences students are expecting. Do you recall their rationale?*

  According to social cognitive theorists, the nonoccurrence of expected reinforcement for appropriate behavior is, in essence, punishment for that behavior. Similarly, the nonoccurrence of expected punishment for inappropriate behavior has the effect of reinforcing the behavior.

- Page 504: *When would it be inappropriate to suggest that parents use e-mail to communicate?*

  Ms. Reilly teaches in a school district where most parents have computers and Internet access at home or at work. Suggesting the use of e-mail would be inappropriate in communities where some families cannot afford computers or where parents have limited knowledge of English.

- Page 505: *To what concept is the teacher referring when she talks about becoming "automatic" with math facts?*

  She is talking about automaticity (see "Factors Affecting Retrieval" in Chapter 6).

- Page 507: *How might a chronically abusive parent react to the conversation with Ms. Johnson?*

  Unfortunately, some parents may overreact and administer severe, abusive punishment. Should you expect that a parent might react in such a manner to a poor report about his or her child's school performance, or should you suspect that one of your students is the victim of abuse, consult with your school principal or guidance counselor *immediately* for guidance about how to proceed.

Sample Test Questions

Items marked with a "**1**)" on the left-hand side are lower-level questions that assess your general knowledge and understanding of the material. Items marked with a "**2**)" on the left-hand side are higher-level questions that assess your ability to apply what you have learned to a new situation.

Multiple-Choice

1) 1. Consider the three teaching strategies described below:
- Giving students an opportunity to plan ahead by letting them know about upcoming assignments well in advance
- Giving students choices about how to do some of their assignments
- Having regular procedures that students should follow for routine activities

What do all three of these classroom management strategies have in common?
- a. They give students a sense of control about certain aspects of classroom life.
- b. They are the three most effective ways of handling transition times.
- c. They make it unnecessary for teachers to set limits.
- d. They facilitate teacher-student interaction.

2) 2. Which one of the statements below is the best example of presenting a classroom rule or procedure in an *informational* manner?
- a. "During the test, please keep your eyes on your own papers at all times."
- b. "You'll get your group projects done more quickly if you decide immediately which group members will do which tasks."
- c. "I will accept your papers only if you have typed them. Handwritten essays are unacceptable."
- d. "You should always wear a T-shirt, loose-fitting shorts, wool socks, and tennis shoes to physical education class, and you should always shower before you go to your next class."

2) 3. Which one of the following examples is most consistent with the textbook's definition of a *misbehavior*?
- a. Angela refuses to participate in the class volleyball lesson.
- b. Brad asks Wally how to spell the word *separate* during a creative writing assignment.
- c. Claudette sucks on a Life Saver during free time.
- d. Dustin does his homework on unlined paper when his teacher specifically asked that it be done on lined paper.

2) 4. Which one of the following strategies is the best example of *cueing*?
- a. Establishing rules at the beginning of the school year
- b. Giving reinforcement for appropriate behavior
- c. Punishing unacceptable behavior
- d. Giving a student a stern look

2)   5.   Which one of the following examples best illustrates *self-monitoring* as a means of changing behavior?

     a. Anna wonders if her obnoxious behavior on the playground is costing her the friendships that she values.

     b. Bill is asked to list the kinds of jobs he will be able to get if, because of his chronic truancy, he never earns his high school diploma.

     c. Cullen keeps a running count of every time an inappropriate curse word slips into his speech in the classroom.

     d. Dale thinks about how he feels when other people borrow school supplies without returning them and realizes that he should not have kept Monte's pencil sharpener as long as he did.

1)   6.   Three of the following are recommended strategies for conducting parent-teacher conferences. Which one is *not* recommended?

     a. Be as flexible as possible when scheduling a time to meet with each child's parents.

     b. Suggest ways in which parents might have caused the child's inappropriate behaviors.

     c. Plan a general agenda for the conference.

     d. Avoid jargon that parents are unlikely to understand.

Essay

1)   7.   Describe six different strategies that you might use to establish and maintain a productive learning environment in your classroom. Your strategies should be based on the textbook's discussion of effective classroom management.

2)   8.   On several occasions, Olivia has been found vandalizing school property—spray-painting walls, breaking windows, damaging equipment, and so on. Describe how you might use behaviorist techniques to change Olivia's behavior.

Answers to Sample Test Questions

1. a—All three of the bulleted items are recommended strategies for giving students a sense of control (see the subsection "Giving Students a Sense of Control" in the section "Creating an Effective Classroom Climate").

2. b—This statement presents a procedure (dividing up tasks at the beginning of the group session) as an item of information, whereas the other three clearly indicate that the teacher is in control. (See the subsection "Presenting Rules and Procedures as Information" in the section "Setting Limits.")

3. a—Angela's behavior interferes with her learning (see the definition of *misbehavior* at the beginning of the section "Dealing with Misbehaviors").

4. d—Cueing sometimes takes the form of body language (see the section "Cueing the Student").

5. c—Having students engage in self-monitoring typically involves asking them to record the frequency with which certain behaviors occur (see the section "Promoting Self-Regulation").

6. b—The textbook suggests that the teacher create a *nonjudgmental* atmosphere and focus on constructive solutions (see Figure 14.3).

7. Numerous strategies are described in the section "Creating an Environment Conducive to Learning." Your response should include at least six of the strategies presented in the text.

8. Ideally, your response should draw from both Chapter 9 (the discussion of behaviorism) and Chapter 14. At a minimum, your response should include reinforcement for appropriate behavior—perhaps for behavior incompatible with vandalism (e.g., you might do something similar to what was done in the litterbug situation in the section "Reinforcing Incompatible Behaviors" in Chapter 9). Your response might also include punishment for further vandalism (e.g., you might use the logical consequence of having to repaint, repair, or replace whatever has been vandalized). And you might take a positive behavioral approach, whereby you determine the purpose(s) that the vandalism serves for Olivia and identify more constructive behaviors that accomplish the same end. Be specific about the responses you intend to reinforce and punish, as well as about the particular consequences that will follow those responses.

Chapter 15

BASIC CONCEPTS AND ISSUES IN ASSESSMENT

Chapter Summary

Assessment is a process of observing a sample of students' behavior and drawing inferences about their knowledge and abilities. It can take any number of forms. For instance, it might be informal or formal, paper-pencil or performance based, traditional or authentic. Occasionally it takes the form of a standardized test, but far more often it consists of a teacher-development assessment instrument.

Classroom assessments are used for a variety of purposes—perhaps to promote learning, guide instructional decision making, diagnose learning and performance problems, promote self-regulation, or determine what students have learned. Regardless of our primary purpose in assessing students' achievement, we must remember that the nature of our assessment instruments will give students messages about what things are most important for them to learn and about how they should study and think about classroom subject matter.

We should keep four "RSVP" characteristics in mind as we develop our classroom assessment strategies. First, an assessment instrument should be *reliable*, yielding consistent results regardless of the circumstances in which we administer and score it. Second, it should be *standardized*, in the sense that it has similar content and is administered and scored in a similar manner for everyone. Third, it should be *valid*, being an accurate reflection of the knowledge or skills we are trying to assess. And finally, it should be *practical*, staying within reasonable costs and time constraints.

A wide variety of standardized tests are available for use in the classroom, including many tests of achievement, general scholastic aptitude, and specific aptitude. As teachers, we must make sure that any standardized test we use meets the RSVP characteristics for our own situation and, if norm-referenced, has appropriate norms to which our students can be compared.

Test scores take a number of forms, with different scores being interpreted in different ways. Raw scores, based on the number or percentage of items answered correctly or the number of points accumulated, have only limited utility unless they can be compared to a criterion for performance or to the performance of a norm group. Criterion-referenced scores tell us specifically what students know and can do. Norm-referenced scores—age and grade equivalents, percentile ranks, and standard scores—enable us to compare our students' test performance to that of others. Because age and grade equivalents are often misinterpreted and percentile ranks distort differences among students, standard scores are preferable whenever they can reasonably be used.

In recent years, we have seen increasing use of standardized achievement tests to make important decisions about students and to hold school personnel accountable for students' achievement. Many experts believe that such *high-stakes testing* creates more problems than it solves, but it is here to stay (at least for the short run), and teachers must become vocal advocates for reasonable and valid assessment practices.

For both legal and pedagogical reasons, we must keep students' assessment results confidential, communicating students' test scores and other information only to the students themselves and to their parents. We must also describe assessment results in ways that students and parents can understand and remember that the ultimate purpose of any assessment is to *help students learn and achieve more effectively*.

Test scores and other assessment results are almost inevitably affected by a variety of factors (motivation, energy level, misinterpretation of assessment tasks, etc.) that impact reliability and validity; such sources of error in these results are especially common in the assessment of young children. Furthermore, excessive test anxiety, limited knowledge of testing procedures, and limited proficiency in English can lead to underestimates of students' ability or achievement, as can cultural bias in the questions or tasks presented. Whenever we suspect that such factors may be affecting students' performance, we should interpret our assessment results cautiously and look for other information that might either confirm or disconfirm those results. As teachers, we must take student diversity into account whenever we design and administer classroom assessments, and we must be especially careful to make appropriate accommodations for students who have been identified as having special educational needs.

Both standardized tests and teacher-developed assessments can be useful tools to help us in instructional decision making. Yet we must remember that any single test score is always subject to error and so must be evaluated in light of other data.

Common Student Beliefs and Misconceptions Related to Chapter Content

Below are several misconceptions that people often have before reading and learning about how to assess academic abilities and achievements, and such misconceptions may interfere with an accurate understanding of effective assessment practice. As you read Chapter 15, be on the lookout for evidence that contradicts these commonly held beliefs:

1. Some people think that classroom assessment must always involve paper and pencil—for instance, that it must always be a "test" of some kind. In fact, many forms of assessment require little or no use of pencil and paper.

2. Many people think of assessment as an activity that is totally separate from the process of classroom learning. In fact, classroom assessment practices significantly influence what and how students learn.

3. Many people seem to think that standardized tests are highly accurate measures of students' abilities and achievements. In reality, standardized tests are imperfect measures at best, and no single test should ever be used to make decisions that affect students over the long run.

4. Many people interpret grade-equivalent scores as indications of appropriate grade placements for students; for instance, they might think that a third grader who performs at a fifth-grade level on achievement tests should be promoted to fourth grade ahead of schedule. Other people believe that grade-equivalent scores should be standards for students' performance; for instance, they might think that something is seriously wrong if some third graders perform at a second-grade level or lower on a test. In fact, many students at any single grade level will perform above or below the average for the grade level on a standardized test; such variability is to be expected in virtually any classroom.

5. Some people think that a *percentile rank* indicates the percentage of test items that a student has answered correctly. Actually, a percentile rank indicates the percentage of peers who have performed at a lower level than that student.

6. Some people (including many politicians and government officials) think that large-scale testing is the best way to enhance instruction and achievement in our schools. For example, they suggest that we reward teachers and schools whose students earn high test scores and in some way "punish" those whose students earn low scores. However, there is no evidence to indicate that such *high-stakes testing* is effective, and many problems are associated with its use.

7. One common practice in schools is having students grade one another's tests and quizzes. Many people (including many experienced teachers) don't realize that, at least in the United States, this practice is illegal. In particular, it violates the Family Educational Rights and Privacy Act passed in 1974.

8. Some people think that test anxiety always interferes with test performance. In fact, a little bit of anxiety can actually enhance performance (recall the distinction between facilitating and debilitating anxiety addressed in Chapter 11).

CHAPTER OUTLINE	FOCUS QUESTIONS
ASSESSMENTS AS TOOLS	• What is *assessment*? What aspects of the textbook's definition are especially important to note?

THE VARIOUS FORMS OF EDUCATIONAL ASSESSMENT	• Explain the difference between:
	  • Informal and formal assessment
	  • Paper-pencil and performance assessment
	  • Traditional and authentic assessment
	  • Standardized tests and teacher-developed assessment instruments

USING ASSESSMENT FOR DIFFERENT PURPOSES
  Promoting Learning
  Guiding Instructional Decision Making
  Diagnosing Learning and Performance Problems
  Promoting Self-Regulation
  Determining What Students Have Learned
	• How are *formative evaluation* and *summative evaluation* different? In what situations is each one appropriate?
	
	• In what ways do classroom assessments influence student learning?
	
	• What strategies are helpful when teachers use assessments to:
	  • Facilitate learning?
	  • Make instructional decisions?
	  • Diagnose learning and performance problems?
	  • Promote self-regulation?

IMPORTANT QUALITIES OF GOOD ASSESSMENTS
  Reliability
  Standardization
  Validity
  Practicality
	• What is *reliability*, and why is it important?
	
	• Explain what the *standard error of measurement* is and how teachers can use it to help them interpret students' test scores.
	
	• How can teachers enhance the reliability of classroom assessments?
	
	• What is *standardization*? Why is it important?
	
	• What is *validity*? How are *construct validity*, *predictive validity*, and *content validity* different? In what situations is each one important?
	
	• How can a *table of specifications* help teachers design assessment instruments that have content validity for classroom objectives?
	
	• What is *practicality*? Why is there sometimes a trade-off between practicality, on the one hand, and reliability and validity, on the other?

CHAPTER OUTLINE	FOCUS QUESTIONS
STANDARDIZED TESTS Types of Standardized Tests Technology and Assessment Guidelines for Choosing and Using Standardized Tests	• Explain how achievement tests, general scholastic aptitude tests, and specific aptitude tests are different. In what situations is each most apt to be useful? • Why are computers increasingly being used in standardized testing? What is *adaptive testing*? • What guidelines does the textbook offer for choosing and using standardized tests?
TYPES OF TEST SCORES Raw Scores Criterion-Referenced Scores Norm-Referenced Scores Norm- Versus Criterion-References Scores in the Classroom Interpreting Test Scores Appropriately	• Explain how *raw scores, criterion-references scores,* and *norm-referenced scores* are different. • What are *grade-equivalents* and *age-equivalents*? Why are they considered to be norm-referenced scores? In what important way are they different from percentile ranks and standard scores? • What are *percentile ranks*? What is their major limitation? • Explain how a *standard score* is determined. (It may help to draw a diagram to illustrate your explanation.) • In what situations might norm-referenced scores be appropriate in the classroom? Why does the textbook suggest that teachers more often use criterion-referenced scores? • What guidelines does the textbook offer for interpreting test scores appropriately?
HIGH-STAKES TESTING AND ACCOUNTABILITY Problems with High-Stakes Testing Potential Solutions to the Problems	• What is *high-stakes testing*? What problems are associated with its use? What suggestions does the textbook offer for addressing such problems?
CONFIDENTIALITY AND COMMUNICATION ABOUT ASSESSMENT RESULTS Communicating Classroom Assessment Results Explaining Standardized Test Results	• In the United States, what implications does the Family Educational Rights and Privacy Act have for teachers and other school personnel? • How can teachers effectively communicate with students and parents about assessment results?

CHAPTER OUTLINE	FOCUS QUESTIONS

TAKING STUDENT DIVERSITY INTO ACCOUNT
  Developmental Differences
  Test Anxiety
  Cultural Bias
  Language Differences
  Testwiseness
  Accommodating Students with Special Needs
	• What issues should teachers keep in mind when using assessment instruments with young children?
	
	• What effects does *test anxiety* have on students' test performance? What groups of students are particularly prone to high test anxiety? How can teachers keep students' test anxiety at a facilitative level?
	
	• When is an assessment instrument *culturally biased*? How can teachers minimize such bias?
	
	• What implication do language differences among students have for classroom assessment practices?
	
	• What is *testwiseness*? What skills does it encompass? How can teachers help students become more "testwise"?
	
	• What characteristics must teachers keep in mind when they assess the achievement of students with special needs? How can teachers accommodate such needs when assessing students' learning and achievement?

THE BIG PICTURE	• What general principles does the textbook offer to guide teachers' classroom assessment practices?

Supplementary Readings

Your instructor may assign either or both of these supplementary readings:
- Appendix A, "Describing Relationships with Correlation Coefficients," in the textbook.
- Supplementary Reading #7, "Calculating Standard Deviations," which appears in the final section of this *Study Guide and Reader*.

Using the CD *Simulations in Educational Psychology and Research*

"Assessment in the Balance" on the *Simulations in Educational Psychology and Research* CD is a hands-on activity that gives you practice assessing student behaviors and products.

Chapter Glossary

Accountability. Holding teachers and other school personnel responsible for students' performance on high-stakes assessments.

Adaptive testing. Computer-based assessment in which students' performance on early items determines which items are presented subsequently; allows more rapid measurement of a characteristic or ability than is possible in traditional paper-pencil testing.

Age-equivalent score. A test score that indicates the age level of students to whom a student's test performance is most similar.

Assessment. The process of observing a sample of students' behavior and drawing inferences about students' knowledge and abilities.

Authentic assessment. Assessment of students' knowledge and skills in an authentic, "real-life" context; in many cases, an integral part of instruction rather than a separate activity.

Confidence interval. A range around an assessment score reflecting the amount of error likely to be affecting the score's accuracy.

Construct validity. The extent to which an assessment accurately measures an unobservable educational or psychological characteristic.

Content validity. The extent to which an assessment includes a representative sample of tasks within the content domain being assessed.

Criterion-referenced score. A test score that specifically indicates what students know and can do.

Cultural bias. The extent to which the items or tasks of an assessment instrument either offend or unfairly penalize some students because of their ethnicity, gender, or socioeconomic status.

ETS score. A standard score with a mean of 500 and a standard deviation of 100.

Family Educational Rights and Privacy Act (FERPA). U.S. legislation passed in 1974 mandating that teachers and other school personnel (a) restrict access to students' test results and school records only to students, their parents, and school employees directly involved in the students' education; (b) upon request, make test scores and other information in students' records available for inspection by students and parents; and (c) help students and parents appropriately interpret this information.

Formal assessment. A systematic attempt to ascertain what students have learned. It is typically planned in advance and used for a specific purpose.

Formative evaluation. An evaluation conducted during instruction to facilitate students' learning.

Grade-equivalent score. A test score that indicates the grade level of students to whom a student's test performance is most similar.

High-stakes testing. Using students' performance on a single assessment instrument to make major decisions about students or school personnel.

Informal assessment. Assessment that results from teachers' spontaneous, day-to-day observations of how students behave and perform in class.

IQ score. A score on an intelligence test. It is determined by comparing one's performance on the test with the performance of others in the same age-group; for most tests, it is a standard score with a mean of 100 and a standard deviation of 15.

Mean (M). The arithmetic average of a set of scores. It is calculated by adding all the scores and then dividing by the total number of people who have obtained those scores.

Normal distribution (normal curve). A theoretical pattern of educational and psychological characteristics in which most individuals lie somewhere in the middle range and only a few lie at either extreme.

Norm-referenced score. A score that indicates how a student's performance on an assessment compares with the average performance of other students (i.e., with the performance of a norm group).

Norms. As related to testing practice, data regarding the typical performance of various groups of students on a standardized test or other norm-referenced assessment. (Note that this term is used in a very different sense in the section "Effects of Culture" in Chapter 3.)

Paper-pencil assessment. Assessment in which students provide written responses to written items.

Percentile rank (percentile). A test score that indicates the percentage of people in the norm group getting a raw score less than or equal to a particular student's raw score.

Performance assessment. Assessment in which students demonstrate their knowledge and skills in a nonwritten fashion.

Practicality. The extent to which an assessment instrument or procedure is inexpensive and easy to use and takes only a small amount of time to administer and score.

Predictive validity. The extent to which the results of an assessment predict future performance.

Raw score. A test score based solely on the number or point value of correctly answered items.

Reliability. The extent to which an assessment instrument yields consistent information about the knowledge, skills, or abilities one is trying to measure.

Reliability coefficient. A numerical index of an assessment tool's reliability; ranges from 0 to 1, with higher numbers indicating higher reliability.

Scholastic aptitude test. A test designed to assess one's general capacity to learn; typically used to predict students' success in future learning situations.

Specific aptitude test. A test designed to predict students' ability to learn in a particular content domain.

Standard deviation (SD). A statistic that reflects how close together or far apart a set of scores are and thereby indicates the variability of the scores.

Standard error of measurement (SEM). A statistic estimating the amount of error likely to be present in a particular score on a test or other assessment instrument.

Standardization. The extent to which assessment instruments and procedures involve similar content and format and are administered and scored in the same way for everyone.

Standardized test. A test developed by test construction experts and published for use in many different schools and classrooms.

Standard score. A test score that indicates how far a student's performance is from the mean with respect to standard deviation units.

Stanine. A standard score with a mean of 5 and a standard deviation of 2; it is always reported as a whole number.

Summative evaluation. An evaluation conducted after instruction is completed and used to assess students' final achievement.

Table of specifications. A two-way grid that indicates both the topics to be covered in an assessment and the things that students should be able to do with each topic.

Teacher-developed assessment instrument. An assessment tool developed by an individual teacher for use in his or her own classroom.

Test anxiety. Excessive anxiety about a particular test or about assessment in general.

Testwiseness. Test-taking know-how that enhances test performance.

Traditional assessment. Assessment that focuses on measuring basic knowledge and skills in relative isolation from tasks more typical of the outside world.

True score. The score a student would obtain if an assessment instrument could measure a characteristic with complete accuracy.

Validity. The extent to which an assessment instrument actually measures what it is intended to measure.

Validity coefficient. A numerical index of an assessment tool's predictive validity; ranges from 0 to 1, with higher numbers indicating more accurate predictions.

***z*-score.** A standard score with a mean of 0 and a standard deviation of 1.

Here is an additional glossary item if your instructor has assigned Appendix A:

Correlation coefficient. A statistic that indicates the nature of the relationship between two variables.

Application Exercise #28: Considering RSVP Characteristics

In each of the situations below, a teacher has failed to address one or more of the RSVP characteristics of good classroom assessment. Identify the problem(s) in each case.

1. Mr. Marshall gives an essay test when three students are absent from class. He worries that the three absent students might learn what the questions are from their classmates and therefore would have an unfair advantage over everyone else. He makes up a test of true-false items for the three students to take instead.

2. Mr. Ermer uses a standardized achievement test as a final exam in his science class. He knows that this test has been carefully developed by its publisher, and he follows the test manual's administration instructions to the letter.

3. Ms. Martino believes she can get a better sense of what students in her advanced literature class have learned when she gives them an oral exam rather than a paper-pencil test. Therefore, she meets with each of her 25 students individually for 30 to 45 minutes apiece to discuss some of the novels they have read. She finds that the individualized format allows her to ask questions specially tailored to each student's interests; she can also ask for more information whenever she doesn't understand what a student is saying.

4. Mr. Thomas has a student teacher in his classroom this semester. Whenever the students do in-class assignments, the two teachers split the stack of papers they take home to grade. This way, they have to grade only 15 assignments apiece—something they can easily do in a single evening—and the students can get feedback about their performance the following day. Although the two have agreed on their scoring criteria ahead of time, Mr. Thomas always grades students' responses more leniently than his student teacher does.

5. Mr. Whitman, the football coach, has learned that more than 100 boys are planning to go out for the football team; this is far too many boys for him to handle at practice. To cut down on the number of potential players, Mr. Whitman gives everyone a multiple-choice test that assesses knowledge of the basic rules of football. He eliminates 30 boys from the team on the basis of their low test scores.

6. On the day of a big geography test, several students are home sick with a 24-hour virus. Their teacher, Ms. Leighton, gives them an equivalent test the following day—a day when the school heating system has broken down and the building is exceptionally chilly. Ms. Leighton notices that the students who took the test late have done more poorly than their classmates, and she wonders if the cold temperature interfered with their concentration.

7. Austin is taking the final exam in Ms. Lundberg's world history class. He has an hour to write two essays on these topics: "Identify two similarities between the government of ancient Rome and the current democratic government of our own country," and "Describe three major turning points of World War II, explaining how each one affected the final outcome of the war." If Austin can successfully answer both questions, he will get an A in the course.

8. Ms. Underwood uses more stringent scoring criteria when she scores the performance of her brightest students so that they will be challenged to do their very best.

Answers to Application Exercise #28

1. The nature of the assessment is not *standardized* for all students. As a result, the *reliability* of the test results is also affected.

2. Mr. Ermer has not determined whether the test has *content validity* for his own class.

3. The assessment does not have *practicality*: It requires a minimum of twelve and a half hours of Ms. Martino's time. Furthermore, it is not *standardized* either in time or in the nature of the questions asked.

4. Because one teacher scores responses more leniently than the other, students' scores are affected by the particular individual who takes their assignments home to grade. This is a source of error in students' scores that lowers the *reliability* of those scores (and indirectly the *validity* of the scores as well).

5. Mr. Whitman has failed to show that his test has *predictive validity* for identifying boys who are most likely to become successful football players.

6. Conditions under which students are taking the test are not *standardized*. The possible effects of room temperature are a source of error that contributes to lower *reliability*.

7. Students' responses to two essay questions are unlikely to provide a representative sample of what they have learned in an entire world history course. Hence, the exam has poor *content validity* in the sense that it is not a good reflection of students' overall achievement in the course.

8. Ms. Underwood's scoring criteria are not *standardized* for all students.

Application Exercise #29: Interpreting Test Scores

For each of the situations below, determine whether the teachers are interpreting test scores appropriately. Justify your decision in each case.

1. Mr. Croot receives the test scores from the standardized achievement tests that his fourth graders took last month. One of his students, Jennifer, has gotten grade equivalents of 6 or 7 on tests in every area—in reading, spelling, math, science, history, and geography. He recommends that Jennifer be placed in sixth grade rather than fifth grade next year.

2. When Mr. Doherty learns that all of his math students have gotten scores at the 90th percentile rank or above on a standardized high school mathematics test, he concludes that they have definitely achieved his instructional objectives in trigonometry.

3. When assessing performance in her driver education class, Ms. Crandall gives her students a separate score for each one of a number of important driving skills: using different gears at appropriate speeds, coming to a complete stop at stop signs, parking successfully in a parallel parking space, and so on. When students have a check mark next to each of these behaviors, Ms. Crandall tells them they are ready to take the state test for a driver's license.

4. Earnest, a high school senior, gets a percentile rank of 48 on a physical fitness test. His teacher concludes that he has performed about as well as the average high school senior.

5. Ms. Thurrell learns that Jason recently got a score of 107 on an IQ test that the school psychologist administered. She concludes that Jason is capable of much more challenging work than the average student and so plans to recommend that Jason be placed in several advanced classes next year.

6. When Ms. Wooten finds that all of her sixth graders have gotten at least 75% of the items correct on a standardized mathematics achievement test, she concludes that they have attained mastery of the school district's instructional objectives for sixth-grade math.

7. Ms. Simons enters her students' scores on yesterday's history test into a computer program that will compute the test's mean and standard deviation. Although she wasn't specifically interested in the students' z-scores, the computer calculates and prints out these scores just the same. She notices that Frieda has a z-score of 3 on the test and concludes that Frieda did exceptionally well on the test compared to her classmates.

8. When Mr. Bedinger gives his fourth graders a test of the week's 20 spelling words, they all get 100% correct. He concludes that they have mastered these words and are ready to move on to next week's list.

9. Mr. Almajbari learns that students in his advanced science class have all gotten stanines of 8 or 9 on a standardized science achievement test. He concludes that his students have done well on the test compared to other students across the nation.

10. Ms. Katz is concerned when she learns that a few students in her eighth-grade social studies class have scored at a sixth-grade level on the reading comprehension subtest of a standardized achievement test. She wonders if her eighth-grade-level textbook might be too difficult for them.

Answers to Application Exercise #29

1. Not appropriate. Although Jennifer has performed as well as the average sixth grader on the tests, this does not necessarily mean that she is capable of sixth-grade work. In any classroom, students are likely to show considerable variability in the grade-equivalent scores they obtain on a standardized test.

2. Not appropriate. Mr. Doherty needs criterion-referenced scores to draw such a conclusion. This test has yielded norm-referenced scores.

3. Appropriate. Ms. Crandall is using criterion-referenced scores to decide whether students have attained mastery of essential driving skills.

4. Appropriate. The test is obviously norm-referenced; Earnest's performance has presumably been compared to a norm group of twelfth graders. The 50th percentile reflects average performance (in a normal distribution, it is the *mean* of the distribution), and the 48th percentile is very close to this average.

5. Not appropriate. An IQ score of 107 is within one standard deviation of the mean, so it is essentially an "average" score.

6. Not appropriate. The score of 75% is a raw score. Standardized achievement tests are designed to yield norm-referenced scores, and raw scores on these tests are relatively meaningless. Ms. Wooten needs a criterion-referenced score to determine whether her students have achieved mastery—a score that this particular test doesn't provide.

7. Appropriate. A *z*-score of 3 indicates that Frieda's performance was three standard deviations above the mean.

8. Appropriate. Mr. Bedinger's test is not assessing just a sample of what students have learned in spelling this week; it is a measure of the entire domain. A score of 100% therefore indicates that his students have mastered all 20 words.

9. Appropriate. His students have all performed more than one standard deviation above the mean.

10. Not appropriate. In any classroom, students will get varying grade-equivalent scores on an achievement test; it is highly unlikely that all of Ms. Katz's eighth graders would get a grade equivalent of *exactly* 8. The low-scoring students will not necessarily have exceptional difficulty with the eighth-grade textbook, although Ms. Katz probably should monitor their academic progress carefully just to be sure.

Application Exercise #30: Evaluating Classroom Assessment Practices

Which of the following assessment practices are consistent with principles and guidelines presented in Chapter 15, and which are not? Defend your choices.

1. At the beginning of his final exam in basic accounting, Mr. Wagner reminds his students, "I want to emphasize once again how important it is to do well on this test. Remember, the score you get is worth one-third of your final grade."

2. Ms. Hovak is planning a homework assignment for students in her middle school literature class. She thinks about asking her students to write an essay comparing a particularly absentminded character in a novel they're reading to the personality of Winnie the Pooh. Although she thinks the question is a good one, she eventually decides *not* to assign it because she suspects that some of her students never read Winnie the Pooh books when they were young.

3. After all of her students have finished a quiz over a recent unit on reptiles and amphibians, Ms. Rosenbloom has them exchange test papers across the aisle and grade one another's work.

4. When Mr. Putnam administers a standardized achievement test to his sixth graders, he has his teacher aide take Danny, who is blind, to a quiet room down the hall. There the aide can read the test questions to Danny and record his responses.

5. Ms. Horrigan sees that Jamie has scored at the 75th percentile on the ABC Standardized Reading Test. She recalls that Jamie scored at the 50th percentile on the California Reading Achievement Test two years ago. "That's great!" she thinks. "Jamie's reading skills have really improved."

6. Ms. Jensen has three students who have recently moved to this country from Nigeria. These students have been raised speaking English, but Ms. Jensen is worried that they may have had little experience with multiple-choice tests and that, as a result, they will do poorly on an upcoming standardized achievement test. She develops a short "practice test" similar to the standardized test the class will be taking so that she can show the three students what a multiple-choice test is like. She also gives the students practice in filling out computer-scorable answer sheets.

7. When Ms. Lewis plans for upcoming parent-teacher conferences, she knows that she must give parents the results of a recent standardized achievement test. She decides that the best way to communicate how students have performed on the test is to use grade-equivalent scores.

8. Mr. O'Hara must give a make-up test to two students who had the flu on the day of his last government exam. He constructs a special test for these students, making sure that the items are similar to those on the original test and being careful to give the students the same instructions and time limits their classmates had.

9. Mr. Norwood has a chart on the wall that lists his students' names in alphabetical order. Every time a student gets 100% on a weekly spelling test, he pastes another gold star next to the student's name.

10. Mr. Quackenbush wants to assess his students' ability to apply the things they have learned in mathematics to real-life situations, so he gives them problems related to three real-world tasks—throwing a football, building a treehouse, and riding a skateboard.

11. Mr. Wilkewicz asks his high school English students to analyze a short story in terms of its underlying themes and the techniques (symbolism, etc.) that the author uses to communicate those themes. The very nature of the task is such that different students are likely to respond in a wide variety of ways. Although Mr. Wilkewicz is able to identify some general criteria to use as he evaluates what students have written, he is also finding that his evaluation of each student's response is somewhat dependent on how it compares with the quality of other students' responses.

12. When choosing a standardized achievement test to get a general idea of how well students are doing in reading, writing, and mathematics, a school district contacts numerous other districts around the country to find out which tests they prefer. It then selects the test that the majority of other districts have been using.

13. The students in Ms. Slobojan's advanced high school math class really enjoy the things they are studying; in fact, many of them are planning careers in mathematics or in such related fields as science and engineering. Ms. Slobojan repeatedly reminds her students how important it is to do well on weekly quizzes, pointing out that their final grades in the class will influence the decisions that college admissions officers make.

14. When Mr. Dietrich hands out the quizzes he has just graded, Melissa is home sick with a 24-hour flu. Her best friend Sallie asks if she can bring Melissa's quiz home to her, as she knows that Melissa is really anxious to find out how well she did on the quiz. "I'm sorry, Sallie," Mr. Dietrich responds, "but Melissa will have to wait until she gets better and comes back to school."

Answers to Application Exercise #30

1. Not consistent. Increasing students' anxiety at this point is unlikely to be helpful. For one thing, it's too late for students to study any more than they already have. Second, Mr. Wagner's statement is likely to raise students' anxiety to a debilitating level.

2. Consistent. Ms. Hovak is attempting to eliminate *cultural bias* in her assignment.

3. Not consistent. This practice violates the confidentiality of students' test scores.

4. Consistent. Generally speaking, administration procedures for standardized tests should be closely followed, but appropriate accommodations must be made for students who have special educational needs. Given that standardized procedures were *not* followed in Danny's case, however, Mr. Putnam and others should interpret Danny's test scores more cautiously.

5. Not consistent. Ms. Horrigan is comparing test scores from two different tests that undoubtedly have different norm groups. Comparing norm-referenced scores makes sense only when they are based on the *same* norm group.

6. Consistent. A test may be *culturally biased* if some students are unfamiliar with its format. By giving the Nigerian students experience with a multiple-choice test, Ms. Jensen increases their *testwiseness* and so increases the likelihood that their test scores will be valid indicators of what they have learned.

7. Not consistent. Grade-equivalents are too easily misinterpreted; for instance, parents may think that such scores reflect the most appropriate grade placement for their children. Percentile ranks and stanines are more generally recommended for communicating test results to parents.

8. Consistent. By keeping the items on both tests similar, and by giving the same instructions and time limits, Mr. O'Hara is keeping the test *standardized* for all students.

9. Not consistent. This practice violates the confidentiality of students' test scores.

10. Not consistent. Males are more likely to have experience in these areas than females, so the test is *culturally biased*.

11. Consistent. Many experts believe that when criteria for a complex skill are difficult to pin down, assigning norm-referenced scores may be the only alternative.

12. Not consistent. The district should determine which test has the greatest *content validity* for its own curriculum.

13. Not consistent. Although tests can be used as motivators, these students are already intrinsically motivated to learn mathematics. Ms. Slobojan's statements may raise students' anxiety to a debilitative level. Furthermore, tests tend to be *extrinsically* rather than intrinsically motivating; if we consider principles of intrinsic motivation (Chapter 12), we should expect such statements to undermine the students' intrinsic motivation for learning mathematics. Ms. Slobojan might instead point out the value of the weekly quizzes for giving students feedback about how well they understand the material.

14. Consistent. If Mr. Dietrich were to give Melissa's graded quiz to Sallie, he would be violating Melissa's right to confidentiality, and he should explain this to Sallie.

Answers to Selected Margin Notes

- Page 516: *Is the emphasis on formative evaluation or summative evaluation here?*
  The emphasis is on formative evaluation: The teacher wants to discover what students know and can do before or during instruction.

- Page 518: *A quick review: What do we call a memory aid such as RSVP?*
  RSVP is an example of a mnemonic—more specifically, a superimposed meaningful structure.

- Page 545: *Look again at the treehouse problem in Figure 8.4. Is this problem culturally biased? Why or why not?*
  It is culturally biased. Students who have experience with carpentry (which is more likely to be true for boys, for instance) may have an advantage over those who do not. This advantage is unrelated to the ability being assessed.

Sample Test Questions

Items marked with a "**1**)" on the left-hand side are lower-level questions that assess your general knowledge and understanding of the material. Items marked with a "**2**)" on the left-hand side are higher-level questions that assess your ability to apply what you have learned to a new situation.

Multiple-Choice

1)   1.   Three of the statements below accurately describe the effects that summative classroom assessments can have on students' learning. Which statement is *not* accurate regarding the effects of summative assessments?
      a. They promote students' intrinsic motivation to learn.
      b. They can provide specific feedback about what students have and have not learned.
      c. They encourage meaningful learning of class material *if* students expect that test items will require meaningful learning.
      d. They provide a mechanism through which students can review important material.

2)   2.   Which one of the following assessment instruments is most likely to have high *reliability*?
      a. A paper-pencil instrument with five multiple-choice questions
      b. A paper-pencil instrument with 50 true-false items
      c. A single comprehensive essay question that requires students to synthesize their knowledge of several topics
      d. Three complex performance tasks that are rated on a scale of 1 to 10

2)   3.   In which of the following situations should a teacher be most concerned about the *predictive validity* of an assessment instrument?
      a. An essay test is used as a final exam in a history class.
      b. A physical fitness test is used to assess the general fitness of students at Emerson Middle School.
      c. A series of mathematics word problems is used to determine whether students have mastered the processes of multiplication and division.
      d. A foreign language aptitude test is used to select students for an accelerated Spanish class.

1)   4.   Three of the strategies below should keep students' anxiety at a facilitative level during a classroom assessment task. Which one will *not*?
      a. Telling students that they will have as much time as they need to finish the task.
      b. Reminding students that their scores will be an important factor in determining final class grades.
      c. Allowing reference materials for things that don't necessarily need to be memorized.
      d. Explaining that the assessment can help students identify the things they know well and the things they still need to work on.

Essay

1)   5.   In a sentence or two, explain what educators mean by *high-stakes testing*. Then, in three separate paragraphs, describe three potential problems that the practice of high-stakes testing may lead to. In a final paragraph, describe two ways in which teachers and others might work to minimize the problems associated with high-stakes tests.

1)   6.   Explain what educational psychologists mean when they say that an assessment is *culturally biased*. Then, describe two different strategies you can use to minimize the cultural bias of the assessment instruments (either standardized tests or teacher-developed instruments) that you use in your classroom.

Answers to Sample Test Questions

1. a—Traditional classroom assessments typically promote extrinsic motivation rather than intrinsic motivation (see the section "Promoting Learning").

2. b—An assessment instrument is more reliable when it has objective items, rather than subjective ones, and when it has many items rather than just a few (see the bulleted list of conditions affecting reliability in the section "Reliability").

3. d—Predictive validity is essential when a test is being used to predict students' future performance (see the section "Validity"). The foreign language aptitude test is being used to predict how well students are likely to do in the accelerated Spanish class. (Content validity is more relevant in the other three situations.)

4. b—Teachers are more likely to keep students' anxiety at a facilitative level when they portray assessments as learning opportunities, rather than as evaluations of student performance (see Table 15.4).

5. *High-stakes testing* means making decisions on the basis of a single assessment instrument. The textbook identifies five potential problems with high-stakes testing (your response should identify three of them):
   - The test doesn't reflect important instructional objectives.
   - Teachers devote considerable class time teaching the content of the test.
   - School personnel have disincentives to include the test results of students with special educational needs and other low achievers.
   - Different criteria lead to different conclusions about how well students are performing.
   - Greater emphasis is placed on punishing low-performing students than on helping those students improve.

   Following are strategies that the text suggests (your final paragraph should identify two of them or offer reasonable alternatives):
   - Work to identify or develop tests that assess what things are most important for students to know and do.
   - Educate the public about what standardized tests can and cannot do for us.
   - Consider alternatives to traditional objective tests.
   - Advocate for the use of multiple measures in high-stakes decisions.

6. An assessment is culturally biased if any of its items either offend or unfairly penalize some students on the basis of their ethnicity, gender, or socioeconomic status (see the section "Cultural Bias"). Strategies for minimizing cultural bias include these:
   - Scrutinize assessment instruments for items that may be offensive to certain groups or items that students may have trouble answering solely because of their cultural backgrounds.
   - Make assessment tasks similar to tasks with which students have had experience.
   - Explain the general nature of the assessments students will be taking when some of them have not had prior experience with such assessments.
   - Give students practice with the assessment format (e.g., answering multiple-choice questions and filling out computer-scorable answer sheets).

   Your response should include at least two of the strategies listed above or reasonable alternatives. (The first strategy comes from the section "Cultural Bias." The other three can be found in the section "Testwiseness.")

Chapter 16

CLASSROOM ASSESSMENT STRATEGIES

Chapter Summary

Our classroom assessment practices will influence how students think about and learn classroom topics and how they conceptualize the very nature of different academic disciplines. Not only is assessment closely interconnected with instruction (see Chapter 13), but in a very real sense it *is* instruction.

As teachers, we may sometimes assess achievement informally, perhaps by simply observing what students do and listening to what they say in normal classroom activities. Informal assessment is flexible and practical and requires little or no advance planning. Unfortunately, it usually doesn't give us a representative sample of what students know and can do, and our judgments will inevitably be biased by our beliefs and expectations about different students. Whenever we must draw firm conclusions about what our students have and have not achieved—for example, when we are assigning final grades—we should base those conclusions largely on formal assessments that have some degree of validity and reliability. Especially important in this context is *content validity*: Our assessment tasks should provide a representative sample of what students have accomplished relative to our instructional objectives.

Paper-pencil assessment tasks take a variety of forms; for instance, they might be multiple-choice questions, interpretive exercises, or essays. Some involve recognition of correct information presented in conjunction with incorrect alternatives; others require students to retrieve information from long-term memory with only minimal retrieval cues. Different formats may be suitable for assessing different instructional objectives, and each format has its advantages and disadvantages. As teachers, we can construct and administer more valid and reliable paper-pencil assessment instruments when we (a) choose item formats suitable for our objectives, (b) clearly communicate what students need to do as they respond to questions and tasks, (c) specify concrete scoring criteria in advance, (d) set parameters for students' responses, and (e) encourage students to ask questions when tasks are not clear.

Performance assessment tasks are often more appropriate for assessing complex achievements that require the integration of numerous skills, and some instructional objectives can be assessed *only* through direct observation of what students can do. Performance assessment may focus on either products or processes, require either independent or small-group work, and involve either short (restricted) or very lengthy (extended) performances. In some instances, it may be *dynamic* in nature, such that it looks at how students learn and change over time, perhaps with the assistance of a teacher or other more competent individual. Performance assessments are typically more effective when they have some structure and when explicit, concrete scoring criteria are identified ahead of time.

When students are actively involved in their own assessments, they will be more intrinsically motivated and can develop important self-regulatory skills. Our classroom assessment practices should also allow leeway for students to take the risks so essential for the pursuit of challenging tasks; no single failure should ever be a fatal one that seriously impacts a student's long-term success.

After we have used a particular assessment instrument, an *item analysis* can help us determine whether the instrument has adequately assessed what students have learned and whether students have, in fact, mastered our instructional objectives. An item analysis also enables us to refine our assessment tasks so that they better serve our purposes in future years.

Most of us will eventually need to boil down the results of our assessments into more general indicators of what students have learned. The most common procedure, of course, is to assign final grades that summarize what students have achieved over the course of the grading term or school year. In most cases, final grades should reflect actual achievement (rather than effort or some other subjective quality) and be based on hard data. The problem with grades, of course, is that they communicate very little about what a student specifically has learned and can do. An alternative to grades—a *portfolio*—provides a means for representing the multifaceted, complex nature of students' achievements.

As teachers, we must always take individual and group differences into account when we develop and administer classroom assessments, and we must make appropriate accommodations for students who have special educational needs. Ultimately, we must be sure that our assessments are closely aligned with important instructional objectives and have reasonable reliability and validity for our purposes.

Common Student Beliefs and Misconceptions Related to Chapter Content

Below are misconceptions that college students sometimes have before studying the topic of classroom assessment; such misconceptions may interfere with an accurate understanding of effective assessment practice. As you read Chapter 16, be on the lookout for evidence that contradicts these commonly held beliefs:

1. Some think (and may even have heard from supposed "experts") that such innovative forms of assessment as performance tests and portfolios are *always* preferable to traditional paper-pencil assessment. In fact, depending on the objective(s) being assessed, paper-pencil assessments can often be a perfectly legitimate way of assessing what students have learned.

2. Many college students think of multiple-choice questions as invariably being "multiple-guess" items that can measure only rote memorization of trivial details. Quite the contrary, multiple-choice, when carefully constructed, can be used to assess many higher-level skills.

3. Many future teachers believe that improvement and effort should be important considerations in determining final grades. Actually, most assessment experts recommend that grades be based primarily on students' actual levels of achievement.

CHAPTER OUTLINE	FOCUS QUESTIONS
ASSESSMENT, COGNITION, AND METACOGNITION	• In what way do classroom assessment practices affect students' study strategies? How do they also affect students' epistemological beliefs?
INFORMAL ASSESSMENT RSVP Characteristics of Informal Assessment	• What various forms can informal assessment take? • What are the potential strengths and weaknesses of informal assessment with respect to the RSVP characteristics?

PLANNING A FORMAL ASSESSMENT
 	
   Selecting Appropriate Tasks
   Obtaining a Representative Sample
	• What issues should teachers consider when choosing the questions and tasks they will use to assess students' learning?
	
	• Why is it important that an assessment instrument be a representative sample of the content domain being assessed?

PAPER-PENCIL ASSESSMENT
 	
   Constructing the Assessment Instrument
   Administering the Assessment
   Scoring Students' Responses
   RSVP Characteristics of Paper-Pencil Assessment
	• What kinds of paper-pencil items can be used to assess higher-level thinking skills?
	
	• How are *recognition tasks* and *recall tasks* different? What are the advantages and disadvantages of each?
	
	• What specific guidelines does the textbook offer for constructing:
	   • Alternative-response items?
	   • Matching items?
	   • Multiple-choice items?
	   • Short-answer and completion items?
	   • Problems and interpretive exercises?
	   • Essays?
	
	• What general guidelines are useful for all paper-pencil item formats?
	
	• What administration procedures can enhance students' performance on paper-pencil assessments?
	
	• How can teachers maximize reliability when they score students' responses on paper-pencil assessment instruments?
	
	• What are the potential strengths and weaknesses of different kinds of paper-pencil instruments with respect to the RSVP characteristics?

CHAPTER OUTLINE	FOCUS QUESTIONS

PERFORMANCE ASSESSMENT
    Choosing Appropriate Performance Tasks
    Planning and Administering the Assessment
    Scoring Students' Responses
    RSVP Characteristics of Performance Assessment
	• On what occasions is performance assessment preferable to paper-pencil assessment?
	
	• Think of an example of a performance assessment that involves assessing a *product*. Think of one that involves assessing a *process*.
	
	• Under what circumstances might assessing *group performance* be appropriate for the subject(s) you plan to teach?
	
	• When might it be appropriate to assess *extended performance*? When might *dynamic assessment* be useful?
	
	• What guidelines does the textbook offer for planning and administering performance assessments? Why is each one important?
	
	• What difficulties are teachers likely to encounter when they score students' responses on a performance assessment? What strategies can teachers use to minimize such difficulties?
	
	• What are the potential strengths and weaknesses of performance assessment with respect to the RSVP characteristics?

INCLUDING STUDENTS IN THE ASSESSMENT PROCESS	• In what ways might teachers get students involved in their own assessments?
ENCOURAGING RISK TAKING	• How can teachers allow for a reasonable amount of student risk-taking through their classroom assessment practices?
EVALUATING AN ASSESSMENT TOOL THROUGH ITEM ANALYSIS	• For what reasons might a teacher conduct an *item analysis* of a classroom assessment instrument? • Explain what *item difficulty* and *item discrimination* are. How is each interpreted when assessment instruments yield norm-referenced scores? when they yield criterion-referenced scores?

CHAPTER OUTLINE	FOCUS QUESTIONS

SUMMARIZING STUDENTS' ACHIEVEMENT
 	
   Determining Final Class Grades
 	
   Using Portfolios
	• Why are traditional grading practices controversial? Why do these practices continue despite the controversy?
	
	• What guidelines does the textbook offer for assigning final grades?
	
	• Why should teachers base grades on hard data, rather than on subjective impressions?
	
	• What problems are associated with grading effort or improvement? What problems are associated with giving students extra credit for special projects?
	
	• What rationale does the textbook offer to support using criterion-referenced grades in most circumstances?
	
	• What is a *portfolio*? What guidelines does the textbook offer regarding the use of portfolios? What are the strengths and weaknesses of portfolios in comparison with traditional class grades?

TAKING STUDENT DIVERSITY INTO ACCOUNT Accommodating Students with Special Needs	• When considering student diversity, why is the *standardization* of a classroom assessment sometimes problematic? In what situations is it most important to standardize assessments? When should they be tailored to individual students' characteristics and special needs? • What approaches might teachers consider when assigning grades to students who have been identified as having special educational needs?

THE BIG PICTURE
 	
   Learning, Motivation, and Assessment
 	
   General Guidelines for Classroom Assessment
	• In what ways is assessment interrelated with learning and motivation?
	
	• What general "big picture" guidelines does the textbook offer for conducting classroom assessments?

Supplementary Readings

Your instructor may assign one or more of these supplementary readings:

• Appendix A, "Describing Relationships with Correlation Coefficients," in the textbook.

• Supplementary Reading #1, "The Seven Themes of the Book," which appears in the final section of this *Study Guide and Reader*.

Chapter Glossary

Analytic scoring. Scoring students' performance on an assessment by evaluating various aspects of their performance separately.

Checklist. An assessment tool with which a teacher evaluates student performance by indicating whether specific behaviors or qualities are present or absent.

Dynamic assessment. Examining how a student's knowledge or reasoning may change over the course of performing a specific task.

Halo effect. A phenomenon whereby people are more likely to perceive positive behaviors in a person they like or admire.

Holistic scoring. Summarizing students' performance on an assessment with a single score.

Item analysis. An analysis of students' responses to the individual items of an assessment instrument; used to identify possibly flawed items.

Item difficulty (p). The proportion of students getting a particular assessment item correct. A high p value indicates an easy item; a low p value indicates a difficult item.

Item discrimination (D). The relative proportion of high-scoring and low-scoring students getting a particular assessment item correct. A positive D indicates that an item appears to discriminate between knowledgeable and unknowledgeable students; a negative D indicates that the item may be providing misinformation about what students know and can do.

Portfolio. A systematic collection of a student's work over a lengthy period of time.

Rating scale. An assessment tool with which a teacher evaluates student performance by rating aspects of the performance on one or more continua.

Recall task. A memory task in which one must retrieve information in its entirety from long-term memory.

Recognition task. A memory task in which one must identify correct information among irrelevant information or incorrect statements.

Rubric. A list of components that performance on an assessment task should ideally include; used to guide the scoring of students' responses.

Test bank. A collection of test items for a particular content domain; sometimes provided by publishers of classroom textbooks.

Here is an additional glossary item if your instructor has assigned Appendix A:

Correlation coefficient. A statistic that indicates the nature of the relationship between two variables.

Application Exercise #31: Evaluating Classroom Assessment Practices

Which of the following assessment practices are consistent with principles and guidelines presented in Chapter 16, and which are not? Defend your choices.

1. Mr. Romero tells his students, "Most of you did a rather mediocre job on yesterday's assignment. Let's see if you can do better today."

2. When grading the research papers students have written in her history class, Ms. Gershwin takes one point off of a student's overall score for every misspelling.

3. When developing a rubric for evaluating students' short stories, Mr. Cornuke asks students for their ideas about the criteria the rubric should include.

4. To meet a school district objective, Mr. Silvestri's sixth graders must know basic history facts about their hometown and their state. A fellow teacher suggests that Mr. Silvestri use a performance test to assess students' knowledge, but Mr. Silvestri instead uses a paper-pencil test made up primarily of short-answer questions.

5. Ms. Roland announces that students' final grades will be largely dependent on the quality and frequency of their class participation.

6. When Mr. Sanderson writes multiple-choice questions for a science quiz, he includes common misconceptions among the incorrect alternatives.

7. Ms. George's class has just finished a unit on World War II. Because she wants her students to be able to synthesize what they have learned, she thinks that an essay test will be more appropriate than a true-false or multiple-choice test would be. Therefore, she asks her students to respond to a single essay question: "What important roles did Winston Churchill play during the war?" She gives her students the entire class period to answer the question.

8. When Mr. Perri asks his students to create portfolios that reflect their improvement in writing over the course of the school year, he tells them which pieces they should include in their portfolios and has them write a brief explanation of what each piece reveals about their writing.

9. To assess her students' mastery of several important mathematical concepts, Ms. Russem asks the students to solve several mathematical problems individually at their desks. To be sure that students don't simply copy their neighbors' answers, she makes three versions of the assignment. Each version has the same problems but presents them in a different order.

10. At the end of a unit on gymnastics, Mr. Valentine administers a performance assessment in which each student must perform a forward roll and a backward roll on the mat, as well as a vault over the horse and a dismount from the parallel bars. He has developed specific criteria for grading student's performance of each skill. Rather than having each student execute all four skills in a row, he first has all of his students, one at a time, do the forward roll. He then has all of his students do a backward roll. Following this, each student does a vault, and then each one executes a dismount from the bars.

11. Mr. Hiratska wants his chemistry students to master the symbols for the basic elements (O is oxygen, C is carbon, Ag is silver, etc.). He constructs a quiz that includes symbols for 20 of the elements, assuming that the elements he has included on the quiz are a representative sample of all the elements. Students who don't get a score of 100% on the quiz the first time must continue to take it until they get all 20 items correct.

12. Mr. Newton instructs his fourth graders to "Write a paragraph describing the solar system we live in. Write the very best paragraph that you can."

13. Ms. Romano has been teaching her students to sew in her junior high school "life skills" class. There are several techniques she wants them to know: how to sew a hem, finish a seam, attach a button, and so on. All of these skills are fairly cut-and-dried: Either students can do them correctly or they can't. To assess what students have learned about sewing, Ms. Romano gives a multiple-choice test on which they choose the correct procedure for each task from among four possibilities.

14. As part of a social studies lesson on cultural differences in family patterns, Ms. Jeffries asks students to interview one another about their family's kinship patterns (closeness and nature of relationships with grandparents, aunts and uncles, cousins, etc.). The students record their findings on interview forms specifically designed for the activity. That night, Ms. Jeffries grades the completed interview forms for completeness and quality, and she plans to consider the results as one of many pieces of data she will use in determining final grades.

15. When assigning final grades, Ms. Grubbs uses a unique set of criteria for Beth, a girl who has dyslexia. In particular, Beth's grades in reading and spelling are based on the extent to which she has achieved the objectives outlined in her IEP.

16. Mr. Orlando looks at the instructional objectives he has established for the unit on microorganisms. He believes that some objectives can be easily assessed by multiple-choice questions, others are better assessed by short-answer questions, and still others can really be assessed only by asking students to perform certain tasks in the lab. He therefore constructs an assessment instrument that includes both performance items and two different kinds of paper-pencil items.

17. Ms. Willis discourages students from asking questions during a test because such questions might be distracting to others.

18. Ms. Katkowski asks her students to write a short story using the writing techniques she has taught them over the past three weeks. Because her students are writing their stories on the computer, she allows them to use the thesaurus and spell-check functions included in the word processing program. She also lets them use a dictionary to check on the meanings of words they might want to use.

19. When grading essay exams, Mr. Urquhart always makes sure he knows whose paper he is grading at any one time. He believes it is important to take students' prior achievement into account when he grades their current performance.

20. Ms. Enriquez gives spelling tests in the traditional manner, asking students to spell each word that she dictates on a lined piece of paper. She finds that she sometimes has trouble grading students' spelling tests accurately because their handwriting is difficult to decipher (an *e* might look like an *i*, an *r* might look like an *n*, etc.). She is worried about the reliability of her tests and wonders if she should instead use a multiple-choice format to test her students' spelling. She eventually decides to continue testing spelling as she has before (i.e., by dictating the words to her students) but to insist that students write more legibly.

21. When grading a paper-pencil quiz in her geography class, Ms. Levinski discovers that only 15% of her students have answered question #5 correctly. Furthermore, all of the high-achieving students in the class have answered it *in*correctly. She decides to leave out question #5 when calculating students' overall quiz scores.

22. Although Justin has gotten higher scores on assignments and tests than Jason, Ms. Rowe gives Jason a higher overall class grade than Justin. After all, Jason has been attending help sessions regularly, and his mother reports that he spends at least two hours on his homework every night. In contrast, Justin never attends help sessions and seems to get high scores even though he invests little time and effort into the class.

23. Mr. Nguyen wants his students to be able to apply the things they learn in physics to new situations. After a unit on simple machines (levers, wedges, inclined planes, and pulleys), he asks students to explain how they might use these devices to solve everyday problems (lifting heavy objects, cutting objects in half, etc.). The particular problems that he asks his students to solve are ones that they have never actually discussed in class.

Answers to Application Exercise #31

1. Not consistent. Mr. Romero's feedback does not provide concrete, constructive information about how students can improve their performance.

2. Not consistent. Ms. Gershwin should evaluate students' writing skills separately from their knowledge of history.

3. Consistent. Mr. Cornuke is including students in the assessment process in an appropriate manner.

4. Consistent. Paper-pencil assessment is often quite appropriate for assessing students' knowledge of basic facts, and it is far more practical than performance assessment.

5. Not consistent. What and how much students say in class falls into the category of *informal assessment*, which is subjective and unreliable and does not provide a representative sample of what students know and can do. Final grades should be based primarily on hard data, in particular on the results of formal assessments.

6. Consistent. The distractors in a multiple-choice item should be plausible to students who haven't mastered the material.

7. Not consistent. First, the single essay question is not a representative sample of what students presumably have studied about WWII. Second, essay tests tend to have lower reliability than objective tests do, and a single essay question would have low reliability indeed; for example, a student who knows the material well but misinterprets the question might get an F rather than the A that he or she should actually get. Third, the question provides insufficient structure regarding how students should respond—a factor that will lead to difficulty scoring the test consistently from one student to the next and therefore will decrease reliability even further. If Ms. George wants to assess students' ability to synthesize what they have learned, she might combine two or three short essay questions with some objective, quick-response items (multiple-choice, short-answer, etc.); this way, she can get a representative sample of what students have learned about WWII.

8. Not consistent. Students should be actively involved in the selection of a portfolio's contents.

9. Consistent. Ms. Russem is taking a reasonable step to discourage cheating while keeping the content of the instrument standardized across students.

10. Consistent. Teachers can score students' performance more consistently when they evaluate it task by task, rather than student by student. If Mr. Valentine had each student perform all four tasks in a row, his judgments of a student's performance on one task might influence his judgments of that student's performance on other tasks.

11. Not consistent. The assessments that students expect influence what and how they study. When students are allowed to retake the same quiz, they may master the specific items on the quiz without necessarily mastering the larger content domain that it represents. A better strategy would be to ask about different symbols on each retake, so that students can do well on the quiz only if they know the symbols of *all* the elements.

12. Not consistent. The task is not clearly defined. Thus, students' responses are likely to vary widely in content and scope, and so they will be difficult to score consistently and reliably.

257

13. Not consistent. Having students actually demonstrate their skills with needle and thread would have greater content validity than simply identifying the correct procedures on a paper-pencil test. Ms. Romano doesn't need to watch every student as he or she performs the skills; she needs to look only at the products that students have created. Therefore, a performance assessment can be as easily administered and scored as a paper-pencil test (i.e., it can be just as practical), and it is undoubtedly a more authentic assessment of whether students have achieved the objectives.

14. Consistent. Performance assessments can often be incorporated into regular instructional activities.

15. Consistent. Using different criteria for a student with special needs is appropriate *if* the criteria are in line with targets identified in the student's IEP.

16. Consistent. It's perfectly acceptable to mix item types on the same instrument, especially if different types are better suited to assessing different objectives.

17. Not consistent. Students can perform well on a test only when they know how they are supposed to respond. Teachers cannot always anticipate the difficulties students will have interpreting test items; they must therefore encourage students to seek clarification whenever an item is unclear. To minimize distractions, Ms. Willis might have students approach her desk when they have a question; that way, she can confer with them without distracting others.

18. Consistent. By allowing students to use a thesaurus, spellchecker, and dictionary, Ms. Katkowski is essentially giving them access to certain reference materials. The point of the assignment is to assess students' ability to write a story; it is *not* meant to assess vocabulary or spelling. Therefore, the use of the three resources is appropriate in this situation.

19. Not consistent. Scoring criteria should be consistently applied from one student to another. Generally speaking, it is *not* appropriate to hold some students to different performance standards than others (possibly excepting students who have been identified as having special educational needs). A better strategy would be to help all students achieve the standards Mr. Urquhart believes are truly important.

20. Consistent. In this situation, a recall test has higher content validity than a recognition test because it more closely resembles what the students must eventually be able to do in real life: remember word spellings without the benefit of four or five possible spellings to choose from.

21. Consistent. Ms. Levinski's item analysis reveals a p value of .15 (reflecting high *item difficulty*) coupled with poor *item discrimination*. There is almost certainly something wrong with the item, and so it should not be considered in determining students' overall performance.

22. Not consistent. Final grades should be based largely on hard data that reflect students' achievement, rather than on subjective qualities such as effort. If Justin has better mastery of the material than Jason, then he should get the higher grade.

23. Consistent. Mr. Nguyen's objective is for students to apply principles of physics to new situations, and the assessment asks them to do exactly that. If he were to limit his assessment only to problems the class had already discussed, it would be measuring knowledge rather than application. Not only does the assessment have high content validity for Mr. Nguyen's objective, but it also provides a new learning experience for his students.

Answers to Selected Margin Notes

- Page 555: *Why do you think affective outcomes are usually assessed informally rather than formally?*
  Airasian (1994) has suggested two reasons. First, affect (e.g., students' feelings, attitudes, interests) is often difficult to assess formally. For example, students can "fake" the responses that they believe to be desirable, and issues of privacy often arise. Second, it is not always possible or appropriate to identify "desired" affective objectives. For example, although we might strive to help our students learn classroom material, it may be inappropriate to insist that they develop a certain set of attitudes or feelings with regard to it.

- Page 559: *Students tend to study more for essay tests than for multiple-choice tests. Why might this be so?*
  Three likely explanations are these:
  - Multiple-choice tests are recognition tests, whereas essay tests are recall tests. Generally speaking, recognition tests provide more retrieval cues than recall tests, making it easier to remember correct answers.
  - Multiple-choice tests typically assess lower-level skills, whereas essays may test either lower-level or higher-level skills. Students must process information more thoroughly (they should engage in elaboration, organization, etc.) to do well on questions involving higher-level skills. (Note that multiple-choice tests *can* assess higher-level skills—as some of the sample test items in this *Study Guide and Reader* illustrate—but those on teacher-developed assessment instruments often *don't*.)
  - Because multiple-choice tests have many more items than essay tests do, students can more easily skip over items related to material they don't understand, knowing that the "holes" in their knowledge will probably not have a major impact on their overall test performance.

- Page 570: *In which category do most performance tasks fall—recognition or recall tasks?*
  Most require recall: Students must retrieve the needed information from memory rather than simply identifying the correct item from among several alternatives.

- Page 574: *Which approach do raters use at the Olympics: analytic or holistic?*
  For the most part, their approach is holistic: Each rater takes into account a variety of criteria but ultimately gives a single rating.

- Page 574: *Use the concept of working memory to explain the value of having only a few criteria.*
  Working memory is the component of the memory system in which active "thinking" takes place. This component appears to have a limited capacity: It can hold only a small amount of information at any one time.

- Page 582: *What are students likely to conclude about these two teachers?*
  They might reasonably conclude that the two teachers do not take the job of evaluating students seriously and/or that they do not have the students' best interests at heart.

- Page 584: *Would a student who does little work all semester but pulls off a passing grade by doing an extra-credit project "learn a lesson" and develop more regular study habits over the long run? Why or why not?*
  From a behaviorist perspective (see Chapter 9), the student would probably not develop more regular study habits because procrastination and asking to do an extra-credit project have been reinforced.

Sample Test Questions

Items marked with a "**1**)" on the left-hand side are lower-level questions that assess your general knowledge and understanding of the material. Items marked with a "**2**)" on the left-hand side are higher-level questions that assess your ability to apply what you have learned to a new situation.

Multiple-Choice

2)   1.   Which one of the following is the best example of *informal assessment*?

       a. Noticing how diligently Tobey is working on his art project

       b. Giving a short quiz each Friday to check students' progress

       c. Having students work in small groups to solve a complex problem and complete a worksheet explaining their solution

       d. Limiting students' oral reports to 15 minutes each to ensure that all students can present them within the same week

1)   2.   Three of the following practices are consistent with the textbook's guidelines for constructing classroom assessment instruments. Which one is *not* consistent with these guidelines?

       a. Assessing lower-level skills if instructional objectives focus on such skills

       b. Combining paper-pencil and performance tasks if such a combination can better assess instructional objectives

       c. Identifying scoring criteria at the same time that you develop the questions or tests you plan to administer

       d. Asking ambiguous questions to see how students respond when they have little or no structure and guidance

2)   3.   When Mr. Johnston conducts an item analysis of a test he has just given to his seventh graders, he calculates p values of .90 or above for every item. Such data indicate that:

       a. His high-achieving students have done very well on the test; his low-achieving students have done poorly.

       b. His low-achieving students have done very well on the test; his high-achieving students have done poorly.

       c. Overall, his students have performed well on the test.

       d. Overall, his students have performed poorly on the test.

1)   4.   The textbook recommends that students' grades always be based on hard data rather than on teachers' subjective judgments. What is the rationale behind this recommendation?

       a. Students will be more motivated to achieve when they are evaluated on the basis of such data.

       b. Actual numbers are more concrete and therefore easier for students to understand.

       c. Students want everything they do to be graded.

       d. Subjective judgments tend to be less accurate assessments of achievement.

Essay

2) 5. As a German teacher, you want your students to carry on a simple conversation entirely
        in German. Describe an appropriate method you can use to assess your students'
        achievement of this objective, being sure to indicate whether your method should:
        a. Be paper-pencil or performance
        b. Assess recall or recognition
        c. Focus on lower-level or higher-level skills
        d. Be scored in a criterion-referenced or norm-referenced fashion
        Justify your decisions.

1) 6. Using what you've learned about self-regulation and motivation from Chapters 10 and
        12, describe two advantages of getting students actively involved in the assessment of
        their own accomplishments. Then, in a separate paragraph, identify three ways in which
        you might involve your students in classroom assessment practices.

Answers to Sample Test Questions

1. a—Informal assessment consists of spontaneous observations of students' day-to-day verbal and nonverbal behaviors. The other three alternatives involve planned assessment tasks. (See the section "Informal Assessment," including the subsection "RSVP Characteristics of Informal Assessment.")

2. d—Ambiguous questions are usually *not* recommended. Regardless of whether students know the answers to the questions, they should at least know what the questions are asking them to do. (See the section "General Guidelines for Constructing Paper-Pencil Assessments" and, under "Performance Assessment," the section "Planning and Administering the Assessment.")

3. c—A *p* value reflects the proportion of students who have gotten an item correct. At least 90% of his students have answered each item correctly; thus, it appears that, as a group, they have done very well on the test. (See the section "Evaluating an Assessment Through Item Analysis.")

4. d—Some teachers are better judges of student achievement than others. Furthermore, teachers often underestimate the achievement of low-ability students (see the section "Determining Final Class Grades").

5. a. Teachers should assess the specific behaviors they want students to acquire (see the section "Selecting Appropriate Tasks"). The best way to assess students' ability to carry on a conversation is to actually have them converse with someone else in German—a performance assessment.

    b. People seldom have the luxury of having several statements to choose from when they talk to someone else. They must instead recall the words and grammatical rules they need from their own long-term memories. Hence, recall tasks provide a more valid measure in this situation (see the discussion of recognition versus recall tasks early in the section "Paper-Pencil Assessment").

    c. You presumably want to assess your students' ability to apply what they have learned to a new conversation. Therefore, you should be testing higher-level skills. (See the discussion of transfer in Chapter 8.)

    d. Because you want to assess what your students can and cannot do rather than how they compare to one another, criterion-referenced scoring is appropriate. (See the section "Norm-Versus Criterion-Referenced Scores in the Classroom" in Chapter 15.")

6. To become self-regulated learners, students must acquire skills in self-monitoring and self-evaluation. Furthermore, self-evaluation enhances students' sense of self-determination, which leads to greater intrinsic motivation. Following are several ways you might involve your students in their own assessments (your response should include three of them or reasonable alternatives):
    * Make evaluation criteria explicit and easy to see.
    * Provide examples of good and poor products and ask students to compare them.
    * Solicit students' ideas about evaluation criteria and rubric design.
    * Have students compare self-ratings with teacher ratings.
    * Have students keep ongoing records of their performance.
    * Have students reflect on their work in class journals or portfolios.
    * Ask students to write practice questions.
    * Ask students to lead parent conferences.

Supplementary Readings

Supplementary Reading #1

COMMON THEMES THROUGHOUT THE BOOK[1]

Throughout the textbook, several themes underlying effective educational practice pop up over and over again. Some particularly prominent ones are these:

- **Interaction:** To learn and develop, students need numerous opportunities to interact both with their physical environments and with other people.

- **Cognitive processes:** How effectively students learn and achieve is a function of how they mentally think about—that is, how they *process*—information. Students need ample time to think about classroom subject matter and develop appropriate responses to tasks and questions.

- **Relevance:** Students must discover how new information and skills are related both to the things they already know and to their own personal lives and needs.

- **Classroom climate:** Students learn more effectively in a supportive classroom atmosphere—one in which they believe that they are valued as human beings, and one in which they feel comfortable taking academic risks.

- **Challenge:** Students are most likely to learn and develop when they encounter challenging tasks—those at which they can succeed only with effort and persistence and those that require them to use newly learned knowledge and procedures. Students should find that they can ultimately be successful at classroom tasks most of the time; however, they must also learn to deal with and benefit from the occasional failures they are likely to encounter along the way.

- **Expectations:** Students achieve at higher levels when their teachers' expectations for their performance are challenging yet attainable. Students exhibit more appropriate and productive classroom behaviors when teachers' expectations for their performance are communicated clearly and concretely.

- **Diversity:** Students will bring a wide variety of backgrounds, abilities, perspectives, and needs to any classroom. As a result, some students may benefit more from one instructional strategy, whereas others may benefit more from a very different approach.

Table 1.1 presents examples of where each theme appears in Chapters 2 through 16 of the book.

---

[1] This reading is an adaptation of text that appeared in the third edition of *Educational Psychology: Developing Learners*. Discussion of common themes was omitted from the fourth edition to make room for new material.

Table 1.1. Seven Themes of the Book

Chapter	Interaction	Cognitive Processes	Relevance	Classroom Climate	Challenge	Expectations	Diversity
Chapter 2: Cognitive and Linguistic Development	In Piaget's theory, interaction with the physical and social environments promotes cognitive development. In Vygotsky's theory, children work with more advanced individuals to accomplish tasks within their zone of proximal development.	In Piaget's theory, children construct knowledge of the world through assimilation and accommodation. According to Vygotsky, children acquire cognitive processes by internalizing their interactions with others. Information processing theorists study developmental changes in how children think about and remember information. Language provides a mechanism through which students can mentally represent their world.	Assimilation and accommodation can occur only when children relate new experiences to existing knowledge. Students show more advanced reasoning capabilities when classroom tasks are related to topics with which they are familiar. According to information processing theory, students' prior knowledge influences the degree to which they can understand, elaborate on, and remember new information.	Many students, especially younger ones, think it is unacceptable to ask their teacher for help, perhaps because they have previously been discouraged from asking questions at school.	Challenge promotes cognitive development, whether the challenge be in the form of disequilibrium (Piaget), a task within the zone of proximal development (Vygotsky), or the increasing need for sophisticated learning strategies (information processing theory). In a cognitive apprenticeship, teacher and student work together to accomplish a challenging task. Children are most likely to develop their linguistic capabilities when challenging tasks require them to do so.	Students may "hear" what they expect their teachers to say, rather than what teachers actually do say.	Students at any given age level vary in their cognitive and linguistic abilities. Some students have special educational needs related to their cognitive or linguistic development.

Table 1.1 (continued)

Chapter	Interaction	Cognitive Processes	Relevance	Classroom Climate	Challenge	Expectations	Diversity
Chapter 3: Personal, Social, and Moral Development	Students' self-concepts and self-esteem are influenced by others' behaviors toward them. Social interaction promotes the development of social skills, moral reasoning, perspective taking, and prosocial behavior.	Some students have trouble looking at a situation from someone else's perspective. Some may also have difficulty interpreting other people's behaviors accurately.	Students may encounter numerous moral dilemmas relevant to the content domains they study in school.	Personal, social, and moral development is most effectively fostered within the context of a warm, supportive, and encouraging environment.	Discussions about controversial moral issues challenge students to think differently about such issues and hence may promote their moral development.	Students' self-concepts are partly the result of expectations that others have for them; their self-concepts, in turn, affect the expectations they have for themselves.	Students differ widely in their social skills, self-concepts, and moral behaviors. Teachers can promote friendships among students with diverse backgrounds by setting up situations in which such students must interact and work closely together.
Chapter 4: Individual and Group Differences	Students often behave more intelligently when they work with the cooperation and support of others. Teachers interact more frequently, and in different ways, with boys than with girls. Students are more tolerant of cultural differences when they interact in a multicultural social environment. Students at risk are less likely to drop out when they get involved in extracurricular activities.	According to Sternberg, numerous cognitive processes are involved in intelligent behavior.	Students are more likely to exhibit creativity when they have considerable knowledge related to the task at hand. Students at risk become more psychologically attached to their school when they believe that school activities are relevant to their own needs.	Creativity is more likely to appear when students feel free to take risks. Students at risk are more likely to feel psychologically attached to school when teachers form close, trusting relationships with them.	Students are more likely to think creatively when teachers ask questions that require using information in new ways.	Boys tend to have higher expectations for themselves than girls. Teachers should not form expectations about individual students based solely on their IQ scores or group membership. Teachers should communicate to at-risk students that school success is both possible and expected.	Considerable diversity is found within any single ethnic group, gender, or socioeconomic group. Students may have trouble adjusting to the school environment when there is a mismatch between home and school cultures. On the average, boys and girls differ with respect to personality, motivation, and career aspirations.

Table 1.1 (continued)

Chapter	Interaction	Cognitive Processes	Relevance	Classroom Climate	Challenge	Expectations	Diversity
Chapter 5: Students with Special Educational Needs	Many students with special needs achieve at higher levels when placed in classrooms with nondisabled classmates. Nondisabled students benefit from interacting with students who have special needs.	Some students with special needs have difficulties with specific cognitive processes. Students who are gifted may have more advanced cognitive processing capabilities.	Students with emotional and behavioral disorders are more likely to be motivated to learn when the curriculum is related to their personal interests and needs.	Teachers should make it clear that they care about students' welfare; this may be especially important for students with emotional and behavioral disorders. Some students with special needs are more successful when the classroom is orderly and predictable.	Students who are gifted often have a higher zone of proximal development than their classmates and so may need more challenging assignments to promote their cognitive development.	Students with special needs are often more successful when expectations for behavior are clearly specified. Teachers should hold similar expectations for all students, with and without special needs, unless there is a specific reason to do otherwise.	Students within any single category of special needs are often very different from one another and so have unique strengths, weaknesses, and educational needs.
Chapter 6: Learning and Cognitive Processes	Increasing teacher wait time can dramatically alter the nature of classroom interactions.	Cognitive psychologists incorporate such concepts as encoding, meaningful learning, elaboration, visual imagery, and retrieval into their explanations of learning. Increasing teacher wait time allows students more time to process information.	Meaningful learning is more likely to occur when students have existing knowledge to which they can relate new information. Making multiple connections between new information and existing knowledge facilitates later retrieval of the information.			When teachers increase their wait time, their expectations for many students, especially previously low-achieving ones, begin to improve.	Individual students encode and store information differently, in part because they have different knowledge bases to which they can relate the information.

Table 1.1 (continued)

Chapter	Interaction	Cognitive Processes	Relevance	Classroom Climate	Challenge	Expectations	Diversity
Chapter 7: Knowledge Construction	Social constructivism focuses on how people can make more sense of an event or phenomenon when they work together to understand and interpret it. Hands-on experimentation with physical objects helps students construct more complete understandings. In a community of learners, students interact regularly to help one another learn.	Students construct their own meanings for the experiences they have and the information they receive. When students explain what they know or think to someone else, they must clarify, organize, and perhaps elaborate on their thoughts.	Students may connect new information to prior misconceptions and misinterpret the information as a result. Authentic activities may help students understand how classroom learning relates to real-life situations.	A classroom dialogue in which students express their ideas openly with one another promotes a better understanding of the topic at hand. A community of learners can create a cooperative spirit in the classroom.	Teachers can correct students' misconceptions by presenting information that conflicts with such misconceptions and by asking challenging questions.	Students and teachers alike may sometimes perceive events in a distorted fashion based on what they expect to see or hear.	Students' diverse backgrounds and knowledge bases lead them to interpret new experiences in different ways. Students from various cultures may derive different, yet equally valid, meanings from the same event.

Table 1.1 (continued)

Chapter	Interaction	Cognitive Processes	Relevance	Classroom Climate	Challenge	Expectations	Diversity
Chapter 8: Higher-Level Thinking Skills	When students study together in small groups, they are exposed to a variety of study strategies, including some that may be more effective than the ones they are currently using.	Metacognition includes students' knowledge about their own cognitive processes and their attempts to regulate those processes. Information learned in one situation is transferred to another situation only when it is retrieved in the second situation. Working memory, encoding, and retrieval affect problem-solving success.	Study strategies are most effectively taught within the context of specific content domains. Students are most likely to transfer their academic knowledge to real-world situations when they perceive its relevance to those situations. Successful problem solving is more likely to occur when students have thorough and integrated knowledge related to the topic in question.	Students are more likely to engage in critical thinking when teachers encourage them to view classroom subject matter with a skeptical eye.	The acquisition of complex study strategies can be facilitated when teachers scaffold students' initial studying efforts.	Students are likely to adopt complex study strategies only when they expect that such strategies will enhance their learning.	Some students have more effective study strategies than others; students with special needs often have few if any effective strategies. Students' differing background knowledge related to the topic at hand will affect their ability to solve problems and use effective study strategies.
Chapter 9: Behaviorist Views of Learning	Social reinforcers and positive feedback are often effective in changing behavior. In a group contingency, students are reinforced only when everyone exhibits desired behavior.	Some behaviorists incorporate cognitive processes into their theoretical explanations of learning.		Skinner recommended that teachers focus their efforts on reinforcing desirable behaviors, rather than on punishing undesirable ones.	Through the process of shaping, students are encouraged to exhibit increasingly complex behaviors over time.	Cueing is a subtle strategy for reminding students about expectations for their behavior. One probable reason for the success of applied behavior analysis, functional analysis, and positive behavioral support is that such techniques let students know exactly what is expected of them.	Because students have had unique previous experiences, they often respond to the same environmental stimuli in different ways.

Table 1.1 (continued)

Chapter	Interaction	Cognitive Processes	Relevance	Classroom Climate	Challenge	Expectations	Diversity
Chapter 10: Social Cognitive Views of Learning	Students learn by observing others; for example, they may learn through vicarious reinforcement and punishment. Students' self-efficacy is affected by others' successes and failures.	Social cognitive theorists view learning as an internal mental process. Students process information more effectively when they expect to be reinforced for learning it. Attention and retention (memory) are necessary for successful imitation of a model's behavior.	Students are most likely to imitate behaviors they believe will help them in their own circumstances.		Students' self-efficacy is enhanced when they set and achieve challenging goals.	Students form expectations about the likely consequences of future responses on the basis of how current responses are reinforced and punished. Students are more likely to engage in certain behaviors when they believe that they can execute those behaviors successfully (i.e., when they have high self-efficacy).	Students differ considerably in their self-efficacy for performing school tasks and in their ability to regulate their own behaviors. Students benefit from observing a wide variety of models, including those of both genders and diverse cultural backgrounds.

Table 1.1 (continued)

Chapter	Interaction	Cognitive Processes	Relevance	Classroom Climate	Challenge	Expectations	Diversity
Chapter 11: Motivation and Affect	All students probably have some need for relatedness. However, students differ in their needs for affiliation and approval. Most students prefer learning activities in which they can take an active, physical role.	Motivation affects what and how information is processed. Cognitive processes are something emotionally charged—a phenomenon known as hot cognition. An excessive level of anxiety interferes with effective cognitive processing.		Many students have a strong need to affiliate with their teachers as well as with their classmates. Some factors in the classroom environment (e.g., excessive demands, threats to self-esteem) lead to debilitating anxiety.	A challenge is a situation in which students believe there is some probability of success with effort; a threat is one in which students believe they have little or no chance of success.	Communicating clear expectations for student performance lessens students' anxiety.	The trait perspective of motivation focuses on how students are apt to be different from one another. Whereas young children often want their teachers' approval, many older ones may be more concerned about gaining the approval of their peers. Students' intrinsic motivation decreases as they get older. On average, students from some ethnic minority groups have more test anxiety than their classmates.

Table 1.1 (continued)

Chapter	Interaction	Cognitive Processes	Relevance	Classroom Climate	Challenge	Expectations	Diversity
Chapter 12: Cognitive Factors in Motivation	A competitive atmosphere undermines many students' motivation to learn and achieve. Some students place higher priority on social goals than on academic goals.	Cognitive processes play a key role in motivation. Students with mastery goals and those who are interested in what they are studying are more likely to use such effective strategies as meaningful learning, elaboration, and comprehension monitoring. Attributions are students' beliefs about what causes what.	Students are more likely to have intrinsic motivation to learn school subject matter when they see its relevance for their personal lives and professional aspirations; such relevance may be especially important for students from lower socioeconomic backgrounds.	Students are more intrinsically motivated when they can control some aspects of classroom life—for example, when they are involved in classroom decision making. Students are more likely to develop the motivation to learn if their teachers commend successful performance but downplay the importance of mistakes. When teachers have high expectations for students' performance, they create a warmer classroom climate, interact with students more frequently, and give more positive feedback.	Students who are intrinsically motivated, and especially those who have a mastery orientation, are more likely to engage in challenging tasks.	Students are more likely to be intrinsically motivated when they expect that they will be able to accomplish a task successfully. Students' expectancies for success are influenced not only by their perceptions of their own ability but also by their perceptions of the support they are apt to get from their teacher and classmates. Students' attributions affect their expectations for future success or failure. Teachers' expectations influence how they treat students and may ultimately lead to a self-fulfilling prophecy.	Students' differing interests affect their intrinsic motivation to pursue various classroom topics. Performance goals become more prevalent as students get older. Researchers have found gender and ethnic differences in students' attributions.

Table 1.1 (continued)

Chapter	Interaction	Cognitive Processes	Relevance	Classroom Climate	Challenge	Expectations	Diversity
Chapter 13: Instructional Strategies	In discovery learning, students acquire firsthand knowledge through their interactions with the environment. Some authentic activities require considerable student interaction. In class discussions, technology-based discussions, reciprocal teaching, cooperative learning, and peer tutoring, students learn through their interactions with one another.	An information-processing task analysis involves identifying the specific cognitive processes that a skill or body of knowledge requires. Classroom lectures are effective only to the extent that they facilitate effective cognitive processing of the information presented. Teacher questions, in-class activities, authentic activities, and homework can promote elaboration of previously learned material. Reciprocal teaching promotes development of metacognitive strategies.	Expository instruction should make frequent connections between new ideas and what students already know. Discovery learning is often most effective when students have relevant background knowledge they can draw on to interpret their observations. Hypermedia enable students to select topics that are relevant to them. Authentic activities are those that closely resemble real-life tasks. Class discussions are more effective when students already know something about the topic at hand.	Class discussions are most effective when students believe that they can speak freely.	In-class activities should become increasingly challenging as students become more proficient. In interactive instructional methods, students often challenge one another's perspectives. Reciprocal teaching provides a setting in which students can more effectively read challenging reading materials.	Instructional objectives enable teachers to describe what they expect students to be able to do at the completion of a lesson. Mastery learning is based on the assumption that all students can eventually master course material. Cooperative learning enhances students' expectations that they will be successful (i.e., it enhances their self-efficacy).	Different instructional strategies may be appropriate for different students; for example, lectures are most appropriate for students who can think abstractly (e.g., gifted students), and mastery learning and direct instruction are more appropriate for students who need to work on basic skills. Computer-based instruction allows students to progress through material at their own speed. Cooperative learning may be especially useful for females and students from diverse ethnic backgrounds. Interactive approaches promote friendships across diverse groups.

Table 1.1 (continued)

Chapter	Interaction	Cognitive Processes	Relevance	Classroom Climate	Challenge	Expectations	Diversity
Chapter 14: Creating and Maintaining a Productive Classroom Environment	One strategy for dealing with a student's problem behavior is a private discussion between teacher and student.			Effective teachers create a classroom climate in which students have a sense of acceptance, belonging, and some degree of control. A productive classroom climate is businesslike without being uncomfortable or threatening. Effective teachers set reasonable limits for classroom behavior.	Some students are likely to behave in counterproductive ways when they are given challenging tasks; one workable strategy is to begin the school year with familiar and easily accomplishable tasks, moving to more difficult tasks after a supportive classroom climate has been established.	Effective teachers give clear directions about how to proceed with classroom tasks. Teachers should inform students in advance about behaviors that are unacceptable and the consequences that will follow such behaviors.	Classroom behaviors considered unacceptable in the dominant culture may be quite acceptable in the cultures of some students.
Chapter 15: Basic Concepts and Issues in Assessment	Teachers must communicate the results of standardized tests in ways that parents and students understand.	How students are assessed influences how they mentally process classroom subject matter.	Authentic assessment involves asking students to perform in situations similar to "real life." Content validity is maximized when assessment tasks are as similar to instructional objectives as possible.			Assessment instruments never have perfect validity; thus, a single assessment should never be used as the sole basis on which to form expectations about students' future performance.	Assessments tend to be less reliable, and so less valid, when administered to young children. Factors affecting students' test performance include test anxiety, cultural bias, language differences, and testwiseness.

Table 1.1 (continued)

Chapter	Interaction	Cognitive Processes	Relevance	Classroom Climate	Challenge	Expectations	Diversity
Chapter 16: Classroom Assessment Strategies	Some classroom assessment activities (especially complex performance tasks) are more appropriate for small groups than for individual students. Although students often decide which products to include in their portfolios, teacher guidance is essential for ensuring that they make appropriate choices.	Classroom assessments can affect students' epistemological beliefs—their views about the nature of various academic disciplines.	Classroom assessment instruments and activities should closely reflect instructional objectives.	Teachers' assessment procedures must be consistent with an atmosphere in which students feel free to take risks and make mistakes.	Dynamic assessment provides a means through which teachers can determine how students respond to instruction and support when engaged in a challenging task.	Teachers' expectations for students can influence their informal assessments and their evaluations of subjectively scorable formal assessment tasks.	Teachers may sometimes need to modify their assessment procedures to accommodate students with special needs.

PHYSICAL DEVELOPMENT ACROSS CHILDHOOD AND ADOLESCENCE[1]

Teresa M. McDevitt and Jeanne Ellis Ormrod

Significant changes take place in size, bodily proportions, strength, coordination, and brain structures throughout childhood and adolescence, and with these changes come visible changes in physical abilities. Key characteristics and acquisitions of four age ranges—early childhood, middle childhood, early adolescence, and late adolescence—are presented in Table 2.1. In the following sections, we look at each age range more closely. We then consider how teachers can accommodate the physical needs of children and adolescents.

Early Childhood (Ages 2-6)

Visit a local playground, and you are likely to see preschool children engaged in non-stop physical activity. Physical movement is a hallmark of early childhood, and dramatic changes occur in both gross motor and fine motor skills. **Gross motor skills** (e.g., running, hopping, tumbling, climbing, and swinging) permit locomotion around the environment. **Fine motor skills** (e.g., drawing, writing, cutting with scissors, and manipulating small objects) involve more limited, controlled, and precise movements, primarily with the hands.

During the preschool years, children typically learn such culture-specific motor skills as riding a tricycle and throwing and catching a ball. Over time, these skills become smoother and better coordinated as a result of practice, longer arms and legs, and genetically-dictated increases in muscular control and strength. Optimism and persistence in motor tasks play a role as well. As an example, consider 4-year-old Alex. He repeatedly asks his parents to throw him a baseball as he stands poised with his bat. Not at all phased that his batting average is abysmal (about .05), Alex frequently exclaims, "I almost got it!" His efforts pay off, as he gradually learns to visually track the ball and coordinate his swing with the ball's path.

A lot of chatter, creative fantasy, and sheer joy accompany gross motor activity in early childhood. Children become superheroes and villains, cowgirls and horses, astronauts and aliens. During *chase play*, a young child may run after another child, pretending to be a lion or other predator (S. A. Owens, Steen, Hargrave, Flores, & Hall, 2000; Steen & Owens, 2000). Both the child doing the chasing and the one being chased work hard to keep the game going. The child wishing to be chased may yell "Chase me!", make a taunting face, and then sprint to avoid capture. The chaser joins in the game and often slows down rather than capture the other, thereby prolonging the fun. The eventual capture occurs in a friendly, if dramatic, manner, with the "victim" often squealing in excitement.

---

[1] This reading is an adaptation of an excerpt from *Child Development and Education,* by Teresa M. McDevitt and Jeanne E. Ormrod (2002), pp. 81–89.

Table 2.1. Physical Development at Different Age Levels

Age Range	What You Might Observe	Diversity in Development	Implications for Teachers
Early Childhood (2–6)	Loss of rounded, babyish appearance, with arms and legs lengthening and taking on more mature proportions Boundless physical energy for new gross motor skills, such as running, hopping, tumbling, climbing, and swinging Acquisition of fine motor skills, such as functional pencil grip and use of scissors Transition away from afternoon nap, which may initially be marked by periods of fussiness in the afternoon	Children differ considerably in the ages at which they master various motor skills. Boys are more physically active than girls, but girls are healthier; these differences will continue throughout childhood and adolescence. Some home environments (e.g., small apartments, homeless shelters) may limit the degree to which children can engage in vigorous physical activity; others may present hazardous environmental conditions (e.g., lead paint, toxic fumes). Children with mental retardation have delayed motor skills.	Provide frequent opportunities to play outside or (in inclement weather) in a gymnasium or other large indoor space. Intersperse vigorous physical exercise with rest and quiet time. Encourage fine motor skills through puzzles, blocks, doll houses, and arts and crafts. Choose activities that accommodate diversity in gross and fine motor skills.
Middle Childhood (6–10)	Steady gains in height and weight Loss and replacement of primary teeth Refinement and consolidation of gross motor skills, and integration of such skills into structured play activities Participation in organized sports Increasing fluency in fine motor skills, such as handwriting and drawing	Variations in weight and height are prominent at any single grade level. Children begin to show specific athletic talents and interests. Gender differences appear in children's preferences for sports and physical activities. Some neighborhoods do not have playgrounds or other safe play areas that foster children gross motor skills. Some children have delays in development of fine motor skills (e.g., their handwriting may be unusually uneven and irregular) as a result of neurological conditions or lack of opportunity to practice fine motor tasks. Some children spend much of their non-school time in sedentary activities (e.g., watching TV, playing video games).	Integrate physical movement into academic activities. Provide daily opportunities for children to engage in self-organized play activities. Teach children the basics of various sports and physical games, and encourage them to participate in organized sports programs. Encourage practice of fine motor skills, but don't penalize children whose fine-motor precision is delayed.

Table 2.1 (continued)

Age Range	What You Might Observe	Diversity in Development	Implications for Teachers
Early Adolescence (10–14)	Periods of rapid growth Beginnings of puberty; self-consciousness about bodily changes Some risk-taking behavior Increased aggression in boys	Onset of puberty may vary over a span of several years; puberty occurs earlier for girls than for boys. Leisure activities may or may not include regular exercise. Young teens differ considerably in strength and physical endurance, as well as in their specific talents for sports. Noticeable gender differences begin to appear, with boys being faster, stronger, and more confident about their physical abilities than girls. Peer groups may or may not encourage risky behavior.	Be a role model in terms of physical fitness and good eating habits. Provide privacy for changing clothes and showering during physical education classes. Explain what sexual harassment is, and do not tolerate it when it appears in the form of jokes, teasing, or physical contact. Encourage after-school clubs and sponsored leisure activities that help teenagers spend their time constructively.
Late Adolescence (14–18)	In girls, completion of growth spurt and attainment of mature height. In boys, ongoing increases in stature. Ravenous appetites, especially in boys Increasing sexual activity Greater risk-taking behavior (e.g., drinking alcohol, taking illegal drugs, engaging in unprotected sexual contact, driving under the influence of drugs or alcohol), due in part to greater independence and acquisition of drivers' licenses	Gender differences in physical abilities increase; boys are more active in organized sports programs. Boys more actively seek sexual intimacy than girls do. Some teens struggle with issues related to sexual orientation. Some teens begin to rebound from earlier risky behaviors and make better decisions. Eating disorders may appear, especially in girls. Adolescents are less likely than younger children to get regular medical care; this is especially true for children from ethnic minority groups.	Make sure that students know "the facts of life" about sexual intercourse and conception. Encourage students to form goals for the future (e.g., going to college, developing athletic skills) as a way of helping them curb risky behaviors. Develop schoolwide policies related to sexual harassment.

Sources: Eaton & Enns, 1986; Eisenberg, Martin, & Fabes, 1996; Gallahue & Ozmun, 1998; Jacklin, 1989; Linn & Hyde, 1989; Logsdon, Alleman, Straits, Belka, & Clark, 1997; National Research Council, 1993; Pellegrini & Smith, 1998; Sadker & Sadker, 1994; Sheridan, 1975; Simons-Morton, Taylor, Snider, Huang, & Fulton, 1994; J. R. Thomas & French, 1985; Wigfield, Eccles, & Pintrich, 1996.

Young children also make major strides in fine motor skills. For example, most begin to scribble with a pencil or crayon when they are 18 to 24 months old, and they can draw shapes such as circles and squares when they are about 3. By age 4 or 5, they can draw rudimentary pictures, perhaps of a "person" that consists of a circle for a head, two smaller circles and a curvy line for eyes and a mouth, and four lines sprouting from the circle that represent arms and legs (Beaty, 1998; R. Kellogg, 1967; McLane & McNamee, 1990). In their writing activities, children create wavy lines or connected loops ("pseudowriting" that resembles adult cursive) when they are about 4, and given sufficient experience with written language, they can often write some letters of the alphabet by age 5 (Graham & Weintraub, 1996).

Children's fine motor skills improve gradually over time with experience, practice, and normal neurological development. Some progressions involve cognitive as well as physical development; for instance, children become more competent at drawing as they are increasingly able to identify basic shapes and contours in the people and objects they want to represent on paper (N. R. Smith et al., 1998).

We see considerable individual differences in young children's fine motor skills. Some children, such as those born with certain chromosomal conditions (e.g., Down syndrome) and those exposed to alcohol during prenatal development, tend to progress more slowly than their age-mates (Barr, Streissguth, Darby, & Sampson, 1990; Bruni, 1998; Goyen, Lui, & Woods, 1998). Furthermore, some evidence indicates that some kinds of fine motor activities (e.g., cursive handwriting) may be easier for girls than boys (Cohen, 1997). Fortunately, explicit instruction and practice can help children improve their fine motor skills, although some individual differences in dexterity will inevitably persist (Bruni, 1998; Case-Smith, 1996).

Middle Childhood (Ages 6-10)

Children in the elementary grades typically show slow but steady gains in height and weight. Body proportions change less than in infancy or early childhood. With these slow, continuous gains come a few losses. Consider the gap-toothed smiles so common in children's elementary school pictures. One by one, children lose their 20 primary ("baby") teeth, replacing them with permanent teeth that at first appear oversized in the small mouths of 6- and 7-year-olds. Girls mature somewhat more quickly than do boys, erupting permanent teeth sooner and progressing toward skeletal maturity earlier.

In middle childhood, children build on their emerging physical capabilities. Many gross motor skills that were once awkward are now executed in a more systematic and proficient fashion. Whereas preschoolers may run for the sheer joy of it, elementary school children put running to use in organized games and sports. They intensify their speed and coordination in running, kicking, catching, and dribbling. Stopping frequently to negotiate over rules, they accompany their physical exercise with important social lessons. Although gender differences in gross motor skills are fairly small at this age, boys begin to outperform girls on some athletic tasks, such as speed in walking long distances (National Children and Youth Fitness Study II, 1987).

Elementary-aged children improve in fine motor skills as well as gross motor ones. Their drawings, fueled by physiological maturation as well as cognitive advances, are more detailed and complex (Case, Okamoto, et al., 1996; N. R. Smith et al., 1998). Their handwriting becomes smaller, smoother, and more consistent (Graham & Weintraub, 1996). And they begin to tackle such fine-motor activities as sewing, model building, and arts and crafts.

As children progress through middle childhood, they become increasing aware of and sensitive about their physical appearance. Consider one fourth grader's viewpoint:

I am the ugliest girl I know. My hair is not straight enough, and it doesn't even have the dignity to be curly. My teeth are crooked from sucking my thumb and from a wet-bathing-suit-and-a-slide accident. My clothes are hand-me-downs, my skin is a greenish color that other people call "tan" to be polite, and I don't say the right words, or say them in the right way. I'm smart enough to notice that I'm not smart enough; not so short, but not tall enough; and definitely, definitely too skinny (Marissa Arillo, in Oldfather & West, 1999).

Physical appearance is a major force in social interactions throughout childhood and adolescence. People respond more favorably to students that they perceive to be physically attractive, and differential treatment leads to variations in how students feel about themselves. In a variety of cultures, physical attractiveness is correlated with, and probably a causal factor in, self-esteem (Chu, 2000; Harter, 1999).

Early Adolescence (Ages 10-14)

The most obvious aspect of physical change in early adolescence is the onset of **puberty**. Ushered in by a cascade of hormones, puberty involves a series of biological changes that lead to reproductive maturity. It is marked not only by the maturation of sex-specific characteristics but also by a **growth spurt**, a rapid increase in height and weight. The hormonal increases of adolescence have other physiological repercussions as well, such as increased oil production in the face (often manifested as acne), increased activity in the sweat glands, mood swings, and emotional sensitivity (Buchanan, 1991).

Just as girls matured more quickly in middle childhood, so too do they reach puberty earlier, initiating the process sometime between ages 8 and 13 (on average, at age 10). The process begins with the onset of the growth spurt, "budding" of the breasts, and the emergence of pubic hair. Whereas such changes are typically gradual, the onset of menstruation (**menarche**) is an abrupt event. The experience can be either positive or frightening, depending on a girl's awareness and preparation ahead of time. The first menstrual period tends to occur rather late in puberty, typically sometime between 9 and 15 years. Nature apparently delays menstruation, and with it the possibility of conception, until girls are physically strong and close to their adult height and so are physiologically better able to have a successful pregnancy.

For boys, puberty gets its start somewhere between 9 and 14 years (on average, at 111 years), when the testes enlarge and the scrotum changes in texture and color. A year or so later, the penis grows larger and pubic hair appears, and the growth spurt begins soon after. At about 13 to 14 years, boys have their first ejaculation experience (**spermarche**), often while sleeping. Boys seem to receive less information from parents about this milestone than girls do about menstruation, and little is known about boys' feelings about it. Later developments include growth of facial hair and deepening of the voice and eventually the attainment of adult height.

Notice that, for girls, the growth spurt is one of the first signs of puberty, but for boys it occurs relatively late in the sequence. The result of this discrepancy is that boys end up taller, partly because they have a longer period of steady prepubescent growth and partly because they grow a bit more during their adolescent growth spurt. With puberty, boys also gain considerably more muscle mass than girls, courtesy of the male hormone *testosterone* (J. R. Thomas & French, 1985).

Accompanying the physical changes of puberty are changes in adolescents' cognitive capacities, social relationships, and feelings about themselves (Brooks-Gunn, 1989; Brooks-Gunn & Paikoff, 1992). Puberty also seems to unleash restraints on problem behaviors. For example, the onset of puberty in boys is associated with increased aggression (Olweus, Mattson, Schalling, & Low, 1998), alcohol and cigarette use (Reifman, Barnes, & Hoffman, 1999), and such behaviors as lying, shoplifting, and burglary (Cota-Robles, & Neiss, 1999).

To some extent, biology affects psychology in young adolescents. The continuing development of the brain's cortex (see Chapter 2 in the textbook) presumably allows more complex thought, and hormonal fluctuations affect emotions. And adolescents' rapidly changing physical characteristics can be a source of either excitement or dismay. For instance, Anne Frank looked very positively on puberty, as this entry in her diary shows:

> I think what is happening to me is so wonderful, and not only what can be seen on my body, but all that is taking place inside. I never discuss myself or any of these things with anybody; that is why I have to talk to myself about them.
> Each time I have a period—and that has only been three times—I have the feeling that in spite of all the pain, unpleasantness, and nastiness, I have a sweet secret, and that is why, although it is nothing but a nuisance to me in a way, I always long for the time that I shall feel that secret within me again (Frank, 1967, p. 146).

Yet others are not at all happy with their changing bodies. In *Reviving Ophelia,* therapist Mary Pipher (1994) describes ninth-grader Cayenne's perspective:

> She hated her looks. She thought her hair was too bright, her hips and thighs too flabby. She tried to lose weight but couldn't. She dyed her hair, but it turned a weird purple color and dried out. She felt almost every girl was prettier. She said, "Let's face it. I'm a dog." (p. 32)

Curiously, psychology also affects biology, in that life experiences influence biological growth in adolescence. Family conflict seems to accelerate puberty in girls, though not in boys (Kenneth, Smith, & Palermiti, 1997). However, pubertal maturation seems to be delayed in girls who grow up in low-income families, quite possibly because of less adequate nutrition (Tremblay, 1999). Also influencing physical well-being is a belief known as the *personal fable*: Young teenagers tend to think of themselves as completely unique beings within the human race (see Chapter 3 in the textbook). This belief often gives teenagers a sense of invulnerability. Because they feel immune from the normal dangers of life, they take many foolish risks, such as experimenting with drugs and alcohol and having unprotected sexual intercourse (DeRidder, 1993; S. P. Thomas, Groër, & Droppleman, 1993).

Diversity in the Onset of Puberty

Compared to boys, girls get a 1½-year head start on puberty. This gender difference is apparent in both the height advantage and the preoccupation with the opposite sex that many girls have in the middle school grades.

Considerable diversity exists in the timing of puberty for both girls and boys, and this diversity causes problems for some teenagers. Researchers have focused primarily on the potential vulnerabilities of *early-maturing girls* and *late-maturing boys*, whose bodies, the researchers hypothesize, are inconsistent with cultural ideals of attractiveness in the Western world. Early-maturing girls become heavier and more curvaceous earlier and so are less likely to resemble the slim and angular professional models that the popular media idealize as icons of beauty. Late-maturing boys are still "boys" when some of their peers are beginning to show signs of adultlike masculinity.

Some evidence indicates that early-maturing girls are, on average, less happy and feel less good about themselves than late-maturing girls (Sussman, Nottelmann, Inoff-Germain, Dorn, & Chrousos, 1987). In addition, their more mature appearance may arouse older boys, ushering them into precocious sexual activity (Hayes & Hofferth, 1987; Stattin & Magnusson, 1990). Early-maturing girls are more likely to partake in other risky behaviors as well, including substance abuse and reckless driving (Irwin & Millstein, 1992).

As for late-maturing boys, research indicates that they get off to a slower start than other boys in several aspects of development. For instance, they tend to be less athletically inclined and less popular with peers, and they less frequently seek leadership positions at school (Gross & Duke, 1980; Simmons & Blyth, 1987). On the plus side, however, they are less likely to engage in risk-taking behaviors such as smoking, drinking, and delinquent activities (Duncan, Ritter, Dornbusch, Gross, & Carlsmith, 1985; Sussman et al., 1985).

The timing of puberty does not necessarily destine adolescents to a life-long fate, however. For instance, the relative popularity of late-maturing girls and early-maturing boys brings only short-term gains that dissipate over time. Admired as teens, late-maturing girls and early-maturing boys may become somewhat rigid, conforming, and discontented as adults (Livson & Peshkin, 1980; Macfarlane, 1971). In contrast, early-maturing girls and late-maturing boys may develop strategies for coping with the trials and tribulations of adolescence, and these strategies may enable them to become independent, flexible, and contented adults.

Adolescents' adjustment to puberty is, to some degree, influenced by their culture, parents, and school setting (Blyth, Simmons, & Zakin, 1985; Hill, Holmbeck, Marlow, Green, & Lynch, 1985; Peterson & Taylor, 1980; Stattin & Magnussun, 1990). In some cultures, the beginning of puberty is joyously welcomed by formal celebrations, such as the Bar Mitzvahs and Bat Mitzvahs for 13-year-olds of the Jewish faith and the *quinceañeras* for 15-year-old girls in Mexican and Mexican American communities. School personnel can ease the transition as well, for instance, by giving some advance warning about the physiological changes that young adolescents are likely to experience and reassuring students that considerable variations in timing are all well within a "normal" range.

Late Adolescence (Ages 14-18)

At about 15 for girls and 17 for boys, the growth spurt ends. And in the later teenage years, most adolescents reach sexual maturation. (Individual differences persist, however, especially for boys, some of whom show few signs of puberty until the high school years.) With sexual maturation comes increasing interest in sexual activity, including hugging, kissing and, for many teens, more intimate contact as well (DeLamateur & MacCorquodale, 1979). (Chapter 3 of the textbook explores several topics related to adolescent sexuality, including dating, sexual intimacy, and sexual orientation.

Even at this point, nature continues to tinker with its handiwork. The brain in particular perseveres in refining its pathways, permitting more thoughtful control of emotions and more deliberate reflection about the possible consequences of various behaviors (Chugani, 1998; Giedd et al., 1999). Perhaps as a result, the false sense of invulnerability tends to decline in later adolescence (Durkin, 1995; Lapsley, Jackson, Rice, & Shadid, 1988). Nevertheless, many older adolescents continue to engage in behaviors that undermine their long-term physical health—for instance, smoking cigarettes, abusing alcohol and drugs, eating too many high-salt and high-fat foods, or, worse still, eating little at all—without thinking about the potential repercussions of such actions (B. J. Guthrie, Caldwell, & Hunter, 1997).

Accommodating the Physical Needs of Children

Following are several suggestions for accommodating the physical development of children in the preschool and elementary school years. Each suggestion is followed by an example of what a teacher might do.

• Make sure that the classroom is free of sharp edges, peeling paint, and other environmental hazards to which young children may be particularly vulnerable.

> After new carpet is installed in his classroom, a preschool teacher notices that several children complain of stomachaches and headaches. He suspects that the recently applied carpet adhesive may be to blame and, with the approval of the preschool's director, asks an outside consultant to evaluate the situation. Meanwhile, he conducts most of the day's activities outdoors or in other rooms in the building.

• Provide frequent opportunities for children to engage in physical activity.

> A preschool teacher schedules "Music and Marching" for mid-morning, "Outdoor Time" before lunch, and a nature walk to collect leaves for an art project after nap time.

• Plan activities that will help children develop their fine motor skills.

> In a unit on transportation, a first-grade teacher has students make mosaics that depict different kinds of transportation. The students glue a variety of small objects (e.g., beads, sequins, beans, colored rice) onto line drawings of cars, trains, boats, airplanes, bicycles, and so on.

• Design physical activities so that students with widely differing skill levels can successfully participate.

> During a unit on tennis, an elementary physical education teacher has students practice the forehand strike using tennis rackets. First she asks them to practice bouncing and then hitting the ball against the wall of the gymnasium. If some students master these basic skills, she asks them to see how many times in succession they can hit the ball against the wall. If any reach 5 successive hits, she tells them to vary the height of the ball from waist high to shoulder high (Logsdon, Alleman, Straits, Belka, & Clark, 1997).

• Integrate physical activity into academic lessons.

> When teaching about molecules and temperature, a fifth-grade teacher asks students to stand in a cluster in an open area of the classroom. To show the students how molecules behave when something is cold, she asks them to stay close together and move around just a little bit. To show them how molecules behave when something is hot, she asks them to spread farther apart and move more actively (courtesy of Michele Minichiello).

• Give children time to rest and rejuvenate.

> After a kindergarten class has been playing outside, their teacher offers a snack of apple slices, crackers, and milk. Once they have cleaned up their milk cartons and napkins, the children gather around him on the floor while he reads them a storybook.

• Respect children's growing ability to care for their own bodies.

> A second-grade teacher allows children to go to the restroom whenever they need to. He teaches the children to hang a clothespin with their name on an "out rope" when they leave the room and then remove the pin when they return.

Accommodating the Physical Needs of Adolescents

Following are several suggestions for accommodating the physical development of adolescents in the middle school and high school years. Each suggestion is followed by an example of what a teacher might do.

- Accommodate the self-conscious feelings that adolescents have about their changing bodies.

    A middle school boys' basketball coach gives students plenty of time to change clothes before and after practice. He also makes sure that the showers have enough curtains that each student can shower in private.

- Keep in mind that menstruation can begin at unexpected and inopportune times.

    An eighth-grade girl comes into class obviously upset, and her best friend approaches their teacher to explain that the two of them need to go to the nurse's office right away. The teacher realizes what has probably just happened and immediately gives them permission to go.

- Make sure students understand what sexual harassment is, and do not tolerate it when it occurs.

    A high school includes a sexual harassment policy in its student handbook, and homeroom teachers explain the policy very early in the school year. When a student unthinkingly violates the policy by teasing a classmate about her "big rack," his teacher takes him aside and privately explains that his comment not only constitutes sexual harassment (and so violates school policy) but also makes the girl feel unnecessarily embarrassed and uncomfortable. The boy admits that he spoke without thinking and, after class, tells the girl he's sorry.

- Be sensitive to students' feelings about early or late maturation.

    In its health curriculum, a middle school clearly describes the biological changes that accompany puberty. It also stresses that the timing of these changes varies widely from one person to the next and that being "normal" takes many forms.

Supplementary Reading #3

PARENTING STYLES AND CHILDREN'S BEHAVIOR[1]

As you've undoubtedly learned from your own experiences, parents use a variety of strategies to guide and discipline their children. Researchers have identified four distinctive patterns of behaviors that parents may use in raising their children and discovered that such **parenting styles** are associated with different behaviors and personality traits in children (Baumrind, 1971, 1989, 1991; Maccoby & Martin, 1983). These four parenting styles—authoritative, authoritarian, permissive, and uninvolved—are summarized in Table 3.1.

As you can see from Table 3.1, an authoritative style seems to be the ideal situation. Children from authoritative homes are well-adjusted, happy, energetic, self-confident, curious, and independent. They are motivated to do well in school; as a result, they are often high achievers (Miller, 1995; Steinberg, Elmen, & Mounts, 1989). They are likable and cooperative, make friends easily, and show strong leadership skills. They also exhibit self-control and concern for the rights and needs of others.

As you examine the four parenting styles in Table 3.1, you may notice that these styles differ in the degree of control exerted over children. At one extreme is the excessively controlling, authoritarian parent; at the other extreme is the noncontrolling (either permissive or uninvolved) parent. The authoritative home appears to be the happy medium: Children thrive when parents establish and consistently enforce standards for acceptable behavior while at the same time considering their children's individual rights and needs. Ideally, adults should tailor the degree of control to the developmental level of the child, gradually loosening restrictions as children become capable of greater responsibility and independence (Maccoby & Martin, 1983). Too much control may lead to a lack of self-confidence and initiative; too little may lead to selfish, impulsive, and possibly delinquent behavior.

Keep in mind, however, that most research on parenting styles is correlational in nature. As you should recall from Chapter 1 in the textbook, only *experimental* studies conclusively demonstrate cause-effect relationships. A few experimental studies of parent training programs *do* support the existence of a general cause-effect relationship between parenting style and children's behavior: Specifically teaching parents to use more effective parenting strategies leads to more desirable behaviors in children (W. A. Collins, Maccoby, Steinberg, Hetherington, & Bornstein, 2000).

---

[1] This reading is based, in part, on a discussion in the third edition of *Educational Psychology: Developing Learners*. The discussion of parenting was greatly reduced in the fourth edition of the book to make room for new material.

...our Parenting Styles

...en parents exhibit this parenting style . . .	Children tend to be . . .
Authoritative: • Provide a loving, supportive, home environment • Hold high expectations and standards for their children's behaviors • Enforce household rules consistently • Explain why some behaviors are acceptable and others are not • Include children in family decision making	• Happy • Self-confident • Curious • Independent and self-reliant • Likable, with effective social skills • Respectful of others • Successful in school
Authoritarian: • Convey less emotional warmth than authoritative parents • Hold high expectations and standards for their children's behaviors • Establish rules of behavior without regard for children's needs • Expect rules to be obeyed without question • Allow little give-and-take in parent-child discussions	• Unhappy • Anxious • Low in self-confidence • Lacking initiative • Dependent on others • Lacking in social and prosocial skills • Coercive in dealing with others • Defiant
Permissive: • Provide a loving, supportive, home environment • Hold few expectations or standards for their children's behaviors • Rarely punish inappropriate behavior • Allow their children to make many of their own decisions (e.g., about eating, bedtime)	• Selfish • Unmotivated • Dependent on others • Demanding of attention • Disobedient • Impulsive
Uninvolved: • Provide little if any emotional support for their children • Hold few expectations or standards for their children's behaviors • Have little interest in their children's lives • Seem overwhelmed by their own problems	• Disobedient • Demanding • Low in self-control • Low in tolerance for frustration • Lacking long-term goals

Sources: Baumrind, 1971, 1989; Dekovic & Janssens, 1992; Lamborn, Mounts, Steinberg, & Dornbusch, 1991; Maccoby & Martin, 1983; Simons, Whitbeck, Conger, & Conger, 1991; Steinberg, 1993; Steinberg, Elmen, & Mounts, 1989.

Following are several additional points to keep in mind about parenting styles:

• *Parent-child interactions are to some extent a two-way street.* Although children's behaviors are often the result of how their parents treat them, sometimes the reverse is true as well: Parents' behaviors may be the result of how *they* are treated by *their children* (Eisenberg & Fabes, 1994; Maccoby & Martin, 1983; Scarr, 1993). One psychologist has made this point by describing her own experiences with her two children:

> I ... reared a pair of very different children. My older daughter hardly ever wanted to do anything that her father and I didn't want her to do. My younger daughter often did. Raising the first was easy; raising the second was, um, interesting....
>
> How do you treat two children both the same when they *aren't* the same—when they do different things and say different things, have different abilities and different personalities? .... I would have been pegged as a permissive parent with my first child, a bossy one with my second....
>
> My husband and I seldom had hard-and-fast rules with our first child; generally we didn't need them. With our second child we had all sorts of rules and none of them worked. Reason with her? Give me a break. Often we ended up taking the shut-your-mouth-and-do-what-you're-told route. That didn't work either. In the end we pretty much gave up. Somehow we all made it through her teens. (J. R. Harris, 1998, pp. 26, 48)

Temperament is, in part, genetically determined: Some children appear to be naturally quieter and more easygoing, whereas others are more lively or irritable (see Chapter 3 in the textbook). When children are quick to comply with their parents' wishes, parents may have no reason to be overly controlling. When children are hot-tempered, parents may have to impose more restrictions on behavior and administer consequences for misbehaviors more frequently. We must be careful that we don't always place total credit or blame on parents for their parenting styles.

• *Different cultures endorse different parenting styles.* Children of authoritative parents appear well adjusted, in part, because they fit well with ideal roles defined in Western cultures: They listen respectfully to others, can follow rules by the time they reach school age, try to be independent, and strive for academic achievement. Yet sometimes other parenting styles are better suited to other cultures. For example, children of very controlling (and so apparently "authoritarian") Asian American parents do quite well in school (Chao, 1994; Dornbusch et al., 1987; Lin & Fu, 1990). In many Asian American families, high demands for obedience are made within the context of a close, supportive mother-child relationship (Chao, 1994). Furthermore, principles of Confucianism teach children that parents are always right and that obedience and emotional restraint are essential for family harmony (Chao, 1994).

• *Impoverished economic conditions may require more authoritarian parenting.* When parents live in low-income, inner-city neighborhoods where danger potentially lurks around every corner, parents may better serve their children by being very strict and directive about activities (Hale-Benson, 1986; McLoyd, 1998). In some cases, the stresses of impoverished financial resources become so overwhelming that they limit parents' ability to solicit children's ideas about family rules (Bronfenbrenner, Alvarez, & Henderson, 1984). Communicating high standards for behavior and negotiating with children when rules seem unfair take considerable time and energy—perhaps more time and energy than some stressful circumstances allow.

• *Parenting styles are just one of the many factors affecting children's personal and social development.* Research findings suggest that, at most, parenting styles have a moderate, rather than strong, influence on children's personalities and social-emotional well-being (W. A. Collins et al., 2000; Weiss & Schwarz, 1996). In fact, children appear to thrive with parents who exhibit a wide variety of parenting styles, provided that their homes aren't severely neglectful or abusive: Most parents provide "good-enough" homes that promote children's social-emotional growth (J. R. Harris, 1995, 1998; Lykken, 1997; Scarr, 1992).

• *Parental neglect and abuse can have significant long-term consequences.* In some cases, parents neglect their children: They fail to provide nutritious meals, adequate clothing, and other basic necessities of life. In other cases, they abuse their children physically, sexually, or psychologically. Systematic research and case studies consistently indicate that parental neglect and abuse have significant adverse effects on children's personal and social development (Dodge, Pettit, Bates, & Valente, 1995; Thompson & Wyatt, 1999). In general, children who have been routinely neglected or abused have low self-esteem, poorly developed social skills, and low school achievement. Many are angry, aggressive, and defiant; others can be depressed, anxious, socially withdrawn, and possibly suicidal.

Implications for Teachers

If you read Chapter 14 in the textbook, you will discover that recommended strategies for classroom management resemble an authoritative parenting style. For instance, experts suggest that we exert some control in the classroom by holding high expectations for student behavior and enforcing classroom rules consistently. At the same time, we should explain to students why some behaviors are acceptable and others are not, provide a supportive environment, and recognize each student's legitimate needs and point of view. We can include students in classroom decision making and encourage them to be independent and self-reliant. And we should gradually loosen the reins as students demonstrate increasing independence and self-control.

As teachers, we can serve as valuable resources to parents about possible strategies for promoting their children's personal and social development. With newsletters, parent-teacher conferences, and parent discussion groups, we can share ways of helping children develop increasingly more appropriate and mature behaviors. The important thing is to communicate information *without* pointing fingers or being judgmental about parenting styles. At the same time, if we suspect parental neglect or abuse, we must, by law, contact proper authorities. Two helpful resources are the National Child Abuse Hotline (1-800-4-A- CHILD®) and the Internet Web site for Childhelp USA® at http://www.childhelpusa.org.

MASLOW'S HIERARCHY OF NEEDS[1]

Abraham Maslow's work (1973, 1987) has been a central aspect of the *humanist* movement, a perspective especially prominent in psychology during the 1960s and 1970s. Humanism, with roots in clinical and counseling psychology, focuses on how individuals acquire emotions, attitudes, values, and interpersonal skills. Humanist views tend to be grounded more in philosophy than in research, but they provide useful insights into human motivation nevertheless.

Maslow proposed that people have five basic kinds of needs that they try to satisfy:

1. **Physiological needs.** People are motivated to satisfy needs related to their physical survival (e.g., needs for food, water, oxygen, warmth, exercise, and rest). For example, thirsty students may request a trip to the drinking fountain, students needing to release pent-up energy may become restless and fidgety, and hungry students may be thinking more about their growling stomachs than a classroom activity.

2. **Safety needs.** People have a need to feel safe and secure in their environment. For instance, students like to know what things are expected of them and are happier when classroom routines are somewhat orderly and predictable.

3. **Love and belonging needs.** People seek affectionate relationships with others and like to feel that they are accepted as part of a group; in other words, they have a need for affiliation. For example, a fourth grader may place great importance on having a "best" friend. And many adolescents take great pains to fit in with the "cool" crowd—for example, by wearing a certain hairstyle or clothes emblazoned with a certain brand name.

4. **Esteem needs.** People have a need to feel good about themselves (a *need for self-esteem*) and to believe that other people also feel positively about them (a *need for esteem from others*). To develop positive self-esteem, students will strive for achievement and mastery of their environment. To attain the esteem and respect of others, they will behave in ways that gain them recognition, appreciation, and prestige. For example, a second grader can partially satisfy the need for self-esteem by reading a book "all by myself" or by achieving a special merit badge in Cub Scouts or Campfire Girls. A high school student may try to satisfy the need for esteem from others by running for Student Council treasurer or becoming a star athlete.

---

[1] This reading is based on material that appeared in the second and third editions of *Educational Psychology: Developing Learners*. The discussion of Maslow's theory was reduced in the fourth edition to make room for greater discussion of contemporary perspectives of motivation.

5. **Need for self-actualization.** People have a need to **self-actualize**—to grow and become all they are capable of becoming. Individuals striving toward self-actualization seek out new activities as a way of expanding their horizons and strive to learn simply for the sake of learning. For example, one student may be driven by her own curiosity to learn everything she can about dinosaurs; another may pursue an active interest in ballet both as a means of developing her muscle tone and as an outlet for creative self-expression.

Maslow further proposed that the five sets of needs form a *hierarchy*, as illustrated in Figure 4.1. When two or more needs are unmet, people tend to satisfy them in a particular sequence. They begin with the lowest needs in the hierarchy, satisfying physiological needs first, safety needs next, and so on. They attempt to fulfill higher needs only when lower needs have already been met. For example, a boy with a need for exercise (a physiological need) may become excessively restless in class even though he is scolded by his teacher for his hyperactivity (thereby *not* satisfying his need for esteem from others). A girl with an unfulfilled need for love and belonging may decide not to enroll in intermediate algebra—a class that would satisfy her desire to learn more math—if the peers whose friendships she most values tell her the class is only for nerds. I once knew a boy living in a Philadelphia ghetto who had a strong interest in learning yet often stayed home from school to avoid the violent gangs that hung out on the local street corner. This boy's need for safety took precedence over any need for self-actualization that he might have had.

The first four needs in the hierarchy—physiological, safety, love and belonging, and esteem—result from things that a person *lacks*; hence, Maslow called them **deficiency needs**. Deficiency needs can be met only by external sources—by people and events in one's environment. Furthermore, once these needs are fulfilled, there is no reason to satisfy them

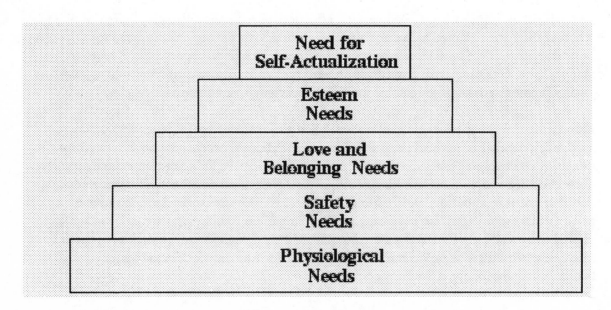

Figure 4.1. Maslow's hierarchy of needs

further. The last need, self-actualization, is a **growth need**: Rather than simply addressing a deficiency in a person's life, it enhances the person's growth and development. The need for self-actualization is never completely satisfied; people seeking to self-actualize continue to strive for further fulfillment. Self-actualizing activities are intrinsically motivating: People engage in them because doing so gives them pleasure and satisfies their desire to know and grow. According to Maslow, total self-actualization is rarely if ever achieved, and then typically only by mature adults.

Contemporary motivation theorists have been somewhat critical of Maslow's perspective. For one thing, little hard evidence exists to substantiate the hierarchical nature of human motivation. Maslow derived his theory from his informal, subjective observations of presumably "self-actualized" personal friends and from published descriptions of such historical figures as Thomas Jefferson and Abraham Lincoln; it would be almost impossible for other investigators to confirm that these individuals had the characteristics Maslow identified. Furthermore, self-actualization is so rare that the hierarchy may not provide an accurate description of people in general (Petri, 1991).

Despite such concerns, aspects of Maslow's theory clearly have merit. For instance, it makes intuitive sense that people will worry about their physiological well-being and personal safety before they strive to address more social needs. It makes sense, too, that students will not show much intrinsic motivation to learn classroom material until they are rested and well-fed, feel safe and secure in their classroom, and enjoy the love and respect of their teachers and classmates.

Implications for Teachers

From Maslow's perspective, we can best pave the way for intrinsically motivated learning by addressing students' deficiency needs. Following are several examples of what we might do (some are based on Wlodkowski, 1978):

- Make sure students' physiological needs are met.

    A teacher who has students for a two-hour block incorporates at least one activity into each class session that allows students to get up, move around, and release any pent-up energy.

    A teacher notices that one student comes to school chronically hungry and tired. The student admits that he is rarely given breakfast at home or money for lunch at school. Knowing that the student's mother has limited knowledge of English, the teacher helps the woman fill out an application for the school's free breakfast and lunch program.

- Create a classroom environment in which students feel safe and secure.

    A teacher has regular and predictable procedures for how materials are handed out and collected, how assignments are to be completed, and how discipline problems are handled.

    When a student is observed threatening his classmates on the playground, his teacher removes him from the situation until it is clear that such behavior will stop.

- Attend to students' needs for love and belonging.

    During the first month of school, a teacher interviews each student personally to find out what students like and dislike, what their outside interests are, and what they hope to learn in his classroom.

    A teacher acknowledges each student's birthday, congratulates students with special personal accomplishments during the year, and sends a card or personal note in times of illness or family tragedy.

- Create situations in which students' self-esteem and esteem from others can be enhanced.

    A teacher provides a sufficient variety of tasks and activities so that virtually all students can find an area in which they can be exceptional.

    A teacher gives awards to recognize special contributions or activities that might otherwise go unnoticed—for example, an award for a student who frequently serves as peacemaker on the playground and an award for a student who has helped her classmates improve skills or grades.

Supplementary Reading #5

EXAMPLE OF A LESSON PLAN[1]

Chapter 13 of the textbook describes the typical components of a lesson plan. I illustrate these components here by presenting an early lesson plan I developed for a middle school unit on culture and migration.

Objectives

- Students will describe what the term *culture* means in their own words.

- Students will give several examples of the ways in which cultures are different from one another.

- Students will give several examples of how the United States is a multicultural nation.

- Students will identify several reasons why people may migrate from one location to another.

Materials

- Chapter 11 of the class's geography textbook

- An enlarged map of Colorado cut into eight pieces, with each piece consisting of two or more counties of the state

- A Spanish dictionary

- Transparency of a map of Colorado, with county lines marked in thick black lines.

- Overhead projector

- Migration homework assignment, as follows:

  In the upcoming unit, we will be looking at migration of various cultures to the United States. We will also be looking at how many of our own families have migrated to Colorado from other states and other nations. To prepare for our discussion, please talk with a family member about the following questions. Fill in as many of the blanks as you can.

  1. In what state of the United States, or in what other country, were you born?_____

---

[1] This lesson plan appeared in the third edition of *Educational Psychology: Developing Learners,* but was omitted from the fourth edition to make room for new material.

2. In what state or country were your parents born?
   Mother_____   Father_____

3. In what state or country were your grandparents born?
   Mother's parents: Grandmother_____   Grandfather_____
   Father's parents: Grandmother_____   Grandfather_____

Instruction—Day 1

Homework

- Ask students to read Chapter 11 during free period today or at home tonight.

Instruction—Day 2

Question/Explanation

- Ask the class, "What is *culture*?"

  - Solicit several possible answers; write students' responses on the board.

  - Integrate students' responses into the general notion that *culture* involves the ways that a particular group of people thinks and acts.

- Ask the class, "What are some ways in which cultures are different from one another?"

  - Write students' responses on the board.

  - List the following ways in which cultures may vary: food, recreation, family life, language, religion. Tie students' responses to these categories; add any other categories that their responses might reflect.

  - Show the map in the textbook that illustrates how different religions are prominent in different parts of the world, and relate the distribution of religions to cultural differences.

- Say, "The United States is *multicultural*. In other words, it includes many different cultures. What are some examples of how the cultures of other countries have become a part of our way of life?"

  - Write students' responses on the board.

  - If students' responses have not been sufficiently diverse, add these examples:
    Mexico—food (e.g., tacos), Spanish words (e.g., *mesa*); France—food (e.g., crepes), words (e.g., *rendezvous*), art; England—soccer (the English call it "football"), literature; China—food (e.g., egg rolls); Africa—fabric designs; Denmark—fairy tales (Hans Christian Andersen); Japan—food (e.g., sushi)

Activity

- Divide the class into eight groups of three or four students each. Ideally, each group should consist of at least one sixth grader, one seventh grader, and one eighth grader. [The class was comprised of an approximately equal number of students from each grade.]

- Give each group one of the eight pieces of the Colorado map. Ask the groups to count the number of Spanish place names (towns, rivers, etc.) for each of the counties in their portion of

296

the map. Tell them that they can refer to the Spanish dictionary if they aren't sure whether a particular name is Spanish.

- When all groups have completed the task, display the Colorado map transparency on the wall with the overhead projector. Ask the groups to give the number of Spanish names in each county, and write these numbers on the transparency.

Question/Explanation

- Ask, "What pattern do you see in these numbers?" Students' responses should reflect the fact that most Spanish names are in the south-central and southwestern portions of the state.

- Explain that the pattern reflects the history of migration to what is now Colorado. Most early settlers in the southern parts of the state came from the south—that is, from what was once Spanish territory. Aspects of Spanish culture (e.g., language) therefore "migrated" as well.

Homework

- Ask students to complete the migration homework assignment with their parent(s).

Instruction—Day 3

Question/Explanation

- Ask, "How do cultures spread from one place to another? For instance, what kinds of experiences do we have that expose us to other cultures?"
  - Write students' responses on the board.
  - Summarize their responses by using the terms *migration, tourism, media, advertising,* and any other categories that seem appropriate.

- Ask, "Why do people migrate from one place to another? Can you remember some of the reasons that Chapter 11 in your textbook described? Can you think of other possible reasons as well?"
  - Solicit of variety of responses.
  - Interpret the responses in terms of *push* and *pull* factors that promote migration. Explain that push and pull factors often change over time.

Activity

- Have students take out their completed migration homework assignment from the night before. Put three columns on the board and label them "You," "Parents," and "Grandparents." Have students go up to the board one table at a time and write the states or countries of origin in each column.

- When all students are seated, ask them to identify any patterns in the data.

- Ask, "If your parents or grandparents migrated to Colorado from another state or country, do you know *why* they did?" Relate students' responses to the push and pull factors identified earlier.

Class Discussion and Explanation

- Have students open their textbooks to the table of immigration figures for the United States. [This was a table that listed the major countries of origin for U.S. immigrants for each decade from the mid-1800s to the present.]

- Ask, "What patterns do you see in this table?"

    - Solicit students' responses; they should reflect the fact that most early immigrants came from Europe, whereas many recent immigrants have come from Mexico and the Far East.

- Ask, "Why do you think the pattern of migration has changed over time? What might be some of the push and pull factors influencing the migration of different groups?"

    - Solicit students' responses and tie them back to the earlier discussion of push and pull.

Assessment

- Informal assessment of students' understanding during class discussions.

- Brief essay asking students to:

    - Describe three reasons that people migrate from one place to another and give an example to illustrate each reason.

    - Describe three kinds of evidence to indicate that the United States is a multicultural nation.

A SHOCKING LESSON[1]

Chapter 13 describes an early approach to computer-based instruction known as **programmed instruction**. This approach, which actually predates modern computer technology, was developed by B. F. Skinner and is based on three principles of operant conditioning:

1. **Active responding.** The learner is continually making responses—for instance, by answering questions or filling in blanks in incomplete statements.

2. **Shaping.** Instruction begins with information the learner already knows, then it breaks new information into tiny pieces and presents them one at a time over the course of a lesson. As the learner acquires more information and answers questions of increasing difficulty, the desired terminal behavior (mastery of the subject matter) is gradually shaped.

3. **Immediate reinforcement.** Because instruction involves such a gradual progression through the material, mastery of each piece is almost guaranteed. Thus, the learner has a high probability of responding correctly to the questions asked and is reinforced immediately by getting feedback that the answers are correct.

The "Experiencing Firsthand" exercise that begins on the next page illustrates these basic elements of programmed instruction by teaching you some of the things you should do to treat a victim of traumatic shock. The lesson is presented in a sequence of boxes known as *frames*. Use a sheet of blank paper to cover all but the first frame. Read the information presented in the first frame and then write the answer to the question at the top of your blank paper. Once you have done so, uncover the next frame and check your response against the answer presented in the upper left-hand corner. Read the new information and again respond to the question. Continue in this manner through all the frames, each time getting feedback to the question you just answered, reading the new information, and answering another question.

---

[1] This Experiencing Firsthand exercise appeared in the third edition of *Educational Psychology: Developing Learners* but was omitted from the fourth edition to make room for an expanded discussion of more contemporary approaches in technology-based instruction.

Frame 1

> When the human body is seriously injured, a condition that frequently results is traumatic shock.
>
> **?** A frequent result of serious injury is traumatic _____ .

Frame 2

> shock
>
> Burns, wounds, and bone fractures can all lead to traumatic shock.
>
> **?** Three common types of injuries can lead to traumatic shock: burns, wounds, and bone _____ .

Frame 3

> fractures
>
> Traumatic shock is a condition in which many normal bodily functions are depressed.
>
> **?** When a person is suffering from traumatic shock, normal bodily functions become _____ .

Frame 4

> depressed
>
> Bodily functions are depressed during shock because not enough blood is circulating through the body.
>
> **?** The depression of bodily functions during shock is due to an insufficient amount of _____ circulating through the body.

Frame 5

> blood
>
> The more blood lost as a result of an injury, the greater the possibility of traumatic shock.
>
> **?** The probability of shock increases when an injury results in the loss of more _____ .

Frame 6

> blood
>
> An injured person who may be suffering from shock should be kept lying down and at a comfortable temperature.
>
> **?** In a cold environment, it is probably best to do which of the following for a person possibly in shock?
>
>   a.   Cover the person with a blanket.
>   b.   Cover the person with cool, damp towels.
>   c.   Leave the person uncovered.

Frame 7

> If you chose **a**, you are correct. Proceed to Frame 9.
> If you chose **b** or **c**, you are incorrect. Continue with this frame.
>
> A person who is possibly suffering from traumatic shock should be kept at a comfortable body temperature.
>
> **?** A possible shock victim should be kept:
>
>   a. as cool as possible
>   b. as warm as possible
>   c. at a comfortable body temperature

Frame 8

> If you chose **c**, you are correct. Continue with this frame.
> If you chose **a** or **b**, you are incorrect. Return to Frame 7.
>
> In a cold environment, the person should be covered with a blanket in order to be kept warm. In a warm environment, little or no covering is needed.
>
> **?** In a cold environment, it is probably best to do which of the following for a person who is possibly suffering from shock?
>
>   a.   Cover the person with cool, damp towels.
>   b.   Leave the person uncovered.
>   c.   Cover the person with a blanket.

Frame 9

> If you chose **c**, you are correct. Continue with this frame.
> If you chose **a** or **b**, you are incorrect. Return to Frame 7.
>
>
> A possible shock victim should be kept lying down. This way, blood will more easily flow to the head and chest, where it is most needed.
>
> **?**   A shock victim should be placed in a _____ position.
>   a. sitting
>   b. lying-down
>   c. standing

Frame 10

> If you chose **b**, you are correct. Proceed to Frame 11.
> If you chose **a** or **c**, you are incorrect. Continue with this frame.
>
>
> It is best to keep a shock victim lying down. This way, blood circulates more readily to the head and chest.
>
> **?**   A shock victim should be kept _____ .
>   a. lying down
>   b. sitting
>   c. standing

Frame 11

> If you chose **a**, you are correct. Continue with this frame.
> If you chose **b** or **c**, you are incorrect. Return to Frame 4.
>
>
> ...the lesson continues...

The first part of the lesson illustrates a **linear program**: All students progress through the same sequence of frames. Beginning with Frame 7, the lesson becomes a **branching program**. At this point, instruction progresses more quickly, presenting larger amounts of information in each frame. As a result, questions are more difficult to answer, and students are more likely to make errors. Whenever students respond incorrectly to a question, they proceed to one or more remedial frames for further clarification or practice before continuing on with new information.

In the 1950s and 1960s, programmed instruction was typically presented through printed materials in much the same way that I presented the first aid lesson to you just now. But with the wide availability of computer technology, it is now presented primarily by means of computers and so is often known as **computer-assisted instruction (CAI)**. Most CAI programs are branching programs, automatically switching to one frame or another depending on how a student responds. Branching programs provide more flexibility than linear programs: Only those students having difficulty with a particular skill or concept proceed to remedial frames. Others can move on to new information, without having to spend time on practice frames they don't need.

Supplementary Reading #7

CALCULATING STANDARD DEVIATIONS

The **standard deviation** (SD) of a set of test scores tells us how close together or far apart these scores are from one another; that is, it tells us the *variability* of the scores. Roughly speaking, the standard deviation tells us the *average distance* of scores from the mean. But more exactly, we take the following steps in order to calculate a standard deviation:

1. Calculate the *mean* for the scores. We calculate the mean by adding all the scores and then dividing by the total number of people involved. We'll use the symbol N for the total number of people and M for the mean.

2. Calculate the *difference* between each score and the mean. We'll use the symbol X for each score, so that $X - M$ equals the difference between each score and the mean.

3. Square each difference—in other words, multiply each difference by itself. This square is symbolized as $(X - M)^2$. Any negative numbers we obtained in Step 2 will become positive when we square them.

4. Add all the squared differences together. The symbol for adding things is $\sum$, so the total of the squared differences is $\sum(X - M)^2$.

5. Divide this total by the number of people (N).

6. Find the square root of the number obtained in Step 5 (most calculators have a square root function). We now have the standard deviation for our set of scores. We'll use the symbol SD for standard deviation.

The formula for calculating a standard deviation, which incorporates the steps I've just listed, is this:

$$SD = \sqrt{\frac{\sum(X - M)^2}{N}}$$

Let's look at how we can calculate the standard deviation for the heights of the 25 students in Ms. Oppenheimer's third-grade class (these are the same heights presented in Appendix C of the textbook), following the same six steps.

Step 1.   We divide the sum of all the heights (1250) by the number of people (25), so the mean height for Ms. Oppenheimer's class is 50.

Steps 2 & 3.   Following are the 25 third graders, their heights, the difference between each height and the mean (Step 2), and the square of that difference (Step 3).

		Step 2 Diff. from Mean	**Step 3** Square of Difference
Child	Height	$X - M$	$(X - M)^2$
Amy	47	3	9
Ben	50	0	0
Cal	52	2	4
Don	48	2	4
Eve	51	1	1
Fay	50	0	0
Gil	49	1	1
Hal	53	3	9
Ivy	49	1	1
Jan	55	5	25
Ken	51	1	1
Les	50	0	0
Max	48	2	4
Nan	49	1	1
Oly	49	1	1
Pat	46	4	16
Roy	53	3	9
Sal	51	1	1
Tom	50	0	0
Una	50	0	0
Val	52	2	4
Wil	47	3	9
Xan	50	0	0
Yul	51	1	1
Zek	49	1	1

Step 4.   We add all the squared differences together. When we add all the numbers in the right-hand column above, we get:

$$\Sigma (X - M)^2 = 102$$

Step 5.   We divide the total obtained in Step 4 by the number of people (or scores), like this:

$$\frac{\Sigma (X - M)^2}{N} = \frac{102}{25} = 4.08$$

Step 6.   We find the square root of the number we calculated in Step 5, like this:

$$\sqrt{4.08} = 2.02$$

We can summarize Steps 4 through 6 this way:

$$SD = \sqrt{\frac{\Sigma (X - M)^2}{N}} = \sqrt{\frac{102}{25}} = \sqrt{4.08} = 2.02$$

As you may have learned if you have read Appendix C in your textbook, you can interpret *standard scores*—IQs, ETS scores (e.g., SAT scores), stanines, and *z*-scores—only when you know both the mean and standard deviation of those scores. But you will encounter standard deviations in other contexts as well. For example, when educational researchers describe their research in professional journals, they typically provide information about the variability of students' performance—variability that is often summarized as a standard deviation. So as you continue to read the educational research literature in your field, you will undoubtedly see reference to this statistic time and time again.

Practice Exercises

Here are two problems in which you can practice the procedure for calculating standard deviations.

1. Fifteen students get the scores below on a geography quiz. What is the standard deviation of these scores?

9	10	4
4	6	8
6	6	9
8	7	8
5	10	5

2. Ms. White's class and Mr. Black's class both take a test over the same 20 spelling words on Friday. Which class has greater variability in its test performance? Answer this question by calculating standard deviations for each class.

Ms. White's Class	Mr. Black's Class
14	16
16	18
20	20
15	17
13	16
10	17
17	14
18	15
12	18
13	16
15	17
17	18
	19
	17

Answers to Practice Exercises

1. There are 15 scores, so $N = 15$. The total of all the scores is 105. Therefore, the mean of the scores is 105/15, or <u>7</u>. Here are $X - M$ and $(X - M)^2$ for each score:

Score	$X - M$	$(X - M)^2$
9	2	4
4	−3	9
6	−1	1
8	1	1
5	−2	4
10	3	9
6	−1	1
6	−1	1
7	0	0
10	3	9

4	−3	9
8	1	1
9	2	4
8	1	1
5	−2	4

The sum of the right-hand column, $\sum(X - M)^2$, is 58. Entering this value and N into the equation, we find that the standard deviation is the square root of 58/15, or 1.97. The standard deviation for the 15 scores, then, is approximately 2.

2. In Ms. White's class, there are 12 scores, so $N = 12$. The total of all the scores is 108. Therefore, the mean of the scores is 180/12, or 15. Here are $X - M$ and $(X - M)^2$ for each score:

Score	$X - M$	$(X - M)^2$
14	−1	1
16	1	1
20	5	25
15	0	0
13	−2	4
10	−5	25
17	2	4
18	3	9
12	−3	9
13	−2	4
15	0	0
17	2	4

The sum of the right-hand column, $\sum(X - M)^2$, is 86. Entering this value and N into the equation, we find that the standard deviation is the square root of 86/12, or 2.68.

In Mr. Black's class, there are 14 scores, so $N = 14$. The total of all the scores is 238, so the mean of the scores is 238/14, or 17. Here are $X - M$ and $(X - M)^2$ for each score:

Score	$X - M$	$(X - M)^2$
16	−1	1
18	1	1
20	3	9
17	0	0
16	−1	1
17	0	0
14	−3	9
15	−2	4
18	1	1
16	−1	1
17	0	0
18	1	1
19	2	4
17	0	0

The sum of the right-hand column, $\sum(X - M)^2$, is 32. Entering this value and N into the equation, we find that the standard deviation is the square root of 32/14, or 1.51.

When we compare the standard deviations of the two classes, we find that Ms. White's class has greater variability.

LEARNING IN THE CONTENT AREAS[1]

What subjects have you especially enjoyed studying in your many years as a student? Do you enjoy classroom topics more when your teachers present them as ideas to be understood, applied, and critically analyzed, rather than just as facts and procedures to be memorized?

When I went to school in the 1950s and 1960s, the general public, as well as many teachers and educational theorists, thought that classroom instruction should be largely a process of teaching specific facts and procedures. But in recent years, theorists and practitioners alike have radically changed their thinking about how school subject matter can most effectively be taught. Although students continue to learn facts and procedures, classroom curricula increasingly focus on helping students develop higher-level thinking skills (transfer, problem solving, critical thinking, metacognitive strategies, etc.) as well (Alleman & Brophy, 1997; Glynn, Yeany, & Britton, 1991; Lester, Lambdin, & Preston, 1997; Newmann, 1997).

---

[1] This reading is an updated version of Chapter 9 in the third edition of *Educational Psychology: Developing Learners*. It was omitted from the fourth edition to make room for expanded discussions of motivation and assessment.

In this supplementary reading, we will apply principles of cognition, knowledge construction, and higher-level thinking to learning and instruction in five areas: reading, writing, mathematics, science, and social studies. As we do so, we will consider questions such as these:

- What general principles seem to hold true regardless of the subject matter we are teaching?

- How do students' reading skills change across the school years, and how can we encourage students at various grade levels to read more effectively?

- What specific processes are involved in writing, and how can we help students develop these processes?

- How can we promote a true understanding and application of mathematics, rather than meaningless memorization of mathematical facts and procedures?

- How can we foster scientific reasoning skills, so that students apply scientific concepts and principles to address real-world problems?

- How can we encourage students to use the things they learn in social studies—in particular, in history and geography—to understand and interpret the societies and cultures in which they live?

- What things should we keep in mind when we teach various content areas to students from diverse populations?

Case Study: *The Birth of a Nation*

Ms. Jackson has asked her second graders to write an answer to this question: *The land we live on has been here for a very long time, but the United States has only been a country for a little more than 200 years. How did the United States become a country?* Following are some of the children's responses:

Bill: The United States began around two hundred years ago, when an Inglish ship from Ingland accadently landed on a big State that wasn't named yet. They named it America, but they didn't know there was already Indians ashore. Soon they found out, and they had a big fight. The Indians trying to fight the Inglish off, and the Inglish trying to fight off the Indians. So finally they talked and after they worked out their problems then they had a big feast for friendship and relationship.

Matt: It all staredid in eginggind they had a wore. Thein they mad a bet howevery wone the wore got a ney country. Called the united states of amarica and amaricins wone the wore. So they got a new country.

Sue: The pilgrums we're sailing to some place and a stome came and pushed them off track and they landed we're Amaraca is now and made friends with the indens and coled that spot AMARACA!

Lisa: We wone the saver wore. It was a wore for fradam and labrt. One cind of labraty is tho stashow of labrt. We got the stashew of labraty from england. Crastaver calbes daskaved Amaraca.[2]

Meg: The United States began around two hundred years ago. The dinosors hav ben around for six taosine years ago. Christfer klumbis salde the May flowr.

Ben: 2000 Days oh go George Washington gave us the Country to Live on.
(responses courtesy of Dinah Jackson)

---

[2] This student's spelling is sufficiently "creative" that a translation is probably in order: "We won the Civil War. It was a war for freedom and liberty. One kind of liberty is the Statue of Liberty. We got the Statue of Liberty from England. Christopher Columbus discovered America."

- What writing skills have all of the second graders mastered? What skills are most of them still developing? In what ways are all of these compositions very different from something a high school student might write?

- What things have the second graders learned about American history? What misconceptions do you see in their responses? In what ways does their knowledge of history fall short of a true understanding of the birth of the United States?

Applying General Principles to Teaching Classroom Subject Matter

These second graders clearly have a basic understanding of the nature of written language. For instance, they know that, at least in English, writing proceeds from left to right and from the top of the page to the bottom. They are aware that written language should follow certain conventions regarding capitalization and punctuation. They have mastered the spellings of many simple words. They know, too, that how a word is spelled is, at least in part, a function of how it is pronounced—in other words, that different letters correspond to different sounds. For example, when Lisa spells *liberty* as "labrt," she is probably thinking that her word would be pronounced "LAB R T."

At the same time, the children do not yet know how to spell many words, and they are still learning the situations in which capitalization and punctuation are and are not appropriate. For instance, Matt spells *England* as "eginggind" and puts a period in the middle of what should be a sentence. Furthermore, most of the compositions consist of short, choppy sentences that are strung together like beads; only Bill's response comes close to telling a story. By the time these students reach high school, most of them should be writing multiple-paragraph compositions that have few spelling and punctuation errors and depict a logical sequence of events.

The children have also learned a few things about American history. They know that Columbus sailed across the ocean, that people from England (the Pilgrims) were early settlers who found Native Americans already living on the land, and that George Washington was a prominent figure when the country was formed. But they don't always have their facts straight. For example, the American Revolution did not involve making a bet, Columbus did not sail on the *Mayflower*, and George Washington did not "give" us the country. In general, the children's knowledge of American history consists of only a few isolated pieces of information; they have little or no understanding of how the country actually came into being.

Like Ms. Jackson's assignment, many classroom tasks involve both language skills, such as reading or writing, and knowledge in one or more academic disciplines, such as mathematics, science, or social studies. As we explore how students learn and achieve in reading, writing, math, science, and social studies, we will repeatedly run into the concepts and principles of learning and development presented in the textbook. But there are several general principles that will feature prominently in our upcoming discussions:

- **Constructive processes.** Learners use the information they receive from various sources to build their own, unique understandings of the world.

- **Influence of prior knowledge.** Learners' interpretations of new information and events are influenced by what they already know and believe about the world.

- **Role of metacognition.** Over time, learners develop cognitive strategies and epistemological beliefs that influence their thinking and performance within a particular content domain.

- **Qualitative changes with development.** The ways in which learners think about and understand academic subject matter are qualitatively different at different points in their cognitive development.

- **Importance of social interaction.** Learners often gain greater understanding and greater metacognitive sophistication in a subject area when they work collaboratively with their peers.

We see two of these principles—constructive processes and prior knowledge—at work in the second graders' history compositions. For instance, Lisa uses her knowledge of letter sounds to construct what is, to her, a reasonable spelling of *liberty*, and Meg knows that someone sailed on the *Mayflower* and assumes (incorrectly) that the sailor must have been Columbus. As Lisa and Meg move to higher grade levels, they will construct more accurate and abstract understandings of historical events, express their thoughts on paper more thoroughly and completely, and have greater metacognitive awareness of what they are doing as they write. Furthermore, their success in learning history and other content areas will increasingly depend on their ability to learn through reading textbooks and other printed materials. Accordingly, virtually *all* teachers should teach reading to some extent, even if they are teaching courses in mathematics, science, social studies, or some other discipline.

Reading

As a topic of instruction per se, reading is taught primarily in elementary school. Many middle school and high school teachers assume that their students have achieved sufficient reading proficiency to learn successfully from textbooks and other printed materials. Such an assumption is not always warranted, however; even at the high school level, many students have not yet mastered some of the skills they need to read effectively.

In this section we will examine the many skills that contribute to reading ability and consider how the quality of students' reading changes over time. We will also identify teaching strategies that researchers and practitioners recommend for enhancing students' ability to read and learn from written language. But first, let's look at the things that many children learn about reading and writing long before they enter school—knowledge and skills that are collectively known as *emergent literacy*.

Emergent Literacy

When you were a young child, perhaps 3 or 4 years old, you may have spent many hours listening to parents or other adults read you storybooks. What might you have learned about the nature of written language from these storybook sessions?

Researchers have consistently found that children who are read to frequently during the preschool years, and especially children who associate reading with pleasure and enjoyment, learn to read more easily once they reach kindergarten and first grade (Baker, Scher, & Mackler, 1997; Crain-Thoreson & Dale, 1992; Frijters, Barron, & Brunello, 2000; Whitehurst et al., 1994). Through storybook reading and other home activities that focus on either oral or written language (storytelling, object and picture identification, practice with the alphabet, rhyming games, etc.), children acquire considerable knowledge and skills essential to the reading process. For instance, they learn that

- Reading proceeds from left to right and from the top of the page to the bottom
- Spoken language is represented in a consistent fashion in written language

- Each letter of the alphabet is associated with one or more sounds in spoken language

They may also learn to recognize their own name in print, and many children begin to recognize the logos of popular products and commercial establishments, such as Coke, Pepsi, McDonalds, and Burger King. Taken together, such knowledge and skills lay a foundation for reading and writing—a foundation that theorists call **emergent literacy**.

The Nature of Skilled Reading

Reading is a complex process that involves considerable knowledge and abilities:
- Recognizing individual sounds and letters
- Using word decoding skills
- Recognizing most words quickly and automatically
- Using context clues to facilitate word recognition
- Constructing an understanding of the writer's intended meaning
- Metacognitively regulating the reading process

Sound and Letter Recognition

A growing body of research indicates that **phonological awareness**—hearing distinct sounds, or *phonemes*, within a spoken word (e.g., detecting the sounds "guh," "ay," and "tuh" in the word *gate*)—is an essential element of successful reading. Children who have trouble identifying the specific phonemes contained in words have more difficulty reading than their classmates. Furthermore, specifically teaching students to hear the individual sounds in words enhances later reading ability (Bus & van IJzendoorn, 1999; Byrne, Fielding-Barnsley, & Ashley, 2000; M. Harris & Hatano, 1999; Torgesen et al., 1999). We can use strategies such as the following to promote students' phonological awareness:
- Ask students to identify objects that all begin with the same sound.
- Show pictures of several objects and ask students to choose the one that begins with a different sound from the others.
- Say several words and ask students which one ends in a different sound.
- Ask students to sound out and blend separate letters into words.
- Play rhyming games. (Bradley & Bryant, 1991; Goswami, 1998; Walton, Walton, & Felton, 2001)

Obviously, another prerequisite for learning to read is learning to distinguish individual letters of the alphabet in uppercase and lowercase forms (Adams, 1990; M. Harris & Giannouli, 1999; W. Schneider, Roth, & Ennemoser, 2000). Although some students will already have learned the written alphabet before they begin school, others may know few if any letters. Especially when we are teaching at the kindergarten or early elementary grade levels, one of our first orders of business must be to determine whether our students have mastered the upper- and lowercase alphabets. Before they begin reading in earnest, our students should be able to identify every letter of the alphabet quickly and effortlessly and associate each letter with one or more sounds that it "makes" in spoken language. To help students learn to recognize letters and their corresponding sounds, we can
- Read alphabet books that embed individual letters in colorful pictures and meaningful stories
- Ask students to make letters with their bodies (e.g., a single student stands with arms outstretched like a Y, or two students bend over and clasp hands to form an M)

311

- Have students practice writing the letters, first by copying them and eventually by retrieving their forms from memory

Word Decoding Skills

When people see a word for the first time, they often engage in **word decoding**: They identify the sounds associated with the word's letters and blend those sounds together to determine what the word probably is. To do this, they must, of course, know how particular letters and letter combinations are typically pronounced. Decoding skills are especially important in the early elementary grades, when students have not yet acquired a large *sight-reading vocabulary*—in other words, when they cannot yet recognize most words quickly and automatically (Gough & Wren, 1998; Tunmer & Chapman, 1998).

Following are examples of how we can promote word decoding skills:

- Teach generalizations that apply most of the time (e.g., an *e* at the end of a word is usually silent).
- Show patterns in similarly spelled and pronounced words (e.g., the *end* in *bend*, *mend*, and *fender*).
- Have students create nonsense words and poems using common letter combinations (e.g., *I know an old lady who swallowed a zwing, I don't why she swallowed the zwing, I guess she'll die*; Reutzel & Cooter, 1999, p. 146).
- Give students lots of practice sounding out unfamiliar words.
- Teach students how to spell the words they are learning to read. (Adams, 1990; Ehri, 1998; Ehri & Wilce, 1987; Reutzel & Cooter, 1999)

Automatic Word Recognition

Try this simple exercise.

EXPERIENCING FIRSTHAND   *An Excerpt from Webster's Dictionary*

Read this sentence as quickly as you can while also trying to make as much sense of it as you can (*Webster's Ninth*, 1991):

> A *zymogram* is an electrophoretic strip or a representation of it exhibiting the pattern of separated proteins or protein components after electrophoresis.

Did you find yourself slowing down at certain points in the sentence? If so, what particular words slowed you down?

I am guessing that three words slowed you down: *zymogram*, *electrophoretic*, and *electrophoresis*. Unless you are a biologist, you had probably never encountered these words before. But I suspect that you read the other words—even *representation*, which has fourteen letters—with virtually no effort because you've read each of them on many previous occasions.

When students must use their limited working memory capacity to decode and interpret individual words, they have little "room" left to understand the overall meaning of what they are reading. It is essential, then, that our students develop automaticity in word recognition. Ultimately, word recognition must become automatic in two ways. First, students must be able to sight-read words: They must be able to identify them in a split second, without having to decode them letter by letter. Second, they must be able to *retrieve the meanings* of words immediately—for example, to know without hesitation what *pattern* and *protein* mean when those words appear in a sentence (Adams, 1990; Hall, 1989; Stanovich, 2000).

As you may recall from Chapter 6 in the textbook, automaticity develops primarily through practice, practice, and more practice. In some instances—perhaps with young children or with students who are having unusual difficulty learning to read—we might use flashcards with individual words. And we can certainly teach the meanings of words through explicit vocabulary lessons. But probably most effective (and certainly more motivating) for promoting automatic word recognition is to encourage students to read as frequently as they possibly can.

Context Clues

Here is another exercise to try.

EXPERIENCING FIRSTHAND   *A Sense of Urgency*

What is the blurry word in the following sentence?

I need to make sure that I get to the ▬▬▬ on time today.

Even when people have learned words to a level of automaticity, they recognize the words faster and more easily when they see them within the context of a sentence than when they see them in isolation (West & Stanovich, 1978). Probably both the syntax and the overall meaning of the sentence provide context clues that help. For instance, when you read the sentence in the exercise just now, you undoubtedly concluded that the blurry word toward the end must be a noun (only a noun would be syntactically correct between *the* and *on*) and that the noun in question must be something that people attend and something for which punctuality is important. These clues, plus the general length and shape of the word, should have led you to identify the blurry word as *meeting*.

Effective use of context clues seems to be especially important for beginning readers and for those older readers who have not fully developed automaticity in word recognition (Goldsmith-Phillips, 1989; Stanovich, 2000; West & Stanovich, 1978). As teachers, we must remember that the English language isn't completely dependable when it comes to letter-sound correspondences; for example, the letters *ough* are pronounced differently in *through*, *though*, *bough*, and *rough*. Accordingly, we should encourage students to use context clues as well as letter-sound correspondences whenever they encounter a word they don't know, perhaps simply by posing the question, "What do you know about the word just by looking at the words around it?"

Meaning Construction

Most reading theorists today believe that reading is very much a constructive process (e.g., E. H. Hiebert & Raphael, 1996; C. A. Weaver & Kintsch, 1991). When people read, they usually go beyond the words themselves: They identify main ideas, draw inferences, make predictions about what the author is likely to say next, and so on. Sophisticated readers may also find symbolism in a work of fiction, evaluate the quality of evidence in a persuasive essay, or identify assumptions or philosophical perspectives that underlie a particular piece of writing.

Effective meaning construction in reading is, of course, enhanced by the amount of knowledge that the reader already has about the topic in question (Beck, McKeown, Sinatra, & Loxterman, 1991; Britton, Stimson, Stennett, & Gülgöz, 1998). For instance, if you were a biologist who knew what *electrophoretic* and *electrophoresis* were, then you would have little difficulty comprehending the *zymogram* definition I gave you earlier. Similarly, second graders who already know a lot about spiders remember more when they read a passage about spiders and can draw inferences more readily than their less knowledgeable classmates (Pearson, Hansen, & Gordon, 1979). Helpful, too, is knowledge about the structures that various types of literature typically follow; for example, the events described in works of fiction usually follow a chronological sequence, and persuasive essays usually begin with a main point and then present evidence to support that point (Byrnes, 1996; Dryden & Jefferson, 1994; Graesser, Golding, & Long, 1991; Mandler, 1987).

Following are several suggestions that experts have offered for helping students construct meaning from the things they read:

• Remind students of the things they already know about the topic.

• Give students specific training in drawing inferences from reading material.

• Relate events in a story to students' own lives.

• Ask students to form mental images of the people or events depicted in a reading passage.

• Ask students to retell or summarize what they have read, perhaps after each sentence, paragraph, or section. (Chi, de Leeuw, Chiu, & LaVancher, 1994; Gambrell & Bales, 1986; Hemphill & Snow, 1996; Johnson-Glenberg, 2000; Morrow, 1989; Oakhill & Yuill, 1996; Pressley, El-Dinary, Wharton-McDonald, & Brown, 1998)

Metacognitive Processes

Not only do good readers work actively to construct meaning from what they read, they also "supervise" their own reading at a metacognitive level. Many of the metacognitive strategies identified in Chapter 8 of the textbook—for instance, elaborating, summarizing, and comprehension monitoring—are particularly important in reading. Good readers also spend more time on parts of a passage that are likely to be critical to their overall understanding, and they frequently make predictions about what they will read next (Gernsbacher, 1994; Hyona, 1994; Palincsar & Brown, 1984). Furthermore, good readers typically set goals for their reading; for example, they may ask themselves questions that they hope to answer as they read (Hall, 1989; Webb & Palincsar, 1996).

The textbook identifies several ways of promoting effective metacognitive strategies, and many of them are certainly applicable to teaching reading. We can further encourage metacognitive processing by explicitly teaching students to use the kinds of strategies that good readers use; for instance, we can teach them to summarize what they read by deleting trivial and redundant information and identifying general ideas that incorporate several more specific ideas (Bean & Steenwyk, 1984). We can also teach them to make predictions as they read—perhaps by looking at the title and section headings, and perhaps by considering the ideas that have already been presented—and then to reflect back on the accuracy of their predictions (Pressley et al., 1994). Group discussions of reading material provide yet another way of enhancing students' metacognitive skills; I describe some techniques along this line later in this section, as well as in the discussion of *reciprocal teaching* in Chapter 13 of the textbook.

Developmental Changes in Reading

As students grow older and gain more experience as readers, their reading processes and skills improve in several ways. A major accomplishment during the kindergarten and early elementary grades is the development of phonological awareness; by second grade, most students are able to divide words into syllables and into the specific phonemes that make up each syllable (Lonigan, Burgess, Anthony, & Barker, 1998; R. E. Owens, 1996). Reading instruction in the early elementary years typically focuses on word recognition and basic comprehension skills, often within the context of reading simple stories (Chall, 1996; R. E. Owens, 1996).

In the upper elementary grades, most students have acquired sufficient linguistic knowledge and reading skills that they can focus almost exclusively on reading comprehension (R. E. Owens, 1996). They are more adept at drawing inferences, and they become increasingly able to learn new information from what they read (Chall, 1996; Paris & Upton, 1976). At this point, they tend to take the things they read at face value, with little attempt to evaluate them critically and little sensitivity to obvious contradictions (Chall, 1996; Johnston & Afflerbach, 1985; Markman, 1979).

As students move into the secondary grades, they become more skillful at identifying main ideas, summarizing passages of text, monitoring their comprehension, and backtracking when they don't understand something the first time they read it (Alvermann & Moore, 1991; Byrnes, 1996; Garner, 1987). They also begin to recognize that different authors sometimes present different viewpoints on a single issue, and they read written material with a critical eye instead of accepting it as absolute truth (Chall, 1996; R. E. Owens, 1996). Furthermore, they become more cognizant of the subtle aspects of fiction, such as the underlying theme and symbolism of a novel (Chall, 1996). We must keep in mind, however, that students' general knowledge of the world and their experiences with a variety of both fictional and nonfictional literature will definitely have an impact on their ability to read challenging material successfully (Byrnes, 1996).

General Strategies for Teaching Reading

As we identified the various processes involved in effective reading, we also identified instructional strategies that should promote the development of those processes. Following are several more general strategies to keep in mind:

• *Make frequent use of authentic reading materials, and give students some choices about what they read.* Chapter 8 in the textbook notes the importance of using *authentic activities* for promoting real-world transfer of the knowledge and skills that students learn in the classroom. Many reading theorists advocate the frequent use of authentic reading materials as well—having students read storybooks, novels, magazine articles, newspaper articles, poems, and so on—rather than a heavy reliance on the traditional "reading" textbooks so common in the 1970s and 1980s. Furthermore, research consistently tells us that students read more energetically and persistently, use more sophisticated metacognitive strategies, and remember more content when they are interested in what they are reading (R. C. Anderson, Shirey, Wilson, & Fielding, 1987; J. T. Guthrie et al., 1998; Sheveland, 1994).

In its most extreme form, this approach is known as **whole language instruction**: teaching reading exclusively by using authentic reading materials (Goodman, 1989; Goodman & Goodman, 1979; C. Weaver, 1990). Basic knowledge and skills related to reading, such as letter-sound correspondences and word recognition, are taught solely within the context of real-world reading and writing tasks, and far less time is devoted to instruction of basic skills than is true in more traditional reading programs. Instead, students spend a great deal of time writing and talking with their classmates about what they have read.

Numerous research studies have been conducted comparing the effectiveness of whole-language and basic-skills approaches to reading instruction. Studies with kindergartners and first graders find that whole-language approaches are often more effective in promoting emergent literacy— familiarity with the nature of print, knowledge that books can be sources of entertainment and pleasure, and so on (Purcell-Gates, McIntyre, & Freppon, 1995; Sacks & Mergendoller, 1997; Stahl & Miller, 1989). When children must actually *read* text, however, basic-skills approaches—in particular, a focus on developing phonological awareness and knowledge of letter-sound relationships—seem to be superior, especially for children from low-socioeconomic backgrounds and for students who show early signs of a reading disability (Adams, 1990; Stahl & Miller, 1989; Stanovich, 2000). Considering such research, many theorists now urge that teachers strike a balance between whole-language activities and basic-skills instruction (Biemiller, 1994; Mayer, 1999; Pressley, 1995).

• *Use motivating activities to teach basic reading skills.* Even when we do teach basic skills such as letter-sound correspondences, word decoding, and use of context clues, we do not necessarily need to teach them through dry, drill-and-practice workbooks. Such workbooks are often not terribly motivating for students, who may see assignments in such books primarily as exercises to complete as quickly as possible (E. H. Hiebert & Raphael, 1996). With a little thought, we can develop interesting activities to teach almost any basic skill. Here are three examples:

  • Playing a game of "Twenty Questions" that begins with a hint such as, "I'm thinking of something in the classroom that begins with the letter *B*"

  • Giving students a homework assignment to bring in three objects that begin with the letter *T* and three more that end with the letter *T*

  • Using children's poems that illustrate common letter patterns (e.g., Dr. Seuss's *The Cat in the Hat* or *Green Eggs and Ham*)

We can also teach these and other basic skills, such as using context clues to identify unfamiliar words and making predictions about what will happen next, while students read interesting storybooks with simple language and colorful illustrations (Clay, 1985).

• *Engage students in group discussions about the things they read.* Our students can often construct meaning more effectively from the things they read when they discuss their readings with their classmates. For instance, we can form "book clubs" in which students lead small groups of classmates in discussions about specific books (McMahon, 1992). We can hold "grand conversations" about a particular work of literature, asking students to share their responses to questions with no single right answers—perhaps questions related to interpretations or critiques of various aspects of a text (Eeds & Wells, 1989; E. H. Hiebert & Raphael, 1996; Keefer, Zeitz, & Resnick, 2000). And we can encourage students to think about a piece of literature from the author's perspective, posing such questions as "What's the author's message here?" or "Why do you think the author wants us to know about this?" (Beck, McKeown, Worthy, Sandora, & Kucan, 1996). Group discussions may not only help students understand what they are reading but may also provide a means through which they can form friendships and in other ways address their social needs (Alvermann, Young, Green, & Wisenbaker, 1999).

Students develop additional insights about reading when they become authors themselves and share their writing with their classmates. We turn our attention now to the nature of writing and to strategies for helping students become proficient writers.

Writing

The second graders in our opening case study clearly have a long way to go in their writing development. This is hardly surprising, because writing is a very complex and multifaceted skill. In addition to mastering the vocabulary and syntax of the English language, students must also master elements of written language—spelling, punctuation, capitalization, indentation, and so on—that aren't directly evident in speech. Yet good writing goes far beyond knowing how to spell words, where to put periods and commas, and when to capitalize. More importantly, it involves putting words together in such a way that readers can construct a reasonable understanding of the author's intended message. Let's look more closely at the processes that skilled writing involves.

The Nature of Skilled Writing

As you might guess, students who are better readers also tend to be better writers; this correlation is undoubtedly due, at least in part, to the fact that general language ability—knowledge and effective use of grammar, vocabulary, and so on—provides a foundation for both reading and writing (Perfetti & McCutchen, 1987; Shanahan & Tierney, 1990). In addition to proficiency in English, the following processes are central to effective writing:

Planning	Setting one or more goals for a writing project Identifying relevant knowledge Organizing ideas
Drafting	Writing a first draft Addressing mechanical issues
Metacognition	Metacognitively regulating the writing process
Revision	Editing (i.e., identifying weaknesses) Rewriting

These processes are summarized in Table 8.1. Skilled writing typically involves moving back and forth among them throughout a writing project (Benton, 1997; Flower & Hayes, 1981; R. T. Kellogg, 1994).

Setting Goals

Certainly the first step in any writing project is to determine what one wants to accomplish by writing. For example, I had two primary goals as I wrote this supplementary reading: (1) to provide an accurate synthesis of what psychologists and educators have discovered about how students learn and develop in the content areas and (2) to help my readers learn this information meaningfully, so that they can easily transfer it to their future instructional practices. But writers may have other goals instead—perhaps to entertain, describe, report, or persuade. I suspect that many students have only one, not terribly beneficial goal when they complete written classroom assignments: to write something that will earn them a good grade.

Expert writers identify specific goals before they begin writing, but beginning writers rarely give much thought to their objectives (Scardamalia & Bereiter, 1986; Sitko, 1998). As teachers, we must help our students establish clear goals for themselves before they begin to write, and such goals should focus more on conveying intended meanings successfully than on addressing such writing mechanics as spelling and punctuation (Langer & Applebee, 1987). For instance, we might ask our students to address questions such as these before they put pen to paper: Why am I writing this? Who am I writing for? (Englert, Raphael, Anderson, Anthony, & Stevens, 1991). By encouraging students to clarify their writing goals, we will almost certainly help them write more effectively (Ferretti, MacArthur, & Dowdy, 2000; Page-Voth & Graham, 1999).

Table 8.1. Components of Skilled Writing

Component	Process(es)	Challenges for Students	Instructional Strategies
Planning	Setting goals	Students must decide what they want to accomplish through their writing.	Ask students to answer questions such as "Why am I writing this?" and "Who am I writing for?" before they begin to write.
	Identifying relevant knowledge	Students must identify what they already know about a topic. In some cases, they must also conduct research to obtain the information they need.	Have students brainstorm ideas before they begin writing. Teach essential research strategies (e.g., finding information in the library or on the Internet).
	Organizing ideas	Students must create a logical sequence in which to present their ideas.	Have students develop an outline before they begin writing. Teach specific structures that students might follow as they write (e.g., a structure for a persuasive essay, the typical elements of a short story).
Drafting	Writing a first draft	Students must get their ideas on paper in a reasonably logical and coherent fashion.	Remind students that they must communicate their ideas in a way that their readers can understand. Give students some strategies for communicating effectively (e.g., using examples, analogies, or rhetorical questions). Ask students not to worry too much about spelling, punctuation, and capitalization in the first draft. When students know how to spell few if any words (especially in the early elementary grades), let them dictate their stories.
	Addressing mechanics	Students must use correct word spellings and apply rules and conventions for grammar, punctuation, and capitalization.	Provide some systematic instruction in spelling, grammar, punctuation, and capitalization. Allow students to use spell and grammar checkers on word processing programs.
Metacognition	Metacognitively regulating the writing process	Students must continually monitor their writing for clarity and logical sequencing, and they must continually keep both their goals and their audience in mind.	Give students a list of questions to consider as they write (e.g., "Am I achieving my goal?" "Am I following a logical train of thought?"). Ask students to write for a specific, concrete audience (e.g., for a younger child or for a member of Congress). Have students write in pairs as a way of encouraging them to verbalize issues related to writing effectively.
Revision	Editing	Students must find mechanical errors; they must also identify problems in organization, clarity, and style.	Provide frequent, concrete, and constructive feedback about both content and mechanics. Have students meet to edit one another's work.
	Rewriting	Students must address the errors and problems they've identified during editing and eventually produce a clear, cohesive, and error-free text.	Encourage students to use a word processing program so that they can make changes more easily. Have students collaborate with one another as they make revisions.

Identifying Relevant Knowledge

Whether they write fiction or nonfiction, writers can write about only the things they know or believe. Thus, they must identify what they have already learned about a topic—knowledge acquired, perhaps, through formal instruction, independent reading, or personal experience—and then, if necessary, supplement it with additional research. Effective writers typically have a solid understanding of the content about which they are writing: They have learned it in a meaningful, well-organized, and elaborated fashion (Benton, 1997; R. T. Kellogg, 1994).

In some situations, we will, of course, need to teach our students various strategies for locating needed information in newspapers, at the library, or on the Internet. In other situations, we may simply need to help them retrieve helpful information from their long-term memories. For instance, as a prewriting activity, we might conduct small-group or whole-class discussions on the topics that students will be writing about (Boiarsky, 1982).

Organizing

After identifying what they know or believe about a topic, good writers typically spend a fair amount of time organizing their ideas (Berninger, Fuller, & Whitaker, 1996; Scardamalia & Bereiter, 1987). For instance, students can organize their thoughts using such tried-and-true methods as making a list, forming clusters of related ideas, or developing an outline (R. T. Kellogg, 1994). Furthermore, we can scaffold their first attempts at particular forms of writing by providing a structure for them. For instance, when asking students to write a persuasive essay, we might suggest that they follow four steps:

1. Develop a topic sentence.
2. List several reasons that support the topic sentence.
3. Determine whether each reason is likely to be convincing to readers; if necessary, modify it so that it is more convincing.
4. Develop an appropriate ending or conclusion. (based on Graham & Harris, 1988)

When we have students write short stories, we can teach them to incorporate the features that most stories have: a setting, a main character with certain thoughts and feelings, a problem situation, an outcome, and so on (Gambrell & Chasen, 1991; Graham & Harris, 1992).

Writing a First Draft

Converting one's ideas into written language—a process known as *translating*—is possibly the most challenging part of effective writing. A good writer uses a wide variety of words and sentence structures to convey ideas, takes into account the prior knowledge that readers are likely to have, and puts words together in such a way that readers can easily construct intended meanings (Burnett & Kastman, 1997; Byrnes, 1996; Spivey, 1997).

Many students at all grade levels think of writing as a process of putting ideas on paper, rather than as a process of presenting ideas in a way that enables their readers to *understand* those ideas. Furthermore, students rarely elaborate in writing on the ideas they present; for instance, they are reluctant to analyze, synthesize, and evaluate them. In general, students' writing tends to be *knowledge telling* rather than *knowledge transforming* (Bereiter & Scardamalia, 1987; Cameron, Hunt, & Linton, 1996; Greene & Ackerman, 1995; McCutchen, 1996). As examples, consider the following two essays, each one written by a small group of fourth graders; both essays were supposedly written to help younger children learn about electric circuits:

Example of knowledge telling:

Electric circuits are wires that when it's closed electricity flows through and it's circular. A generator is a magnet that spins around in coils. It powers up a city or town. A conductor is what makes electricity. It powers up electrical things. (Chambliss, 1998, p. 8; reprinted by permission)

Example of knowledge transforming:

Electric Circuits They'll Shock You

You have energy inside of you that allows you to walk, run, jump, etc. There's also another source of energy, electrical energy. It lets you turn on your light, run your computer, listen to the radio, and many other things.

But before you experiment let us caution you that electricity can be very dangerous so don't experiment without adult supervision. Here are some safety precautions for when you experiment: Never touch the copper part of a wire. Do NOT leave liquid substances near electrical equipment. Do not open a battery without protection (it contains acid).

Now that you know the rules let me tell you about electricity. When you turn on your light that means you have made a circuit flow, when you turn off the light that means you broke the circuit. How does a light bulb light you ask? Well you have to have a complete circuit. Let all the equipment touch each other. The wires must touch the battery. The battery must touch the light. The light must touch the battery.

If you don't understand how the circuit breaks, here is an example. When you are using the refrigerator, you open it, and all the air comes out. When you are not using the refrigerator, you close it, and the air no longer comes out.

Now that you know about electricity it won't shock you the way it works. (Chambliss, 1998, p. 8; reprinted by permission)

When students engage in knowledge telling, they are likely to write their thoughts in the order in which they retrieve them from long-term memory, with little regard for constructing a cohesive, logical, and complete piece of written work. In contrast, when students engage in knowledge transforming, they tailor their presentation to the things that their intended audience is likely to know and systematically lead their readers toward a better understanding of the topic in question.

Students may knowledge-tell, rather than knowledge-transform, partly because they must consider *so* many different things—the content, the audience, spelling, grammar, punctuation, handwriting, and so on—when they write that their working memories simply cannot handle the load (Benton, 1997; Flower & Hayes, 1981; McCutchen, 1996). It is usually beneficial, then, to have students address only one or two aspects of the writing process at a time; for instance, we might ask them to plan and organize their thoughts *before* they actually begin writing and to ignore the mechanics of writing until after they have written their first draft (K. R. Harris & Graham, 1992; Treiman, 1993). We may also want to brainstorm with students about strategies for communicating ideas effectively—for instance, using examples, analogies, graphics, and rhetorical questions—to a particular audience (Chambliss, 1998). And we can illustrate knowledge transforming by showing students actual examples of how expert writers communicate their ideas (Byrnes, 1996; Englert et al., 1991).

Addressing Writing Mechanics

Expert writers have typically learned the mechanical aspects of writing—spelling, punctuation, capitalization, and proper syntax (correct word order, subject-verb agreement, etc.)—to a level of automaticity. Given the limited capacity of working memory, such automaticity is probably essential if we want students to communicate their thoughts in a logical, well-organized, knowledge-transforming manner. Yet it makes little sense to postpone writing tasks until students have completely mastered writing mechanics; if we did so, our students might never have a chance to write!

Too much emphasis on writing mechanics is likely to discourage our students from wanting to write very much in the future. When we put writing mechanics aside for awhile—for the first draft in the case of older students and perhaps altogether in the case of very young ones—we are likely to see our students write more frequently and create longer and more complex texts (Clarke, 1988; Leu & Kinzer, 1995; Treiman, 1993). For instance, kindergartners and first graders can write a great deal using "invented spellings" that often only vaguely resemble actual words. Consider this kindergartner's creation entitled "My Garden" (note that "HWS" is *house*):

> THIS IS A HWS
> THE SUN
> WL SHIN
> ND MI
> GRDN
> WL GRO
> (Hemphill & Snow, 1996, p. 192)

If time and resources allow, and especially if we are teaching in the early elementary grades, we might even have our students initially dictate stories and compositions for someone else to write down (Scardamalia, Bereiter, & Goelman, 1982).

Eventually, of course, we must teach our students the conventions of written language and stress the importance of using those conventions for effective communication (Treiman, 1993). For instance, we should teach general rules of punctuation and capitalization, stress the importance of subject-verb agreement, and introduce various kinds of simple and complex sentences. And we will undoubtedly want to provide some explicit instruction in spelling. Theorists and practitioners have offered several strategies for spelling instruction:

- Point out letter-sound correspondences in how words are spelled.
- Draw analogies among words that are spelled similarly.
- Have students write each word several times as they study it.
- Stress the importance of correct spelling for enhancing a writer's credibility.
  (Berninger et al., 1998; K. J. Brown, Sinatra, & Wagstaff, 1996; Kernaghan & Woloshyn, 1994; Nation & Hulme, 1998; W. Schneider et al., 2000; M. H. Thomas & Dieter, 1987)

Metacognition

Throughout the writing process, expert writers are metacognitively active: They monitor their progress and the effectiveness of what they have written, addressing questions such as these:

- Am I achieving my goal(s) for writing this piece?
- Am I explaining myself clearly?
- Am I following a logical train of thought?
- Am I giving examples to illustrate my ideas?
- Am I supporting my opinions with valid arguments?

The answers to such questions influence their subsequent courses of action.

Furthermore, skillful writers continually keep their anticipated readers in mind (R. T. Kellogg, 1994; Paris & Cunningham, 1996). When we speak with other people, we get constant verbal and nonverbal feedback from them; for instance, they ask questions when they don't understand and let us know when they disagree with us. But when we write, we do so in isolation from our audience. We must therefore make assumptions about our readers' prior knowledge, vocabulary level, cognitive maturity, and motivation for reading what we have written.

All too often, elementary and secondary students don't metacognitively "supervise" what they are doing as they write; for instance, they give little thought to who their audience might be, and they engage in knowledge telling rather consciously trying to communicate their thoughts in a way that someone else can easily understand (Graham, Harris, & Troia, 1998; Sitko, 1998). This state of affairs is probably not surprisingly given the fact that, in most cases, the only person who actually reads their work is a teacher who may already be familiar with the ideas they are trying to present.

One way to enhance students' metacognitive awareness and regulation of what they do (mentally) as they write is to explicitly teach and model various writing strategies—identifying the goals to be accomplished in a writing project, organizing one's thoughts before starting to write, asking oneself questions about what has already been written, and so on—and initially give students the scaffolding they need to use these strategies (Graham et al., 1998). A second approach is to meet with students one-on-one and ask them to reflect on the strategies they've used while writing (e.g., "How did you decide to start the piece in this way?"; Sitko, 1998, p. 107). Yet another technique is to ask students to write for a particular audience, as the fourth graders who wrote the "Electric Circuits They'll Shock You" essay did (Burnett & Kastman, 1997; Cameron et al., 1996; Sperling, 1996). For example, we might ask students to write a letter to people their own age who live in environments very different from their own—perhaps in a large city or in farm country (Benton, 1997; Kroll, 1984). Or we might ask them to imagine themselves in particular roles—perhaps as reporters investigating a news story or as travelers hoping to spread peace throughout the world (J. J. Schneider, 1998). Students as young as 7 or 8 can adapt their writing to different audiences when they understand who those audiences are (J. J. Schneider, 1998).

Editing

Try your hand at editing in the following exercise.

EXPERIENCING FIRSTHAND   *What's Wrong?*

Here is how one eighth-grade girl responded to the question, *How did the United States become a country?* As you read it, mark places that need revision.

> The first people here were what we called the Native Americans they crossed over to
>
> America on a land Bridge or as some people say.
>
> In Europue people where thinking the world was flat and if you sailed on and on you
>
> would fall of the world but Christopher Columbus did not beleave that he believed it was
>
> round. So Christopher Columbus sailed to America. Soon after Pilgrims came to get
>
> away from the Cathalic religion. More people came over and keept pushing the Indians
>
> off their land and taking what was not theirs the Indians where willing to share it but

americans just took it. Then the people wanted to break away from Brittany. Then

Americans fought with each other over many things like slaver. And North won.

(courtesy of Dinah Jackson)

Now count how many times you marked these kinds of errors:

Spelling errors	____	Indentation errors	____
Punctuation errors	____	Run-on sentences	____
Capitalization errors	____	Unclear writing	____
Factual errors	____	Problems of style	____

What kinds of problems did you focus on when you edited the student's composition?

How much did you focus on writing mechanics (spelling, capitalization, etc.) in your editing? Did you identify any problems *other* than mechanical errors? Did you find the two factual errors? The Pilgrims wanted to leave the Church of England, not the Catholic church, and they left Britain, not Brittany (a region in France). Did you note any instances of unclear writing? For instance, in the phrase "taking what was not theirs" in the second paragraph, the meanings of *what* and *theirs* are not clear. And what about the overall style of the piece? The phrase "or as some people say" serves no purpose, and the last sentence is short and choppy. In general, the student has engaged in knowledge telling rather than knowledge transforming: She has simply written down her thoughts, apparently in the order in which she retrieved them from long-term memory, and made no attempt to tie them together into a coherent whole.

Unfortunately, when teachers provide feedback about students' writing, they tend to focus more on mechanical errors than on problems with style, clarity, or cohesiveness (Byrnes, 1996). So it is not surprising that when students edit their own work, they, too, focus on mechanics (Berninger et al., 1996; Kellch, 1999; McCutchen, Kerr, & Francis, 1994). Many students, especially those in the elementary grades, believe that they are expressing themselves more clearly than they actually are; they have difficulty reading their own writing as another person might read it (Bartlett, 1982; Beal, 1996).

Our students can edit their writing more successfully when we give them criteria that they can use to judge their work (McCormick, Busching, & Potter, 1992). It is essential, too, that we provide feedback that addresses style, clarity, and cohesiveness as well as mechanics (Benton, 1997; Covill, 1997). (We should be careful, of course, that we balance criticism with a healthy dose of feedback about what students are doing *well*, so that we don't discourage them from writing altogether!) Furthermore, we can ask students to read and respond to one another's work (Benton, 1997; Cameron et al., 1996; Sperling, 1996); in the process, they may become better able to examine their own writing from the perspective of potential readers.

Rewriting

Good writers almost invariably revise the things they write; in the process, they tend to focus on problems of clarity and organization while keeping in mind the overall goals of their writing (Fitzgerald, 1992; Scardamalia & Bereiter, 1986). In contrast, children and adolescents rarely revise unless a teacher or other adult specifically urges them to do so; when they *do* rewrite, they tend to make only small, superficial changes (Beal, 1996; Fitzgerald, 1987).

Sometimes, students fail to address problems in clarity and organization because they haven't located these problems to begin with (Fitzgerald, 1987). But our students may also not know *how* to revise their work. Researchers have identified several strategies through which we can help our students as they revise the things they've written:

- Schedule in-class time for revising so that students can get assistance when they need it.

- Before students begin rewriting, ask them to list five things they can do to make their writing better.

- Provide questions that students should ask themselves as they rewrite (e.g., "Is this confusing?" "Do I need another example here?" "Who am I writing this for?").

- Occasionally have students work in pairs or small groups to help one another revise. (Benton, 1997; Bereiter & Scardamalia, 1987; Cameron et al., 1996; De La Paz, Swanson, & Graham, 1998; Graham, MacArthur, & Schwartz, 1995; Graves, 1983; Kish, Zimmer, & Henning, 1994; Sitko, 1998; Webb & Palincsar, 1996)

Writing as a Facilitator of Learning

As you must surely have noticed in the preceding discussion, writing involves several cognitive processes that promote learning. Writers must retrieve from long-term memory the things that they already know about a topic. They must clarify and organize their thoughts sufficiently to communicate them to their readers. And a knowledge-transforming approach to writing requires writers to elaborate on the things they know—for instance, to put ideas in language that the intended audience can understand, to think of good examples, and to anticipate readers' questions. So it is not surprising that writing about a topic, phenomenon, or problem-solving strategy enhances students' understanding (Benton, 1997; Greene & Ackerman, 1995; Johanning, D'Agostino, Steele, & Shumow, 1999; Klein, 1999, 2000). As teachers, then, we should ask students to write frequently for two reasons: to enhance their writing ability *and* to enhance their learning more generally.

Developmental Changes in Writing

The nature and quality of students' writing change in many ways throughout the elementary and secondary school years. In the early elementary years, writing projects typically involve narratives: Students write about their own personal experiences and create short, fictional stories (Hemphill & Snow, 1996). They have a hard time writing for an imagined audience and, as a result, engage in knowledge telling (rather than knowledge transforming) almost exclusively (Knudson, 1992; Perfetti & McCutchen, 1987). And of course, as was evident in the second graders' compositions in the opening case study, students in the lower elementary grades are still working on the "basics" of spelling, grammar, punctuation, and capitalization.

In the later elementary grades, writing mechanics (e.g., many word spellings) are beginning to become automatic, enabling students to use more complex sentence structures and devote more effort to communicating their thoughts effectively on paper (R. E. Owens, 1996). Furthermore, they begin to think about how their readers might respond to what if they have written and so are more likely to proofread and revise their work (R. E. Owens, 1996). At this point, however, they do very little planning before they begin to write, and their writing continues to involve knowledge telling rather than knowledge transforming (Berninger et al., 1996).

We see several changes as students move through the secondary grades. First, students are more capable of analyzing and synthesizing their thoughts when they write, and so they are better able to write research papers and argumentative essays (Knudson, 1992; McCann, 1989; Spivey, 1997).

They are more likely to consider specific goals when they write and therefore to include only content directly relevant to those goals (Scardamalia & Bereiter, 1987). When asked to write about a particular topic, they retrieve and generate many more ideas than students in the elementary grades do (Scardamalia & Bereiter, 1986). Their sentences are more likely to vary in structure and frequently contain one or more dependent clauses (Byrnes, 1996). And in general, they compose more cohesive, integrated texts (Berninger et al., 1996; Byrnes, 1996; R. E. Owens, 1996; Spivey, 1997). At this point, too, although many students continue to engage in knowledge telling, we start seeing regular signs of knowledge transforming as well (Spivey, 1997). As an example, consider how this eighth grader answered the question, *How did the United States become a country?*

> We became a country by way of common sense. The inhabitants on American soil thought it rather silly and ridiculus to be loyal to, follow rules and pay taxes to a ruler who has never seen where they live. King George III had never set foot (as far as I know) on American soil, but he got taxes and other things from those who lived here. When America decied to unit and dishonnor past laws and rules, England got angry. There was a war. When we won, drew up rules, and accepted states America was born.

> In a more poetic sense, we became a country because of who lived here and what they did. They actions of heros, heroines, leaders, followers, and everyday people made America famous, an ideal place to live. The different cultures and lifestyles made America unique and unlike any other place in the world. If you think about it, it's like visiting the worlds at Epcot in Florida. You can go from country to country without leaving home. (courtesy of Dinah Jackson)

The student's analogy between the United States and Disney World's Epcot Center is knowledge transforming at its finest.

General Strategies for Teaching Writing

We've already identified numerous strategies for helping students develop specific aspects of the writing process. Here are several additional strategies to promote writing development more generally:

• *Assign authentic writing tasks.* Although we would like students to be able to write for a variety of audiences, in reality most of them write primarily for one person: their teacher (Applebee, 1984; Benton, 1997). By giving our students authentic, real-world writing tasks—having them write short stories for their classmates, letters to businesses and lawmakers, editorials for the local newspaper, e-mail messages to people in distant locations, and so on—we can encourage them to consider the language abilities and prior knowledge of their readers (e.g., Englert et al., 1991; Sugar & Bonk, 1998). Such tasks can also prompt students to set specific goals for writing and to acquire the writing skills they need to achieve those goals.

• *Offer students some choices about writing topics.* Students write more frequently, and in a more organized and logical fashion, when they are interested in what they are writing about (Benton, 1997; Garner, 1998). For instance, one high school English teacher, who noticed that several very capable students were failing his class because they weren't completing assigned writing tasks, began having his students write about their own personal experiences and share them on the Internet with students in other classrooms; the teacher monitored their compositions for vulgar language but imposed no other restrictions. The students suddenly began writing regularly, presumably because they could write for a real audience and could now choose their own topics (Garner, 1998). As Chapter 12 of the textbook points out, choices enhance students' sense of *self-determination*, which in turn enhances their intrinsic motivation to complete assigned tasks and, hence, to develop their academic skills.

INTO THE CLASSROOM: *Promoting Reading and Writing Skills*

- Help young children develop phonological awareness.

    A kindergarten teacher suggests to his class, "Let's see how many words we can think of that rhyme with the word *gate*. I'll write the words on the chalkboard. Let's see if we can think of at least eight words that rhyme with *gate*."

- Help students develop automaticity in word recognition and spelling, but do so within the context of authentic reading and writing activities as much as possible.

    A second-grade teacher has her students read Dr. Seuss's *The Cat in the Hat*, a book that repeats many of the same words (e.g., *cat*, *hat*, *thing*) over and over again.

- Have students discuss with peers the things they are reading and writing.

    A middle school teacher has his students meet in small groups to read their short stories to one another. As each student reads his or her story, other group members ask questions for clarification and make suggestions about how to make the story better. Later, students consider their classmates' comments as they revise their stories.

- Scaffold students' efforts as they work on increasingly more challenging reading and writing tasks.

    A high school English teacher gives students a format to follow when writing a research paper: an introductory paragraph that describes the topic of the paper, at least three different sections within the paper that address different aspects of the topic (each one beginning with a new heading), and a "Conclusion" section that summarizes and integrates the main ideas of the paper.

- Address reading and writing skills in all areas of the curriculum.

    An eighth-grade social studies teacher gives her students an article to read from *Newsweek* magazine. Knowing that the reading level of the article may be challenging for many of her students, she gives them specific questions to answer as they read the article.

• *Use peer groups to promote effective writing skills.* Earlier we noted the value of using peer groups to help students edit and revise their writing. In fact, we may want to have our students actually *write* together as well. Several studies have shown that when students collaborate on writing projects, they produce longer and more complex texts, revise more, and enhance one another's writing skills (Daiute, 1986, 1989; Daiute & Dalton, 1993).

• *Encourage students to use word processing programs.* Word processing programs encourage students to revise; after all, it is much easier to change words and move sentences when one is working on a computer rather than on paper (Cochran-Smith, 1991; R. T. Kellogg, 1994). Furthermore, by taking over some of the mechanical aspects of writing, word processing can lessen the load on working memory, enabling students to devote more working memory capacity to the overall quality of writing (Jones & Pellegrini, 1996). As an illustration, consider what the same first grader wrote by hand and by computer (Jones & Pellegrini, 1996):

By hand:

Some busy wut to play boll But thay cnat play Boll Be cus the Big Busys and the grul wit to tale on them (p. 711)

By computer:

The man cooks some soup and he cooks carrots in the soup and the king gives the man a big hat, and the man goes to the house and the man shows the hat cap to the children. (p. 711)

A big difference, wouldn't you say?

• *Include writing assignments in all areas of the curriculum.* Writing shouldn't be a skill that only elementary teachers and secondary English teachers teach. In fact, writing takes different forms in different disciplines; for instance, writing fiction is very different from writing a science laboratory report, which in turn is very different from writing an analysis of historical documents. Ideally, *all* teachers should teach writing to some degree, and, especially at the secondary level, they should teach the writing skills specific to particular academic disciplines (Burnett & Kastman, 1997; Sperling, 1996).

Not only is writing often very different in different subject areas, but the very nature of thinking and learning can be quite different as well. You will see what I mean as we explore mathematics, science, and social studies.

Mathematics

Mathematics probably causes more confusion and frustration, for more students, than any other subject in the school curriculum. The hierarchical nature of the discipline may be partly to blame: To the extent that students don't completely master mathematical concepts and procedures at one grade level, they lack necessary prerequisites for learning math successfully in later grades. As increasingly more complex and abstract concepts and procedures are introduced over the years, students must resort more and more frequently to rote, meaningless learning.

Mathematics is actually a cluster of domains—arithmetic, algebra, geometry, statistics and probability, and so on—that comprise different methods of representing situations and strategies for solving problems (De Corte, Greer, & Verschaffel, 1996). Nevertheless, we can identify several key components that underlie effective mathematical reasoning across the board. As we do so, we will also identify many strategies that can help our students become successful mathematical thinkers.

The Nature of Mathematical Reasoning

Mathematical thinking and problem solving typically require the following:
  • Understanding numbers and counting
  • Understanding central mathematics concepts and principles
  • Encoding problem situations appropriately
  • Mastering a variety of problem-solving procedures
  • Relating problem-solving procedures to mathematical concepts and principles
  • Relating mathematical principles to everyday situations
  • Developing effective metacognitive processes and beliefs

Understanding Numbers and Counting

Many children begin counting before their third birthday, and most 3- and 4-year-olds can count to ten correctly (Geary, 1994). Five-year-olds can often count far beyond ten (perhaps to 50), but they may get confused about the order of such numbers as 70, 80, and 90 (Fuson & Hall, 1983). Furthermore, most 5-year-olds have mastered several basic principles of counting, including these:

- *One-one principle.* Each object in the group being counted must be assigned one and only one number word; in other words, you say "one" while pointing to one object, "two" while pointing to another, and so on until every object has been counted once.

- *Cardinal principle.* The last number word counted indicates the number of objects in the group; in other words, if you count up to five when counting objects, then there are five objects in the group.

- *Order-irrelevance principle.* A group of objects has the same number regardless of the order in which they are counted. (Gallistel & Gelman, 1992; Gelman & Gallistel, 1978)

Many 5-year-olds have also developed simple procedures for adding and subtracting, procedures that they have, in most cases, developed on their own (Bermejo, 1996; Correa, Nunes, & Bryant, 1998; Geary, 1994). If they want to add a group of five objects and a group of three objects, they won't necessarily begin counting with *one*; instead, they may begin with *five* and then count the smaller group: "Five, six, seven, eight." They might do something similar for subtracting, starting with the original number of objects and then counting down the number of objects removed: "Eight, seven, six, five." Eventually, children no longer need to have the objects in front of them when they add and subtract; instead, they use their fingers to represent the objects (Bermejo, 1996).

Certainly not all young children acquire the basic understanding of counting, numbers, addition, and subtraction just described. Yet such understanding forms the basic foundation for the arithmetic that we teach in the early elementary years. Especially if we are teaching kindergartners or first graders, we must determine what our students do and do not know about numbers and remediate any weaknesses in their understanding. Numerous activities and games involving counting, comparing quantities, adding, and subtracting—always using concrete objects—are likely to be beneficial. We may also want to use a number line to help young children develop an understanding of how numbers relate to one another (Greeno, Collins, & Resnick, 1996; Griffin, Case, & Capodilupo, 1995; Griffin, Case, & Siegler, 1994).

Understanding Central Concepts and Principles

In addition to a basic understanding of numbers, mathematical reasoning requires an understanding of many concepts and principles. For instance, students must eventually master such concepts as *negative number*, *right angle*, and *variable* and such principles as these:

- Multiplying a positive number by a negative number always yields a negative number.
- The three angles of a triangle always have a total of 180°.
- When an equation of the form $ax + by + c = 0$ is plotted on a graph, all possible solutions for x and y form a straight line.

Growing children are unlikely to develop such concepts and principles on their own; instead, some degree of formal instruction seems to be necessary (De Corte et al., 1996; Geary, 1994; Ginsburg, Posner, & Russell, 1981).

The more abstract mathematical concepts and principles are, the more difficulty our students are likely to have understanding them (Byrnes, 1996). With a little creativity, we can translate many abstract mathematical ideas into concrete form; Figure 8.1 provides examples.

Encoding Problems Appropriately

As noted in Chapter 8 of the textbook, an essential step in solving a problem is to encode it—that is, to think of it as being a certain *kind* of problem. For instance, you would immediately categorize the following problem:

TEACHING FRACTIONS

Pizza A is divided into six equal pieces. Each piece is $\frac{1}{6}$ of the pizza.

Pizza B is divided into eight equal pieces. Each piece is $\frac{1}{8}$ of the pizza.

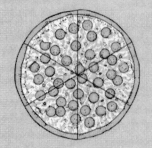

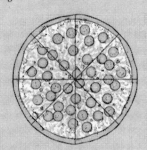

- *Which is bigger, $\frac{1}{6}$ or $\frac{1}{8}$?*

$$\frac{1}{6} > \frac{1}{8}$$

- *How many pieces equal $\frac{1}{2}$ of each pizza?*

3 pieces $= \frac{1}{2}$ 4 pieces $= \frac{1}{2}$

$\frac{1}{6} + \frac{1}{6} + \frac{1}{6} = \frac{3}{6}$ $\frac{1}{8} + \frac{1}{8} + \frac{1}{8} + \frac{1}{8} = \frac{4}{8}$

In other words, $\frac{3}{6} = \frac{1}{2}$ In other words, $\frac{4}{8} = \frac{1}{2}$

- *Which is more, $\frac{2}{3}$ of a pizza or $\frac{5}{8}$ of a pizza?*

Four pieces of Pizza A are more pizza than five pieces of Pizza B.

So $\frac{2}{3} > \frac{5}{8}$

TEACHING NEGATIVE NUMBERS

(Based on a strategy used by Jaime Escalante in *Stand and Deliver* [Musca & Menendez, 1988])

Imagine that you dig a hole in the ground like this:

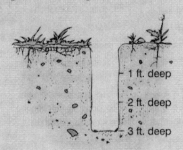

1 ft. deep
2 ft. deep
3 ft. deep

The bottom of the hole is 3 feet below ground level. If you think of the ground as 0, then the bottom of the hole is –3.

You want to put a wooden post in the hole so that it rises 5 feet above the ground. *How long does the post need to be?*

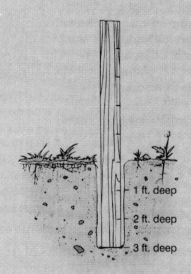

1 ft. deep
2 ft. deep
3 ft. deep

The pole needs to be 8 feet long.
–3 + 8 = 5

Figure 8.1 Illustrating abstract mathematical concepts and principles in concrete ways

> Mary has five marbles. John gave her seven more. How many does she have altogether?

as an addition problem. And you should recognize this problem:

> I have a carpet that is 45 square feet in area. It is 4 feet longer than it is wide. What are the dimensions of my carpet?

as an area-of-a-rectangle problem. You might also identify it as an algebra problem, because the two numbers you need to calculate the area (the width and length) are unknowns.

At the high school level, encoding algebra problems poses a challenge for many students (Clement, 1982; Geary, 1994). Furthermore, students of all ages tend to have difficulty encoding *relational problems*—problems in which only comparative numbers are given—and hence are often unable to solve problems such as this one:

> Laura is 3 times as old as Maria was when Laura was as old as Maria is now. In 2 years Laura will be twice as old as Maria was 2 years ago. Find their present ages. (Mayer, 1982, p. 202)

Even college students have trouble encoding and solving this problem (Mayer, 1982). (Laura is 18 and Maria is 12.)

Chapter 8 in the textbook offers several suggestions for helping students encode problems more effectively: We can give them real objects or pictures that can help them think about a problem in concrete terms, encourage them to draw their *own* pictures or diagrams, and point out features of a problem that should remind them of similar problems. Several additional strategies are useful as well (Mayer, 1999). We can give students a large number of problems and ask them only to categorize the problems, not to solve them. We can give them problems with irrelevant as well as relevant information (e.g., in the "carpet" problem presented earlier, we might include information about how old the carpet is or how much it costs per square yard). And we should definitely mix different kinds of problems together (e.g., problems requiring addition, subtraction, multiplication, and division) so that students get in the habit of encoding different problems differently.

Mastering Problem-Solving Procedures

Many mathematical problem-solving procedures involve specific algorithms that, when correctly applied, always yield a correct answer. For instance, students learn algorithmic procedures for doing long division, multiplying and dividing fractions, and solving for *x* in algebraic equations. Problem-solving heuristics sometimes come into play as well. For instance, there aren't always specific algorithms that students can use in geometric proofs. As an illustration, let's use the following problem from Chapter 8 in the textbook:

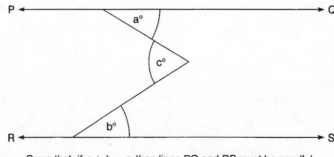

Prove that, if *a* + *b* = *c*, then lines PQ and RS must be parallel.

There is no single "right" way to prove this point. Instead, we might experiment with the situation, perhaps extending some of the lines and considering other angles, like this:

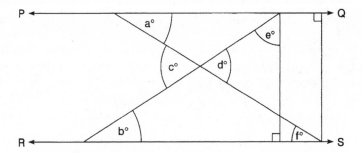

By using principles related to the angles of triangles and intersecting lines, we can eventually prove that, yes, lines PQ and RS must be parallel.

As teachers, we can do several things to help students master mathematical procedures. In some cases—for instance, in basic addition, subtraction, multiplication, and division—we may want to replace algorithms with quickly retrievable facts; after all, retrieving 5 + 3 = 8 uses less working memory capacity than an algorithm such as counting "five . . . and six, seven, eight." We should also encourage students to use external forms of "storage" to reduce the working memory load, perhaps by using their fingers or pencil and paper to keep track of numbers or other elements of a problem. We can use concrete manipulatives to illustrate what might otherwise be fairly abstract procedures (Fuson & Briars, 1990). For example, we might demonstrate the rationale behind "borrowing" in subtraction by using toothpicks, some of which have been bundled into groups of ten or one hundred (see Figure 8.2). We can provide worked-out examples to illustrate such complex procedures as solving quadratic equations (Mayer & Wittrock, 1996; Mwangi & Sweller, 1998; Zhu & Simon, 1987). Ultimately, however, we must help our students understand *why* the mathematical procedures they use are appropriate. This particular point is so important that I address it separately in the following discussion.

Relating Procedures to Concepts and Principles

EXPERIENCING FIRSTHAND   *Quarters and Dimes*

See whether you can solve this problem before you read further.

> The number of quarters a man has is seven times the number of dimes he has. The value of the dimes exceeds the value of the quarters by two dollars and fifty cents. How many has he of each coin? (Paige & Simon, 1966, p. 79)

If you found an answer to the problem—any answer at all—then you overlooked an important point: Quarters are worth more than dimes. If there are more quarters than dimes, the value of the dimes cannot possibly be greater than the value of the quarters. The problem makes no sense, and so it cannot be solved.

Unfortunately, when our schools teach mathematical problem solving, they often focus on teaching procedures for solving problems while omitting explanations of why the procedures work; in other words, they don't relate the procedures to basic concepts and principles of mathematics (Cooney,

1991; J. Hiebert & Lefevre, 1986; Perkins & Salomon, 1989). For example, perhaps you can recall learning how to solve a long division problem, but you probably don't recall learning *why* you multiply the divisor by each digit in your answer and then write the product in a particular location below the dividend. Or perhaps you were taught that the words *all together* in a word problem indicate that addition is called for and that the word *left* means you should subtract.

When students learn mathematical procedures at a rote level, without understanding the concepts, principles, and general logic behind them, they may often apply them "unthinkingly" and inappropriately (Carr & Biddlecomb, 1998; Perkins & Simmons, 1988; Resnick, 1989; Silver, Shapiro, & Deutsch, 1993). As a result, they may obtain illogical or physically impossible results. Consider the following instances of meaningless mathematical problem solving as examples:

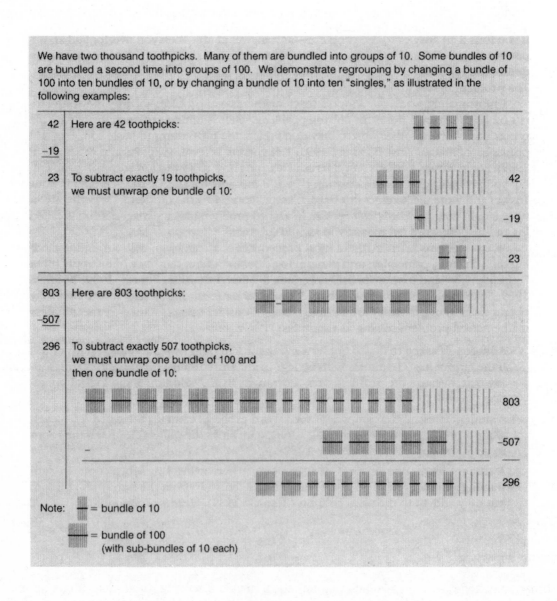

Figure 8.2 Illustrating a problem-solving algorithm with concrete manipulatives

- A student is asked to figure out how many chickens and how many pigs a farmer has if the farmer has 21 animals with 60 legs in all. The student adds 21 and 60, reasoning that, because the problem says "how many in all," addition is the logical operation (Lester, 1985).

- A student uses subtraction whenever a word problem contains the word *left*—even when a problem actually requiring addition includes the phrase "John left the room to get more apples" (Schoenfeld, 1982).

- A student learns the process of regrouping ("borrowing") in subtraction. In subtracting a number from 803, the student may "borrow" from the hundreds column, but only add 10 to the ones column (Resnick, 1989). Here is an example:

$$\begin{array}{r} \overset{7}{\cancel{8}}\,\overset{1}{0}\,3 \\ -\ 5\,0\,7 \\ \hline 2\,0\,6 \end{array}$$

(The correct answer, of course, is 296.)

Rather than simply teach mathematical procedures at a rote level, we should help students understand *why* they do the things they do to solve problems (Greeno, 1991; Griffin & Case, 1996; Perry, 1991; Rittle-Johnson, Siegler, & Alibali, 2001). For instance, we can relate regrouping procedures ("carrying" and "borrowing") in addition and subtraction to the concept of *place value*—the idea that a number in the second column from the right indicates the number of *tens*, the number in the third column indicates the number of *hundreds*, and so on (Byrnes, 1996). By showing our students the logic behind problem-solving procedures, we increase the likelihood that they will apply those procedures at appropriate times and obtain plausible results.

Relating Mathematics to Everyday Situations

Ultimately, learning mathematics is of little use unless students can apply it to real-world situations. Word problems are often used to help students make the connection between formal mathematics and everyday life. Yet traditional word problems alone are probably insufficient to enable most students to bridge the gap between classroom math and everyday situations (De Corte et al., 1996). First, word problems are typically well-defined: They provide all the information students need to know and pose a specific question that students must answer. In contrast, the real world rarely presents such problems: Some necessary numbers or measures may be missing, irrelevant information may be present, and perhaps the exact question to be answered is not clearly specified. (See Chapter 8 in the textbook for a discussion of well-defined versus ill-defined problems.)

In the following exercise, we discover a second difficulty with word problems.

EXPERIENCING FIRSTHAND *Busing the Band*

Take a minute to solve the following problem. Feel free to use a calculator if you have one handy.

> The Riverdale High School marching band is traveling to Hillside High School to perform in the half-time show at Saturday's football game. The school buses owned by the Riverdale School District can transport 32 passengers each. There are 104 students in the Riverdale band. How many buses will the band director need to request to transport the band to Hillside on Saturday?

Did you get the answer 3.25? If so, think about it for a moment. How is it possible to have 3.25 *buses*? What in the world is .25 of a bus? In actuality, the band director must request four buses for Saturday's game. If you fell into my trap, you're not alone. Many students develop the habit of solving word problems based on numerical information alone and overlook the realities of the situation with which they are dealing (De Corte et al., 1996).

In addition to using word problems, then, many theorists suggest that we engage students in tasks that require them to identify, on their own, the specific mathematical problems they need to solve in order to complete the tasks successfully (De Corte et al., 1996; J. Hiebert et al., 1996; Lester et al., 1997). For example, we might have our students work collaboratively to collect and then analyze large sets of data while studying their local ecology (Roth, 1996). We might take them grocery shopping, asking them to consider not only the "best buys" for various products but also how much cupboard space they have for storage (Lave, 1988). And we can ask them to bring to class some of the mathematical problems they encounter at home (Resnick, Bill, Lesgold, & Leer, 1991).

Developing Metacognitive Processes and Beliefs

Like virtually any other complex cognitive task, mathematical problem solving involves metacognition: The successful student must choose one or more appropriate problem-solving strategies, monitor progress toward the problem goal, and recognize when a solution has been reached (Carr & Biddlecomb, 1998; Schoenfeld, 1992). Rather than assume that our students will acquire these metacognitive processes on their own, we should probably teach such processes explicitly (Cardelle-Elawar, 1992). For instance, we can give students practice in identifying situations in which they don't have all the information they need to answer a question. We can also give them problems requiring two or more separate procedures, ask them to list the specific steps necessary to solve the problems, and suggest that they cross off each step as they accomplish it.

An additional aspect of metacognition is being *aware* of the processes one is using, yet many elementary and secondary school students do not actively reflect on what they are doing as they solve mathematical problems (Carr & Biddlecomb, 1998). We can encourage such reflection by engaging students in group discussions about how best to approach particular problems (more about such discussions shortly) and by asking them to explain in writing why they solved a problem as they did (Carr & Biddlecomb, 1998; Johanning et al., 1999).

We must make sure, too, that our students' beliefs about mathematics are conducive to effective learning and problem solving in math. Unfortunately, many students, even at the high school level, have several counterproductive beliefs:

- Mathematics is a collection of meaningless procedures that must simply be memorized.

- Mathematical problems always have one and only one right answer.

- One will either solve a problem within a few minutes or else not solve it at all.

- There's only one right way to solve any particular math problem. (Schoenfeld, 1988, 1992)

When we teach mathematics, we must certainly be aware of students' beliefs about math and take steps to correct any erroneous ones. For instance, as mentioned before, we can make mathematical procedures meaningful by relating them to concepts and principles students have already learned, and we can engage students in discussions about the variety of approaches possible for any particular problem. In addition, we can present problems that have multiple answers or require considerable time and persistence to solve.

Developmental Changes in Mathematical Understanding

As noted earlier, many (but not all) students first enter school having some proficiency in counting and some understanding of numbers. In the early elementary grades, we need to solidify these capabilities and expand them to include an understanding of addition and subtraction; later, we must expand them to include multiplication and division as well. But rather than ignore any strategies that students may have developed on their own—for instance, using their fingers to keep track of numbers or to add and subtract—we should probably encourage them to use existing strategies that seem to work effectively for them. They will eventually discard their early strategies as they acquire more efficient ones (Geary, 1994; Siegler, 1989).

The mathematics curriculum at the upper elementary grades typically includes an introduction to such proportions as fractions and decimals. Even first graders can understand simple fractions (e.g., 1/2, 2/3) if they can relate such fractions to their own, concrete reality (Empson, 1999). Yet the ability to reason more generally and effectively about proportions typically does not appear until students are, on average, about 11 or 12 years old (see Chapter 2 in the textbook). If school district objectives give us little choice about teaching proportions or other concepts that, from a developmental perspective, are going to be especially challenging for students, then we must present as many concrete and real-world examples of these concepts as possible.

In the middle school, junior high, and high school grades, mathematics instruction focuses increasingly on abstract ideas such as *irrational numbers, pi* (π), *infinity*, and *variable*. Over time, mathematical concepts and principles gradually become more and more removed from the concrete realities with which students are familiar. Perhaps it is no surprise, then, that students' anxiety about mathematics peaks during the high school years (Geary, 1994). Two general strategies can help us keep math anxiety within reasonable limits. First, we must continue to use concrete examples and experiences to illustrate mathematical ideas even in high school. And second, we must make sure that our students truly master the concepts and procedures they will need when they proceed to more difficult topics.

General Strategies for Teaching Mathematics

Throughout this section we have identified specific strategies for helping students learn and use mathematics effectively. Following are three more general strategies:

• *Have students tutor one another in mathematics.* When students tutor one another in math, both the tutor and the student being tutored seem to learn from the interaction. Peer tutoring can occur within a single classroom, with students pairing off differently on different occasions, depending on which students have and have not mastered a particular idea (Fuchs, Fuchs, & Karns, 1995; Fuchs et al., 1996). But it can also happen in a cross-age fashion, with older students tutoring younger ones. In one situation, for instance, fourth graders who were doing relatively poorly in math served as arithmetic tutors for first and second graders; the tutors themselves showed a substantial improvement in arithmetic problem-solving skills (Inglis & Biemiller, 1997).

Why does peer tutoring help the tutors as well as the students being tutored? Theorists believe that by explaining something to someone else, the tutors must first clarify it in their own minds. Furthermore, tutors may have to provide several examples to help their partners understand a concept or procedure; developing such examples requires the tutors to *elaborate* on what they know—always a good strategy from a cognitive processing perspective.

• *Hold small-group or whole-class discussions about mathematical problems.* A growing body of research supports the effectiveness of group discussions for enhancing students' mathematical understanding (Carr & Biddlecomb, 1998; Cobb et al., 1991; J. Hiebert & Wearne, 1992; Lampert,

1990). One common strategy is to ask students to identify (perhaps invent) and defend various ways of solving a particular problem (Brenner et al., 1997; Ginsburg-Block & Fantuzzo, 1998; Kline & Flowers, 1998; Lampert, 1990). For example, at the second grade level, students might develop their own strategies for adding two- and three-digit numbers (J. Hiebert & Wearne, 1996). At the high school level, they might derive their own set of geometric theorems (Healy, 1993).

Many theorists believe—and some research supports their belief—that when we encourage students to invent and justify mathematical procedures and principles within a group context, we also encourage them to construct a more meaningful understanding of mathematics (Cobb, 1994; J. Hiebert et al., 1997; Lampert, Rittenhouse, & Crumbaugh, 1996). Furthermore, if particular students have misconceptions that lead them to develop inappropriate procedures or principles, then their classmates may quickly object to their ideas. But to create a climate in which students feel free to argue with one another about mathematics, we must communicate two messages very clearly—that as a group, we "agree to disagree" and that, as lifelong learners, we are all apt to be wrong some of the time (J. Hiebert et al., 1997; Lampert et al., 1996).

• *Have students use calculators and computers frequently.* On some occasions, we will probably want students to do calculations by hand; for instance, this will often be the case when students are first mastering such operations as addition, subtraction, multiplication, and division. But eventually, especially as students begin dealing with complex mathematical situations and problems, we may want to help them ease the load on working memory by encouraging them to use calculators or computers to do simple calculations. Calculators and computers also enable students to experiment with mathematics—for example, to graph an equation and then see how the graph changes when the equation is modified in particular ways (De Corte et al., 1996; Pressley, 1995).

Chapter 4 in the textbook introduces the notion of *distributed intelligence*—the idea that people can perform more complex tasks, and therefore can behave in a more "intelligent" fashion, when they have the support of their social and physical environments. Peer groups and technology are two examples of such environmental support. There is no reason why we or our students should think of mathematics as something that must be done in isolation from other people and without the use of modern technology. The same is true for science as well, and we turn to this subject area now.

Science

Historically, science as a discipline has had two major goals: to describe and to explain what people observe in nature (Mayer, 1999). Some of the things you studied in science were primarily descriptive in content. For instance, you probably studied characteristics of the planets in our solar system, discovered that water expands when it freezes, and examined the ways in which vertebrates and invertebrates are different. But you probably also studied possible explanations—*theories*—about natural phenomena. For instance, you may have considered theories about how the universe began, why water expands when it freezes, or how various animal species evolved.

Actually, you began learning science long before you entered school as a kindergartner or first grader. In your early explorations of the world, you learned that objects usually fall toward the earth when you let go of them, that water freezes when it gets cold, and that dogs and cats have four legs whereas birds have two legs and fish have none. Children rarely come to school as "blank slates" when it comes to science.

Not only have young learners already made numerous observations about the world, but they have also constructed their own explanations—their **personal theories**—for those observations. In some cases, these theories are reasonably accurate. For example, by the time children are 6 years old, most of them have an intuitive understanding of differences between living things and inanimate objects: Both plants and animals grow and reproduce, and animals can typically move themselves around, whereas inanimate objects can neither grow nor go of their own accord (Hatano & Inagaki, 1996; Massey & Gelman, 1988). Yet children also acquire many misconceptions about the world. For example, most of them initially believe that the earth is flat and motionless and that the sun and stars revolve around it (Vosniadou, 1991).

Most contemporary theorists suggest that learning science is very much a constructive process: As learners gather more and more information about the world around them, they construct increasingly complex and integrated theories (diSessa, 1996; Driver, 1995; Wellman & Gelman, 1992; Wittrock, 1994). Children's early observations of the world provide a foundation upon which formal science instruction in school can more effectively build. At the same time, the misconceptions that emerge in the early years often hinder children's ability to develop more scientifically acceptable understandings of natural phenomena.

The Nature of Scientific Reasoning

Ideally, a school science curriculum must help students begin to think about the phenomena they observe in the same ways that adult scientists do. Here are some abilities that such reasoning includes:

- Investigating scientific phenomena objectively and systematically
- Constructing theories and models
- Revising theories and models in light of new evidence or better explanations
- Applying scientific principles to real-world problems
- Metacognitively supervising the reasoning process

Investigating Scientific Phenomena

At this point, I hope that you have already conducted experiments with a pendulum, either by completing the "Pendulum Problem" exercise presented in Chapter 2 of the textbook or by doing "The Pendulum Experiment" on the *Simulations in Educational Psychology and Research* CD at the back of the text. (If you have not done one of these, now would be a good time.) If you experimented as a true scientist would, then you engaged in two processes essential to scientific reasoning: *formulation and testing of hypotheses* and *separation and control of variables*. In particular, you identified several possible causes of a pendulum's oscillation rate (your hypotheses), perhaps including the *weight* of the hanging object, the *length* of the string, the *force* with which the pendulum is pushed, and the *height* from which the object is dropped. You then tested your hypotheses by changing one variable at a time and keeping the other three constant. For instance, you might have varied the weight at the bottom of the pendulum while always keeping the length of string, force of push, and height of drop the same. If the oscillation rate changed each time you changed the weight, then you would know that weight has an effect; if it *didn't* change, then you would know that weight is irrelevant. You might have experimented with length, force, and height in a similar manner (always keeping the other three variables constant) and once again looked for resulting differences in oscillation rate.

To study a phenomenon objectively, scientists follow a systematic sequence of steps, or *scientific method*, that commonly includes formulating and testing hypotheses as well as separating and controlling variables. Furthermore, scientists must make observations that specifically relate to their hypotheses. This task is not necessarily as easy as it might seem, as the following exercise demonstrates.

EXPERIENCING FIRSTHAND   *Four Cards*

Each of the cards above has a letter on one side and a number on the other side. Consider the following rule, which may or may not be true about the cards:

> *If a card has a vowel on one side, then it has an even number on the other side.*

Which one or more cards *must* you turn over to determine whether the rule is true for this set of cards? Don't turn over any more cards than you have to. Make your selection(s) before you continue reading. (modeled after Wason, 1968)

Which card or cards did you turn over to test the rule? You probably identified the E card as one that you should turn over; after all, if the other side has an odd number, then the rule is false. If you are like most people, then you also decided that you need to turn over the 4 card (Wason, 1968). But in fact, you do *not* need to turn over the 4 card. If it has a consonant on the other side, you haven't disproved the rule, which says nothing about what cards with consonants have on the flip side. Instead, you need to turn over the 7 card: If you find a vowel on the other side, then you have a card that violates the rule. In other words, then, you need to look both for evidence that confirms the rule and for evidence that *contradicts* it.

Many students, especially those in the elementary grades, fail to separate and control variables when they test their hypotheses (e.g., they might change weight and length simultaneously when experimenting with a pendulum), making their observations essentially uninterpretable (Pulos & Linn, 1981; Schauble, 1990, 1996). Furthermore, students of all ages (even college students) have a tendency to look for evidence that confirms their hypotheses but to ignore evidence that runs counter to their hypotheses—a phenomenon known as **confirmation bias** (Kuhn, Amsel, & O'Loughlin, 1988; Minstrell & Stimpson, 1996; Schauble, 1990). For example, when students in a high school science lab observe results that contradict what they expected to happen, they might complain that "Our equipment isn't working right" or "I can never do science anyway" (Minstrell & Stimpson, 1996).

In our science lessons and courses, we want our students to be able to separate and control variables so that they can test various hypotheses in a systematic fashion. We also want them to be able to determine whether the information they obtain confirms or disconfirms their existing hypotheses and beliefs. One obvious way to accomplish both objectives, of course, is to engage them regularly in experimentation. Such experiments can occur in both traditional school laboratories and outside (field) settings. A growing body of research tells us, however, that students often need considerable scaffolding to conduct meaningful experiments and to interpret the results appropriately. Following are several ways to provide such scaffolding:

- Present situations in which only two or three variables need to be controlled, especially when working with elementary students.

- Use situations with which students are familiar and so have relevance to students' lives (e.g., see the fishing situation depicted in Figure 2.4 in the textbook).

- Ask students to identify several possible hypotheses about cause-effect relationships before beginning to experiment.

- Provide regular guidance, hints, and feedback regarding the need to control variables and evaluate observations objectively.

- Ask questions that encourage students to make predictions and reflect appropriately on their observations (e.g., "What do you think will happen?" "What is your evidence?" "Do you see things that are inconsistent with what you predicted?").

- Point out occasions when students obtain information that contradicts the hypotheses they are testing.

- Ask students to summarize their findings. (Byrnes, 1996; Carey, Evans, Honda, Jay, & Unger, 1989; Howe, Tolmie, Greer, & Mackenzie, 1995; Kuhn et al., 1988; Metz, 1995; Minstrell & Stimpson, 1996; Ruffman, Perner, Olson, & Doherty, 1993; White & Frederiksen, 1998)

Constructing Theories and Models

An essential part of learning science is acquiring increasingly complex and integrated understandings of various natural phenomena. Scientific understanding sometimes takes the form of a **theory**—an organized body of concepts and principles that have been developed to explain certain scientific phenomena. For example, when you studied biology, you probably studied the theory of evolution, a theory that encompasses interrelationships among such concepts as *mutation*, *adaptation*, and *natural selection*. Scientific understanding may also take the form of a **model**—knowledge of the components of a particular scientific entity and the interrelationships among those components. For instance, you probably have a mental model of our solar system that includes the sun and nine planets revolving around it at varying distances. If you look at Figures 3.1, 4.3, and 6.3 in the textbook, you'll see physical representations of the models that some educational psychologists have developed for *self-concept*, *intelligence*, and *human memory*, respectively.

To some extent, students may acquire their knowledge of science through their own experimentation. But they should also study the concepts, principles, theories, and models that professional scientists currently use to make sense of the physical world (Driver, 1995; Hatano & Inagaki, 1996; Linn, Songer, & Eylon, 1996). The trick is for students to pull all of the things they learn into integrated, meaningful bodies of knowledge. Theorists have offered several suggestions for helping students learn science as integrated, cohesive theories and models:

- Introduce a new unit with a lesson or experiment that illustrates the important issues that the unit will address (science educators use the terms **benchmark lesson** and **benchmark experiment**).

- Use analogies that help students relate new ideas to prior knowledge.

- Present physical models of the phenomena being described, perhaps in the form of diagrams, flowcharts, or physical replicas.

- Ask students to organize the material they have learned (e.g., by drawing diagrams, making concept maps, or writing summaries).

- Have students reflect on and write about what they've observed and concluded.
(A. L. Brown & Campione, 1994; D. E. Brown, 1992; Edens & Potter, 2001; Klein, 2000; Mayer, 1999; Mayer & Wittrock, 1996; Minstrell & Stimpson, 1996; Wittrock, 1994)

Revising Theories and Models

EXPERIENCING FIRSTHAND *Water and Earth*

Do these two problems before you read further.

1. A glass half full of water is lifted from the table on which it is resting and tilted at a 45-degree angle. Draw a line in the glass to mark the water's surface.

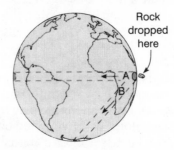

Rock dropped here

2. A rock is dropped at the equator, at the entrances to two tunnels that go through the earth. Tunnel A comes out at the equator on the opposite side of the earth. Tunnel B comes out at the South Pole. Into which tunnel will the rock fall?

Your water line in the tilted glass should be parallel to the top of the table; in other words, it should be horizontal. Did you instead draw a line that slanted one way or the other? If so, you're hardly alone; many adults have difficulty with this task (Pulos, 1997). I hope that you had an easier time with the "tunnels" question: The rock will fall into Tunnel A, toward the center of the earth.

Many middle school students have difficulty with both of these problems involving gravity. They draw a slanted line to indicate that the water's surface tilts upward toward one side of the glass or the other, and they answer that the rock will fall into Tunnel B, thinking, apparently, that gravity always pulls something "down." They respond in these ways despite many personal experiences with tilted water glasses and despite explicitly learning that gravity pulls objects toward the center of the earth (Pulos, 1997).

Just as scientific theories and models evolve over time as new evidence emerges, so, too, must our students continually revise their understanding of natural phenomena as they acquire more information; in other words, they must undergo *conceptual change*. Yet students often cling tenaciously to their naive ideas about scientific phenomena despite considerable experience and instruction to the contrary (diSessa, 1996; Keil & Silberstein, 1996; Reiner, Slotta, Chi, & Resnick, 2000; Vosniadou, 1991). (As an example, go to "Intuitive Physics" on the *Simulations in Educational Psychology and Research* CD that accompanies the textbook.)

Chapter 7 of the textbook identifies several strategies for promoting conceptual change. Following are additional strategies that relate specifically to science:

- Portray science as a dynamic, evolving collection of theories and models to be understood, rather than as a collection of discrete facts to be memorized.

- Identify and discuss students' existing scientific beliefs (e.g., the idea that gravity pulls objects toward the South Pole), so that such beliefs are in working memory and, as a result, more likely to be modified.

- Relate abstract ideas to concrete and familiar experiences; for instance, illustrate the abstract concept *density* by showing how a can of diet soft drink floats in water while a can of regular soft drink sinks.

- Give students opportunities to discuss competing perspectives within a classroom environment that communicates the message, "It's OK to make errors and to change our minds." (Brandes, 1996; Byrnes, 1996; Duit, 1991; Keil & Silberstein, 1996; Minstrell & Stimpson, 1996)

At the same time, we must recognize that in some cases scientific explanations may be inconsistent with students' personal belief systems; for instance, the theory of evolution may be inconsistent with the creationist views of a student's religion. In such circumstances, our best approach may be to help students *understand* scientific explanations rather than convince them to accept these explanations as "truth" (Sinatra & Southerland, 2001; Southerland, Sinatra, & Matthews, 2001).

Applying Science to Real-World Problems

All too often, students have trouble relating the things they learn in science to real-world situations (Linn et al., 1996; Mayer, 1996). For instance, despite formal instruction about the nature of heat and insulation, it never occurs to many students that they can use wool to keep something *cold* as well as to keep it warm (Linn et al., 1996).

Ideally, any science curriculum should make frequent connections between school science and everyday situations (Linn et al., 1996; White & Frederiksen, 1998). Accordingly, we should provide numerous opportunities for students to apply scientific principles to the kinds of problems they are likely to encounter in their outside lives.

Metacognition

Students' beliefs about the nature of science (i.e., their epistemological beliefs) will undoubtedly affect the approaches they take (mentally) when they study science. Students who believe that "knowing" science means understanding how various concepts and principles fit together and using those concepts and principles to explain everyday phenomena are going to study and learn more effectively than students who think that learning science means memorizing facts (Linn et al., 1996). Students who recognize that scientific theories will inevitably change over time are more likely to evaluate theories with a critical eye (Bereiter, 1994; Kuhn, 1993, 2001; Linn et al., 1996). Through both our lessons and our assessment techniques, we must continually communicate the message that "mastering" science means understanding concepts and principles in a meaningful fashion, integrating concepts and principles into a cohesive whole, revising personal theories in the light of new evidence, and applying science to real-world situations (Schauble, 1996; C. L. Smith, Maclin, Houghton, & Hennessey, 2000; Wittrock, 1994).

We can also promote metacognitive development in science by encouraging students to reflect on how they and their classmates are reasoning about scientific phenomena (Herrenkohl & Guerra, 1998; Palincsar & Herrenkohl, 1999; Van Meter, 2001). In one approach, which has been used effectively with fourth graders, students engage in short experiments and other activities in small groups. For each activity, they (a) make initial predictions and develop initial theories about what they think they will observe, (b) perform the activity and summarize their results, and (c) relate their results to their initial predictions and theories. The students then meet as an entire class to present and evaluate each group's findings and conclusions; at this time, some students act as "reporters" and others act as a critical audience, asking such questions as "What is your theory?" and "Did what you think was going to happen really happen?" Students who participate in such activities are more engaged in class, more likely to monitor their own understanding, and more likely to challenge one another's explanations (Herrenkohl & Guerra, 1998; Palincsar & Herrenkohl, 1999).

Developmental Changes in Scientific Reasoning

As noted earlier, children acquire considerable knowledge about science long before they begin school. But their ability to *think about* science is apt to be limited throughout the elementary grades. As Chapter 2 in the textbook points out, abstract and hypothetical reasoning capabilities and the ability to separate and control variables all appear to be fairly limited until adolescence. Perhaps for this reason, elementary school teachers focus most science instruction on descriptions of natural phenomena rather than on explanations of why those phenomena occur (Byrnes, 1996). Yet even at the elementary level, it is probably counterproductive to portray science as primarily a collection of facts. By having students engage in simple experiments almost from the very beginning of the science curriculum, we convey the message that science is an ongoing, dynamic process of unraveling the mysteries of our world.

At the middle school level, students' increasing ability to think about abstract ideas enables us to begin addressing some of the causal mechanisms that underlie natural phenomena. Yet even at this point, we may not want to introduce ideas completely removed from students' everyday, concrete experiences (Linn & Muilenburg, 1996; Linn et al., 1996; Reiner et al., 2000). For instance, when teaching eighth graders about heat, we may have better success if we talk about heat as something that "flows" from one object to another rather than as something that involves molecules moving and colliding with one another at a certain rate. Although the heat-flow model is, from a chemical perspective, not entirely accurate, students can effectively apply it to a wide variety of everyday situations; for instance, they can use it to explain why a bathtub filled with warm water heats the air around it, why packing food in ice helps to keep it cold, and why using a wooden spoon is safer than using a metal one to stir something that's cooking on the stove (Linn & Muilenburg, 1996).

When students reach high school, they are more likely to have acquired the scientific knowledge they need to begin thinking in truly abstract ways about natural phenomena (Linn et al., 1996). Nevertheless, we should continue to engage students in frequent hands-on science activities, not only through systematic laboratory experiments but also through informal, exploratory activities that relate scientific concepts and principles to everyday experiences. Secondary students in general, but especially females, are likely to achieve at higher levels when they have regular hands-on experiences with the phenomena they are studying (Burkam, Lee, & Smerdon, 1997).

General Strategies for Teaching Science

Throughout this section we have identified specific strategies for helping students learn various aspects of science more effectively. Following are three more general strategies to keep in mind:

• *Engage students regularly in authentic scientific investigations.* Historically, most science laboratory activities have been little more than cookbook recipes: Students are given specific materials and instructions to follow in a step-by-step manner (Committee on High School Biology Education, 1990). Although such activities can certainly help make scientific phenomena more concrete for students, they are unlikely to encourage students to engage in thinking processes—

INTO THE CLASSROOM: *Promoting Mathematical and Scientific Reasoning Skills*

- Take students' cognitive development into account when teaching concepts and principles.

  A fourth-grade teacher asks his students to conduct experiments to find out what kinds of conditions influence the growth of sunflower seeds. He knows that his students probably have only a limited ability to separate and control variables, so he asks them to study the effects of just two things: the amount of water and the kind of soil. He has the students keep their growing plants on a shelf by the window, where temperature and amount of sunlight will be the same for all of the plants.

- Use concrete manipulatives and analogies to illustrate abstract ideas.

  A high school physics teacher has learned from experience that, even though her students are, in theory, capable of abstract thought, they are still likely to have trouble understanding this principle: *When an object rests on a surface, the object exerts a force on the surface, and the surface also exerts a force on the object.* To illustrate the principle, she places a book on a large spring. The book compresses the spring somewhat, but not completely. "So you see, class," she says, "the book pushes downward on the spring, and the spring pushes upward on the book. An object compresses even a hard surface, such as a table, a little bit, and the surface pushes back up in response." (based on D. E. Brown & Clement, 1989)

- Ask students to apply math and science to real-world problems.

  A third-grade teacher gives his students copies of a menu from a local family restaurant. He tells them, "Imagine that you have eight dollars to spend. Figure out what you might order for lunch so that your meal includes each of the food groups we've discussed."

- Ask students to identify several strategies or hypotheses regarding a particular task or situation, and to explain and justify their ideas to one another.

  A middle school math teacher is beginning a unit on how to divide numbers by fractions. After students convene in small groups, she says, "You've already learned how to multiply one fraction by another. For example, you've learned that when you multiply 1/3 by 1/2, you get 1/6. But now imagine that you want to *divide* 1/3 by 1/2. Do you think you'll get a number smaller than 1/3 or larger than 1/3? And what kind of number might you get? Discuss these questions within your groups. In a few minutes we'll all get back together to talk about the ideas you've come up with."

- Foster metacognitive strategies that students can use to regulate their experimentation and problem solving.

  When a high school science teacher has his students conduct lab experiments, he always has them keep several questions in mind as they work: (1) As I test the effects of one variable, am I controlling for possible effects of other variables? (2) Am I seeing anything that supports my hypothesis? (3) Am I seeing anything that contradicts my hypothesis?

- Have students use mathematics and scientific methods in other content domains.

  A junior high school social studies teacher asks his students to work in small groups to conduct experiments regarding the effects of smiling on other people's behavior. As the groups design their experiments, he reminds them about the importance of separating and controlling variables, and he insists that each group identify an objective means of measuring the specific behavior or behaviors that it intends to study. Later, he has the groups tabulate their results and report their findings to the rest of the class.

---

testing and formulating hypotheses, separating and controlling variables, and so on—that characterize true scientific reasoning (Keil & Silberstein, 1996; Padilla, 1991; Singer, Marx, Krajcik, & Chambers, 2000). So in addition, we must give students many opportunities to conduct investigations in which the procedures and outcomes are not necessarily predetermined. In some cases, we can provide materials that allow students to explore phenomena closely related to known scientific principles; for instance, we might ask them to address questions such as "How does the amount of electric current affect electromagnetic strength?" or "How does temperature affect the germination rate of seeds?" (Padilla, 1991). In other situations, we can have students apply their developing experimentation skills to address everyday problems; for instance, we might pose a question such as "Does one fast food chain provide more meat in a hamburger than others?" or "Is one brand of paper towel stronger or more absorbent than the others?" (Padilla, 1991). We may also want to engage our students in long-term, outdoor field work, perhaps studying the quality of air in the local environment or analyzing the bacterial content of neighborhood rivers and lakes (Singer et al., 2000).

• *Use class discussions to promote conceptual change.* A growing body of research indicates that small-group and whole-class discussions help students acquire more accurate and integrated understandings of scientific phenomena—for many of the reasons that Chapter 7 in the textbook identifies (Bereiter, 1994; Greeno et al., 1996; Hatano & Inagaki, 1991; Minstrell & Stimpson, 1996; C. L. Smith et al., 2000). In the following essay, one sixth grader who has participated in an interactive, inquiry-oriented science curriculum throughout the elementary grades portrays science as the dynamic process that it truly is and explains how discussing science with peers has contributed to this epistemological belief:

> I think science changes because people's ideas change over time. This even happens in school science. For example, when someone tells you their ideas you may or may not understand it. However, if they change their explanation a little then you can understand it. Or when different people in a class explain their thinking about something we are all working on, soon different people in class begin to change their thinking and so do I. That's how I develop my ideas. I discuss with other students and I listen to their explanations. I try to see things from their perspectives and they try to see things from mine. All of us begin to develop ideas that are a combination of what we hear or discuss—that's how I change my thinking. I think people who are scientists do the same thing. Only when they change their ideas or describe them from a different perspective then science itself changes. (C. L. Smith et al., 2000, p. 396)

• *Make use of computer technology.* Many software programs now enable students to explore scientific phenomena in ways that might not be possible in real life. Some programs let students "explore" human anatomy—the heart, the lungs, the eye, and so on—or conduct "dissections" of frogs, cats, and other species. Other programs create "virtual" environments that allow students to manipulate and experiment with such phenomena as friction, gravity, and thermodynamics, allowing them to separate and control variables in ways that the real world would prohibit (Greeno et al., 1996; Schauble, 1990; White & Frederiksen, 1998). Furthermore, electronic mail (e-mail) and the Internet provide means through which students can communicate with one another and with outside experts, enabling them to share information and test their hypotheses and ideas (Pea, 1992).

Over the past few decades, many psychologists and educators have studied how students learn mathematics and science and how teachers can help them master these content domains more effectively. Only recently, however, have a significant number of theorists and researchers turned their attention to that part of the school curriculum collectively known as *social studies*. In the next section we will explore some of the ideas that are beginning to emerge in this area.

Social Studies

Many theorists believe that the ultimate goal of social studies education should be to help students make informed decisions about matters of public policy, social welfare, and personal growth (Alleman & Brophy, 1997; Byrnes, 1996). In my own mind, social studies should also promote tolerance for diverse perspectives and cultures, with the understanding that such diversity of ideas is essential for the social, moral, and cultural advancement of the human race over time.

If we want our students to draw on the things they learn in social studies when they make decisions as adult citizens, it is essential that we focus on meaningful learning and higher-level thinking skills —transfer, problem solving, and so on—in the social studies curriculum, rather than on the learning of discrete facts (Alleman & Brophy, 1997; Newmann, 1997). In this section we will consider how we might focus the curriculum in two specific areas: history and geography.

The Nature of Historical Knowledge and Thinking

A true understanding of history, both as a body of knowledge and as an academic discipline, requires several abilities and processes:

- Understanding the nature of historical time
- Drawing inferences from historical documents
- Identifying cause-effect relationships among events
- Recognizing that historical figures were real people

Understanding Historical Time

In the case study at the beginning of this reading, Ben accounts for America's origins as follows:

> 2000 Days oh go George Washington gave us the Country to Live on.

As a second grader, Ben obviously has little sense of how long a time span "2000 days" is. Like Ben, children in the early elementary grades have little understanding of historical time (Barton & Levstik, 1996). For instance, they might refer to events that happened "a long, long time ago" or "in the old days" yet tell you that such events happened in 1999. And they tend to lump historical events into two general categories: those that happened very recently and those that happened many years ago. Not until about fifth grade do students show a reasonable ability to sequence historical events and to attach them to particular periods of time (Barton & Levstik, 1996).

Perhaps it is not surprising, then, that systematic history instruction typically does not begin until fifth grade (Byrnes, 1996). In the earlier grades, any instruction about history should probably focus on students' own, personal histories and on events that have occurred locally and in the recent past (Byrnes, 1996).

Drawing Inferences from Historical Documents

History textbooks often describe historical events in a very matter-of-fact manner, communicating the message that "This is what actually happened" (Britt, Rouet, Georgi, & Perfetti, 1994; Paxton, 1999; Wineburg, 1994). In reality, however, historians often don't know exactly how particular events occurred. Instead, they construct a reasonable interpretation of events after looking at a variety of historical documents that, in many cases, provide differing perspectives of what transpired (Leinhardt & Young, 1996; Seixas, 1996; Wineburg, 1994).

The idea that history is often as much a matter of perspective and opinion as it is a matter of fact is a fairly abstract notion that students may not be able to comprehend until they reach adolescence (Byrnes, 1996; Seixas, 1996). In the secondary grades, we can begin to have them read multiple accounts of significant historical events and then draw conclusions both about what *definitely* happened and about what *might* have happened (Leinhardt, Beck, & Stainton, 1994; Paxton, 1999; Seixas, 1996). For instance, when students study racial strife in the American South, they might learn about the Montgomery, Alabama, bus boycott of 1955 both by reading newspaper articles published at the time and by reading Rosa Parks' own account of why she refused to give up her bus seat for a white person (Banks, 1994). When they study the Mexican-American War, they should be exposed to the Mexican perspective as well as that of the United States. Ultimately, students at the secondary grade levels must discover that history is not as cut-and-dried as some present it—that learning history involves constructing a reasonable interpretation of events based on the evidence at hand and that some aspects of history may never be known for certain.

Identifying Cause-Effect Relationships Among Events

To some extent, an integrated knowledge of history includes an understanding of how some events led to others. For instance, it might be helpful for students to learn that economic hardship in the Southern states was a contributing factor to the Northern victory in the American Civil War and that paranoia about expanding empires was partly responsible for World War II, the Korean War, and the Vietnam War. One way we can help students learn such cause-effect relationships is, of course, is to describe them ourselves. But we can also engage students in discussions in which they develop their *own* explanations of why certain events may have occurred (Leinhardt, 1993). And we can indirectly help them discover causal relationships by asking them to consider how things might have been different if certain events had *not* taken place (Byrnes, 1996).

Thinking of Historical Figures as Real People

Students will learn historical events in a more meaningful fashion when they discover that historical figures had particular goals, motives, and personalities and that these individuals often had to make decisions based on incomplete information—in other words, that they were, in many respects, just ordinary human beings. For instance, we might ask students to read Rosa Parks' explanation about why she refused to give up her bus seat for a white person:

> People always say that I didn't give up my seat because I was tired, but that isn't true. I was not tired physically, or no more tired than I usually was at the end of a working day. I was not old, although some people have an image of me being old then. I was 42. No, the only tired I was, was tired of giving in. (Parks, 1992, cited in Banks, 1994)

As another example, we might ask students to read newspaper accounts of World War II just prior to Harry Truman's decision to drop an atomic bomb on Hiroshima—accounts that give students a better sense of what Truman probably did and did not know at the time (Yeager et al., 1997). Following are several additional strategies we can use to foster perspective taking:

- Assign works of fiction that realistically depict people living in particular times and places.
- Conduct a simulated legislative session or town meeting in which students debate the pros and cons of a particular course of action.
- Have "journalists" (two or three students) interview people (other students) who "participated" in various ways in a historical event.
- Role-play family discussions and decision making during critical times (e.g., British soldiers demand to be housed in American colonists' homes, or a son wants to enlist and go off to war). (Brophy & Alleman, 1996; Brophy & VanSledright, 1997)

When students understand why historical figures behaved as they did, they are more likely to empathize with them, and such empathy makes historical events just that much more understandable (Seixas, 1996; Yeager et al., 1997).

The Nature of Geographic Knowledge and Thinking

Many people conceive of geography as consisting of little more than the locations of various countries, capital cities, rivers, and so on, perhaps because geography is often taught this way (Bochenhauer, 1990). In fact, the discipline of geography involves not only *where* things are but also *why* and *how* they got there (National Geographic Education Project, 1994). For instance, geographers study why and how rivers and mountain ranges end up where they do, why people are more likely to settle in some locations than in others, and how people in various locations interact with one another.

Mastering geography involves at least three things:

- Understanding maps as symbolic representations
- Identifying interrelationships among people, places, and environments
- Appreciating cultural differences

Understanding Maps as Symbolic Representations

Central to geographical thinking is the realization that maps depict the arrangement and characteristics of particular locations. Yet young children have trouble interpreting maps and using them effectively (Blades & Spencer, 1987; Liben & Downs, 1989b). Children in the early elementary grades don't truly appreciate the symbolic nature of maps: They take what they see on a map too literally (Gardner, Torff, & Hatch, 1996; Liben & Downs, 1989b). For instance, they may think that roads depicted in red are paved with red concrete and that the lines separating states and countries are actually painted on the earth. Young children also have difficulty maintaining a sense of scale and proportion (Liben & Downs, 1989b). For instance, they might deny that a road could actually be a road because it's "too skinny for two cars to fit on" or insist that mountains depicted on a three-dimensional relief map can't possibly be mountains because "they aren't high enough."

One major goal of any geography curriculum, especially in the elementary grades, must be to foster an understanding of the symbolic nature of maps. Students probably need explicit instruction in map interpretation skills (Liben & Downs, 1989a). We can certainly do this by giving students practice in interpreting a wide variety of maps, including maps that depict different kinds of information (e.g., those that depict physical landforms, those that depict roads and highways, those that depict varying elevations) and maps that use different kinds of symbols (Liben & Downs, 1989a). We can also teach map interpretation skills by having students create their *own* maps, perhaps of their neighborhoods or even of the entire country (Forbes, Ormrod, Bernardi, Taylor, & Jackson, 1999; Gregg & Leinhardt, 1994a).

Students must learn, too, that different maps are drawn to different scales, reflecting various proportions between graphic representation and reality (Liben & Downs, 1989b). We must keep in mind that, because proportional reasoning typically does not emerge until adolescence (see Chapter 2 in the textbook), we probably do not want to study scale in any systematic way until the middle school years. At this point, we can specifically talk about the scales used in different maps (one inch per mile, one centimeter per ten kilometers, etc.).

Identifying Interrelationships Among People, Places, and Environments

Much of geography centers on principles that identify how people, places, and environments interact. Consider the following geographical principles as examples:

- People are more likely to settle in areas that are easily accessible—for instance, along navigable rivers or near major roadways.

- People tend to migrate from places with limited or decreasing resources to places with more plentiful resources.

- Historically, people who were separated by significant physical barriers—mountain ranges, large rivers, deserts, and so on—interacted with one another rarely, if at all, and so tended to develop different languages and cultures.

We can teach our students to use maps as tools not only to help them locate places but also to look for patterns in what they see and to speculate about why those patterns exist (Gregg & Leinhardt, 1994b; Liben & Downs, 1989a). For instance, we can ask them to consider questions such as these as they peruse maps like those in Figures 9.3 and 9.4:

- Why did Chicago become the major railroad center of the American Midwest in the middle of the nineteenth century? (Use Figure 9.3.)

- Why are the languages of the Far East so distinctly different from those of the Middle East? (Use Figure 9.4.)

Appreciating Cultural Differences

An important goal of any geography curriculum must be to help students develop an understanding and appreciation of cultural diversity. In Chapter 4 of the textbook, the section "Creating a More Multicultural Classroom Environment" identifies strategies for promoting cultural awareness and tolerance. Those strategies are probably worth repeating again in this context:

- Incorporate the values, beliefs, and traditions of many cultures into the curriculum.

- Work to break down ethnic and cultural stereotypes.

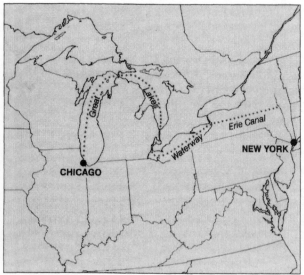
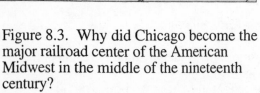
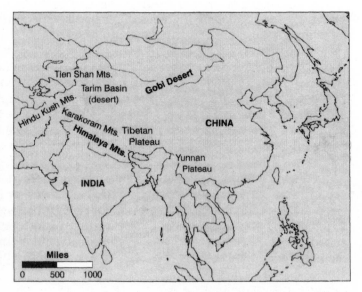

Figure 8.3. Why did Chicago become the major railroad center of the American Midwest in the middle of the nineteenth century?

Figure 8.4. Why are the languages of the Far East so distinctly different from those of the Middle East?

348

- Promote positive social interaction among students from various ethnic groups.
- Foster democratic ideals.

Although not all of these strategies fall within the discipline of geography, certainly they all fall within the more general domain of social studies.

An additional strategy is to show students that, despite superficial differences among cultures, human beings often behave in similar ways and for similar reasons. I found an excellent example of this strategy a few years ago when I visited Colorado's Mesa Verde National Park, once the home of cliff-dwelling Native Americans now called the Anasazi (a Navajo word meaning "ancient ones"). The National Park Service distributed a pamphlet that compared the Anasazi lifestyle in the thirteenth century with that of people living in Europe during the same time period. Following are some excerpts from the pamphlet:

> The romantic notion that the Middle Ages were filled with knights in shining armor and ladies-in-waiting is exaggerated. In reality, 80 to 90 percent of Europeans at that time were serfs or peasants. The thirteenth-century peasant was surrounded by a world just as difficult for him to understand as it was for the average Anasazi. In Europe famines, plagues and diseases were rampant and decimated populations almost overnight. . . . During a lunar eclipse, many Europeans might spend a night in terror behind their cottage walls of mud and wattle. It is no wonder that religion played a major role in the lives of both cultures, influencing a great deal of their daily activities. Given the problems of drought and overuse of natural resources, it is understandable that the Anasazi would seek outside assistance in the form of ceremonies and special rites, just as the Europeans were governed by their superstitious beliefs. In certain respects, the way the two cultures looked at their world was not so different at all.
>
> . . . Sanitation was a major problem for both cultures. Today's visitors [to Mesa Verde National Park] think it is appalling that the Anasazi would throw their refuse—broken pottery vessels, used sandals, food remnants, etc.—right out in front of the dwelling. However, European city dwellers threw their trash out their windows and onto the streets.... Since the humidity levels in the American Southwest are less than most areas of Europe, the stench and decay may have been worse in Europe than it was for the Anasazi. (Mesa Verde Museum Association, n.d.)

Developmental Changes in Thinking About History and Geography

Students' understanding of social studies is, of course, dependent on their growing cognitive abilities. At the elementary level, students tend to think in relatively concrete terms. For example, in history, they may conceptualize the birth of the United States as resulting from a single, specific event (e.g., the Boston Tea Party) or as involving nothing more than constructing new buildings and towns (Ormrod, Jackson, Kirby, Davis, & Benson, 1999). In geography, they may think that an airplane symbol on a map represents an airport with only one airplane (Liben & Downs, 1989b).

As students develop the ability to think abstractly, so, too, can they more readily comprehend the abstract principles that underlie historical events and geographical patterns. Furthermore, as they acquire an increasing ability to look at events from other people's perspectives (see Chapter 3 in the textbook), they become more capable of empathizing with historical figures (Ormrod et al., 1999). And as they develop proportional reasoning, they can more effectively consider the concept of *scale* in map making.

General Strategies for Teaching Social Studies

In addition to the specific strategies we've considered for teaching history and geography, following are three more general strategies for teaching social studies:

INTO THE CLASSROOM: *Facilitating Learning in Social Studies*

- Help students organize and integrate the things they are learning.
  During a unit on ancient civilizations (e.g., Mesopotamia, Egypt, Greece, Rome), a middle school teacher has her students mark the location of each civilization on a map of the Eastern Hemisphere. She also has them develop a time line that depicts the rise and fall of the various civilizations.

- Ask students to draw inferences.
  A geography teacher displays a map showing European countries and their capital cities. "Notice how almost all of the capital cities are located either by seaports or on major rivers," he points out. "Why do you suppose that is?"

- Identify cause-effect relationships.
  A history teacher asks her students to consider the question, "What effects did the Japanese bombing of Pearl Harbor have on the course and final outcome of World War II?"

- Encourage empathy for people from diverse cultures and different periods of time.
  A fourth-grade teacher encourages his students to imagine themselves as Native Americans who are seeing Europeans for the first time. "You see some strange-looking men sail to shore on big boats—boats much larger than the canoes your own people use. As the men disembark from their boats and approach your village, you see that they have very light skin; in fact, it is almost white. Furthermore, some of them have yellow hair and blue eyes. 'Funny colors for hair and eyes,' you think to yourself. How might you feel as these people approach?"

• *Choose content that helps students discover important principles and ideas within the discipline.* Social studies cover a broad range of topics—far too many to include in just twelve or thirteen years of schooling. So what exactly *do* we include in a social studies curriculum? Theorists suggest that we develop lessons and units that help students discover the key principles—the "big ideas"—that underlie social studies (Alleman & Brophy, 1997; Newmann, 1988; Olsen, 1995). For instance, when teaching students about various wars, we might focus on cause-effect relationships and general trends (e.g., the role of women on the home front and in the military) rather than on the details of specific battles (Olsen, 1995). Or, when exploring the geography of Africa, we might consider how different environments (tropical rain forests, desert plains, etc.) lead to very different lifestyles among the residents of various regions.

• *Determine what students do and do not already know about a new topic.* Many history textbook writers assume their readers have knowledge that the students probably *don't* have (Beck, McKeown, & Gromoll, 1989; McKeown & Beck, 1994). For instance, textbook writers may assume that fifth graders can appreciate why the early American colonists resented the British policy of "taxation without representation," yet such a situation is far removed from students' own personal experiences. In the history compositions previously presented in this supplementary reading, we saw numerous errors of fact—errors that might easily lead to confusion as students study history in later grades. For example, one second grader in the opening case study believed that the dinosaurs were around as recently as six thousand years ago. And the eighth grader whose composition appeared in the "What's Wrong?" exercise didn't know that Britain and Brittany are different places. When we begin with what our students definitely know, not with what we think they *should* know, and proceed from there, our students' comprehension of social studies will almost certainly improve (Brophy & VanSledright, 1997; McKeown & Beck, 1994).

• *Have students conduct their own research using primary source materials.* Our students must eventually learn that history and geography are, like science, evolving disciplines and that, even as students, they can contribute to the knowledge bases in these disciplines. For instance, we might have them study the history of their own community using old newspapers, brochures, personal letters, and other artifacts; they can then display their findings in a local museum (A. Collins, Hawkins, & Carver, 1991). Or we might have them compile data about the populations of people living in various parts of their state, province, or country (perhaps voting records, occupations, or frequency of various health problems) and then construct maps that depict patterns in these data.

As you have seen, each of the content domains we've considered—reading, writing, mathematics, science, and social studies—involves numerous skills and abilities that are somewhat domain-specific. Accordingly, different teaching strategies may be more or less applicable for each of them.

Before we close, we should consider how we can accommodate student diversity as we teach various content areas. Then, as we look at the "Big Picture," we will revisit the five general principles we identified at the beginning of the chapter.

Taking Student Diversity into Account

As we teach reading and writing, we must remember that students' early experiences with language and literature are likely to vary considerably. For instance, students in some African American families may have had few experiences reading storybooks but a great deal of experience with storytelling, jokes, rhymes, and other creative forms of oral language (Trawick-Smith, 2000). Some Native American communities may value nonlinguistic forms of expression, such as art and dancing, more than reading and writing (Trawick-Smith, 2000). We must be sensitive to what students' early language and literacy experiences have been and use the specific knowledge and skills that they *have* developed as the basis for future instruction in reading and writing. For instance, students who can use their local dialect when they write stories may write more imaginatively than students who must use standard English (Smitherman, 1994).

When teaching mathematics and science, we must keep in mind that these two disciplines have, historically, been considered "male" domains. As a result, the boys in our classes are more likely to believe that they can be successful in these areas; this will be the case even though there are no substantial gender differences in *ability* in these areas (see Chapter 4 in the textbook). We must make a concerted effort to convey the message that mathematics and science are important for girls as well as boys. We should also use instructional strategies—small-group discussions, hands-on activities, cooperative learning, and so on—that encourage males and females alike to become actively involved in studying, talking about, and mastering math and science.

As we teach social studies, we must remember that students' perspectives on history and geography will, in part, be a function of the cultures in which they have been raised and the early family experiences they have had. For instance, a student with a Japanese heritage is likely to have a very different perspective on Truman's decision to bomb Hiroshima than a student with English ancestors. Students who have traveled extensively are apt to have a greater appreciation of distance, a greater knowledge of differing environmental landscapes, and a better understanding of how maps are used (Trawick-Smith, 2000). A friend of mine once described her experience taking children raised in a lower-income, inner-city Denver neighborhood on a field trip into the Rocky Mountains. Even though these children had seen the Rockies many times from downtown Denver, some of them, upon seeing the mountains up close for the very first time, were amazed at how big they were. And a few children were quite surprised to discover that the white stuff on the mountaintops was snow!

Accommodating Students with Special Needs

Many students with special needs have difficulty with reading and writing. The majority of poor readers, whether they've been identified as having a learning disability, attention-deficit hyperactivity disorder (ADHD), or some other disability, appear to have a significant deficit in phonological awareness: They have difficulty hearing the individual sounds in words and connecting those sounds with letters (Hulme & Joshi, 1998; Morris et al., 1998; Stanovich, 2000; Swanson, Mink, & Bocian, 1999). A few poor readers have other cognitive processing deficits; for example, they may have greater-than-average difficulty retrieving words and word meanings based on what they see on the page (Stanovich, 2000). Such difficulties with literacy can have wide-ranging effects, not only for achievement in other disciplines but also for self-esteem. Tom, a second grader, describes his feelings when first trying to learn how to read in first grade:

> I falt like a losr. Like nobad likde me. I was afrad then kais wod tec me. Becacz I wased larning wale ... I dan not whet to raed. I whoe whte to troe a book it my mom.
>
> *(I felt like a loser. Like nobody liked me. I was afraid that kids would tease me. Because I wasn't learning well ... I did not want to read. I would want to throw a book at my mom.)* (Knapp, 1995, p. 9)

Students' difficulties are not always limited to reading and writing, of course; for instance, some students with learning disabilities have difficulty with mathematics as well (Cawley & Miller, 1989). So when we teach various content domains, we must often make special accommodations for those students who have special educational needs. Table 8.2 presents some specific strategies that may be helpful as we work with these students.

The Big Picture

In this final section we summarize what we've learned about each of the content areas. We then revisit the five general principles identified at the beginning of the chapter.

Reading

Most children learn some things about literacy (e.g., that particular words are always spelled in the same way) before they begin school; such knowledge is called *emergent literacy*. Skilled reading involves knowing letter-sound correspondences, recognizing both individual letters and entire words quickly and automatically, using context clues to facilitate decoding, constructing meaning from the words on the page, and metacognitively regulating the reading process. Strategies for helping students become proficient readers include promoting phonological awareness, scaffolding students' efforts to make sense of what they read, giving students many opportunities to read authentic literature, and engaging students in discussions about what they are reading.

Writing

Skilled writing involves planning, drafting, metacognition, and revision, and good writers move back and forth flexibly among these processes. We can help students learn to write effectively by asking them to clarify their goals for writing and the audience for whom they are writing, to organize their thoughts before they begin to write, and to focus more on clear communication than on writing mechanics in early drafts. We should also assign writing tasks in all areas of the curriculum and provide sufficient criteria and feedback to guide students as they revise what they've written.

Table 8.2. Helping Students with Special Needs Achieve in Various Content Domains

Category	Characteristics You Might Observe	Suggested Classroom Strategies
Students with specific cognitive or academic difficulties	Difficulties in word recognition and reading comprehension, often as a result of poor phonological awareness Difficulties in spelling and handwriting Tendency to focus on mechanics (rather than meaning) during the revision stage of writing Less developed writing skills (if students have learning disabilities) Greater than average difficulty learning basic facts in math, science, and social studies	Assign reading materials appropriate for students' reading skills. Provide extra scaffolding for reading assignments (e.g., shorten assignments, identify main ideas, have students look for answers to specific questions). Provide extra scaffolding for writing activities (e.g., ask students to set goals for their writing, give students a specific structure to follow as they write, encourage use of word processing programs with grammar and spell checkers). Use concrete manipulatives to teach math and science. Use mnemonics to help students remember basic facts.
Students with social or behavioral problems	Less motivation to achieve academic success in some or all content domains In some instances, achievement two or more years below grade level in one or more content domains	Have students read and write about topics of personal interest. Ask students to apply math, science, and social studies to situations relevant to their own lives. (Also use strategies listed for students with specific cognitive or academic difficulties.)
Students with general delays in cognitive and social functioning	Delayed language development (e.g., in reading, writing) Less developed knowledge base to which new information can be related Difficulty remembering basic facts Lack of learning strategies such as rehearsal or organization Reasoning abilities characteristic of younger children (e.g., inability to think abstractly in the secondary grades)	Minimize reliance on reading materials as a way of presenting new information. Provide experiences that help students learn the basic knowledge and skills that other students may have already learned on their own. Have students conduct simple scientific experiments in which they need to consider only one or two variables at a time. (Also use strategies listed for students with specific cognitive or academic difficulties.)
Students with physical or sensory challenges	More limited reading and writing skills, especially if students have hearing loss Less awareness of the conventions of written language, especially if students have visual impairments Fewer outside experiences and less general world knowledge upon which instruction in math, science, and social studies can build	Locate Braille texts for students with visual impairments. When students have difficulty with motor coordination, allow them to dictate the things that they write. Conduct demonstrations and experiments to illustrate basic scientific concepts and principles. Use drama and role playing to illustrate historical events. If students have visual impairments, use three-dimensional relief maps and embellish two-dimensional maps with dried glue or nail polish.
Students with advanced cognitive development	Development of reading at an early age Advanced reading comprehension ability More sophisticated writing abilities Greater ability to construct abstract and integrated understandings	Provide challenging tasks (e.g., higher-level reading assignments, more advanced writing assignments). Form study groups in which students can pursue advanced topics in particular domains.

Sources: Bassett et al., 1996; Butterfield & Ferretti, 1987; Cone, Wilson, Bradley, & Reese, 1985; Ferretti et al., 2000; Garner, 1998; Graham, Schwartz, & MacArthur, 1993; Hallenbeck, 1996; Hulme & Joshi, 1998; Mastropieri & Scruggs, 1992, 2000; Page-Voth & Graham, 1999; Piirto, 1999; Salend & Hofstetter, 1996; Swanson, Cooney, & O'Shaughnessy, 1998; Tompkins & McGee, 1986; Turnbull, Turnbull, Shank, & Leal, 1999; Wood, Frank, & Wacker, 1998.

Mathematics

To master mathematics, students must understand key mathematical concepts and principles, encode problems in ways that facilitate correct solutions, relate problem-solving procedures to the mathematical concepts and principles that underlie them, and acquire appropriate metacognitive processes and beliefs. We can facilitate students' mathematics learning by using concrete situations to illustrate abstract concepts, promoting automaticity in basic facts and skills, giving students a great deal of practice solving a wide variety of problems, and teaching students how to monitor their problem-solving efforts.

Science

Scientific reasoning involves investigating natural phenomena objectively and systematically, constructing theories and models that explain these phenomena, revising those theories and models in light of new evidence or better explanations, and metacognitively overseeing the reasoning process. We can help students learn science and scientific methods by scaffolding their efforts to conduct meaningful and authentic investigations, encouraging them to learn how scientific concepts and principles are interconnected and related to everyday situations, and engaging them in discussions about their hypotheses and predictions.

Social Studies

Effective learning in history involves understanding the nature of historical time, drawing inferences from historical documents, identifying causal relationships among events, and recognizing that historical figures were real people. Effective learning in geography involves understanding that maps are symbolic representations of places, identifying interrelationships among people and their environments, and appreciating cultural differences. When we teach social studies, we should choose topics that encompass important general principles, point out cause-effect relationships, identify similarities among diverse cultures, and have students conduct some their own research.

Revisiting the Five General Principles

Although the various domains considered in this chapter involve cognitive processes that are, to some degree, quite specific to those content areas, many general principles of learning and development (e.g., the importance of meaningful learning and elaboration, the increase in abstract thinking over time) kept popping up in our discussion. Five principles, summarized in Table 8.3, have been especially prominent:

• *Learners use the information they receive from various sources to build their own, unique understandings of the world.* We've seen this principle at work in how students construct meaning from what they read, engage in knowledge transforming as they write, and build increasingly complex and integrated understandings as they study mathematics, science, and social studies.

• *Learners' interpretations of new information and events are influenced by what they already know and believe about the world.* Students draw on their prior knowledge to interpret what they read, and they write more effectively about the things they know well. Their success in learning mathematics depends on how well they've mastered prerequisite concepts and procedures. Their ability to learn and apply scientific principles is influenced by their personal theories about scientific phenomena. Their understanding of social studies is enhanced when they relate historical events and geographical phenomena to their personal experiences.

Table 8.3. Applying Five General Principles in Different Content Domains

Principle	Reading	Writing	Mathematics
Constructive processes	Students construct an understanding of an author's intended meaning using the clues that the text provides. Good readers go beyond the specific things that they read, drawing inferences, making predictions, finding symbolism, and so on.	Effective writing is a process of knowledge transforming rather than knowledge telling.	Beginning with a basic understanding of numbers and counting, students build an increasingly complex and integrated understanding of mathematical concepts and principles.
Influence of prior knowledge	Students use what they already know about a topic to help them construct meaning from text. Their knowledge of typical text structures (e.g., the usual sequence of events of stories, the usual structure of expository text) also assists them in comprehension.	Students write more effectively about things that they know well.	Mathematics is an especially hierarchical discipline—one in which advanced concepts and principles almost always build on ideas learned in earlier years.
Role of metacognition	Good readers monitor their comprehension and engage in processes that are likely to increase their comprehension (setting goals, asking questions that they try to answer, etc.).	Good writers set goals for their writing, consider what their audience is likely to know about their topic, and think consciously about how to help the audience understand the message they are trying to communicate.	Effective problem solvers monitor their progress toward problem solutions. They also have epistemological beliefs conducive to problem-solving success; for instance, they recognize that mathematical procedures make logical sense and know that they may need to try several different approaches before they are successful.
Qualitative changes with development	In the preschool and early elementary years, students begin to develop and use word decoding skills, and they are capable of comprehending simple text. At the upper elementary grades, word recognition is largely automatic, enabling students to focus almost exclusively on comprehension. In the secondary years, students acquire more sophisticated metacognitive skills and become more critical of what they read.	Young writers have difficulty writing for an imaginary audience and engage almost exclusively in knowledge telling. As writing mechanics become more automatic in the upper elementary grades, students begin to use complex sentence structures and to focus on communicating effectively. Secondary school students produce more comprehensive and organized texts, and some (but not all) of them engage in knowledge transforming.	In the elementary grades, students' understanding of mathematics is limited to concrete situations and focuses on simple operations (e.g., addition, multiplication). In the middle and secondary school years, students become increasingly able to think about abstract concepts and procedures (e.g., solving for an unknown x in algebra).
Social interaction	Students more effectively construct meaning from what they read when they discuss their readings with their classmates.	Students write more effectively when their peers read and critique their work and when they collaborate on writing projects.	Students gain a better understanding of math when they tutor classmates or younger students. They gain greater metacognitive awareness of their strategies, and they may also modify inappropriate ones, when they must explain and justify their reasoning to others.

Table 8.3 (continued)

Principle	Science	Social Studies
Constructive processes	Learning science effectively involves constructing an integrated understanding of concepts and principles related to a particular topic.	Mastery of history and geography involves constructing integrated understandings of cause-effect relationships.
Influence of prior knowledge	Students often develop personal theories about natural phenomena long before they have formal instruction about these phenomena. To the extent that such theories represent inaccurate understandings, they may interfere with students' ability to learn more scientifically acceptable explanations.	Students learn social studies more effectively when they can relate historical events and geographical phenomena to their own personal experiences.
Role of metacognition	Students' beliefs about what science is influence how they study and learn science; for instance, those who believe that science consists of isolated facts are likely to focus on meaningless memorization. Furthermore, students' ability to conduct meaningful experiments is influenced by the extent to which they ask themselves questions about their observations and interpretations (e.g., "Have I confirmed my prediction?").	A true understanding of history involves the recognition that a great deal of historical "knowledge" is interpretive rather than factual.
Qualitative changes with development	In the elementary grades, students have difficulty thinking about abstract scientific concepts, and they can separate and control variables only in simple and familiar situations. In the middle school grades, students still have limited abstract reasoning capabilities and so may benefit from concrete models of scientific phenomena (e.g., the idea of heat "flow"). High school students can comprehend abstract scientific explanations, especially after they have studied a topic in depth.	Elementary school students (especially those in the lower grades) have difficulty comprehending the nature of historical time and appreciating the symbolic nature of maps. At the secondary level, students' understanding of both history and geography becomes increasingly abstract. Secondary students are more capable of empathizing with historical figures; in addition, they can apply their proportional reasoning skills to interpreting the scales of various maps.
Social interaction	Students revise misconceptions about scientific phenomena and acquire more sophisticated scientific reasoning processes when they jointly wrestle with puzzling findings and critique one another's conclusions.	Students can better appreciate the perspectives of historical figures when they role-play historical events.

• *Over time, learners develop cognitive strategies and epistemological beliefs that influence their thinking and performance within a particular content domain.* Good readers, writers, mathematicians, and scientists continually monitor their progress toward goals and ask themselves questions that guide their thinking. Furthermore, certain epistemological beliefs—for example, beliefs that mathematical procedures make logical sense and that much of history is interpretive rather than factual—increase the likelihood that students will learn and achieve at high levels.

• *The ways in which learners think about and understand academic subject matter are qualitatively different at different points in their cognitive development.* Several trends in cognitive development influence students' learning and performance in the content domains, including the increasing automaticity of basic skills and growing ability to think abstractly, separate and control variables, reason about proportions, and take the perspectives of others.

• *Learners often gain greater understanding and greater metacognitive sophistication in a subject area when they work collaboratively with their peers.* Throughout the chapter, we've repeatedly seen the benefits of having students work together. Small-group and whole class discussions help students construct meaning from what they read in fiction and textbooks and from what they observe in scientific investigations. Students who work together create better written compositions and can tackle more challenging mathematical problems. When students must justify their actions to someone else, they develop greater awareness of their reasoning and problem-solving processes. And when they role-play historical events, they gain a better appreciation of the very "human" nature of historical figures.

Case Study: *All Charged Up*

Jean, Greg, Jack, and Julie are working on a laboratory assignment in Mr. Hammer's high school physics class. They are using a ball of crumpled aluminum hanging from a piece of string (a device known as a *pith ball*) to determine whether various objects have an electric charge; objects that are charged will make the aluminum ball swing either toward or away from them, and objects that aren't charged will have no effect on the ball. The students have attached two plastic straws—one wrapped in aluminum foil—to opposite sides of an aluminum pie plate, which they have placed on a Styrofoam cup. The materials before them look like this:

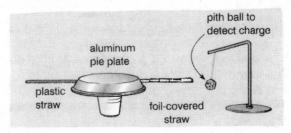

The students put a charge on the aluminum pie plate and discover that the aluminum-covered straw becomes electrically charged (it attracts the pith ball), but the uncovered plastic straw remains uncharged. As Mr. Hammer approaches, Greg explains what the group thinks it has just observed:

Greg: The plate is aluminum, right? And the foil-covered straw is the same thing. The plate charges the foil straw because they're both aluminum.

Mr. H.: Hmmm... do you think that if the plate were plastic, then the plastic straw would become charged?

Greg: If the plate was charged and if it was plastic, then yes.

Mr. H.: So your idea is that one object can charge another only if both objects are made of the same kind of material—that aluminum charges aluminum, and plastic charges plastic?

Greg agrees with Mr. Hammer's statement, as do Julie and Jack. Jean is hesitant, however, and suggests another experiment.

> Jean: I don't know, could we try it with the foam? Charge a foam plate, maybe, and then put a foam cup on it.
> Mr. H.: That's a great experiment.

Mr. Hammer is delighted. He knows that Styrofoam does not conduct electricity, so a foam plate cannot possibly share a charge with a foam cup. He fully expects that the experiment Jean has proposed will force the students to discard their hypothesis that any object can be charged but will transfer its charge only to other objects of the same material (in reality, some materials can be charged but others cannot). He gives the group a couple of foam plates to add to their experimental materials and then moves on to converse with other students.

Later in the lab session, Mr. Hammer returns to the foursome to inquire about their observations in the second experiment. He is quite taken aback at what they tell him.

> Jack: It worked. The charge on the foam plate spread to the foam cup.
> Julie: We even tried it in a different way. We put one foam plate on top of another one, and it gave us the same result.

All four students are quite confident about the conclusion they have drawn from their experiments: Charge moves from foam to foam in the same way that it moves from aluminum to aluminum. (based on Hammer, 1997, p. 486)

- Why do the students draw an erroneous conclusion from their experiments with the foam objects? What common error in scientific reasoning are they making?

- What strategies might Mr. Hammer use to encourage the students to reject their current hypothesis and adopt one more consistent with the laws of physics?

Once you have answered these questions, compare your responses with those presented following the Glossary for this *Study Guide and Reader*.

Using the Student Artifact Library

You can find many examples of actual classroom assignments and students' work in language arts, mathematics, science, and social studies on the Companion Website for *Educational Psychology: Developing Learners*. You can find this site at http://www.prenhall.com/ormrod. Once you're there, click on the "Student Artifact Library" module on the navigation bar on the left side of the screen.

GLOSSARY FOR THE SUPPLEMENTARY READINGS

Authoritarian parenting style. A parenting style characterized by rigid rules and expectations for behavior that children are expected to obey without question.

Authoritative parenting. A parenting style characterized by emotional warmth, high expectations and standards for behavior, consistent enforcement of rules, explanations regarding the reasons behind these rules, and the inclusion of children in decision making.

Benchmark lesson or experiment. Lesson or experiment that begins a new unit by illustrating the issues that the unit will address.

Branching program. A form of programmed instruction in which students responding incorrectly to a question proceed to one or more remedial frames for further clarification or practice before continuing on with new information.

Computer-assisted instruction (CAI). Programmed instruction presented by means of a computer; it is one form of computer-based instruction.

Confirmation bias. A tendency to look for evidence that confirms a hypothesis and to ignore evidence that contradicts the hypothesis.

Deficiency need. In Maslow's hierarchy, a need that results from something a person lacks.

Emergent literacy. Knowledge and skills that lay a foundation for reading and writing; typically develops in the preschool years as a result of early experiences with oral and written language.

Fine motor skills. Small, precise movements of particular parts of the body, especially the hands.

Gross motor skills. Large movements of the body that permit locomotion around the environment.

Growth spurt. Rapid increase in height and weight during puberty.

Growth need. In Maslow's hierarchy, a need that serves to enhance a person's growth and development and is never completely satisfied.

Linear program. A form of programmed instruction in which all students proceed through the same sequence of instructional frames.

Menarche. First menstrual period in an adolescent female.

Model. In science, knowledge of the components of a particular scientific entity and the interrelationships among those components.

Parenting style. The general pattern of behaviors that a parent uses to raise his or her children.

Permissive parenting style. A parenting style characterized by emotional warmth but few expectations or standards for children's behavior.

Personal theory. A self-constructed explanation for one's observations about a particular aspect of the world; it may or may not be consistent with generally accepted explanations of scientific phenomena.

Phonological awareness. The ability to hear the distinct sounds (phonemes) within a word.

Programmed instruction (PI). An approach to instruction whereby students independently study a topic that has been broken into small, carefully sequenced segments.

Puberty. Physiological changes that occur during adolescence and lead to reproductive maturation.

Self-actualization. The tendency for human beings to enhance themselves and fulfill their potential—to strive toward becoming everything that they are capable of becoming.

Spermarche. First ejaculation in an adolescent male.

Standard deviation (SD). A statistic that reflects how close together or far apart a set of scores are and thereby indicates the variability of the scores.

Theory. An organized body of concepts and principles developed to explain certain phenomena; a description of possible underlying mechanisms to explain why certain principles are true.

Uninvolved parenting style. A parenting style characterized by a lack of emotional support and a lack of standards regarding appropriate behavior.

Whole language instruction. An approach to teaching reading and writing in which basic skills are taught solely within the context of authentic reading and writing tasks.

Word decoding. In reading, identifying the sounds associated with a word's letters and then determining what the word probably is.

ENDING CASE STUDY ANALYSIS
(for Supplementary Reading #8)

Why do the students draw an erroneous conclusion from their experiments with the foam objects? What common error in scientific reasoning are they making?

Their expectations are influencing the meanings they construct from their experiences: They expect the charge on the foam plate to spread to the foam cup, so they "observe" such an effect (see the discussion of the effects of prior knowledge and expectations on learning in Chapter 7 of the textbook). Their reasoning reflects *confirmation bias*.

What strategies might Mr. Hammer use to encourage the students to reject their current hypothesis and adopt one more consistent with the laws of physics?

Following are several possibilities (you and your classmates might identify others as well):

- Have students repeat the experiments they've conducted (both those with metal objects and those with plastic objects) to see if they can replicate their results.

- Have students use an objective approach to measuring how much the pith ball moves (e.g., they might use a ruler to measure the distance that the ball moves from a stationary position each time).

- Have the students perform experiments with other plastic objects to further test their hypothesis.

- Have all student groups conduct the same experiment that these four students have just conducted, then have each group report its results to the entire class. (Presumably some groups should find that the electric charge does not transfer from the foam plate to the foam cup.)

REFERENCES

Adams, M. J. (1990). *Beginning to read: Thinking and learning about print.* Cambridge, MA: MIT Press.

Airasian, P. W. (1994). *Classroom assessment* (2nd ed.). New York: McGraw-Hill.

Alleman, J., & Brophy, J. (1997). Elementary social studies: Instruments, activities, and standards. In G. D. Phye (Ed.), *Handbook of classroom assessment: Learning, achievement, and adjustment.* San Diego, CA: Academic Press.

Alvermann, D. E., & Moore, D. W. (1991). Secondary school reading. In R. Barr, M. L. Kamil, P. B. Mosenthal, & P. D. Pearson (Eds.), *Handbook of reading research: Vol. II.* New York: Longman.

Alvermann, D. E., Young, J. P., Green, C., & Wisenbaker, J. M. (1999). Adolescents' perceptions and negotiations of literacy practices in after-school read and talk clubs. *American Educational Research Journal, 36,* 221-264.

Anderson, J. R. (1987). Skill acquisition: Compilation of weak-method problem solutions. *Psychological Review, 94,* 192-210.

Anderson, R. C., Shirey, L., Wilson, P., & Fielding, L. (1987). Interestingness of children's reading materials. In R. Snow & M. Farr (Eds.), *Aptitude, learning, and instruction: III. Conative and affective process analyses.* Hillsdale, NJ: Erlbaum.

Applebee, A. N. (1984). *Contexts for learning to write: Studies of secondary school instruction.* Norwood, NJ: Ablex.

Baker, L., Scher, D., & Mackler, K. (1997). Home and family influences on motivations for reading. *Educational Psychologist, 32,* 69-82.

Banks, J. A. (1994). Transforming the mainstream curriculum. *Educational Leadership, 51*(8), 4-8.

Barr, H. M., Streissguth, A. P., Darby, B. L., & Sampson, P. D. (1990). Prenatal exposure to alcohol, caffeine, tobacco, and aspirin: Effects on fine and gross motor performance in 4-year-old children. *Developmental Psychology, 26,* 339-348.

Bartlett, E. J. (1982). Learning to revise: Some component processes. In M. Nystrand (Ed.), *What writers know: The language, process, and structure of written discourse.* New York: Academic Press.

Barton, K. C., & Levstik, L. S. (1996). "Back when God was around and everything": Elementary children's understanding of historical time. *American Educational Research Journal, 33,* 419-454.

Bassett, D. S., Jackson, L., Ferrell, K. A., Luckner, J., Hagerty, P. J., Bunsen, T. D., & MacIsaac, D. (1996). Multiple perspectives on inclusive education: Reflections of a university faculty. *Teacher Education and Special Education, 19,* 355-386.

Baumrind, D. (1971). Current patterns of parental authority. *Developmental Psychology Monographs, 4*(1, Pt. 2).

Baumrind, D. (1989). Rearing competent children. In W. Damon (Ed.), *Child development today and tomorrow.* San Francisco: Jossey-Bass.

Baumrind, D. (1991). Parenting styles and adolescent development. In R. Lerner, A. C. Petersen, & J. Brooks-Gunn (Eds.), *The encyclopedia of adolescence.* New York: Garland Press.

Beal, C. R. (1996). The role of comprehension monitoring in children's revision. *Educational Psychology Review, 8,* 219-238.

Bean, T. W., & Steenwyk, F. L. (1984). The effect of three forms of summarization instruction on sixth graders' summary writing and comprehension. *Journal of Reading Behavior, 16,* 297-306.

Beaty, J. J. (1998). *Observing development of the young child* (4th ed.). Upper Saddle River, NJ: Merrill/Prentice Hall.

Beck, I. L., McKeown, M. G., & Gromoll, E. W. (1989). Learning from social studies texts. *Cognition and Instruction, 6,* 99-158.

Beck, I. L., McKeown, M. G., Sinatra, G. M., & Loxterman, J. A. (1991). Revising social studies text from a text-processing perspective: Evidence of improved comprehensibility. *Reading Research Quarterly, 26,* 251-276.

Beck, I. L., McKeown, M. G., Worthy, J., Sandora, C. A., & Kucan, L. (1996). Questioning the author: A yearlong classroom implementation to engage students with text. *The Elementary School Journal, 96,* 385-414.

Benton, S. L. (1997). Psychological foundations of elementary writing instruction. In G. D. Phye (Ed.), *Handbook of academic learning: Construction of knowledge.* San Diego, CA: Academic Press.

Bereiter, C. (1994). Implications of postmodernism for science, or, science as progressive discourse. *Educational Psychologist, 29*(1), 3-12.

Bereiter, C., & Scardamalia, M. (1987). *The psychology of written composition.* Hillsdale, NJ: Erlbaum.

Bermejo, V. (1996). Cardinality development and counting. *Developmental Psychology, 32,* 263-268.

Berninger, V. W., Fuller, F., & Whitaker, D. (1996). A process model of writing development across the life span. *Educational Psychology Review, 8,* 193-218.

Biemiller, A. (1994). Some observations on beginning reading instruction. *Educational Psychologist, 29,* 203-209.

Biemiller, A., Shany, M., Inglis, A., & Meichenbaum, D. (1998). Factors influencing children's acquisition and demonstration of self-regulation on academic tasks. In D. H. Schunk & B. J. Zimmerman (Eds.), *Self-regulated learning: From teaching to self-reflective practice* (pp. 203–224). New York: Guilford Press.

Blades, M., & Spencer, C. (1987). Young children's strategies when using maps with landmarks. *Journal of Environmental Psychology, 7,* 201-217.

Blyth, D. A., Simmons, R. G., & Zakin, D. F. (1985). Satisfaction with body image for early adolescent females: The impact of pubertal timing within different school environments. *Journal of Youth and Adolescence, 14,* 207-225.

Bochenhauer, M. H. (1990, April.) *Connections: Geographic education and the National Geographic Society.* Paper presented at the annual meeting of the American Educational Research Association, Boston.

Boiarsky, C. (1982). Prewriting is the essence of writing. *English Journal, 71,* 44-47.

Bradley, L., & Bryant, P. E. (1991). Phonological skills before and after learning to read. In S. A. Brady & D. P. Shankweiler (Eds.), *Phonological processes in literacy.* Hillsdale, NJ: Erlbaum.

Brandes, A. A. (1996). Elementary school children's images of science. In Y. Kafai & M. Resnick (Eds.), *Constructionism in practice: Designing, thinking, and learning in a digital world.* Mahwah, NJ: Erlbaum.

Brenner, M. E., Mayer, R. E., Moseley, B., Brar, T., Durán, R., Reed, B. S., & Webb, D. (1997). Learning by understanding: The role of multiple representations in learning algebra. *American Educational Research Journal, 34,* 663-689.

Britt, M. A., Rouet, J.-F., Georgi, M. C., & Perfetti, C. A. (1994). Learning from history texts: From causal analysis to argument models. In G. Leinhardt, I. L. Beck, & C. Stainton (Eds.), *Teaching and learning in history.* Hillsdale, NJ: Erlbaum.

Britton, B. K., Stimson, M., Stennett, B., & Gülgöz, S. (1998). Learning from instructional text: Test of an individual differences model. *Journal of Educational Psychology, 90,* 476-491.

Bronfenbrenner, U., Alvarez, W. F., & Henderson, C. R., Jr. (1984). Working and watching: Maternal employment status and parents' perceptions of their three-year-old children. *Child Development, 55,* 1362-1379.

Brooks-Gunn, J. (1989). Pubertal processes and the early adolescent transition. In W. Damon (Ed.), *Child development today and tomorrow* (pp. 155-176). San Francisco, CA: Jossey-Bass.

Brooks-Gunn, J., & Paikoff, R. L. (1992). Changes in self-feelings during the transition toward adolescence. In H. R. McGurk (Ed.), *Childhood social development: Contemporary perspectives* (pp. 63-97). Hillsdale, NJ: Erlbaum.

Brophy, J. E., & Alleman, J. (1996). *Powerful social studies for elementary students.* Fort Worth, TX: Harcourt Brace.

Brophy, J. E., & VanSledright, B. (1997). *Teaching and learning history in elementary schools.* New York: Teachers College Press.

Brown, A. L., & Campione, J. C. (1994). Guided discovery in a community of learners. In K. McGilly (Ed.), *Classroom lessons: Integrating cognitive theory and classroom practice.* Cambridge, MA: MIT Press.

Brown, D. E. (1992). Using examples and analogies to remediate misconceptions in physics: Factors influencing conceptual change. *Journal of Research in Science Teaching, 29,* 17-34.

Brown, D. E., & Clement, J. (1989). Overcoming misconceptions via analogical reasoning: Abstract transfer versus explanatory model construction. *Instructional Science, 18,* 237-262.

Brown, K. J., Sinatra, G. M., & Wagstaff, J. M. (1996). Exploring the potential of analogy instruction to support children's spelling development. *Elementary School Journal, 97,* 81-90.

Bruni, M. (1998). *Fine-motor skills in children with Down syndrome: A guide for parents and professionals.* Bethesda, MD: Woodbine House.

Buchanan, C. M. (1991). Pubertal status in early adolescent girls: Relations to moods, energy, and restlessness. *Journal of Early Adolescence, 11*(2), 185-200.

Buckhout, R. (1974). Eyewitness testimony. *Scientific American, 231*(6), 23-31.

Burkam, D. T., Lee, V. E., & Smerdon, B. A. (1997). Gender and science learning early in high school: Subject matter and laboratory experiences. *American Educational Research Journal, 34*, 297-331.

Burnett, R. E., & Kastman, L. M. (1997). Teaching composition: Current theories and practices. In G. D. Phye (Ed.), *Handbook of academic learning: Construction of knowledge.* San Diego, CA: Academic Press.

Bus, A. G., & van IJzendoorn, M. H. (1999). Phonological awareness and early reading: A meta-analysis of experimental training studies. *Journal of Educational Psychology, 91*, 403-414.

Butterfield, E. C., & Ferretti, R. P. (1987). Toward a theoretical integration of cognitive hypotheses about intellectual differences among children. In J. G. Borkowski & J. D. Day (Eds.), *Cognition in special children: Approaches to retardation, learning disabilities, and giftedness.* Norwood, NJ: Ablex.

Byrne, B., Fielding-Barnsley, R., & Ashley, L. (2000). Effects of preschool phoneme identity training after six years: Outcome level distinguished from rate of response. *Journal of Educational Psychology, 92*, 659–667.

Byrnes, J. P. (1996). *Cognitive development and learning in instructional contexts.* Boston: Allyn & Bacon.

Cameron, C. A., Hunt, A. K., & Linton, M. J. (1996). Written expression as recontextualization: Children write in social time. *Educational Psychology Review, 8*, 125-150.

Cardelle-Elawar, M. (1992). Effects of teaching metacognitive skills to students with low mathematics ability. *Teaching and Teacher Education, 8*, 109-121.

Carey, S., Evans, R., Honda, M., Jay, E., & Unger, C. (1989). "An experiment is when you try it and see if it works": A study of grade 7 students' understanding of the construction of scientific knowledge. *International Journal of Science Education, 11*, 514-529.

Carr, M., & Biddlecomb, B. (1998). Metacognition in mathematics from a constructivist perspective. In D. J. Hacker, J. Dunlosky, & A. C. Graesser (Eds.), *Metacognition in educational theory and practice* (pp. 69–91). Mahwah, NJ: Erlbaum.

Case, R., & Okamoto, Y., in collaboration with Griffin, S., McKeough, A., Bleiker, C., Henderson, B., & Stephenson, K. M. (1996). The role of central conceptual structures in the development of children's thought. *Monographs of the Society for Research in Child Development, 61*(1, Serial No. 246).

Case-Smith, J. (1996). Fine motor outcomes in preschool children who receive occupational therapy services. *American Journal of Occupational Therapy, 50*(1), 52-61.

Cawley, J. F., & Miller, J. H. (1989). Cross-sectional comparisons of the mathematical performance of children with learning disabilities: Are we on the right track toward comprehensive programming? *Journal of Learning Disabilities, 22*, 250–254, 259.

Chall, J. S. (1996). *Stages of reading development* (2nd ed.). Fort Worth, TX: Harcourt Brace.

Chambliss, M. J. (1998, April). *Children as thinkers composing scientific explanations.* Paper presented at the annual meeting of the American Educational Research Association, San Diego, CA.

Chao, R. K. (1994). Beyond parental control and authoritarian parenting style: Understanding Chinese parenting through the cultural notion of training. *Child Development, 65*, 1111-1119.

Chi, M. T. H., de Leeuw, N., Chiu, M., & LaVancher, C. (1994). Eliciting self-explanations. *Cognitive Science, 18*, 439-477.

Chu, Y-W. (2000). *The relationships between domain-specific self-concepts and global self-esteem among adolescents in Taiwan.* Unpublished doctoral dissertation, University of Northern Colorado, Greeley.

Chugani, H. T. (1998). Biological bases of emotions: Brain systems and brain development. *Pediatrics, 102*(5, Suppl. E), 1225-1229.

Clarke, L. K. (1988). Invented versus traditional spelling in first graders' writings: Effects on learning to spell and read. *Research in the Teaching of English, 22*, 281-309.

Clay, M. M. (1985). *The early detection of reading difficulties: A diagnostic survey with recovery procedure.* Portsmouth, NH: Heinemann.

Clement, J. (1982). Algebra word problem solutions: Thought processes underlying a common misconception. *Journal for Research in Mathematics Education, 13*, 16-30.

Cobb, P. (1994). Where is the mind? Constructivist and sociocultural perspectives on mathematical development. *Educational Researcher, 23*(7), 13-20.

Cobb, P., Wood, T., Yackel, E., Nicholls, J., Wheatley, G., Trigatti, B., & Perlwitz, M. (1991). Assessment of a problem centered second-grade mathematics project. *Journal for Research in Mathematics Education, 22*, 3-29.

Cochran-Smith, M. (1991). *The making of a reader.* Norwood, NJ: Ablex.

Cohen, M. R. (1997). Individual and sex differences in speed of handwriting among high school students. *Perceptual and Motor Skills, 84*(3, Pt. 2), 1428-1430.

Collins, A., Hawkins, J., & Carver, S. M. (1991). A cognitive apprenticeship for disadvantaged students. In B. Means, C. Chelemer, & M. S. Knapp (Eds.), *Teaching advanced skills to at-risk students.* San Francisco: Jossey-Bass.

Collins, W. A., Maccoby, E. E., Steinberg, L., Hetherington, E. M., & Bornstein, M. H. (2000). Contemporary research on parenting: The case for nature and nurture. *American Psychologist, 55,* pp. 218–232.

Committee on High School Biology Education. (1990). *Fulfilling the promise: Biology education in the nation's schools.* Washington, DC: National Academy Press.

Cone, T. E., Wilson, L. R., Bradley, C. M., & Reese, J. H. (1985). Characteristics of LD students in Iowa: An empirical investigation. *Learning Disability Quarterly, 8,* 211-220.

Cooney, J. B. (1991). Reflections on the origin of mathematical intuition and some implications for instruction. *Learning and Individual Differences, 3,* 83-107.

Correa, J., Nunes, T., & Bryant, P. (1998). Young children's understanding of division: The relationship between division terms in a noncomputational task. *Journal of Educational Psychology, 90,* 321-329.

Cota-Robles, S., & Neiss, M. (1999, April). *The role of puberty in non-violent delinquency among Anglo-American, Hispanic, and African American boys.* Paper presented at the Biennial Meeting of the Society for Research in Child Development, Albuquerque, NM.

Covill, A. E. (1997, March). *Students' revision practices and attitudes in response to surface-related feedback as compared to content-related feedback on their writing.* Paper presented at the annual meeting of the American Educational Research Association, Chicago.

Crain-Thoreson, C., & Dale, P. S. (1992). Do early talkers become early readers? Linguistic precocity, preschool language, and emergent literacy. *Developmental Psychology, 28,* 421-429.

Daiute, C. (1986). Do 1 and 1 make 2? *Written Communication, 3,* 382-408.

Daiute, C. (1989). Play as thought: Thinking strategies of young writers. *Harvard Educational Review, 59*(1), 1-23.

Daiute, C., & Dalton, B. (1993). Collaboration between children learning to write: Can novices be masters? *Cognition and Instruction, 10,* 281-333.

Davidson, J. E., & Sternberg, R. J. (1998). Smart problem solving: How metacognition helps. In D. J. Hacker, J. Dunlosky, & A. C. Graesser (Eds.), *Metacognition in educational theory and practice* (pp. 47–68). Mahwah, NJ: Erlbaum.

De Corte, E., Greer, B., & Verschaffel, L. (1996). Mathematics teaching and learning. In D. C. Berliner & R. C. Calfee (Eds.), *Handbook of educational psychology.* New York: Macmillan.

Dekovic, M., & Janssens, J. M. (1992). Parents' child-rearing style and child's sociometric status. *Developmental Psychology, 28,* 925-932.

DeLamateur, J., & MacCorquodale, P. (1979). *Premarital sexuality.* Madison, WI: University of Wisconsin Press.

De La Paz, S., Swanson, P. N., & Graham, S. (1998). The contribution of executive control to the revising by students with writing and learning difficulties. *Journal of Educational Psychology, 90,* 448-460.

DeRidder, L. M. (1993). Teenage pregnancy: Etiology and educational interventions. *Educational Psychology Review, 5,* 87-107.

diSessa, A. A. (1996). What do "just plain folk" know about physics? In D. R. Olson & N. Torrance (Eds.), *The handbook of education and human development: New models of learning, teaching, and schooling.* Cambridge, MA: Blackwell.

Dodge, K. A., Pettit, G. S., Bates, J. E., & Valente, E. (1995). Social information-processing patterns partially mediate the effect of early physical abuse on later conduct problems. *Journal of Abnormal Psychology, 104,* 632-643.

Dornbusch, S. M., Ritter, P. L., Leiderman, P. H., Roberts, D. F., & Fraleigh, M. J. (1987). The relation of parenting style to adolescent school performance. *Child Development, 58,* 1244-1257.

Driver, R. (1995). Constructivist approaches to science teaching. In L. P. Steffe & J. Gale (Eds.), *Constructivism in education.* Hillsdale, NJ: Erlbaum.

Dryden, M. A., & Jefferson, P. (1994, April). *Use of background knowledge and reading achievement among elementary school students.* Paper presented at the annual meeting of the American Educational Research Association, New Orleans, LA.

Duit, R. (1991). Students' conceptual frameworks: Consequences for learning science. In S. M. Glynn, R. H. Yeany, & B. K. Britton (Eds.), *The psychology of learning science.* Hillsdale, NJ: Erlbaum.

Duncan, P. D., Ritter, P. L., Dornbusch, S. M., Gross, R. T., & Carlsmith, J. M. (1985). The effects of pubertal timing on body image, school behavior, and deviance. *Journal of Youth and Adolescence, 14,* 227-235.

Durkin, K. (1995). *Developmental social psychology: From infancy to old age.* Cambridge, MA: Blackwell.

Eaton, W. O., & Enns, L. R. (1986). Sex differences in human motor activity level. *Psychological Bulletin, 100,* 19-28.

Edens, K. M., & Potter, E. F. (2001). Promoting conceptual understanding through pictorial representation. *Studies in Art Education, 42,* 214–233.

Eeds, M., & Wells, D. (1989). Grand conversations: An explanation of meaning construction in literature study groups. *Research in the Teaching of English, 23,* 4-29.

Ehri, L. C. (1998). Word reading by sight and by analogy in beginning readers. In C. Hulme & R. M. Joshi (Eds.), *Reading and spelling: Development and disorders.* Mahwah, NJ: Erlbaum.

Ehri, L. C., & Wilce, L. S. (1987). Does learning to spell help beginners learn to read words? *Reading Research Quarterly, 22,* 47-65.

Eisenberg, N., & Fabes, R. A. (1994). Mothers' reactions to children's negative emotions: Relations to children's temperament and anger behavior. *Merrill-Palmer Quarterly, 40,* 138-156.

Eisenberg, N., Martin, C. L., & Fabes, R. A. (1996). Gender development and gender effects. In D. C. Berliner & R. C. Calfee (Eds.), *Handbook of educational psychology.* New York: Macmillan.

Elkind, D. (1981). *Children and adolescents: Interpretive essays on Jean Piaget* (3rd ed.). New York: Oxford.

Empson, S. B. (1999). Equal sharing and shared meaning: The development of fraction concepts in a first-grade classroom. *Cognition and Instruction, 17,* 283–342.

Englert, C. S., Raphael, T. E., Anderson, L. M., Anthony, H. M., & Stevens, D. D. (1991). Making strategies and self-talk visible: Writing instruction in regular and special education classrooms. *American Educational Research Journal, 28,* 337-372.

Ferretti, R. P., MacArthur, C. A., & Dowdy, N. S. (2000). The effects of an elaborated goal on the persuasive writing of students with learning disabilities and their normally achieving peers. *Journal of Educational Psychology, 92,* 694–702.

Fitzgerald, J. (1987). Research on revision in writing. *Review of Educational Research, 57,* 481-506.

Fitzgerald, J. (1992). Variant views about good thinking during composing: Focus on revision. In M. Pressley, K. R. Harris, & J. T. Guthrie (Eds.), *Promoting academic competence and literacy in school.* San Diego, CA: Academic Press.

Flower, L. S., & Hayes, J. R. (1981). A cognitive process theory of writing. *College Composition and Communication, 32,* 365-387.

Forbes, M. L., Ormrod, J. E., Bernardi, J. D., Taylor, S. L., & Jackson, D. L. (1999, April). *Children's conceptions of space, as reflected in maps of their hometown.* Paper presented at the annual meeting of the American Educational Research Association, Montreal, Canada..

Frank, A. (1967). *The diary of a young girl* [B. M. Mooyaart-Doubleday, Trans.]. New York: Doubleday.

Frijters, J. C., Barron, R. W., & Brunello, M. (2000). Direct and mediated influences of home literacy and literacy interest on prereaders' oral vocabulary and early written language skill. *Journal of Educational Psychology, 92,* 466–477.

Fuchs, L. S., Fuchs, D., & Karns, K. (1995). Acquisition and transfer effects of classwide peer-assisted learning strategies for students with varying learning histories. *School Psychology Review, 24,* 604-620.

Fuchs, L. S., Fuchs, D., Karns, K., Hamlett, C. L., Dutka, S., & Katzaroff, M. (1996). The relation between student ability and the quality and effectiveness of explanations. *American Educational Research Journal, 33,* 631-664.

Fuson, K. C., & Briars, D. J. (1990). Using a base-ten blocks learning/teaching approach for first- and second-grade place-value and multidigit addition and subtraction. *Journal for Research in Mathematics Education, 21,* 180-206.

Fuson, K. C., & Hall, J. W. (1983). The acquisition of early word meanings: A conceptual analysis and review. In H. P. Ginsburg (Ed.), *Children's mathematical thinking.* New York: Academic Press.

Gallahue, D. L., & Ozmun, J. C. (1998). *Understanding motor development: Infants, children, adolescents, adults.* Boston: McGraw-Hill.

Gallistel, C. R., & Gelman, R. (1992). Preverbal and verbal counting and computation. *Cognition, 44,* 43-74.

Gambrell, L. B., & Bales, R. J. (1986). Mental imagery and the comprehension-monitoring performance of fourth- and fifth-grade poor readers. *Reading Research Quarterly, 21,* 454-464.

Gambrell, L. B., & Chasen, S. P. (1991). Explicit story instruction and the narrative writing of fourth- and fifth-grade below-average readers. *Reading Research and Instruction, 31,* 54-62.

Gardner, H., Torff, B., & Hatch, T. (1996). The age of innocence reconsidered: Preserving the best of the progressive traditions in psychology and education. In D. R. Olson & N. Torrance (Eds.), *The handbook of education and human development: New models of learning, teaching, and schooling.* Cambridge, MA: Blackwell.

Garner, R. (1987). Strategies for reading and studying expository texts. *Educational Psychologist, 22,* 299-312.

Garner, R. (1998). Epilogue: Choosing to learn or not-learn in school. *Educational Psychology Review, 10,* 227-237.

Geary, D. C. (1994). *Children's mathematical development: Research and practical applications.* Washington, DC: American Psychological Association.

Gelman, R., & Gallistel, C. R. (1978). *The child's understanding of number.* Cambridge, MA: Harvard University Press.

Gernsbacher, M. A. (1994). *Handbook of psycholinguistics.* San Diego, CA: Academic Press.

Giedd, J. N., Blumenthal, J., Jeffries, N. O., Rajapakse, J. C., Vaituzis, A. C., Liu, H., Berry, Y. C., Tobin, M., Nelson, J., & Castellanos, F. X. (1999). Development of the human corpus callosum during childhood and adolescence: A longitudinal MRI study. *Progress in Neuro-Psychopharmacology and Biological Psychiatry, 23,* 571-588.

Ginsburg, H. P., Posner, J. K., & Russell, R. L. (1981). The development of mental addition as a function of schooling and culture. *Journal of Cross-Cultural Psychology, 12,* 163-178.

Ginsburg-Block, M. D., & Fantuzzo, J. W. (1998). An evaluation of the relative effectiveness of NCTM standards-based interventions for low-achieving urban elementary students. *Journal of Educational Psychology, 90,* 560-569.

Glynn, S. M., Yeany, R. H., & Britton, B. K. (1991). A constructive view of learning science. In S. M. Glynn, R. H. Yeany, & B. K. Britton (Eds.), *The psychology of learning science.* Hillsdale, NJ: Erlbaum.

Goldsmith-Phillips, J. (1989). Word and context in reading development: A test of the interactive-compensatory hypothesis. *Journal of Educational Psychology, 81,* 299-305.

Goodman, K. S. (1989). Whole-language research: Foundations and development. *Elementary School Journal, 90,* 207-221.

Goodman, K. S., & Goodman, Y. M. (1979). Learning to read is natural. In L. B. Resnick & P. A. Weaver (Eds.), *Theory and practice of early reading* (Vol. 1). Hillsdale, NJ: Erlbaum.

Goswami, U. (1998). Rime-based coding in early reading development in English: Orthographic analogies and rime neighborhoods. In C. Hulme & R. M. Joshi (Eds.), *Reading and spelling: Development and disorders.* Mahwah, NJ: Erlbaum.

Gough, P. B., & Wren, S. (1998). The decomposition of decoding. In C. Hulme & R. M. Joshi (Eds.), *Reading and spelling: Development and disorders.* Mahwah, NJ: Erlbaum.

Goyen, T. A., Lui, K., & Woods, R. (1998). Visual-motor, visual-perceptual, and fine-motor outcomes in very-low-birthweight children at 5 years. *Developmental Medicine and Child Neurology, 40*(2), 76-81.

Graesser, A., Golding, J. M., & Long, D. L. (1991). Narrative representation and comprehension. In R. Barr, M. L. Kamil, P. Mosenthal, & P. D. Pearson (Eds.), *Handbook of reading research* (Vol. II). New York: Longman.

Graham, S., & Harris, K. R. (1988). Instructional recommendations for teaching writing to exceptional children. *Exceptional Children, 54,* 506-512.

Graham, S., & Harris, K. R. (1992). Self-regulated strategy development: Programmatic research in writing. In B. Y. L. Wong (Ed.), *Contemporary intervention research in learning disabilities: An international perspective.* New York: Springer-Verlag.

Graham, S., Harris, K. R., & Troia, G. A. (1998). Writing and self-regulation: Cases from the self-regulated strategy development model. In D. H. Schunk & B. J. Zimmerman (Eds.), *Self-regulated learning: From teaching to self-reflective practice* (pp. 20–41). New York: Guilford Press.

Graham, S., MacArthur, C., & Schwartz, S. (1995). Effects of goal setting and procedural facilitation on the revising behavior and writing performance of students with writing and learning problems. *Journal of Educational Psychology, 87,* 230-240.

Graham, S., Schwartz, S. S., & MacArthur, C. A. (1993). Knowledge of writing and the composing process, attitude toward writing, and self-efficacy for students with and without learning disabilities. *Journal of Learning Disabilities, 26,* 237-249.

Graham, S., & Weintraub, N. (1996). A review of handwriting research: Progress and prospects from 1980 to 1994. *Educational Psychology Review, 8,* 7-87.

Graves, D. (1983). *Writing: Teachers and children at work.* Portsmouth, NH: Heinemann.

Greene, S., & Ackerman, J. M. (1995). Expanding the constructivist metaphor: A rhetorical perspective on literacy research and practice. *Review of Educational Research, 65,* 383-420.

Greeno, J. G. (1991). A view of mathematical problem solving in school. In M. U. Smith (Ed.), *Toward a unified theory of problem solving: Views from the content domains.* Hillsdale, NJ: Erlbaum.

Greeno, J. G., Collins, A. M., & Resnick, L. B. (1996). Cognition and learning. In D. C. Berliner & R. C. Calfee (Eds.), *Handbook of educational psychology.* New York: Macmillan.

Gregg, M., & Leinhardt, G. (1994a, April). *Constructing geography.* Paper presented at the annual meeting of the American Educational Research Association, New Orleans, LA.

Gregg, M., & Leinhardt, G. (1994b). Mapping out geography: An example of epistemology and education. *Review of Educational Research, 64,* 311-361.

Griffin, S. A., & Case, R. (1996). Evaluating the breadth and depth of training effects when central conceptual structures are taught. In R. Case & Y. Okamoto (Eds.), The role of central structures in the development of children's thought. *Monographs of the Society for Research in Child Development, 61* 1-2, (Serial No. 246).

Griffin, S. A., Case, R., & Capodilupo, A. (1995). Teaching for understanding: The importance of the central conceptual structures in the elementary mathematics curriculum. In A. McKeough, J. Lupart, & A. Marini (Eds.), *Teaching for transfer: Fostering generalization in learning.* Mahwah, NJ: Erlbaum.

Griffin, S. A., Case, R., & Siegler, R. S. (1994). Rightstart: Providing the central conceptual prerequisites for first formal learning of arithmetic to students at risk for school failure. In K. McGilly (Ed.), *Classroom lessons: Integrating cognitive theory and classroom practice.* Cambridge, MA: MIT Press.

Gross, R. T., & Duke, P. M. (1980). The effect of early versus late physical maturation in adolescent behavior. *Pediatric Clinics of North America, 27,* 71-77.

Guthrie, B. J., Caldwell, C. H., & Hunter, A. G. (1997). Minority adolescent female health: Strategies for the next millennium. In D. K. Wilson, J. R. Rodrigue, & W. C. Taylor (Eds.), *Health-promoting and health-compromising behaviors among minority adolescents* (pp. 153-171). Washington, DC: American Psychological Association.

Guthrie, J. T., Cox, K. E., Anderson, E., Harris, K., Mazzoni, S., & Rach, L. (1998). Principles of integrated instruction for engagement in reading. *Educational Psychology Review, 10,* 177-199.

Hale-Benson, J. E. (1986). *Black children: Their roots, culture, and learning styles.* Baltimore: Johns Hopkins University Press.

Hall, W. S. (1989). Reading comprehension. *American Psychologist, 44,* 157-161.

Hallenbeck, M. J. (1996). The cognitive strategy in writing: Welcome relief for adolescents with learning disabilities. *Learning Disabilities Research and Practice, 11,* 107-119.

Hammer, D. (1997). Discovery learning and discovery teaching. *Cognition and Instruction, 15,* 485-529.

Harris, J. R. (1995). Where is the child's environment? A group socialization theory of development. *Psychological Review, 102,* 458-489.

Harris, J. R. (1998). *The nurture assumption: Why children turn out the way they do.* New York: Free Press.

Harris, K. R., & Graham, S. (1992). Self-regulated strategy development: A part of the writing process. In M. Pressley, K. R. Harris, & J. T. Guthrie (Eds.), *Promoting academic competence and literacy in school.* San Diego, CA: Academic Press.

Harris, M., & Giannouli, V. (1999). Learning to read and spell in Greek: The importance of letter knowledge and morphological awareness. In M. Harris & G. Hatano (Eds.), *Learning to read and write: A cross-linguistic perspective.* Cambridge, England: Cambridge University Press.

Harris, M., & Hatano, G. (Eds.). (1999). *Learning to read and write: A cross-linguistic perspective.* Cambridge, England: Cambridge University Press.

Harter, S. (1999). *The construction of the self.* New York: Guilford Press.

Hatano, G., & Inagaki, K. (1991). Sharing cognition through collective comprehension activity. In L. B. Resnick, J. M. Levine, & S. D. Teasley (Eds.), *Perspectives on socially shared cognition.* Washington, DC: American Psychological Association.

Hatano, G., & Inagaki, K. (1996). Cognitive and cultural factors in the acquisition of intuitive biology. In D. R. Olson & N. Torrance (Eds.), *The handbook of education and human development: New models of learning, teaching, and schooling.* Cambridge, MA: Blackwell.

Hayes, C. D., & Hofferth, S. L. (1987). *Risking the future: Adolescent sexuality, pregnancy, and childbearing* (Vol. 2). Washington, DC: National Academy Press.

Healy, C. C. (1993). Discovery courses are great in theory, but . . . In J. L. Schwartz, M. Yerushalmy, & B. Wilson (Eds.), *The geometric supposer: What is it a case of?* Hillsdale, NJ: Erlbaum.

Hemphill, L., & Snow, C. (1996). Language and literacy development: Discontinuities and differences. In D. R. Olson & N. Torrance (Eds.), *The handbook of education and human development: New models of learning, teaching, and schooling.* Cambridge, MA: Blackwell.

Herrenkohl, L. R., & Guerra, M. R. (1998). Participant structures, scientific discourse, and student engagement in fourth grade. *Cognition and Instruction, 16,* 431–473.

Hiebert, E. H., & Raphael, T. E. (1996). Psychological perspectives on literacy and extensions to educational practice. In D. C. Berliner & R. C. Calfee (Eds.), *Handbook of educational psychology.* New York: Macmillan.

Hiebert, J., Carpenter, T. P., Fennema, E., Fuson, K., Human, P., Murray, H., Olivier, A., & Wearne, D. (1996). Problem solving as a basis for reform in curriculum and instruction: The case of mathematics. *Educational Researcher, 25*(4), 12-21.

Hiebert, J., Carpenter, T. P., Fennema, E., Fuson, K. C., Wearne, D., Murray, H., Olivier, A., & Human, P. (1997). *Making sense: Teaching and learning mathematics with understanding.* Portsmouth, NH: Heinemann.

Hiebert, J., & Lefevre, P. (1986). Conceptual and procedural knowledge in mathematics: An introductory analysis. In J. Hiebert (Ed.), *Conceptual and procedural knowledge: The case of mathematics.* Hillsdale, NJ: Erlbaum.

Hiebert, J., & Wearne, D. (1992). Links between teaching and learning place value with understanding in first grade. *Journal for Research in Mathematics Education, 23,* 98-122.

Hiebert, J., & Wearne, D. (1996). Instruction, understanding, and skill in multidigit addition and subtraction. *Cognition and Instruction, 14,* 251-283.

Hill, J. P., Holmbeck, G. N., Marlow, L., Green, T. M., & Lynch, M. E. (1985). Menarchal status and parent-child relations in families of seventh-grade girls. *Journal of Youth and Adolescence, 14,* 301-316.

Howe, C., Tolmie, A., Greer, K., & Mackenzie, M. (1995). Peer collaboration and conceptual growth in physics: Task influences on children's understanding of heating and cooling. *Cognition and Instruction, 13,* 483-503.

Hulme, C., & Joshi, R. M. (Eds.). (1998). *Reading and spelling: Development and disorders.* Mahwah, NJ: Erlbaum.

Hyona, J. (1994). Processing of topic shifts by adults and children. *Reading Research Quarterly, 29,* 76-90.

Inglis, A., & Biemiller, A. (1997, March). *Fostering self-direction in mathematics: A cross-age tutoring program that enhances math problem solving.* Paper presented at the annual meeting of the American Educational Research Association, Chicago.

Irwin, C. E. Jr., & Millstein, S. G. (1992). Biopsychosocial correlates of risk-taking behaviors during adolescence: Can the physician intervene? *Journal of Adolescent Health Care, 7* (Suppl. 6), 82S-96S.

Jacklin, C. N. (1989). Female and male: Issues of gender. *American Psychologist, 44,* 127-133.

Johanning, D. I., D'Agostino, J. V., Steele, D. F., & Shumow, L. (1999, April). *Student writing, post-writing group collaboration, and learning in pre-algebra.* Paper presented at the annual meeting of the American Educational Research Association, Montreal, Canada.

Johnson-Glenberg, M. C. (2000). Training reading comprehension in adequate decodes/poor comprehenders: Verbal versus visual strategies. *Journal of Educational Psychology, 92,* 772–782.

Johnston, P., & Afflerbach, P. (1985). The process of constructing main ideas from text. *Cognition and Instruction, 2,* 207-232.

Jones, I., & Pellegrini, A. D. (1996). The effects of social relationships, writing media, and microgenetic development on first-grade students' written narratives. *American Educational Research Journal, 33,* 691-718.

Keefer, M. W., Zeitz, C. M., & Resnick, L. B. (2000). Judging the quality of peer-led student dialogues. *Cognition and Instruction, 18,* 53–81.

Keil, F. C., & Silberstein, C. S. (1996). Schooling and the acquisition of theoretical knowledge. In D. R. Olson & N. Torrance (Eds.), *The handbook of education and human development: New models of learning, teaching, and schooling.* Cambridge, MA: Blackwell.

Kellch, M. A. (1999). The writing process: Secondary students' perspectives. *McNair Scholars Journal* (publication of the University of Northern Colorado), *4,* 1-24.

Kellogg, R. (1967). *The psychology of children's art.* New York: CRM-Random House.

Kellogg, R. T. (1994). *The psychology of writing.* New York: Oxford University Press.

Kenneth, K., Smith, P. K., & Palermiti, A. L. (1997). Conflict in childhood and reproductive development. *Evolution and Human Behavior, 18,* 109-142.

Kernaghan, K., & Woloshyn, V. E. (1994, April). *Explicit versus implicit multiple strategy instruction: Monitoring grade one students' spelling performances.* Paper presented at the annual meeting of the American Educational Research Association, New Orleans, LA.

Kish, C. K., Zimmer, J. W., & Henning, M. J. (1994, April). *Using direct instruction to teach revision to novice writers: The role of metacognition.* Paper presented at the annual meeting of the American Educational Research Association, New Orleans, LA.

Klein, P. D. (1999). Reopening inquiry into cognitive processes in writing-to-learn. *Educational Psychology Review, 11,* 203-270.

Klein, P. D. (2000). Elementary students' strategies for writing-to-learn in science. *Cognition and Instruction, 18,* 317–348.

Kline, K., & Flowers, J. (1998, April). *A comparison of fourth graders' proportional reasoning in reform and traditional classrooms.* Paper presented at the annual meeting of the American Educational Research Association, San Diego, CA.

Knapp, N. F. (1995, April). *Tom and Joshua: Two at-risk readers at home and at school.* Paper presented at the annual meeting of the American Educational Research Association, San Francisco.

Knudson, R. E. (1992). The development of written argumentation: An analysis and comparison of argumentative writing at four grade levels. *Child Study Journal, 22,* 167-181.

Kroll, B. M. (1984). Audience adaptation in children's persuasive letters. *Written Communication, 1,* 407-427.

Kuhn, D. (1993). Connecting scientific and informal reasoning. *Merrill-Palmer Quarterly, 39,* 74-103.

Kuhn, D. (2001). How do people know? *Psychological Science, 12,* 1–8.

Kuhn, D., Amsel, E., & O'Loughlin, M. (1988). *The development of scientific thinking skills.* San Diego, CA: Academic Press.

Lamborn, S. D., Mounts, N. S., Steinberg, L., & Dornbusch, S. M. (1991). Patterns of competence and adjustment among adolescents from authoritative, authoritarian, indulgent, and neglectful families. *Child Development, 62,* 1049-1065.

Lampert, M. (1990). When the problem is not the question and the solution is not the answer: Mathematical knowing and teaching. *American Educational Research Journal, 27,* 29-63.

Lampert, M., Rittenhouse, P., & Crumbaugh, C. (1996). Agreeing to disagree: Developing sociable mathematical discourse. In D. R. Olson & N. Torrance (Eds.), *The handbook of education and human development: New models of learning, teaching, and schooling.* Cambridge, MA: Blackwell.

Langer, J. A., & Applebee, A. (1987). *How writing shapes thinking: A study of teaching and learning.* Champaign, IL: National Council of Teachers of English.

Lapsley, D. K., Jackson, S., Rice, K., & Shadid, G. (1988). Self-monitoring and the "new look" at the imaginary audience and personal fable: An ego-developmental analysis. *Journal of Adolescent Research, 3,* 17-31.

Lave, J. (1988). *Cognition in practice: Mind, mathematics and culture in everyday life.* Cambridge, England: Cambridge University Press.

Leinhardt, G. (1993). Weaving instructional explanations in history. *British Journal of Educational Psychology, 63,* 46-74.

Leinhardt, G., Beck, I. L., & Stainton, C. (Eds.). (1994). *Teaching and learning in history.* Hillsdale, NJ: Erlbaum.

Leinhardt, G., & Young, K. M. (1996). Two texts, three readers: Distance and expertise in reading history. *Cognition and Instruction, 14,* 441-486.

Lester, F. K. (1985). Methodological considerations in research on mathematical problem-solving instruction. In E. A. Silver (Ed.), *Teaching and learning mathematical problem solving: Multiple research perspectives.* Hillsdale, NJ: Erlbaum.

Lester, F. K., Lambdin, D. V., & Preston, R. V. (1997). A new vision of the nature and purposes of assessment in the mathematics classroom. In G. D. Phye (Ed.), *Handbook of classroom assessment: Learning, achievement, and adjustment.* San Diego, CA: Academic Press.

Leu, D., & Kinzer, C. (1995). *Effective reading instruction* (3rd ed.). Upper Saddle River, NJ: Merrill/Prentice Hall.

Liben, L. S., & Downs, R. M. (1989a). Educating with maps: Part I, the place of maps. *Teaching Thinking and Problem Solving, 11*(1), 6-9.

Liben, L. S., & Downs, R. M. (1989b). Understanding maps as symbols: The development of map concepts in children. In H. W. Reese (Ed.), *Advances in child development and behavior* (Vol. 22). San Diego, CA: Harcourt Brace Jovanovich.

Lin, C. C., & Fu, V. R. (1990). A comparison of child-rearing practices among Chinese, immigrant Chinese, and Caucasian-American parents. *Child Development, 61,* 429-433.

Lindsay, D. S. (1993). Eyewitness suggestibility. *Current Directions in Psychological Science, 2,* 86-89.

Linn, M. C., & Hyde, J. S. (1989). Gender, mathematics, and science. *Educational Researcher, 18*(8), 17-19, 22-27.

Linn, M. C., & Muilenburg, L. (1996). Creating lifelong science learners: What models form a firm foundation? *Educational Researcher, 25*(5), 18-24.

Linn, M. C., Songer, N. B., & Eylon, B. (1996). Shifts and convergences in science learning and instruction. In D. C. Berliner & R. C. Calfee (Eds.), *Handbook of educational psychology*. New York: Macmillan.

Livson, N., & Peshkin, H. (1980). Perspectives on adolescence from longitudinal research. In J. Adelson (Ed.), *Handbook of adolescent psychology* (pp. 47-98). New York: Wiley.

Loftus, E. F. (1991). Made in memory: Distortions in recollection after misleading information. In G. H. Bower (Ed.), *The psychology of learning and motivation: Advances in research and theory* (Vol. 27). San Diego, CA: Academic Press.

Loftus, E. F. (1992). When a lie becomes memory's truth: Memory distortion after exposure to misinformation. *Current Directions in Psychological Science, 1*, 121-123.

Logsdon, B. J., Alleman, L. M., Straits, S. A., Belka, D. E., Clark, D. (1997). *Physical education unit plans for grades 5–6* (2nd ed.). Champaign, IL: Human Kinetics.

Lonigan, C. J., Burgess, S. R., Anthony, J. L., & Barker, T. A. (1998). Development of phonological sensitivity in 2- to 5-year-old children. *Journal of Educational Psychology, 90*, 294-311.

Lykken, D. T. (1997). The American crime factory. *Psychological Inquiry, 8*, 261-270.

Maccoby, E. E., & Martin, J. A. (1983). Socialization in the context of the family: Parent-child interaction. In E. M. Hetherington (Ed.), *Handbook of child psychology: Vol. 4. Socialization, personality, and social development*. New York: Wiley.

Macfarlane, J. W. (1971). From infancy to adulthood. In M. C. Jones, N. Bayley, J. W. Macfarlane, & M. P. Honzik (Eds.), *The course of human development* (pp. 406-410). Waltham, MA: Xerox College Publishing.

Mandler, J. M. (1987). On the psychological reality of story structure. *Discourse Processes, 10*, 1-29.

Markman, E. M. (1979). Realizing that you don't understand: Elementary school children's awareness of inconsistencies. *Child Development, 50*, 643-655.

Maslow, A. H. (1973). Theory of human motivation. In R. J. Lowry (Ed.), *Dominance, self-esteem, self-actualization: Germinal papers of A. H. Maslow*. Monterey, CA: Brooks/Cole.

Maslow, A. H. (1987). *Motivation and personality* (3rd ed.). New York: Harper & Row.

Massey, C. M., & Gelman, R. (1988). Preschoolers' ability to decide whether a photographed unfamiliar object can move itself. *Developmental Psychology, 24*, 307-317.

Mastropieri, M. A., & Scruggs, T. E. (1992). Science for students with disabilities. *Review of Educational Research, 62*, 377-411.

Mastropieri, M. A., & Scruggs, T. E. (2000). *The inclusive classroom: Strategies for effective instruction*. Upper Saddle River, NJ: Merrill/Prentice Hall.

Mayer, R. E. (1982). Memory for algebra story problems. *Journal of Educational Psychology, 74*, 199-216.

Mayer, R. E. (1996). Learning strategies for making sense out of expository text: The SOI model for guiding three cognitive processes in knowledge construction. *Educational Psychology Review, 8*, 357-371.

Mayer, R. E. (1999). *The promise of educational psychology: Learning in the content areas*. Upper Saddle River, NJ: Merrill/Prentice Hall.

Mayer, R. E., & Wittrock, M. C. (1996). Problem-solving transfer. In D. C. Berliner & R. C. Calfee (Eds.), *Handbook of educational psychology*. New York: Macmillan.

McCann, T. M. (1989). Student argumentative writing knowledge and ability at three grade levels. *Research in the Teaching of English, 23*, 62-72.

McCormick, C. B., Busching, B. A., & Potter, E. F. (1992). Children's knowledge about writing: The development and use of evaluative criteria. In M. Pressley, K. R. Harris, & J. T. Guthrie (Eds.), *Promoting academic competence and literacy in school*. San Diego, CA: Academic Press.

McCutchen, D. (1996). A capacity theory of writing: Working memory in composition. *Educational Psychology Review, 8*, 299-325.

McCutchen, D., Kerr, S., & Francis, M. (1994, April). *Editing and revising: Effects of knowledge of topic and error location*. Paper presented at the annual meeting of the American Educational Research Association, New Orleans, LA.

McKeown, M. G., & Beck, I. L. (1994). Making sense of accounts of history: Why young students don't and how they might. In G. Leinhardt, I. L. Beck, & C. Stainton (Eds.), *Teaching and learning in history*. Hillsdale, NJ: Erlbaum.

McLane, J. B., & McNamee, G. D. (1990). *Early literacy.* Cambridge, MA: Harvard University Press.

McLoyd, V. C. (1998). Socioeconomic disadvantage and child development. *American Psychologist, 53,* 185-204.

McMahon, S. (1992). Book club: A case study of a group of fifth graders as they participate in a literature-based reading program. *Reading Research Quarterly, 27*(4), 292-294.

Mesa Verde Museum Association, Inc. (no date). *Balcony house trail guide.* Mesa Verde National Park, CO: Author.

Metz, K. E. (1995). Reassessment of developmental constraints on children's science instruction. *Review of Educational Research, 65,* 93-127.

Miller, L. S. (1995). *An American imperative: Accelerating minority educational advancement.* New Haven, CT: Yale University Press.

Minstrell, J., & Stimpson, V. (1996). A classroom environment for learning: Guiding students' reconstruction of understanding and reasoning. In L. Schauble & R. Glaser (Eds.), *Innovations in learning: New environments for education.* Mahwah, NJ: Erlbaum.

Morris, R. D., Stuebing, K. K., Fletcher, J. M., Shaywitz, S. E., Lyon, G. R., Shankweiler, D. P., Katz, L., Francis, D. J., & Shaywitz, B. A. (1998). Subtypes of reading disability: Variability around a phonological core. *Journal of Educational Psychology, 90,* 347-373.

Morrow, L. M. (1989). *Literacy development in the early years: Helping children read and write.* Boston: Allyn & Bacon.

Musca, T. (Producer), & Menendez, R. (Director). (1988). *Stand and deliver* [videorecording]. Burbank, CA: Warner Home Video.

Mwangi, W., & Sweller, J. (1998). Learning to solve compare word problems: The effect of example format and generating self-explanations. *Cognition and Instruction, 16,* 173-199.

Nation, K., & Hulme, C. (1998). The role of analogy in early spelling development. In C. Hulme & R. M. Joshi (Eds.), *Reading and spelling: Development and disorders.* Mahwah, NJ: Erlbaum.

National Children and Youth Fitness Study II. (1987). *Journal of Physical Education, Recreation and Dance, 58*(9), 49-96.

National Geographic Education Project. (1994). *Geography for life: National geography standards.* Washington, DC: National Geographic Research and Education, National Geographical Society.

National Research Council. (1993). *Understanding child abuse and neglect.* Washington, DC: National Academy Press.

Nelson, T. O., & Dunlosky, J. (1991). When people's judgments of learning (JOLs) are extremely accurate at predicting subsequent recall: The "delayed-JOL effect." *Psychological Science, 2,* 267-270.

Newmann, F. M. (1988). Can depth replace coverage in the high school curriculum? *Phi Delta Kappan, 70,* 345-348.

Newmann, F. M. (1997). Authentic assessment in social studies: Standards and examples. In G. D. Phye (Ed.), *Handbook of classroom assessment: Learning, achievement, and adjustment.* San Diego, CA: Academic Press.

Northup, J. (2000). Further evaluation of the accuracy of reinforcer surveys: A systematic replication. *Journal of Applied Behavior Analysis, 33,* 335–338.

Oakhill, J., & Yuill, N. (1996). Higher order factors in comprehension disability: Processes and remediation. In C. Cesare & J. Oakhill (Eds.), *Reading comprehension difficulties.* Mahwah, NJ: Erlbaum.

Oldfather, P., & West, J. (1999). *Learning through children's eyes: Social constructivism and the desire to learn.* Washington, DC: American Psychological Association.

Olsen, D. G. (1995, March). "Less" can be "more" in the promotion of thinking. *Social Education, 59*(3), 130-134.

Olweus, D., Mattson, A., Schalling, D., & Low, H. (1988). Circulating testosterone levels and aggression in adult males: A causal analysis. *Psychosomatic Medicine, 42,* 253-269.

Ormrod, J. E. (1989). *Using your head: An owner's manual.* Englewood Cliffs, NJ: Educational Technology Publications.

Ormrod, J. E., Jackson, D. L., Kirby, B., Davis, J., & Benson, C. (1999, April). *Cognitive development as reflected in children's conceptions of early American history.* Paper presented at the annual meeting of the American Educational Research Association, Montreal, Canada.

Owens, R. E., Jr. (1996). *Language development* (4th ed.). Boston: Allyn & Bacon.

Owens, S. A., Steen, F., Hargrave, J., Flores, N., & Hall, P. (2000). Chase play: The neglected structure of a type of physical activity play. Paper submitted for publication.

373

Padilla, M. J. (1991). Science activities, process skills, and thinking. In S. M. Glynn, R. H. Yeany, & B. K. Britton (Eds.), *The psychology of learning science*. Hillsdale, NJ: Erlbaum.

Page-Voth, V., & Graham, S. (1999). Effects of goal setting and strategy use on the writing performance and self-efficacy of students with writing and learning problems. *Journal of Educational Psychology, 91*, 230-240.

Paige, J. M., & Simon, H. A. (1966). Cognitive processes in solving algebra word problems. In B. Kleinmuntz (Ed.), *Problem solving*. New York: Wiley.

Palincsar, A. S., & Brown, A. L. (1984). Reciprocal teaching of comprehension-fostering and comprehension-monitoring activities. *Cognition and Instruction, 1*, 117-175.

Palincsar, A. S., & Herrenkohl, L. R. (1999). Designing collaborative contexts: Lessons from three research programs. In A. M. O'Donnell & A. King (Eds.), *Cognitive perspectives on peer learning* (pp. 151–177). Mahwah, NJ: Erlbaum.

Paris, S. G., & Cunningham, A. E. (1996). Children becoming students. In D. C. Berliner & R. C. Calfee (Eds.), *Handbook of educational psychology*. New York: Macmillan.

Paris, S. G., & Upton, L. R. (1976). Children's memory for inferential relationships in prose. *Child Development, 47*, 660-668.

Paxton, R. J. (1999). A deafening silence: History textbooks and the students who read them. *Review of Educational Research, 69*, 315–339.

Pea, R. D. (1992). Augmenting the discourse of learning with computer-based learning environments. In E. De Corte, M. C. Linn, H. Mandl, & L. Verschaffel (Eds.), *Computer-based learning environments and problem solving*. Berlin, Germany,: Springer-Verlag.

Pearson, P. D., Hansen, J., & Gordon, C. (1979). The effect of background knowledge on young children's comprehension of explicit and implicit information. *Journal of Reading Behavior, 11*, 201-209.

Pellegrini, A. D., & Smith, P. K. (1998). Physical activity play: Consensus and debate. *Child Development, 69*, 609-610.

Perfetti, C. A., & McCutchen, D. (1987). Schooled language competence: Linguistic abilities in reading and writing. In S. Rosenberg (Ed.), *Advances in applied psycholinguistics*. Cambridge, England: Cambridge University Press.

Perkins, D. N., & Salomon, G. (1989). Are cognitive skills context-bound? *Educational Researcher, 18*(1), 16-25.

Perkins, D. N., & Simmons, R. (1988). Patterns of misunderstanding: An integrative model for science, math, and programming. *Review of Educational Research, 58*, 303-326.

Perry, M. (1991). Learning and transfer: Instructional conditions and conceptual change. *Cognitive Development, 6*, 449-468.

Peterson, A. C., & Taylor, B. (1980). The biological approach to adolescence: Biological change and psychological adaptation. In J. Adelson (Ed.), *Handbook of adolescent psychology* (pp. 117-155). New York: Wiley.

Petri, H. L. (1991). *Motivation: Theory, research, and applications* (3rd ed.). Belmont, CA: Wadsworth.

Piirto, J. (1999). *Talented children and adults: Their development and education* (2nd ed.). Upper Saddle River, NJ: Merrill/Prentice Hall.

Pipher, M. (1994). *Reviving Ophelia: Saving the selves of adolescent girls*. New York: Putnam.

Pressley, M. (with McCormick, C. B.). (1995). *Advanced educational psychology for educators, researchers, and policymakers*. New York: HarperCollins.

Pressley, M., Almasi, J., Schuder, T., Bergman, J., Hite, S., El-Dinary, P. B., & Brown, R. (1994). Transactional instruction of comprehension strategies: The Montgomery County Maryland SAIL program. *Reading and Writing Quarterly, 10*, 5-19.

Pressley, M., El-Dinary, P. B., Wharton-McDonald, R., & Brown, R. (1998). Transactional instruction of comprehension strategies in the elementary grades. In D. H. Schunk & B. J. Zimmerman (Eds.), *Self-regulated learning: From teaching to self-reflective practice* (pp. 42–56). New York: Guilford Press.

Pulos, S. (1997). Adolescents' implicit theories of physical phenomena: A matter of gravity. *International Journal of Behavioral Development, 20*, 493-507.

Pulos, S., & Linn, M. C. (1981). Generality of the controlling variables scheme in early adolescence. *Journal of Early Adolescence, 1*, 26-37.

Purcell-Gates, V., McIntyre, E., & Freppon, P. A. (1995). Learning written storybook language in school: A comparison of low-SES children in skills-based and whole language classrooms. *American Educational Research Journal, 32*, 659-685.

Reifman, A., Barnes, G. M., & Hoffman, J. H. (1999, April). *Physical maturation and problem behaviors in male adolescents: A test of peer and parent relations as mediators*. Paper presented at the biennial meeting of the Society for Research in Child Development, Albuquerque, NM.

Reiner, M., Slotta, J. D., Chi, M. T. H., & Resnick, L. B. (2000). Naïve physics reasoning: A commitment to substance-based conceptions. *Cognition and Instruction, 18*, 1–34.

Resnick, L. B. (1989). Developing mathematical knowledge. *American Psychologist, 44*, 162-169.

Resnick, L. B., Bill, V. L., Lesgold, S. B., & Leer, M. N. (1991). Thinking in arithmetic class. In B. Means, C. Chelemer, & M. S. Knapp (Eds.), *Teaching advanced skills to at-risk students.* San Francisco: Jossey-Bass.

Reutzel, D. R., & Cooter, R. B., Jr. (1999). *Balanced reading strategies and practices.* Upper Saddle River, NJ: Merrill/Prentice Hall.

Rittle-Johnson, B., Siegler, R. S., & Alibali, M. W. (2001). Developing conceptual understanding and procedural skill in mathematics: An iterative process. *Journal of Educational Psychology, 93*, 346–362.

Roth, W. (1996). Where is the context in contextual word problems?: Mathematical practices and products in grade 8 students' answers to story problems. *Cognition and Instruction, 14*, 487-527.

Ruffman, T., Perner, J., Olson, D. R., & Doherty, M. (1993). Reflecting on scientific thinking: Children's understanding of the hypothesis-evidence relation. *Child Development, 64*, 1617-1636.

Sacks, C. H., & Mergendoller, J. R. (1997). The relationship between teachers' theoretical orientation toward reading and student outcomes in kindergarten children with different initial reading abilities. *American Educational Research Journal, 34*, 721-739.

Sadker, M. P., & Sadker, D. (1994). *Failing at fairness: How our schools cheat girls.* New York: Touchstone.

Salend, S. J., & Hofstetter, E. (1996). Adapting a problem-solving approach to teaching mathematics to students with mild disabilities. *Intervention in School and Clinic, 31*(4), 209-217.

Scardamalia, M., & Bereiter, C. (1986). Research on written composition. In M. C. Wittrock (Ed.), *Handbook of research on teaching* (3rd ed.). New York: Macmillan.

Scardamalia, M., & Bereiter, C. (1987). *The psychology of written composition.* Hillsdale, NJ: Erlbaum.

Scardamalia, M., Bereiter, C., & Goelman, H. (1982). The role of production factors in writing ability. In M. Nystrand (Ed.), *What writers know: The language, process, and structure of written discourse.* New York: Academic Press.

Scarr, S. (1992). Developmental theories for the 1990s: Development and individual differences. *Child Development, 63*, 1-19.

Scarr, S. (1993). Biological and cultural diversity: The legacy of Darwin for development. *Child Development, 64*, 1333-1353.

Schauble, L. (1990). Belief revision in children: The role of prior knowledge and strategies for generating evidence. *Journal of Experimental Child Psychology, 49*, 31-57.

Schauble, L. (1996). The development of scientific reasoning in knowledge-rich contexts. *Developmental Psychology, 32*, 102-119.

Schneider, J. J. (1998, April). *Developing multiple perspectives and audience awareness in elementary writers.* Paper presented at the annual meeting of the American Educational Research Association, San Diego, CA.

Schneider, W., Roth, E., & Ennemoser, M. (2000). Training phonological skills and letter knowledge in children at risk for dyslexia: A comparison of three kindergarten intervention programs. *Journal of Educational Psychology, 92*, 284-295.

Schoenfeld, A. H. (1982). Measures of problem-solving performance and problem-solving instruction. *Journal for Research in Mathematics Education, 13*, 31-49.

Schoenfeld, A. H. (1988). When good teaching leads to bad results: The disasters of "well-taught" mathematics courses. *Educational Psychologist, 23*, 145-166.

Schoenfeld, A. H. (1992). Learning to think mathematically: Problem solving, metacognition, and sense making in mathematics. In D. A. Grouws (Ed.), *Handbook of research on mathematics teaching and learning.* New York: Macmillan.

Seixas, P. (1996). Conceptualizing the growth of historical understanding. In D. R. Olson & N. Torrance (Eds.), *The handbook of education and human development: New models of learning, teaching, and schooling.* Cambridge, MA: Blackwell.

Shanahan, T., & Tierney, R. J. (1990). Reading-writing connections: The relations among three perspectives. In J. Zutell & S. McCormick (Eds.), *Literacy theory and research: Analyses from multiple paradigms. Thirty-ninth yearbook of the National Reading Conference.* Chicago: National Reading Conference.

Sheridan, M. D. (1975). *Children's developmental progress from birth to five years: The Stycar Sequences.* Windsor, England: NFER Publishing Company.

Sheveland, D. E. (1994, April). *Motivational factors in the development of independent readers.* Paper presented at the annual meeting of the American Educational Research Association, New Orleans, LA.

Siegler, R. S. (1989). Mechanisms of cognitive growth. *Annual Review of Psychology, 40*, 353-379.

Silver, E. A., Shapiro, L. J., & Deutsch, A. (1993). Sense making and the solution of division problems involving remainders: An examination of middle school students' solution processes and their interpretations of solutions. *Journal of Research in Mathematics Education, 24*, 117–135.

Simmons, R. G., & Blyth, D. A. (1987). *Moving into adolescence: The impact of pubertal change in school context.* New York: A. de Gruyter

Simons, R. L., Whitbeck, L. B., Conger, R. D., & Conger, K. J. (1991). Parenting factors, social skills, and value commitments as precursors to school failure, involvement with deviant peers, and delinquent behavior. *Journal of Youth and Adolescence, 20*, 645-664.

Simons-Morton, B. G., Taylor, W. C., Snider, S. A., Huang, I. W., & Fulton, J. E. (1994). Observed levels of elementary and middle school children's physical activity during physical education classes. *Preventive Medicine, 23*, 437-441.

Sinatra, G. M., & Souterland, S. (2001, April). *Intentions, beliefs, and acceptance of evolutionary theory.* Paper presented at the annual meeting of the American Educational Research Association, Seattle, WA.

Singer, J., Marx, R. W., Krajcik, J., & Chambers, J. C. (2000). Constructing extended inquiry projects: Curriculum materials for science education reform. *Educational Psychologist, 35*, 165–178.

Sitko, B. M. (1998). Knowing how to write: Metacognition and writing instruction. In D. J. Hacker, J. Dunlosky, & A. C. Graesser (Eds.), *Metacognition in educational theory and practice* (pp. 93–115). Mahwah, NJ: Erlbaum.

Smith, C. L., Maclin, D., Houghton, C., & Hennessey, M. G. (2000). Sixth-grade students' epistemologies of science: The impact of school science experiences on epistemological development. *Cognition and Instruction, 18*, 349–422.

Smith, N. R., Cicchetti, L., Clark, M. C., Fucigna, C., Gordon-O'Connor, B., Halley, B. A., & Kennedy, M. (1998). *Observation drawing with children: A framework for teachers.* New York: Teachers College Press.

Smitherman, G. (1994). "The blacker the berry the sweeter the juice": African American student writers. In A. H. Dyson & C. Genishi (Eds.), *The need for story: Cultural diversity in classroom and community.* Urbana, IL: National Council of Teachers of English.

Southerland, S. A., Sinatra, G. M., & Matthews, M. R. (2001). Belief, knowledge, and science education. *Educational Psychology Review, 13*, 325-351..

Sperling, M. (1996). Revisiting the writing-speaking connection: Challenges for research on writing and writing instruction. *Review of Educational Research, 66*, 53-86.

Spivey, N. N. (1997). *The constructivist metaphor: Reading, writing, and the making of meaning.* San Diego, CA: Academic Press.

Stahl, S. A., & Miller, P. D. (1989). Whole language and language experience approaches for beginning reading: A quantitative research synthesis. *Review of Educational Research, 59*, 87-116.

Stanovich, K. E. (2000). *Progress in understanding reading: Scientific foundations and new frontiers.* New York: Guilford Press.

Stattin, H., & Magnusson, D. (1990). *Pubertal maturation in female development.* Hillsdale, NJ: Erlbaum.

Steen, F., & Owens, S. A. (2000, March). *Implicit pedagogy: From chase play to collaborative worldmaking.* Paper presented at the Evolution and Social Mind Speaker Series, University of California at Santa Barbara.

Steinberg, L. (1993). *Adolescence* (3rd ed.). New York: McGraw-Hill.

Steinberg, L., Elmen, J., & Mounts, N. (1989). Authoritative parenting, psychosocial maturity, and academic success among adolescents. *Child Development, 60*, 1424-1436.

Sugar, W. A., & Bonk, C. J. (1998). Student role play in the World Forum: Analyses of an Arctic learning apprenticeship. In C. J. Bonk & K. S. King (Eds.), *Electronic collaborators: Learner-centered technologies for literacy, apprenticeship, and discourse.* Mahwah, NJ: Erlbaum.

Sussman, E. J., Nottelmann, E. D., Inhoff-Germain, G., Dorn, L. D., & Chrousos, G. P. (1987). Hormonal influences on aspects of psychological development during adolescence. *Journal of Adolescent Health Care, 8*, 492-504.

Sussman, E. J., Nottelmann, E. D., Inhoff-Germain, G. E., Dorn, L. D., Cutler, G. B. Jr., Loriaux, D. L., & Chrousos, G. P. (1985). The relation of development and social-emotional behavior in young adolescents. *Journal of Youth and Adolescence, 14*, 245-264.

Swanson, H. L., Cooney, J. B., & O'Shaughnessy, T. E. (1998). Learning disabilities and memory. In B. Y. L. Wong (Ed.), *Learning about learning disabilities* (2nd ed.). San Diego, CA: Academic Press.

Swanson, H. L., Mink, J., & Bocian, K. M. (1999). Cognitive processing deficits in poor readers with symptoms of learning disabilities and ADHD: More alike than different? *Journal of Educational Psychology, 91*, 321-333.

Thomas, J. R., & French, K. E. (1985). Gender differences across age in motor performance: A meta-analysis. *Psychological Bulletin, 98*, 260-282.

Thomas, M. H., & Dieter, J. N. (1987). The positive effect of writing practice on integration of foreign words in memory. *Journal of Educational Psychology, 79*, 249-253.

Thomas, S. P., Groër, M., & Droppleman, P. (1993). Physical health of today's school children. *Educational Psychology Review, 5*, 5-33.

Thompson, R. A., & Wyatt, J. M. (1999). Current research on child maltreatment: Implications for educators. *Educational Psychology Review, 11*, 173-201.

Tompkins, G. E., & McGee, L. M. (1986). Visually impaired and sighted children's emerging concepts about written language. In D. B. Yaden, Jr., & S. Templeton (Eds.), *Metalinguistic awareness and beginning literacy: Conceptualizing what it means to read and write.* Porstmouth, NH: Heinemann.

Torgesen, J. K., Wagner, R. K., Rashotte, C. A., Rose, E., Lindamood, P., Conway, T., & Garvan, C. (1999). Preventing reading failure in young children with phonological processing disabilities: Group and individual responses to instruction. *Journal of Educational Psychology, 91*, 579–593.

Trawick-Smith, J. (2000). *Early childhood development: A multicultural perspective* (2nd ed.). Upper Saddle River, NJ: Merrill/Prentice Hall.

Treiman, R. (1993). *Beginning to spell: A study of first-grade children.* New York: Oxford University Press.

Tremblay, L. (1999, April). *Acceleration hypothesis: A meta-analysis of environmental stressors impact on puberty onset.* Paper presented at the biennial meeting of the Society for Research in Child Development, Albuquerque, NM.

Tunmer, W. E., & Chapman, J. W. (1998). Language prediction skill, phonological recoding ability, and beginning reading. In C. Hulme & R. M. Joshi (Eds.), *Reading and spelling: Development and disorders.* Mahwah, NJ: Erlbaum.

Turnbull, A., Turnbull, R., Shank, M., & Leal, D. (1999). *Exceptional lives: Special education in today's schools* (2nd ed.). Upper Saddle River, NJ: Merrill/Prentice Hall.

Van Meter, P. (2001). Drawing construction as a strategy for learning from text. *Journal of Educational Psychology, 93*, 129–140.

Vosniadou, S. (1991). Conceptual development in astronomy. In S. M. Glynn, R. H. Yeany, & B. K. Britton (Eds.), *The psychology of learning science.* Hillsdale, NJ: Erlbaum.

Walton, P. D., Walton, L. M., & Felton, K. (2001). Teaching rime analogy on letter recoding reading strategies to prereaders: Effects on prereading skills and word reading. *Journal of Educational Psychology, 93*, 160–180.

Wason, P. (1968). Reasoning about a rule. *Quarterly Journal of Experimental Psychology, 20*, 273-281.

Weaver, C. (1990). *Understanding whole language: From principles to practice.* Portsmouth, NH: Heinemann.

Weaver, C. A., III, & Kelemen, W. L. (1997). Judgments of learning at delays: Shifts in response patterns or increased metamemory accuracy? *Psychological Science, 8*, 318-321.

Weaver, C. A., III, & Kintsch, W. (1991). Expository text. In R. Barr, M. L. Kamil, P. B. Mosenthal, & P. D. Pearson (Eds.), *Handbook of reading research* (Vol. 2). New York: Longman.

Webb, N. M., & Palincsar, A. S. (1996). Group processes in the classroom. In D. C. Berliner & R. C. Calfee (Eds.), *Handbook of educational psychology.* New York: Macmillan.

Weiss, L. H., & Schwarz, J. C. (1996). The relationship between parenting types and older adolescents' personality, academic achievement, adjustment, and substance use. *Child Development, 67*, 2101-2114.

Wellman, H. M., & Gelman, S. A. (1992). Cognitive development: Foundational theories of core domains. In M. R. Rosenzweig & L. W. Porter (Eds.), *Annual review of psychology* (Vol. 43). Palo Alto, CA: Annual Reviews.

West, R. F., & Stanovich, K. E. (1978). Automatic contextual facilitation in readers of three ages. *Child Development, 49*, 717-727.

White, B. Y., & Frederiksen, J. R. (1998). Inquiry, modeling, and metacognition: Making science accessible to all students. *Cognition and Instruction, 16*, 3-118.

Whitehurst, G. J., Arnold, D. S., Epstein, J. N., Angell, A. L., Smith, M., & Fischel, J. E. (1994). A picture book reading intervention in day care and home for children from low-income families. *Developmental Psychology, 30*, 679-689.

Wigfield, A., Eccles, J. S., & Pintrich, P. R. (1996). Development between the ages of 11 and 25. In D. C. Berliner & R. C. Calfee (Eds.), *Handbook of educational psychology.* New York: Macmillan.

Wineburg, S. S. (1994). The cognitive representation of historical texts. In G. Leinhardt, I. L. Beck, & C. Stainton (Eds.), *Teaching and learning in history.* Hillsdale, NJ: Erlbaum.

Wittrock, M. C. (1994). Generative science teaching. In P. J. Fensham, R. F. Gunstone, & R. T. White (Eds.), *The content of science: A constructivist approach to its teaching and learning.* London: Falmer Press.

Wlodkowski, R. J. (1978). *Motivation and teaching: A practical guide.* Washington, DC: National Education Association.

Wood, D. K., Frank, A. R., & Wacker, D. P. (1998). Teaching multiplication facts to students with learning disabilities. *Journal of Applied Behavior Analysis, 31,* 323–338.

Yeager, E. A., Foster, S. J., Maley, S. D., Anderson, T., Morris, J. W., III, & Davis, O. L., Jr. (1997, March). *The role of empathy in the development of historical understanding.* Paper presented at the annual meeting of the American Educational Research Association, Chicago.

Zhu, X., & Simon, H. A. (1987). Learning mathematics from examples and by doing. *Cognition and Instruction, 4,* 137-166.